P9-CIU-457

The Luftwaffe

MODERN WAR STUDIES

The Luftwaffe

Creating the Operational Air War 1918–1940

James S. Corum

University Press of Kansas

Published by the University Press of Kansas (Lawrence, Kansas 66049), which was organized by the Kansas Board of Regents and is operated and funded by Emporia State University, Fort Hays State University, Kansas State University, Pittsburg State University, the University of Kansas, and Wichita State University

Library of Congress Cataloging-in-Publication Data

Corum, James S.
The Luftwaffe : creating the operational air war, 1918–1940 / by James S. Corum
p. cm. — (Modern war studies)
Includes bibliographical references and index.
ISBN 0-7006-0836-2
1. Germany. Luftwaffe—History. 2. Maneuver warfare—History—20th century. 3. Air power—Germany—History. 4. Aeronautics, Military—Germany—History. I. Title. II. Series.
UG635.G3C68 1997
358.4′00943—dc21 97-6943

British Library Cataloguing in Publication Data is available.

Printed in the United States of America
10 9 8 7 6 5 4 3 2 1

The paper used in this publication meets the minimum requirements of the American National Standard for Permanence of Paper for Printed Library Materials Z39.48-1984.

To Major James E. Corum
United States Army, 1940–1965

Contents

Acknowledgments

A great many people have helped me in the research and writing of this book, and it would be fair to say that I could not have done it without the offering of time and effort by these people. I wish to take a moment to gratefully acknowledge the time, effort, and wisdom of a few of these people. First of all, my colleagues at the U.S. Air Force School of Advanced Airpower Studies have provided support, encouragement, and critical advice for the last few years, and I wish to thank Colonel Phil Meilinger USAF, Colonel Rob Owen USAF, and Professor Dave Mets (Lieutenant Colonel USAF Ret.) for giving me the benefit of their broad understanding of air power history. The staff of the U.S. Air Force Historical Research Agency, headed by Colonel Rauschkalb, is the best of any major military archive I have seen. They set a high standard of competence and friendly service.

Members of the German Military History Office (Militärgeschichtliches Forschungsamt) in Potsdam have provided advice, assistance, and encouragement for the last few years. Professor Horst Boog, probably the best Luftwaffe historian anywhere, has sent me documents and often provided sound advice. Colonel Klaus Maier, Ph.D., and Dr. Jürgen Förster have been consistently helpful in my research. Archivist Völker Ernst is one of the most knowledgeable and helpful archivists anywhere. All these people have tracked down sources and documents that I could not have found on my own.

I wish to give special thanks to Freiherr Götz von Richthofen, son of Field Marshal Wolfram von Richthofen, Hans-Joachim Wilberg, son of General der Flieger Helmuth Wilberg, and Frau Siess and Professor von Sietencron of Tübingen, daughter and stepson of General der Flieger Robert Knauss, all of whom have been extremely generous in providing me with full access to family photos and papers and have helped me gain a personal understanding of three of Germany's premier air power thinkers. All these people have been enormously helpful in broadening my understanding of the Luftwaffe in the interwar period and during World War I.

The most important person who has helped me in this work has been my wife, Lynn Corum. Lynn is a first-rate scholar in her own right and is the best proofreader and assistant that a historian could hope for.

Introduction

From 1939 to the winter of 1941, the German military won a series of victories rarely equaled in the annals of war. Poland, Norway, France, Belgium, Holland, Yugoslavia, Denmark, and Greece all fell victim to the armed forces of the Third Reich. In the summer and fall of 1941, the USSR came close to total defeat at the hands of the Wehrmacht, losing millions of soldiers on the battlefield and witnessing the occupation of a large portion of Russia and the Ukraine. The German air force, the Luftwaffe, played a central role in this remarkable string of victories. During the first two years of World War II the German military experienced only one major setback at the hands of the Royal Air Force, when the Luftwaffe attempted to gain superiority in the air over Britain. On the other hand, the rapid conquest of Norway, Holland, France, and Greece would have been impossible without the superb performance of the Luftwaffe.

The Luftwaffe was an integral part of the modern doctrine of maneuver warfare that was used so effectively by the German military in the early years of World War II and which was eventually learned by the Allied powers and used against the Germans in the latter years of the war. The Luftwaffe demonstrated to the world what a joint air/ground campaign could accomplish. In some cases, the success of the Luftwaffe can be attributed to simply overwhelming the opponent by sheer weight of numbers and superior technology—witness the campaigns in Poland, Yugoslavia, and Greece. However, in other very successful air campaigns, the Luftwaffe's margin of superiority in numbers and technology was fairly slim—witness the campaign against two major modern air powers, Britain and France, in the spring of 1940.[1]

Even after the Luftwaffe lost the production battle and by 1942 fought outnumbered on all fronts, it remained a formidable enemy able to hold air superiority in the east until 1944 and able to successfully defend Germany against the American daylight bomber offensive until the spring of 1944. The Luftwaffe was able to hold its own even after it lost the qualitative advantage it held early in the war and had to face Allied aircraft that were often faster, better-armed, and more capable.

The study of air power history in general and of the Luftwaffe in particular tend to focus overwhelmingly on aircraft technology. There are hundreds, if not thousands, of books published since 1945 on the aircraft that the Luftwaffe flew. If the writing on air power history does not emphasize technology, it emphasizes the stories of individual aerial daring—usually the stories of fighter pilots told in the "there I was at 10,000 feet with three bogies on my tail" style. While this kind of literature abounds on the Luftwaffe, there is very little that is written in articles or books about the operational doctrine of the Luftwaffe or the air power theories that helped form the framework for planning and executing numerous successful air campaigns. The Luftwaffe is not alone in this; it is a trademark of air power history in general. One can make almost the same comments about the history of the U.S. Army Air Forces or the RAF in World War II. At this time, more than fifty years after World War II only one major American air command, the Eighth Air Force—the U.S. strategic bombing force against Germany—has had a thorough operational history written about it.[2] Other major commands, such as the Ninth U.S. Air Force, an organization of over 200,000 men and fielding thousands of aircraft in combat, has yet to see an operational history.

In the matter of air leaders there is a similar story. Serious biographies have been written for only a few of the senior air commanders of World War II—and it becomes especially notable when one compares the scholarship on air leaders with the extensive scholarship that has been done on ground and naval commanders of the war. If the scholarship of naval and army historians followed the example of the air historians there might be biographies of Eisenhower, Montgomery, and Patton—and that's all.

However, it is in the study of air power ideas that the research and scholarship is most lacking today. For example, there is no scholarly book available on vital subjects such as the air power concepts developed at the U.S. Air Corps Tactical School in the interwar era.[3] For the history of the Luftwaffe, the serious literature on the study of operational doctrine and air power theory is equally thin. There have been more books written on the Luftwaffe aircraft tail markings (at least three) than there have been on the Luftwaffe's operational doctrine and air theory (none).

At its heart, warfare is the clash of armed men and of leaders striving to defeat the other. Therefore, books about warfare will always emphasize the leaders and the weapons. However, warfare is also a clash of ideas. Military theory provides a guide for military leaders in organizing their forces for war, theory forms the basis for officer education about war, and it plays a central role in determining which weapons will be built to fight a future war. Operational doctrine comes from theory and is constantly evolving. Doctrine is the practical expression of theory in that it is the stated manner in which the military leadership expects the large and small units of the military to conduct movement, logistics, and combat so as to successfully win a campaign or war. In warfare it is not always the case that the biggest battalions or the best weapons win. There are innumerable examples from military history that show that the smaller or more poorly armed force has often won because it had the superior ideas and a more effective combat doctrine than its opponent.

This book is about the ideas and operational doctrines of the German air force as they developed during the interwar period and up to the early days of World War II. This work is primarily interested in how the concepts of air power in Germany were developed, how the theories about air war were translated into practical operational doctrine for war, how the German military approached the study of air warfare, and how the air staff interpreted the experience of World War I and the Spanish Civil War, as well as the experiences of other air forces, and translated these into a practical doctrine for the German armed forces. Central to the issue are the debates concerning air power that took part in German military circles and the leaders that guided the debates. The issue of how technology affects the employment of air power and the organization of an air force is also a central issue. By using primary sources as much as possible I hope to accurately recreate the nature of the air power debate in Germany and, hopefully, provide some insights into the manner in which air forces create an operational doctrine for war and how they adapt that doctrine from experience gained in exercises and war games as well as in combat.

I have selected the interwar period as the parameters of this study because, for air power as well as for the development of land warfare, the period between the two world wars remains the most important era in the development of military theory in the twentieth century. Most of the theories of warfare that provide a guide for present-day military operational doctrine come from this fascinating era. World War I saw the introduction of most of the modern weapons and technology that have characterized war in the twentieth century. In World War I tank warfare, the extensive use of motor vehicles, radio communications, strategic bombing, close air support, submarine warfare, and the exponential increase in firepower of all kinds saw their genesis and even reached a degree of maturity. World War I even saw the first use of aircraft carriers. Virtually the only major new weapon or method of warfare that cannot trace its development and use back to World War I was the atom bomb. After World War I every major military establishment in the world was forced to come to grips in analyzing the impact of the new weapons and technology and to adapt old theories and devise new ones to meet the challenge posed by the introduction of so many innovations in warfare.

After the war, all the major militaries engaged in extensive internal debates as to how the organization of the armed forces and the operational doctrine of those forces should be shaped in regard to the lessons of World War I and each military's vision of what a future war would look like. In some cases, the process was extremely successful. The German army and the Soviet army developed concepts and doctrine for maneuver warfare that combined the capabilities of modern firepower, communications, and mechanized and motorized forces with air power. These concepts developed in the 1920s and 1930s are still central to the planning and execution of conventional wars even at the end of the century. The theory of strategic air war grew out of the experience of World War I and was developed into a coherent theory and doctrine of strategic targeting and attack in the Royal Air Force and U.S. Army Air Corps in the 1920s and 1930s and still provides the foundation for much of modern U.S. Air Force doctrine. In some cases, the attempt to reform military forces and doctrine in light of the innovations of World War I were terribly flawed. The French army and air force provide one of the best historical case studies of armed forces that misinterpreted the lesson of World War I. Guided by poor analysis and a faulty vision of what a future war would look like, the French entered World War II with a large and well-equipped military, but with little appreciation for the capability that mechanization and air power had brought to the battlefield. France would pay for having poor doctrine and an unsound theory of war with catastrophic defeat on the battlefield in 1940.

As important as the air war is to modern military thought and as important as the interwar period is to understand the evolution of modern military doctrine, there has been surprisingly little written about air theory and doctrine in this period. The typical history of the Luftwaffe or other air forces will gloss over the prewar development of air thought in a few pages before getting into the examination of air operations in World War II. Readers of military history are normally left with only a sketchy idea of how the German military actually thought of using air power in a war before they are thrown headlong into a rendition of the air operations themselves. Filling this large gap in the study of air war is the author's primary motivation for writing this book. The air war in World War II and the Luftwaffe's operations are two of the most important topics in the military history of this century. By studying the evolution of air war theory and doctrine in the Luftwaffe in the interwar period, I hope to help military history readers and scholars to put the air operations of the Luftwaffe into a clearer context and to make the employment of air power by the German Reich during World War II more understandable.

One of the major difficulties in writing about the development of air power thought in Germany is the large number of myths that have grown up around the study of the Luftwaffe since the end of World War II and how—usually by constant repetition—they have become established in the history of air war as accepted fact. To properly write about the Luftwaffe one has to get beyond the clichés that have driven many historians to inaccurate conclusions about the Luftwaffe and how it, as a military service, viewed the conduct and planning of war. The most prevalent myth—and the one most damaging to the historical record—is the view that the Luftwaffe was merely a tactical air force geared to army support operations. There are several corollary beliefs tied into this assertion: that the Luftwaffe doctrine did not recognize the importance of strategic air war and that the Luftwaffe ultimately failed because it did not build more than a handful of strategic bombers and institute a doctrine of strategic air war. Variations of this argument are found in dozens of books and articles written about the Luftwaffe. A few examples of this view of Luftwaffe doctrine can be found in even some of the best books on World War II and on air power history. John Keegan in *The Second World War*[4] says that "the Luftwaffe of 1939–1940 did not espouse any strategic bombing theory at all," and that the Luftwaffe's leaders, mostly ex-army officers, "devoted themselves to building the Luftwaffe into a ground support arm."[5] Telford Taylor in *The March of Conquest* argues, "The Luftwaffe's fundamental limitations were not the consequence of its immaturity but of a deliberate decision, taken in 1937, to design it for short-range operations in support of the army, rather than for long-range strategic undertakings of its own."[6] In *The Evolution of Weapons and Warfare,* Trevor Dupuy states that "Germany . . . used its air power almost exclusively as an adjunct of land and (to a limited extent) naval power."[7] This view of the Luftwaffe's doctrine has become an established dogma in air power history today. One of the primary authors of this view of the Luftwaffe was the U.S. Air Force. In the official history of the U.S. Army Air Forces in World War II it is asserted that "official policy regarded the airplane primarily as a tactical weapon for use in support of ground armies" and that the Luftwaffe "bombers were suited to the close support for ground armies."[8] In the period right after World War II air power historians from the victorious—and strategically oriented air forces—

promulgated the position that the Luftwaffe was designed to be purely an army support force.[9] This interpretation of history has been carried on right into the most recent books on air power history.[10]

The Luftwaffe would never have recognized this narrow definition of its doctrine, because it had developed a large body of theory and doctrine of strategic air warfare before World War II. While it was quite capable of supporting the army, the Luftwaffe never saw itself primarily as an army support force. Indeed, at the start of World War II, the Luftwaffe was the only air force in the world that had the equipment, the training for nighttime and poor weather operations, and the necessary long-distance navigation aids to enable it to conduct strategic bombing. The Luftwaffe even had a rudimentary pathfinder force. It took the air forces that were strategically oriented years to catch up with the skills for strategic air war that the Luftwaffe had in 1939–1940. When it conducted a highly successful, large night-bombing raid against the important British war industries of Coventry in November 1940, the Luftwaffe was the only air force capable of accurately locating and bombing such a target under night conditions.[11] Putting 450 bombers on target in the dark is scarcely the trademark of an air force that had been designed purely for army support.

The historians who characterize the Luftwaffe as an army support force tell us far more about their own prejudices than they do about the Luftwaffe's understanding of air warfare. This view of the Luftwaffe stems largely from a U.S. Air Force, and to a lesser degree the RAF, theory of war. Since the 1930s and continuing down to the present day, the predominant doctrine of the U.S. Air Force has been in favor of independent strategic bombing campaigns. U.S. Air Corps officers in the Air Corps Tactical School taught the primacy of the strategic bombing campaign almost to the exclusion of other forms of air warfare in the 1930s. At the start of World War II and right through the war, senior American airmen believed that Germany could be defeated by strategic bombing alone and a strategic campaign that paralyzed the nodes of German industrial production would push Germany to surrender without requiring a land invasion of Germany.[12] For the USAF, strategic air campaigns became the "proper" use of air power and anything smacking of the use of the air force as an "army support weapon" has been generally disdained as a misuse of air power if not a violation of true air power dogma.[13] That such a view persists and is still held as dogma can be seen in the statements of the U.S. Air Force chief of staff General Michael Dugan who, while commenting on the planning for an air campaign against Iraq in the summer of 1990, told the press that the Air Force alone could defeat Saddam Hussein and Iraq and that ground forces were unnecessary to win a war.

Another prevalent myth about the Luftwaffe is that the Luftwaffe had a doctrine of "terror bombing" in which civilian populations were deliberately targeted in order to break the morale of an enemy nation and bring about rapid collapse of an enemy. Such a view, promulgated by the great Italian air power theorist General Giulio Douhet in the 1920s, had a significant effect on airmen of all nations in the interwar period. After the bombing of Guernica by the Luftwaffe in 1937 and the bombing of Rotterdam in 1940 it was commonly assumed by military commentators in Europe and America that terror bombing was part of the Luftwaffe's operational doctrine. The assumption that the Luftwaffe made civilians a primary target certainly seemed to fit the public's understanding of the ideology and aims of Germany's Nazi leadership. Since World War II it has become generally accepted by many historians that the Luftwaffe employed terror bombing as part of its doctrine prior to World War II.[14] Even as distinguished a historian as Gerhard Weinberg refers to the bombing of Guernica and Rotterdam as Nazi "terror bombing."[15] In fact, the Luftwaffe did not have a policy of terror bombing civilians as part of its doctrine prior to World War II. As will be discussed later, Guernica in 1937 and Rotterdam in 1940 were bombed for tactical military reasons in support of military operations. Civilians were certainly killed in both incidents, but in neither case was that the goal or intent of the bombing. Indeed, the Luftwaffe leadership specifically rejected the concept of terror bombing in the interwar period, and one must look well into World War II, starting with the night bombing of selected British towns in 1942, to see a Luftwaffe policy of terror bombing in which civilian casualties are the primary desired result.

Yet another myth about the Luftwaffe's concept of air war comes from the specialists in social history who imply that the popular culture of Germany, as well as the Nazi ideology and the Nazis' use of propaganda in support of air power, had some genuine influence on the way the military thought of air warfare. The claim that popular culture influenced the conduct of the air war in World War II is made by Dominick Pisano, editor of *Legend, Memory and the Great War in the Air:* "The evolution of the popular perception of aviation's role in World War I reveals how legend colors the memory of an event. The myths of the 'knights of the air', born during World War I, have formed the basis for commonly held attitudes about the first major war in the air. In fact, these myths have influenced the planning and use of air power in World War II and are still with us today."[16] Peter Fritzsche, in *A Na-*

tion of Fliers: German Aviation and the Popular Imagination, discusses the influence of aviation hero literature on the German public in the interwar period, as well as the effect of the Nazi propaganda campaigns for aviation on the population. More subtly, he implies an important role for popular culture in affecting the actual German employment of air power in the interwar period.[17] This may be mostly social historians overestimating the importance of their own subject. Certainly, aviation was popular with the public, and the Nazis used many aviation themes in their propaganda campaigns. In the 1930s aviation was a symbol of modernity, and all fascist regimes tried to show how "modern" they were. While propaganda did affect the perceptions of the public, there is simply no evidence that popular conceptions of air power—or even the specifically Nazi concepts of war and politics—had any real effect on the professional military men who developed the actual operational doctrine of the air force. German air doctrine was created by experienced professional officers who were well educated in aviation and in the operational art and, with the exception of encouraging the public campaign for civil defense training, seemed to have had little interest in how the public or even the Nazi leadership conceived of the use of air power in a future war.

Misconceptions about the Luftwaffe and the Luftwaffe's concepts of warfare are, in large part, simply caused by a lack of basic skills of many who write about the Luftwaffe. For some inexplicable reason, many historians—especially, Americans—believe they can write books about the German army and air force without knowing German. This entails authors researching and writing about complex historical events without being able to read either any primary documents, or most of the secondary literature. This is an awfully small base to work from, yet it has not deterred some from writing popular books about the Luftwaffe. Edwin Hoyt's *Angels of Death: Goering's Luftwaffe*[18] and Samuel Mitcham's *Men of the Luftwaffe*[19] spring to mind as examples of works so filled with basic errors that they illustrate the problem of trying to write without access to original sources. Even the judicious use of every available secondary source, and of numerous translations, cannot substitute for looking at the primary documents themselves. In *To Command the Sky: The Battle for Air Superiority Over Germany, 1942–1944,*[20] Stephen McFarland and Wesley Newton attempted a scholarly work about the air war over Europe, but their lack of primary sources led them to numerous misconceptions about the Luftwaffe, its doctrine, its air defense system, and its technology. Newton and McFarland's work contains numerous errors of fact that would be quickly caught by a knowledge of German sources. For example, they give Hermann Göring credit for organizing the secret reklame squadrons during rearmament, although these units were actually operating long before Göring's appointment as air minister.[21] They argue that Luftwaffe Regulation 16 was Douhetian in tone—which it was not.[22] They confuse the Bf 109 with the Bf 108, describing the Bf 109 as a transition trainer.[23] What emerges is essentially a "party line" view of history in which the U.S. Army Air Forces do almost everything right, and the Luftwaffe stumbles from one mistake to the next; the language is telling. Luftwaffe claims against U.S. aircraft that are 50 percent too high are labeled "bloated claims." When U.S. fighters and bombers claim 400 percent of actual German losses, they are referred to as "claims."[24] The reader is left wondering how the Germans managed to defeat even the Polish air force in 1939.

An understanding of the human dimension in the development of Luftwaffe theory and doctrine is sorely lacking. David Irving has written biographies of Hermann Göring and Erhard Milch, at one end of the Luftwaffe's command spectrum, but both of these works are seriously flawed by Irving's tendency to defend his subject's behavior rather than provide an objective analysis.[25] There are also numerous books about the experiences of the fighter aces of the Third Reich, on the other end of the command spectrum. But in the middle, at the level of the senior commanders of the Luftwaffe—the men who created an air power doctrine—there is next to nothing. There are the memoirs of Field Marshal Kesselring, but while telling the reader a great deal about Kesselring's experience as a theater commander in World War II, they tell us little about his views on air doctrine while he was the chief of staff of the Luftwaffe in the 1930s.

As a result of this dearth of literature about the senior commanders and air theorists of the Luftwaffe it is common to find blithe statements about the Luftwaffe's leadership, such as Telford Taylor's comment that 'the Luftwaffe was shaped by aviators who were amateur soldiers and by soldiers who were amateur aviators."[26] Stephen McFarland and Wesley Newton characterize the leadership of the Luftwaffe as "an odd collection of personalities," adding, "almost all were eccentric."[27] Such is almost certainly true of Hermann Göring, but one can scarcely describe Walter Wever, Field Marshal Hugo Sperrle, Field Marshal Albert Kesselring, generals Helmuth Wilberg, Kurt Student, Helmuth Felmy, Wilhelm Wimmer, or Wolfram von Richthofen as being especially odd or eccentric. It is also hard to describe any of these men as being amateur soldiers or amateur aviators. In reality, the Luftwaffe had some excellent leadership in the top ranks and this largely accounts for the effectiveness of the Luftwaffe in combat in World War II.

If most of the literature on the leadership of the Luftwaffe is about Göring, a man who actually knew very little about air power ideas or the capabilities of the air force that he nominally commanded, then it is easy to understand how a relatively facile judgment that implies that the Luftwaffe was an army support force and simply got its ideas from the army can take hold. In fact, the Luftwaffe had a great many very competent air commanders and air thinkers in the top ranks who made a major contribution to the development of air power theory and doctrine in their time. Unfortunately, there has been so little written about the senior Luftwaffe leaders and their air concepts that their contribution to the history of military and air power ideas has been generally overlooked. There is much to do in this field to remedy this deficiency. A proper biography of Lieutenant General Walter Wever, the Luftwaffe's first chief of staff, is certainly called for. General der Flieger Helmuth Wilberg, the senior air officer of the Reichswehr in the 1920s and Field Marshal Wolfram von Richthofen, an important figure in the Luftwaffe in the 1930s as well as World War II air fleet commander Hugo Sperrle, all deserve their own biographies. The roles of General Robert Knauss, Wilhelm Wimmer, and Herhudt von Rohden in creating strategic air war concepts in the 1930s have also been largely ignored.

I hope to deal with some of this historical vacuum in this work. Even in an era of mass movements and mass culture, individual effort still plays the central role in developing ideas and in leading military forces. The German military contained a great many first-rate air power thinkers in the interwar period, and the army air staff, and later the Luftwaffe, nurtured these talented men who made a significant original contribution to air power thought and doctrine. The German military developed a wide range of ideas and practical doctrines about air power and, it can be argued, had by the start of World War II the most comprehensive systematic body of thought about air power of all the major powers. This book rightly concentrates on the efforts of these individuals and the contribution that they made to military thought. If I cannot do the theoretical contribution of each full justice, I can at least provide the reader with an overview of the ideas of each of these officers and provide a historical and technological context for their contribution.

A REVIEW OF LITERATURE ON THE LUFTWAFFE

While the literature on the air theory and doctrine of the Luftwaffe is slim, a number of excellent books and articles have addressed various aspects of German air doctrine. I have taken these works as a starting point for my own investigations. No historian truly works alone, and I could not have written this book without relying on the work of some skilled historians who have written about the Luftwaffe. Certainly the most useful and thorough histories of the Luftwaffe in the interwar period, which detail the history of both the secret Luftwaffe of the Weimar Republic and the open Luftwaffe of the post-1935 era, have been written by Karl-Heinz Völker. In his *Entwicklung der Militärischen Luftfahrt in Deutschland 1920–1933*[28] and his *Die Deutsche Luftwaffe 1933–1939: Aufbau, Führung, Rüstung,*[29] Völker has provided a sober and detailed history of the development of German air power. In *Dokumente und Dokumentarfotos zur Geschichte der Deutschen Luftwaffe,*[30] Völker has edited and published a selection of many of the most important documents of Luftwaffe history including much of the correspondence on air power between the senior German military leaders.

On all matters relating to the Luftwaffe's leadership, the Luftwaffe's general staff system, and Luftwaffe organization, Horst Boog's *Die deutsche Luftwaffenführung 1935–1945* is the definitive work.[31] Boog provides some invaluable insights into the relationships among the Luftwaffe's senior leaders. Dr. Boog has also written numerous articles about Luftwaffe operational history, German military strategy, and the Luftwaffe leadership. Although Boog's focus is on the post-1935 period, the latter part of the period I am studying, some of his work provides important background to the Luftwaffe's early views of strategic bombing.[32]

There have been several book chapters and articles that have specifically addressed German air theory in the interwar period and should be necessary reading for anyone attempting to understand the interwar Luftwaffe. Klaus Maier has outlined the tensions evident in German air doctrine and the nature of the debates about air theory in the 1930s and 1940s in a chapter of the German official history of World War II. In a later chapter of the same work, Maier provides an excellent short history of the Luftwaffe's early wartime operations from Poland to the Battle of Britain.[33] Richard Muller, in the first chapter of his book *The German Air War in Russia,*[34] has written an insightful essay on the Luftwaffe's conception of "operative Luftkrieg" (operational air war), which does a fine job of laying to rest the concept that the Luftwaffe thought of itself as a "tactical" air force. I find Muller's chapter to be the best historical analysis in English on the nature of the Luftwaffe's conception of air war at the start of World War II.

Some excellent books and articles are available that cover in detail many of the subsidiary themes of this work. John Morrow's *German Air Power in World War I*[35] and his more recent book, *The Great War in the Air,*[36] provide the most detailed and thorough coverage available of the German air service in the First World War. Raymond Proctor's book, *Hitler's Luftwaffe in the Spanish Civil War,*[37] remains the best scholarly work to cover the history of the Luftwaffe's involvement in Spain from 1936–1939. One important historical event for the German military that has been shrouded in secrecy for more than seventy years—the story of the German-Soviet military cooperation and joint training from 1922–1933—has been thoroughly examined in Manfred Zeidler's book, *Reichswehr und Rote Armee 1920–1933.*[38] Zeidler has employed the extant German, and many of the Russian, sources to argue for the importance of the German-Russian relationship in the evolution of military doctrine in both countries. Bernd Stegemann, in his chapters on the German navy in the German official history of World War II, has provided a very useful examination of the German navy's understanding—or lack of understanding—of the role of air power in naval warfare in the 1930s, and the early years of World War II.[39]

There have been numerous books on the economic side of the Luftwaffe and its programs for rearmament and aircraft production. The one I have found the most useful is Edward Homze's *Arming the Luftwaffe: The Reich Air Ministry and the German Aircraft Industry, 1919–1939.*[40] Homze not only provides a detailed and critical history of the development and production of Luftwaffe aircraft, but has also effectively related the problems of planning and production to how the Luftwaffe staff conceived of aerial warfare. For details on the development and production of Luftwaffe aircraft, the definitive work has been done by William Green in his *Warplanes of the Third Reich.*[41] Green assesses the performance and combat effectiveness of each aircraft produced for the Luftwaffe, explaining why each aircraft was developed and how it fit into German doctrine at the time.

There are several good histories of the Luftwaffe that touch on the interwar period in the first chapter or so, but there are few that concentrate on the interwar period. One of the few books that deals with the interwar period is a short book by Hanfried Schliephake, *The Birth of the Luftwaffe.*[42] The best recent work on this period in English is E. R. Hooton's *Phoenix Triumphant: The Rise and Rise of the Luftwaffe.*[43] Hooten provides a sound general history of the Luftwaffe from 1918–1940, based on thorough research of primary documents.

A NOTE ON SOURCES

As much as possible, I have tried to research and write this book from original and contemporary documents. I have also tried to look at as many of the military periodicals and aviation periodicals of the period as possible. The popular and military literature about air power in this period is vast, but I hope that I have looked at enough to give a "feel" for the issues and opinions widely held during the period under study.

The primary official documents such as manuals, correspondence, maneuver reports, and war plans used in the research of this book have been found primarily in the German military archives located in Freiburg im Breisgau, Germany, and in the German Records Collection of the U.S. National Archives in Washington, D.C. I have also sought out contemporary periodicals in libraries and special collections in Germany, Canada, and the United States. The research was made much easier by the events of 1989 and 1990 and the reunification of Germany. I have been able to find some important periodical collections and documents in the military archives of the former East Germany in Potsdam. These documents had been generally unavailable to Western scholars prior to 1990. For example, detailed historical monographs on the German air service and on air war in the interwar period were written by the staff of the military history section of the prewar Reichs Archives, and these ended up in East German hands after World War II. Such documents and collections have been significant additions to our understanding of the interwar period. Unfortunately, finding and obtaining documents relating to the German military relationship with the Russians in this era is extremely difficult on the Russian side due to the sheer chaos of the Russian archives. Hopefully, someday in the future the archives will be sorted out and the access to historians will be made easy. Until that time, however, any research on this topic will have to work around a relative scarcity of hard information.

During the last few years I have interviewed many former Luftwaffe officers to gain some background into the Luftwaffe of World War II and the immediate prewar era. What is even more important, the families of some of Germany's most important air thinkers and commanders have granted me access to letters, photos, and other documents relating to the background and personality of men such as Helmuth Wilberg, Robert Knauss, and Wolfram von Richthofen. I have incorporated this information into this book to provide a fuller explanation of the nature of the air power debates of the 1930s.

ON TERMINOLOGY

In writing this book I have translated or adapted many specific German terms for greater readability. The German army, for example, officially abolished the general staff in 1920 in accordance with the Treaty of Versailles. The general staff was replaced by the "Troops Office" (Truppenamt), and the general staff officers were renamed "leadership assistants" (Führergehilfen). However, in reality only the names had changed. The Troops Office *was* the general staff for all practical purposes and the "leadership assistants" thought of themselves as general staff officers, even referring to themselves as such outside of Allied hearing. Therefore, I simply use the term general staff and Troops Office interchangeably, even though the general staff did not officially exist between 1920 and 1935.

I also do much the same in employing the term "air staff" to the air officers who served in the army headquarters and staff from 1920 to 1933. Of course, no air staff officially existed. However, the special slots for pilot officers in the Troops Office and the Weapons Office for all practical purposes fulfilled the functions of an air staff—they made war plans, wrote doctrine, and set requirements for aircraft development and procurement. For simplicity's sake, I refer to these officers as "the air staff" and the secret air projects of the German army as the "shadow Luftwaffe" or "Luftwaffe" for 1920 to 1935—although the Luftwaffe did not come officially into being until March 1935.

CHAPTER ONE

The Lessons of World War I

During the First World War, air power came of age. Although it was not yet a weapon that was capable of achieving decision on the battlefield, between 1914 and 1918 it became, at the very least, an important weapon used in a variety of ways by all the major combatants. During the First World War, the German Imperial Air Service, the Luftstreitkräfte, fashioned an extensive air theory and air doctrine. Even before the start of World War I, however, Germany had become a serious air power, and had already laid the foundations for an air doctrine. The important weapon that the air service had become by 1918 had already been fashioned prior to 1914. Before 1914, the German army had established a methodology, and laid down some basic principles that would govern the development of German air power in a unique way. In this chapter, I will examine the foundations of German air theory and doctrine from the early years through World War I.

PRE-WORLD WAR I

Prior to World War I and during most of the war, the primary missions of the aircraft, airship, and stationary balloon were reconnaissance and artillery spotting. Making reconnaissance the top priority mission of the air arm was based on an accurate understanding of the nature of warfare and technology of that time. The Franco-German War of 1870 had been studied in minute detail by the French and German general staffs, as well as by the militaries of the other major powers. One of the most notable lessons of the Franco-German War was the vital importance of good intelligence and reconnaissance. Most of the early battles of the 1870 war—Spicheren (6 August), Fröschwiller (6 August), Beaumont (29–30 August)—were unplanned battles, instances when the French and German armies simply blundered into each other. The result was a series of bloody slugging matches in which the Germans prevailed more by luck and by the mistakes of the French commanders than by any operational finesse.[1] "The fighting at Spicheren, Fröschwiller,

Colombey, and Vionville had come as a surprise to the high command on both sides as an interruption and distraction to totally different plans."[2] After the 1870 war, both the French and German general staffs therefore placed a high priority on improving their long-range operational reconnaissance.

Another lesson from the Franco-Prussian War was the significance of the new, rapid-firing, rifled-steel, breech-loading Krupp guns. Artillery assumed greater importance on the battlefield, and the longer range of the rifled guns required more precise observation at greater distances than the bronze muzzle-loaders that were used for most of the nineteenth century.

In the decades following the war of 1870, both the German and French armies emphasized reconnaissance in their general staff education and their war games. Both the French and the Germans looked to fixed hydrogen balloons as part of the solution for better reconnaissance and artillery observation. The Franco-Prussian War was scarcely over when both sides created committees that undertook experiments with balloons.[3] By 1884, the Prussian army had created its first permanent balloon unit.[4] The French had established their first balloon units in 1879.[5]

The French/German rivalry and arms race prior to World War I was a primary factor in driving the development of aviation in both countries. After creating stationary observation balloon units in the 1880s and 1890s, both countries turned their attention to powered airship flight. By July 1900, Count Zeppelin was able to fly his dirigible airship, powered by gasoline engines turning propellers, over the Bodensee. German officers were on hand to observe the first flight.[6] The general staff showed great interest in the development of the powered airship. One of General Helmuth von Moltke's first acts as new chief of the general staff in January 1906 was to advise the inspector of the transport troops to study the use of the airship as a weapon.[7] By 1906, the Prussian war ministry was providing 550,000 reichsmarks a year for development of powered airships.[8] From 1906 to 1910, the war ministry, navy ministry, and general staff put considerable effort into developing airships as weapons. In 1908, the army paid 225,000 reichsmarks for one airship, the P-1.[9] In 1909, the first real air maneuvers took place, with four airships participating.[10]

The development of the airship provided the impetus for the army and war ministry to begin thinking about the missions and capabilities of the air weapon. With their long range, airships were first considered for a strategic reconnaissance role, but by the 1909 maneuvers the possibility of developing the airship to drop bombs on military and transportation targets was considered.[11] However, despite the great public enthusiasm for the Zeppelin dirigibles and other powered airships of pre-World War I Germany, the general staff quickly lost its enthusiasm for the airship. Airships were expensive, difficult to build and maintain, required special docking and hangar facilities, and were extremely vulnerable to accidents in winds over 25 knots. The airship's only real advantages were its range and load-carrying capacity.

In 1908, the army high command had recommended acquiring fifteen airships, but the airship and army maneuvers of 1909 and 1910 showed that the airships were unable to meet the standards set by the army. Trials in 1910 proved that the airship was extremely vulnerable to fire from howitzers and rapid-fire antiballoon guns.[12] Europe's first great air show at Rheims in 1909, moreover, dramatically changed the air power paradigm by demonstrating the capabilities of a new invention: the airplane. Although the German war ministry—which controlled army spending—remained enthusiastic about the airship, the general staff, under the direction of von Moltke, turned its attention to the airplane as being a more fruitful means of developing the potential of military aviation.

In January 1908, the general staff assigned Captain von der Lieth-Thomsen the duty of following domestic and foreign aviation development.[13] Lieth-Thomsen's study section was assigned to Captain Erich Ludendorff's mobilization branch of the general staff in October 1908, and both officers became enthusiasts for, and advocates of, the airplane.[14] By 1912, von Moltke was pushing the war ministry for funds and personnel for airplane units, arguing that the French were far ahead in heavier-than-air aviation, and were spending far more money on aviation than the Germans.[15]

Under the pressure of the French/German arms race, the Prussian army airplane budget grew from 36,000 reichsmarks in 1909 to 25,920,000 reichsmarks in 1914 out of a total aviation expenditure, including airships, of 52,525,950 reichsmarks.[16] The Bavarian army created its own air service, and developed a Bavarian aircraft industry as well.[17] On the other hand, the German navy lagged behind in developing the airplane, due to its reliance on the long-range airship. Between 1911 and August 1914, only thirty-nine airplanes (seaplanes) had been acquired. By the start of World War I, army aviation had passed out of its infancy to become a considerable force, while naval aviation remained in the experimental stage.[18]

By 1909, at the urging of the general staff, the war ministry decided to directly subsidize civilian aviation companies to produce airplanes.[19] By 1910, the army was committed to developing airplane technology through subsidies to the new airplane companies, purchases of airplanes, and contracting to train officers as pilots and observers. In 1910, Germany's first military pilot training began at Döberitz, near Berlin.[20] By 1911, an organizational framework had been developed, and a flight command created and placed under the direction of the inspectorate of transport troops.[21]

After 1910, the airplane program of the German army gained momentum. Eight army aircraft flew in the Kaiser's maneuvers of 1911, and performed well. The inspector of military transport, Colonel Messing, reported that "Outstanding progress has been made in the construction of airplanes in the last year, although the airplane is not yet a truly effective reconnaissance and observation machine."[22] Henceforth, the army was committed to the rapid development of an aviation branch.

AVIATION AND THE GENERAL STAFF

Military aviation in Germany was very much a child of the general staff, which spurred its development prior to World War I. The Prussian war ministry, however, had more direct control of the aviation force—it controlled the military budget, procurement of weapons, and the organization of the army. Even though it commanded army operations in wartime, the general staff had less control of the army in peacetime. In peacetime, the general staff was responsible for army training and education, doctrine, and most important, war planning. While the general staff could not order the creation of an air force or directly procure aircraft, it did advise the war ministry on such matters.[23] The prestige of the general staff prior to World War I was such that its advice was usually taken with a great deal of respect by the war ministry.

The general staff had rightly earned its prestige. Although the modern Prussian general staff was a product of the era of General Scharnhorst's reforms in the early 1800s, it was scarcely noticed until the dramatic victories of 1866 and 1870 showed that Germany's general staff system gave it a decisive edge in war planning, and command and control. The general staff, as developed by the most famous chief of the general staff, Count Helmut von Moltke, was an impressive institution and a true meritocracy. Once admitted to the general staff, an officer was transferred to a separate branch of the army, and his career was carefully managed. Officers of this general staff corps, identified by the carmine stripes on their uniform trousers, received preference for promotion and command, and had greater opportunities to reach senior command positions than the average line officer.[24]

Admittance to the general staff was earned. About ten years into their careers, officers—usually, as senior first lieutenants—could take the examination for admittance to the general staff school (Kriegsakademie). About forty officers a year were selected and underwent an intensive course at the Kriegsakademie in Berlin. The three-year course emphasized military planning, war gaming, and the study of military theory and history. In the exercises, originality was encouraged. No rigid "school solutions" were taught, and a high standard of clear and logical thought was expected in war games, papers, and exercises. After a thorough professional grounding of ten years in regimental service, the general staff students learned to think at the operational level of war: military operations at the division, corps, and army level. The Prussian Kriegsakademie, open also to officers of the Sachsen, Württemberg, and Bavarian armies, provided the most thorough advanced military education in the world prior to World War I.

Of the approximately 29,000 officers in the German army in 1914, there were 622 officers (2.14 percent of the active officer corps) who were members of the General Staff Corps.[25] One advantage of this elite group of officers was its size. Officers of the general staff corps knew each other well. Intimacy bred debate and discussion, but also some tolerance for views outside the mainstream. Erich von Ludendorff's pre-World War I views on total war were considered extreme by most of his colleagues of the general staff, but his undoubted brilliance as a thinker and tactician kept him in influential positions on the greater general staff, while such views would have earned Ludendorff at least exile to provincial postings in other armies. Another advantage that accrued thanks to the prestige of the general staff corps was that even junior captains and majors were given positions of real responsibility, and lower-ranking members of the general staff could be assured of a serious hearing at the highest levels of the army. This fostered discussion, and the flow of accurate information to the top that other armies of the time could not equal.

In contrast to the images of the reactionary and intellectually stagnant officer corps of the pre-World War I era, the German general staff and its chief, General Helmut von Moltke (nephew of Generalfeldmarschall von Moltke), took a lively interest in technological developments. Under his tenure, the general staff assumed a leading role in developing military aviation as rapidly as possible. In early 1911, von Moltke advised the war ministry that the nine airships assigned to the army were sufficient, and requested that the requirement for fifteen airships set in 1908 be reconsidered. In the meantime, the general staff would study the degree to which airplanes could carry out reconnaissance.[26] After some serious study, by 1912, von Moltke had come down firmly on the side of the airplane, and made the following recommendations:

- The creation of a separate inspectorate of aviation troops, and the release of aviation from the transportation inspectorate;
- An increase in aviation organization, assigning aircraft units to corps and developing antiaircraft guns.[27]

While the aircraft's role remained primarily that of reconnaissance, developing the airplane as an offensive weapon was urged. In March 1912, von Moltke questioned the inspectorate of transport on the following points:

1. With what firing weapons should airplanes be equipped, and are there difficulties in mounting these weapons?
2. What weights have been dropped from our planes up to this time, and what was the degree of accuracy?

I would recommend that, by dropping bombs during flights on main and secondary roads, the accuracy of aircraft against these targets at wartime altitude be determined.[28]

A month later, von Moltke recommended equipping aircraft with machine guns, and requested a report on the Euler machine-gun mount.[29] He also requested information on the largest weights that could be dropped from airplanes to recommend procurement of aerial bombs for the aviation force.[30] By September 1912, von Moltke proposed that an aviation organization be created by 1914, which would consist of air detachments for each army and cavalry corps, as well as aviation detachments for border fortresses. The aircraft units would be available for reconnaissance and artillery spotting, and would comprise a force of 388 aircraft—not including aircraft in air parks or replacement units. The recommended air units were, moreover, to be highly mobile, with motor vehicles, motorized workshops, tents, spare parts, and fuel supplied to the air units so they could operate closely with the army. A standard air detachment would consist of eight aircraft.[31] Von Moltke noted his belief that the French were superior in aviation and proposed creating a reserve force of civilian pilots who could be quickly mobilized by the army in wartime. While the aircraft was still seen primarily as a reconnaissance weapon, von Moltke concluded, "The practice and experiments using the aircraft as a fighting machine, such as those being conducted at Döberritz . . . need to produce practical results as soon as possible."[32]

By 1913, Ludendorff, who enjoyed flying as a passenger in airplanes and visited aviation units at every opportunity, had revised the general staff's plans for aviation. He proposed to the war ministry that by 1914, the army should have 528 airplanes and by April 1916, an air service with 1,796 airplanes.[33] Von Moltke's and Ludendorff's interest in aviation reflected the development, at an early date, of an enthusiasm for the airplane within the general staff and the officer corps. The new aviation arm tended to attract many of the army's best officers. In 1911—right after the army's first aircraft fatalities—more than 900 line officers applied for flight training.[34] It took a considerable degree of courage to apply for aviation training at this time because the fatality rate for pilots was horrendous. In 1911 three military pilots died in air accidents. In 1912 thirteen died and this figure increased to more than thirty in 1913. Prior to the outbreak of World War I more than seventy German army and navy personnel had been killed in aviation accidents.[35] This figure amounted to about a 20 percent death rate for military aviators. Yet, the new aviation branch had no problem in recruiting personnel.

Within the general staff, several officers already had experience with aviation. Major Hermann von der Lieth-Thomsen had served with airships, and Major Wilhelm Siegert had paid out of pocket in 1910 to learn to fly. Both would hold senior positions in early German aviation.[36] In 1911, four general staff captains, Buckrucker, von Stülpnagel, Würtz, and Zimmerman, underwent pilot training.[37] First Lieutenant Helmuth Wilberg received his pilot's license in 1910, after beginning the Kriegsakademie course, and after completion in 1913, he was assigned as adjutant of the air service. Between 1910 and 1914, general staff officers Wilhelm Haehnelt, Hugo Sperrle, and Helmuth Felmy transferred to the aviation branch.[38] By the outbreak of the war in 1914, two to three dozen general staff officers had undergone pilot and observer training. The small new service had succeeded in attracting a disproportionate share of the army's best talent.

The aviation forces were organized into the Prussian *Fliegertruppe* (Flying Troops) in 1912, and became a separate inspectorate in October 1913, under the command of Colonel Walter Eberhardt.[39] The general staff had recommended in 1912 that each corps have its own air detachment, and by 1913 this was becoming a reality. As the force grew, several corps air detachments were combined under a senior air commander—equivalent to a battalion commander—who was responsible for training, administration, and logistics. By 1913, four aviation battalions existed in the Prussian air service and one in the Bavarian air arm.[40] In March 1913, even before the creation of the new inspectorate, the first doctrine manual for the new force was published. *Guidelines for Training the Troops about Aircraft and Means of Resisting Aircraft* described the missions of aircraft (balloons, airships, and airplanes) as "strategic and tactical reconnaissance, artillery observation, transmission of orders and information, transport of people and objects, dropping bombs, fighting aircraft."[41] The doctrine provided descriptions of the aircraft types in common use, provided advice on the tactics of conducting air reconnaissance, and advised ground troops on methods of camouflage and dispersal to protect themselves against enemy reconnaissance.[42] The latter part of the manual provided firing tables for machine guns and artillery to shoot down aircraft.[43] The army had been experimenting with specially designed antiaircraft guns for several years and conducted its first antiaircraft exercises in 1910. The army recognized that an antiaircraft artillery force was required, and by 1914 a small number of motorized antiaircraft guns had been procured.[44]

Maneuvers and other studies were important in moving the air service to a more detailed tactical and operational doctrine. The airplane played an important role in the 1913 army maneuvers with six air detachments with a total of thirty-six aircraft participating. For the first time in maneuvers, the air units conducted night flights.[45] In early 1914, working with the experience of the maneuvers and exercises, the evaluation board for the transportation inspectorate of the army wrote a memo listing nine specific roles for the airplane in military operations:[46]

1. Strategic reconnaissance
2. Tactical reconnaissance
3. Artillery observation
4. Reconnaissance for cavalry divisions
5. Fighting enemy airplanes
6. Fighting ground troops
7. Destroying enemy installations
8. Liaison (carrying messages)
9. Transporting troops

The German army was moving quickly to develop specialized types of aircraft and specialized units that could most effectively carry out each of these missions.

In January 1914, Wilhelm Siegert wrote a memorandum to the general staff in which he referred to the Italian use of aircraft in bombing operations in Libya in 1911–1912. He asserted that the airplane was now more than a reconnaissance machine—it was a fighting machine. "It will not be possible to operate without weapons. Every reconnaissance flight will result in an encounter with enemy aircraft . . . It is likely that an aircraft which is capable of shooting an enemy will have the advantage . . . The most suitable weapon is a light, air-cooled machine gun. The army which succeeds in knocking the enemy's aerial reconnaissance system out of operation . . . will have the advantage. With these facts in mind, it is essential that aircraft are designed which permit the use of weapons in the widest possible sector above, below, and on both sides of the airplane."[47]

When World War I began in August 1914, only France and Germany could be considered serious air powers. Both nations had well developed air arms with over 250 operational front aircraft each, and reserves of both airplanes and pilots. After mobilization in August 1914, the German flying forces had the following units and equipment available: thirty-three field aviation detachments, with six aircraft each; eight fortress detachments, with four aircraft each; eight rear depots, with three aircraft each (reserve); twenty-four balloon detachments; twelve airship units; and eighteen antiaircraft units.[48] From 1909 to 1914, the German general staff—notably its chief, General Helmuth von Moltke—showed considerable foresight and innovation in developing an air arm. Germans entered the war with a rational organization, and a well-trained cadre of senior and junior officers for its air arm, an aviation industry, and most important a doctrine that was workable and effective for the era, and which foresaw the evolution of the aircraft from the reconnaissance and artillery-spotting role to a genuine combat weapon.

THE OUTBREAK OF WAR: THE AIRPLANE PROVES DECISIVE

In the first months of World War I, the airplane proved its worth in the reconnaissance and spotting roles. In August and September of 1914, German aircraft units flew extensive reconnaissance over the Russian offensive into East Prussia, and kept the German Eighth Army informed of Russian troop movements.[49] The good intelligence thus provided enabled the German Eighth Army to encircle and destroy the Russian Second Army at the Battle of Tannenberg. As to the worth of the aircraft, Eighth Army Commander General von Hindenburg remarked, "Without the airplane, there is no Tannenberg."[50] On the western front, the aircraft proved a worthy support weapon for the Allies, when Allied aircraft spotted the gap between the German armies before Paris, allowing the French army to counterattack and drive the Germans back at the "Miracle of the Marne" in September 1914. Once the battle lines were stabilized in late fall 1914 and trench warfare became the norm, the reconnaissance mission of the aircraft became less urgent, and both sides looked for means to best employ their aviation arms. In late fall 1914, the Germans created a special bombing unit in Ostend, Belgium, with the mission of attacking deep behind enemy lines. Already, at the very start of the war, both sides had carried out limited bombing attacks against targets behind each other's lines.[51] The new German bombing unit, given the cover name *Carrier Pigeon Detachment Ostend,* began to prepare itself for a unique mission: the Germans planned a strategic bombing campaign against the British home isles.

In early 1915 German army and navy airships began direct attacks on London. These attacks continued sporadically throughout 1915. The material effect of bombing London was actually fairly minimal: The casualties were low, and the material damage slight.[52] The first strategic bombing attacks were, however, remarkable for the psychological effect they had on the British population. There were instances of panic in London, and widespread absenteeism in the munitions plants for a time.[53] To deal with flagging civilian morale, the British military began a crash program of building up defenses for Great Britain as a reaction to the German attacks.[54] Despite the impressive psychological effect on its enemies, the first German strategic bombing offensive can be considered a failure. Zeppelin airships, for the reasons noted earlier, were not particularly suitable as bombing aircraft. In the 1915–1916 campaign, German losses of Zeppelin airships—primarily from operational accidents caused by weather and wind conditions rather than by any enemy resistance—were relatively high.[55] The Germans' first strategic bombing offensive confirmed their general staffs' prewar dislike of the Zeppelin airship. Zeppelin construction was nevertheless stepped up after the outbreak of the war, and Zeppelins were employed as strategic bombers, because they were the only aircraft available with the necessary range and carrying load for bombing targets at a significant range.

In 1915 and 1916 a wide range of new aircraft models and technologies was developed on both sides, to meet new combat needs on the western front. The most significant innovation of the era came in 1915, with the development of the single-seat fighter aircraft by both sides. Single-seat fighter aircraft were primarily defensive weapons, developed for the sole purpose of attacking other aircraft. They had limited range and firepower, but the necessary speed and maneuverability to gain the advantage in aerial combat. The fighter plane was the result of an understanding that, for aircraft to operate in their primary roles—that is, as reconnaissance aircraft and as bombers, air superiority must be won and maintained. Reconnaissance and bombing aircraft needed to be protected from other enemy airplanes.

The next major step in the development of German air doctrine came in early 1916, with the planning for the great German army offensive at Verdun. At Verdun, the German army planned to use its fighter force in an air superiority campaign, so that German artillery-spotting aircraft could freely conduct observation flights and then assist German artillery to destroy the French army. In this instance, aircraft were a support weapon, but a very important support arm for the German army. If the German plan was to work effectively, control of the air would have to be maintained, or else accurate artillery fire could not be sustained. To control the air, the Germans placed a major proportion of their air power on the Verdun front, and organized their fighters to fly a pattern of patrols along the front lines to protect German observation craft against French fighters and to prevent French fighters and observation planes from carrying out artillery spotting against the German army. The German air campaign at Verdun was the first major failure for the Luftstreitkräfte. Noting the rigid pattern of German patrols, the French could wait and amass their aircraft, and simply break the German air barrier at a time and place of their own choosing. As the battle over Verdun continued, the Germans lost air superiority over their front, which inhibited their artillery-spotting aircraft considerably.[56]

REORGANIZATION OF THE GERMAN AIR SERVICE

The year 1916 saw a massive restructuring of the German aerial arm and was a decisive period for the development of German air doctrine. In March 1916, Lieutenant Colonel Hermann von der Lieth-Thomsen, chief of field flying forces, proposed that the German air service, including the naval air arm, ought to be combined, and given the status of a separate and independent branch of the armed forces, coequal with the army and navy, and with its own general staff and commander.[57] The German airmen argued that air power had come of age, and had proven its importance on the battlefield as a decisive arm of battle. The Prussian war ministry and the general staff of the army supported the proposal to create an air force as a separate and independent branch of the armed services and called for the "free development of the whole arm."[58] The debate bogged down, however, because of strong opposition to an independent air force from the German navy. The navy ostensibly opposed the move because naval aviation was a specialized branch of the navy and its development would not be handled effectively in a service dominated by land pilots.[59] The navy, arguing that such a force would be against the imperial constitution, placed sufficient roadblocks in the way of the army and war ministry to prevent the establishment of an air force in early 1916. The navy's true opposition to an independent air force was based on service politics: the creation of an independent air force, as a coequal branch of the military, would require the establishment of a new ministry of defense to serve as the cover ministry for all services. This would reduce the influence of the navy, and give the army a greater voice on the defense councils of the empire.[60]

The argument for an independent air force did, however, result in a new organization for the German air arm. In October 1916, the German air service was granted its own commander in chief, its own general headquarters, its own general staff, and effective centralized control of most aviation assets of the German army. The principle of centralized control meant that all aspects of aviation—from production of aircraft to the training of airmen, to the disposition of air logistics units, to civil air defense, to army flak units—now came under the single direction of the air service.[61] The Luftstreitkräfte headquarters had staff sections for operations, weather, flak, home air defense, and medical services as well as the logistics and administrative sections. An army air commander had a staff with communications, operations, intelligence, personnel, airfield engineers, transport, and equipment sections. A commander of flak served under the direction of the army commander. While the Luftstreitkräfte operated under the command and direction of the army high command, its senior air officers operated at the direction of the air service commander. Units attached to an army reported to a single air commander for that army, and squadron commanders no longer reported, or were directly subordinate to, the army's lower echelon ground commanders. By the end of 1916, the air service had complete control of its own weather service, communications network, flak units, and the entire infrastructure necessary for a modern air force.

The first commander in chief of the German air service was General der Kavallerie Ernst Hoeppner.[62] Though not an airman, Hoeppner was a highly experienced general staff officer who had proven himself as a division commander, and who had long been an advocate of a strong air arm. The commander of the field flying force—that is, the commander of the German air units serving at the front, was the experienced airman, Colonel Hermann von der Lieth-Thomsen.[63] Chief of staff of the air service was Colonel Wilhelm Siegert, an experienced airman who served brilliantly as director of procurement and air service logistics.

With the creation of a central headquarters and an air general staff in 1916, the Luftstreitkräfte had a mechanism by which it could effectively evaluate and create air doctrine. In early 1917, numerous new manuals and regulations appeared, including *Instructions on the Mission and Utilization of Flying Units Within an Army.*[64] The new doctrine manuals provided the air

General von Hoeppner, commander, Luftstreitkräfte, visiting the strategic bomber force in Flanders in 1917. He is conferring with Navy Lieutenant von Frankenberg, the bomber group navigation officer. (Courtesy of the U.S. National Air and Space Museum, Washington, D.C.)

service with clear guidelines for operational doctrine. The early doctrine of the air service provided the air arm with a set of clear doctrinal principles for the execution of an air campaign. These principles were essentially the traditional principles of war of the German army, adapted to aerial conditions and technologies. For example, the new air doctrine emphasized the importance of troop leadership, and stressed that the principles of command and leadership were inherently no different in the air than they were for the ground. As in the case of the ground forces, while realizing the power of the defense, the experience of Verdun had taught the Luftstreitkräfte that a purely defensive battle could not lead to decisive results. To gain a notable effect and keep the initiative, the air force needed to conduct an offensive, including an air superiority battle, in which the fighter planes would conduct sweeps and offensive operations to control the air over the battlefield.[65] The 1917 doctrine of the air service also stressed, as in the case of the army ground force doctrine, the importance of using air power in mass, and preventing the piecemeal dispersion of air units.[66] German air doctrine, following the army tradition, stressed the importance of maintaining a reserve, and employing the reserve in mass at the decisive point of the battle.[67]

The German general staff system, the foundation for the general staff of the new Luftstreitkräfte headquarters, gave the Germans an advantage throughout the war, by enabling them to react quickly to technological and operational changes on the battlefield. Although German technology was generally equal to that of the Allies, the Luftstreitkräfte was often able to employ its more limited resources more effectively and more decisively than the Allies. In the Luftstreitkräfte, commanders were granted greater authority and responsibility for the operational employment of their units than in the Allied air arms. The air general staff officers serving with every army on the eastern and western fronts constantly reported to the commander in chief of the air service, and made recommendations for changing doctrine and technology. The status and prestige of the general staff officer in the Imperial army meant that even such relatively junior officers as captains were granted more consideration, and were listened to more closely, than company-grade officers in the British, French, and American armies. The Luftstreitkräfte also made a practice of obtaining reports from successful squadron commanders on the front. Commanders such as Rittmeister Baron Manfred von Richthofen, a squadron commander in 1916 and 1917 and a wing commander from 1917 until his death in 1918, provided the air service commander with numerous critical reports detailing the state of German equipment and tactics, as well as his evaluation of Allied technology and operational methodology.[68] Von Richthofen's reports were so highly valued that the acceptance of the Fokker D-7 fighter plane in late 1917 was primarily due to von Richthofen's advice.

Another German air service advantage in conducting the air war in 1917 was the thorough training customarily provided for the German army. By 1916, German pilots underwent an extensive training program that included both short-range and long-range flying, night flying, and day and night landings. In 1916, by the time a German pilot had his wings, he had flown approximately sixty-five hours. That amount of training did not, however, qualify a pilot for combat duties. New German pilots were sent to a special training center at Valenciennes, in occupied France. There, the fledgling airmen were given an intensive, one-month course in combat techniques, taught by experienced airmen who had just completed tours of several months flying in the front lines.[69] The thorough training that was provided to the German pilots gave them a distinct edge over the battlefield. Throughout 1916 and 1917, the pilots of the Royal Flying Corps, Britain's air service, commonly entered combat with no more than seventeen total flying hours, only a few of them solo.[70] At this stage of the war, British losses of pilots, flying against the more experienced German pilots, were horrendous. During the air battles of "Bloody April" in 1917, the Royal Flying Corps lost aircraft at a more than 3:1 ratio when opposing the Luftstreitkräfte.[71]

FLANDERS AIR CAMPAIGN

German historians writing after World War I have argued that the Luftstreitkräfte had reached its highest point of combat efficiency in the air over Flanders during the campaign from May to November 1917.[72] In May 1917, the British army began its major offensive in Flanders, which was to last for six months, petering out in the mud of a Belgian autumn. For both the Allies and the Germans, Flanders can be regarded as the first truly comprehensive modern air campaign. The air over Flanders saw all aspects of modern aviation incorporated: an integrated air defense air network on the German side; interdiction bombing against enemy transport and logistics targets carried out by both the British and the Germans; air superiority and fighter superiority campaigns conducted against enemy aircraft and airfields; and, on the German side, extensive use of close air support in defensive and offensive battles.

When the British offensive began in the early summer of 1917, the German air units under the Fourth Army in Flanders consisted of approximately 300 aircraft. The Luftstreitkräfte quickly reinforced the sector. By the end of July 1917, 600 aircraft were operational, under the command of Captain Helmuth Wilberg, commander of aviation forces for the Fourth Army. At this point, by July 1917, the Germans were opposing approximately 840-plus Allied aircraft in the area with about 600 of their own. The ratio of fighter aircraft was approximately 350 Allied fighters against 200 German fighters.[73]

The Flanders campaign saw some distinctive innovations in aerial warfare. The Germans formed Jagdgeschwader I (Fighter Wing 1) in June 1917. The Luftstreitkräfte had formed a provisional wing organization in April by putting four squadrons together as an operational unit under one commander. Once the concept was proven in combat, the Luftstreitkräfte reacted quickly, forming other fighter wings as well as JG 1.[74] Now, several fighter squadrons would be formally organized as a consistent tactical and operational unit. Rittmeister Baron Manfred von Richthofen was named as the first commanding officer of JG 1. The fighter squadron organization was also reorganized in the spring of 1917, and the German Jagdstaffel now consisted of twelve aircraft and fourteen pilots.[75] The fighter wings would now have approximately fifty aircraft and were made highly mobile with motorized transport and the ability to move quickly from one section of the front to another. The appearance of such a large tactical unit over the air in Flanders meant that it soon became common for the Air Service to conduct aircraft sweeps of fifty aircraft, whereas before 1917, an aircraft mission of even ten aircraft at a time was considered exceptional. The battle in the air over Flanders in 1917 proved the effectiveness of using aircraft in mass.

Another innovation of the Flanders air battle was Wilberg's organization of the two-seater observation plane squadrons into two- and three-squadron groups, and their employment as specialized close air support craft during the battle. The German two-seater observation aircraft of World War I, such as the Hannoveraner and the Halberstadt CL IV, were fast, well armed, and rugged. Provided with a small load of hand-droppable bombs, they became an effective weapon in providing support to German ground forces. While ground attack missions had been conducted regularly before 1917, the air campaign in Flanders saw the first use of specialized close air support craft employed in mass.[76]

In early 1917, the first doctrine manual for the ground attack squadrons was issued by the high command.[77] The normal squadron size for the armored two-seaters was six aircraft. Three squadrons were combined to operate as a group.[78] The ground attack squadrons would normally come under

Senior officers and staff of the German Fourth Army Aviation Force, summer 1917. Captain Wilberg, commander, Fourth Army Aviation, seated second from left. Rittmeister Baron Manfred von Richthofen, commander, Jagdgeschwader 1, seated third from left. First lieutenant Lothar von Richthofen, Manfred's brother and also a leading ace, seated second from right. (Photo from the Wilberg family.)

the operational control of an infantry division, and squadrons would be attached to divisions based on the army and army aviation commanders' assessment of support requirements.[79] However, as it was understood that the division commander would only be interested in combat to his immediate front, the army aviation commander was enjoined to keep some of the ground attack squadrons under army headquarters control as an operational reserve that could be available to attack lucrative targets found well behind the enemy's front lines.[80] The high command placed a great deal of hope in the new ground attack branch of the aviation forces. The morale effect of low-level bombing and strafing attacks on enemy infantry and artillery was seen as especially important—"the object of the battle flights is to shatter the enemy's nerve by repeated attacks in close formation."[81]

The British approach to the same issue was very different. The Royal Fly-

Halberstadt CL II, two-seat observer and ground attack plane, ca. 1917. With three machine guns and a bombload, this was one of the most popular and effective German aircraft for close support duties. (Photo from the U.S. Army Center for Military History.)

ing Corps employed unmodified single-seat fighters and sent them singly or in small flights over the front to find and attack any suitable targets they found. The British pilots had no specialized training for the role; it was just another duty of a fighter pilot.[82] The German air service set up a training program for the ground attack pilots behind the front and exercised them in group attacks on simulated targets.[83] The Luftstreitkräfte found the idea of small harassment raids as wasteful of scarce airmen and aircraft. One or two aircraft hitting random targets in the rear were unlikely to have any real impact on troop morale. The Germans preferred to mass their forces and wait to attack a specified target. It was believed that a large number of aircraft attacking one target would have far greater effect than a series of small attacks on dispersed targets. The German approach proved to be much more effective on the battlefield. Wilberg and his Fourth Army aviators massed their ground attack squadrons and then flung them at the British front lines and reserve positions in support of major counterattacks. A strong German counterattack on 10/11 July was preceded by squadrons of ground attack Halberstadts and Hannoveraner pinning down British troops and artillery. Under cover of their aircraft, the German army made some rapid gains and virtually destroyed two battalions of British troops.[84]

One of the most interesting aspects of the Flanders air campaign was the antiair campaign conducted by the Luftstreitkräfte. During the summer and fall of 1917, German heavy bombers carried out a series of raids against British and French airfields and air depots supporting the Allied offensive in Flanders. The German bombers attacked by night and dropped parachute flares to illuminate their targets. The airfield raids turned out to be surprisingly successful. On one raid the night of 6/7 July against the British airfield at Bray Dunes, the Luftstreitkräfte damaged twelve British aircraft.[85] The German bombers struck the British airfield and depot at St. Pol on the night of 24 September and caused heavy damage to the base. One hundred forty aircraft engines were destroyed by a German bomber hit on a hanger.[86] On the night of 1/2 October, the German night bombers returned to St. Pol and destroyed twenty-nine British aircraft and seven French aircraft, and caused heavy damage to hangers and the depot.[87] In several attacks, the Luftstreitkräfte was able to destroy a considerable number of Allied aircraft on the ground with negligible losses, mostly landing accidents, to their own forces.

An important feature of the 1917 air battles was a major interdiction campaign conducted by both sides against targets in their enemy's rear. The British bombers concentrated on bombing German rail yards, and the Germans hit French rail yards supporting the British army and made numerous night attacks on the ports that supplied the British Expeditionary Force (BEF)—especially Calais and Dunkirk. Both sides hoped to interrupt the logistics flow to the other. Neither the British nor the Germans were able to seriously disrupt their opponent's supply lines, but serious damage was inflicted and the bombing was a major inconvenience. In June and July 1917, the German First and Fourth Bomber Wings were assigned to support the Fourth Army's campaign in Flanders, and they quickly mounted a program of night raids on the enemy Channel ports.[88] Throughout August the British munitions dumps at Dunkirk were attacked with severe damage. The attacks on rail yards and ports were almost a nightly occurrence and, after a particularly devastating attack on Dunkirk on 3 October, it took four days to put out the fires.[89] Just as fighter aces were being made heroes, some bomber commanders were gaining renown. Captain Alfred Keller, commander of Bomber Wing 1 and a specialist in night bombing, was awarded the Pour le Mérite by the Kaiser after his unit dropped 100,000 kilograms of bombs on Dunkirk. On the whole, the German bombers on the Flanders front dropped 300,000 kilograms of bombs on the British during the 1917 campaign.[90]

The 1917 campaign in Flanders saw several other important innovations in air warfare. The Luftstreitkräfte was ahead of the Allied powers in applying radio technology to the air war. By early 1917, the Germans had radios small and rugged enough so that they could be mounted in two-seater observation planes used for artillery spotting.[91] The Luftstreitkräfte saw the potential that immediate communication between the aerial spotters and the artillery could have for combat efficiency and quickly developed a formal system of radio nets and simple codes for the aircraft observers. The aircraft radios of the time used Morse code, and a two- or three-letter message to the battery would tell the artillerymen the target location and help adjust fire.[92]

Some radios were also mounted in the ground attack aircraft, and Captain Wilberg used the radio to direct his ground attack squadrons at the height of the battle. The German Schutzstaffel were able to react quickly, and the employment of his ground attack squadrons at Messines Ridge on 6–14 June, helped slow and control the British offensive.[93] Wilberg also used his artillery observation aircraft to support the ground battle by dropping ammunition, food, and medical supplies on forward German infantry units that were hard-pressed by British attacks and unable to get ammunition forward.[94] Captain Wilberg gained a reputation as the Luftstreitkräfte's premier expert on ground attack aviation. General Freiherr von Bülow described Wilberg as "having the deepest understanding of the employment of the aircraft in the ground battle."[95] The German army and air service came out of the Flanders campaign deeply impressed with the value of ground attack aviation. The tactics that the Germans had developed for their ground attack squadrons and groups in Flanders were summarized in a detailed manual that was published by the Luftstreitkräfte staff circulated to the air units in September 1917.[96]

THE GERMAN STRATEGIC BOMBING CAMPAIGN

By early 1917, the Germans had developed an effective twin-engine bomber, the Gotha G IV, which could carry a 1,100-lb bombload over a long range to its target. During the early months of 1917, the Germans massed a force of forty-plus heavy bombers at airfields in Flanders on the North Sea coast under the command of Captain Ernst Brandenburg, who then trained his aircrew for the world's first strategic bombing campaign. The Luftstreitkräfte heavy bomber force was to conduct a bombing campaign against the British cities—primarily London—at the same time the German navy would begin an unrestricted submarine warfare campaign against British shipping. The German high command hoped that the double blow would seriously demoralize the British and knock Britain out of the war.

Gotha G IV heavy bomber, ca. 1917. This was the bomber that conducted most of the strategic raids against England in 1917–1918. (Photo from the U.S. Army Center for Military History.)

The earlier raids by Zeppelins were more in the nature of harassment raids by single airships or small flights of two or three airships. Brandenburg's conception was to use his bombers in mass to provide a greater impact. Because this was a new conception, there was no doctrine or experience to guide Brandenburg. The German bomber commander had to establish targeting guidelines, plan the operations, create formations for massed flight, and decide on the bombing altitude—all from scratch. All of this was done and in May 1917, the German bombers started raiding cities on the south coast of England. On 13 June 1917 a force of eighteen Gothas flying at 8,000 feet in daylight bombed London and killed 162 civilians and wounded 432. There was no effective air defense and no Gothas were shot down.[97] There was immediate panic on the part of the British public. Absenteeism in the factories soared, and the German raids soon became a cabinet-level crisis.[98] The crisis resulted in the recall of British fighter squadrons from the front and the creation of the Royal Air Force—whose first mission was to assure the strategic defense of Britain.[99]

The German bomber raids continued into early 1918. As the British defenses grew in scope, Brandenburg switched to night attacks. By 1918 the Germans were able to employ their *Riesen* (giant) bombers, which had four engines and could carry a one-ton bombload. As impressive as the psychological effects were on British civilians, however, the actual damage caused by the German air offensive was fairly small. The total British casualties from the May 1917–May 1918 strategic bombing raids were 836 dead and 1,982 wounded.[100] Brandenburg's problem was the limitations of the 1917 aviation technology. The German losses on the campaign were severe. Sixty-two German bombers were lost in the twenty-seven raids made by the "England Wing" of the Luftstreitkräfte. The primary cause of the losses was not the British defenses. Of the sixty-two planes lost, only nineteen were lost due to British aircraft or ground fire. The other forty-three were lost due to operational accidents. Of these, no fewer than thirty-seven bombers were lost due to landing accidents. These were large and heavy aircraft, and sorely underpowered. The landing gear of the time was weak, and the heavy aircraft were unforgiving of any mistakes. Because of the heavy losses, the high command and the Luftstreitkräfte finally concluded that the costs outweighed the benefits and called off the strategic bombing campaign. The German bomber force was, however, used for other purposes and employed constantly for the rest of the war in attacks on enemy airfields and in interdiction campaigns against British and French depots and rail yards.

PREPARING FOR THE 1918 OFFENSIVE

The German high command put a great deal of emphasis on enlarging and reequipping the Luftstreitkräfte in preparation for the March 1918 offensive on the western front that it hoped would quickly end the war. The flying schools were enlarged, and forty new fighter squadrons and seventeen new observation detachments were created.[101] The ground attack units were now being equipped with the Junkers J1, the first all-metal aircraft that was purpose-built for the low-level attack mission. With armor plate protecting the crew and engine, three machine guns, and a 150-lb bombload, it was an impressive weapon for that time.[102] The new J1s and the reliable armored Halberstadts and Hannovers proved their worth in the successful German counterattack at Cambrai in December 1917 when the surprise attack was led by waves of ground attack squadrons pinning down the British reserves and artillery while the storm troops swept forward using the new infiltration tactics.[103]

The high command issued new doctrinal directives that stressed the role of air support in the offensive.[104] *The Attack in Trench Warfare,* published in January 1918, discussed the operational air campaign and the need to gain surprise by quietly moving air units to the sector to be attacked at night and then camouflaging and dispersing them thoroughly.[105] The use of the air force in surprise attacks was central to the new offensive doctrine. The infantry would attack after a short artillery barrage under the cover of ground attack squadrons, which would seek out the enemy reserves and artillery, as well as preplanned strikes on the frontline strong points.[106] The heavy bomber force would be directed primarily against the enemy airfields to assist the air superiority battle.[107] To ensure that good air/ground coordination was achieved for the great offensive, infantry units were pulled out of the line, and the first-wave assault units conducted live-fire exercises with ground attack squadrons against mock trench lines.[108] Tactical experience was quickly assimilated by the air staff, and additional guidance was issued in a regular series of "Tactical Guidelines" issued by the Luftstreitkräfte, which advised air unit commanders on formations, tactics, and task organization of their forces.[109]

THE 1918 AIR CAMPAIGN

The German air service was well prepared to play a major role in the March 1918 offensive in the west. By March, the Luftstreitkräfte had amassed 3,668 frontline aircraft on the western front. The Germans had 307 aircraft operating on other fronts and had built up a reserve of 1,600 aircraft for the expected attrition.[110] In the west, the Germans had about 1,000 combat aircraft fewer than the Allies but, to gain air superiority for the offensive, the Luftstreitkräfte concentrated a powerful force of thirty-five fighter squadrons, twenty-two ground attack squadrons, forty-nine observation detachments, and four bomber wings to support the three ground armies mounting the attack on the British held front.[111] The offensive plan detailed the ground attack units to attack British frontline positions and then concentrate their efforts on the British troop reserves and artillery. The fighters would fly cover for the observation and ground attack craft and aggressively engage any Allied fighters. The bombers were detailed to conduct night attacks on Allied headquarters and airfields.

As the offensive began on 21 March, the Luftstreitkräfte was initially successful. The Germans gained air superiority over the attack front, and the German assault divisions swept rapidly forward under the cover of the ground attack squadrons. In the first days of the offensive, the ground attack units successfully pounded the British reserves strung out on the open roads and caused considerable British casualties.[112] The Germans maintained some of their ground attack squadrons in reserve and available to support the ground troops and attack an enemy position thirty minutes after receiving a call for air support.[113]

However, the German aerial superiority did not last very long. The Allied

Friedrichhafen G III bomber. Lighter than the Gotha and with a smaller bomber load, it was used extensively in short-range interdiction missions in 1917–1918. (Photo from the U.S. Army Center for Military History.)

air services were far better prepared to fight an air campaign in 1918 than they were in 1917. The Royal Flying Corps had reorganized its training program in the late 1917, and the new British pilots were far better trained.[114] While the Germans were introducing the superb Fokker D 7 fighter plane to their forces in the spring of 1918, the Allies had equipped their fighter squadrons with the Spad VII, Spad XIII, the Bristol two-seat fighter, the SE 5A, and other first-rate aircraft. Moreover, the Allies had a lot more good aircraft than the Germans and, as the German ground offensive bogged down, the war in the French skies became an attrition battle that the Germans could not hope to win.

The German bomber force was heavily engaged in 1918 and, after the strategic bombing campaign against England was called off, the Luftstreitkräfte turned its attention to Paris, which it bombed on numerous occasions in 1918. However, it may have been that civilian populations were adjusting to aerial bombardment or that the French civilians could take more punishment than the English, for the German bombing of Paris caused no panic or drop in the morale of the Parisians. In the bombing of Paris, 303 civilians were

First Lieutenant Hermann Göring as a fighter pilot, ca. 1918. (Photo from USAF HRA.)

killed and 539 wounded before the Germans called off the bombing campaign due to their own losses.[115]

By the summer of 1918 the German ground and air effort had petered out and the Allies were mounting powerful counteroffensives under the cover of an overwhelming numerical advantage in the air. For the rest of the war, the German Air Service would be outnumbered two or three to one in the west as the aircraft production superiority of the Allies made itself felt. Bolstered by good leadership, good equipment, and sound doctrine, the Luftstreitkräfte remained a potent fighting force to the end of the war. In the latter months of the war, the Germans regularly shot down their Allied opponents at a two or three to one ratio. In August 1918 the Germans shot down 487 Allied aircraft for a loss of 150 of their own planes.[116] Jagdgeschwader 2 shot down eighty-one Allied aircraft in September 1918, with only two losses of their own.[117] The Luftstreitkräfte inflicted an especially high toll on the inexperienced American air units.[118] For example, the 80th U.S. Aero Squadron had averaged a 75 percent monthly loss of their aircrew from March to November 1918.[119]

By the end of the war in November 1918, the Luftstreitkräfte still had

4,500 aircrew and 2,709 aircraft serving on the western front, a considerable drop from their 3,600 aircraft available in March.[120] The Allied air forces, despite massive losses in the air in 1918, had a total of 7,200 combat aircraft on the western front.[121]

STRATEGIC BOMBING AND AIR DEFENSE

Impressed by Germany's capability to directly target the British homeland in a strategic bombing campaign, in 1918 the Royal Air Force instituted its own program of bombing the German homeland. The Independent Air Force comprising several heavy bomber wings was set up under the command of Air Marshal Hugh Trenchard. Although German cities and industrial areas along the French border and in the Ruhr had been subject to a few attacks between 1914 and 1917, the 1918 RAF offensive would carry the war fairly deep into Germany. The British strategic offensive would make the Ruhr a primary target but would also range fairly deep into Germany with attacks on Mainz, Frankfurt am Main, Ludwigshafen, and Aschaffenburg from July to October 1918.[122] During 1918 the Allied air forces would make 353 raids on Germany, dropping 7,717 bombs and killing 797 Germans while wounding another 380. The total cost of the damages inflicted on Germany was 15,522,000 reichsmarks (approximately $3.6 million).[123]

The Allied bombing campaign against Germany was less successful than the German campaign against England in terms of costs and benefits. Although the Allied effort was far greater, the casualties and damage inflicted was less. Moreover, the Allies faced a very heavy attrition rate for their bomber units. The RAF's Independent Air Force, the leading participant in the campaign, dropped 543 tons of bombs on Germany for a loss of 352 aircraft badly damaged or destroyed for a wastage rate of 1.54 tons of bombs dropped for every aircraft lost.[124] The RAF suffered casualties of 29 aircrew dead, 64 wounded, and 235 missing.[125] The expense of the RAF's destroyed aircraft exceeded the cost of the damage it inflicted on Germany, and the heavy aircrew losses meant that the British and Allied air forces were trading one aircrew, trained at great length and at great expense, for one or two German civilian bystanders—certainly not a means to win an attrition war.

The German air staff studied the effect of the Allied strategic raids against Germany and concluded that they posed no major threat to the population or to war production. A general staff study of August 1918 examined every Allied raid on Germany in minute detail and came to some surprising

Heavy 88-mm flak gun in position in 1918. (Photo from Kriegsgeschichtliche Abteilung der Luftwaffe, *Entwicklung und Einsatz der deutschen Flakwaffe und des Luftschutzes im Weltkreige,*" vol. 1. Berlin, 1942.)

conclusions. Many of the 122 civilians killed or wounded in the thirty-one bombing raids that month were casualties that could have been avoided by taking proper precautions such as taking shelter. Many of the dead and wounded had actually gone outside to watch the bombing raids. The author of the report, Captain Hoth, noted that the population quickly adjusted to bombing raids and that most casualties occurred the first time a city was bombed. After that, people learned to take cover when the alarms sounded and the casualty rate fell. The Allied night raids were a nuisance but the bombing was notoriously inaccurate and ineffective. In ten of the largest Allied raids in July 1918 the Allied bombers had inflicted no casualties at all.[126] The Germans were, quite rightly, not impressed with the Allied strategic bombing campaign.

One of the reasons for the poor Allied showing in strategic bombing in World War I was the size and effectiveness of the German air defense forces. By 1918 the Luftstreitkräfte had developed a fairly sophisticated system for defense of Germany's western cities. The western portion of the country had been divided into five air defense zones, each with its own commander, and air reporting and communications service, as well as several separate air de-

German heavy flak gun in battle, 1918. (Photo from USAF HRA.)

fense commands set up to protect industrial areas.[127] By 1918 the German Home Defense Forces of the air service were equipped with a total of 896 heavy flak guns, 454 searchlights, and 204 flak machine guns backed up by nine fighter squadrons.[128] Strong antiaircraft defenses meant that the Allied bombers were forced to fly at their extreme ceilings with consequent poor bombing accuracy.

The Germans placed a great deal more faith in the antiaircraft arm than the Allies did during World War I. Along the front and in the army rear areas, the Luftstreitkräfte set up air defense commands with good communications nets and a system of ground reporting and warning of impending air attacks. The Germans also developed a wide variety of flak guns ranging from a rapid-fire 37-mm cannon to long-range and high-velocity 88-mm guns. Each army aviation headquarters had a flak commander and, where the aerial action was the heaviest, the Germans would reinforce their air commanders with sizable flak forces. In the Flanders campaign of 1917, the German Fourth Army flak force eventually totaled 130 units with 252 flak guns and 28 searchlights under the control of seven sector commanders.[129] The British reported that the German flak fire over the front was deadly and effective, and fear of flak pushed the Royal Flying Corps to maximum altitudes.[130]

The German flak force grew quickly during the war and by 1918 the Luftstreitkräfte fielded a force of 2,558 flak cannon in size from 37 mm to 105 mm.[131] The performance of the flak force justified the effort that the air service had put into it. The flak arm shot down 322 Allied aircraft in 1916, 467 aircraft in 1917, and 748 in 1918. Late in the war, improved munitions and fuses dramatically improved the lethality of the flak guns, so that the German flak gunners shot down a total of 132 Allied planes in September 1918, and 129 in October.[132]

THE GERMAN NAVAL AIR ARM

The German navy built up a small but very effective seaplane force for patrol and antishipping strikes in the Baltic Sea and North Sea theaters. The navy consistently fought for a larger force but, as the army's Luftstreitkräfte controlled the airframe and engine allocations and was reluctant to divert any resources, the navy had to make do with the engines and airframes allocated to it.[133] However, the navy made good use of the 1,740 aircraft that it acquired and deployed during the war.[134]

Although the naval air arm performed useful service in the Baltic, the

A flight of Hansa Brandenburg twin-seat seaplane fighters, 1918. These aircraft gave the Germans air superiority over the North Sea in 1917–1918.

most impressive performance of the German naval air service was in the air campaign over the North Sea in 1917–1918. German seaplane patrol craft covered by the forty naval fighters of Lieutenant Friedrich Christiansen's Seaplane Detachment 1, based in Flanders, roamed the North Sea to the English coast, attacking Allied shipping and warships. In June 1917 three British merchant ships were sunk in the channel by bombs and torpedoes carried by German naval aircraft.[135] In 1917–1918 the naval aircraft operating over the North Sea sank four merchant vessels, four patrol boats, three Allied submarines, twelve other ships, and a Russian destroyer.[136]

The success of the antishipping attacks was made possible by the excellent two-seat seaplane fighters designed by Ernst Heinkel and produced by the Hansa-Brandenburg Company. The W 12 biplane fighter of 1917 and the W 19 naval biplane fighter of 1918 with the later addition of the W 29 monoplane seaplane fighter of 1918 were far superior to the British and Allied naval aircraft they were opposing over the North Sea.[137] The Germans gained air superiority over the North Sea in 1917 and held it to the end of the war. In aerial combat, the German naval air arm shot down 270 Allied airplanes for a loss of 170 of their own.[138]

By 1918, the German navy had come to appreciate the potential for naval aviation as a striking arm of the fleet and ordered the 11,300-ton passenger ship *Ausonia* to be redesigned and converted into a true fleet aircraft carrier with a 128.5-meter landing deck and space for nineteen to twenty conventional aircraft. The German naval construction office gave the *Ausonia* top priority in its construction program in 1918, but the German navy's first aircraft carrier was not completed before the armistice.[139]

TECHNOLOGY AND AIR POWER

Air forces are more dependent on and sensitive to technological development than other branches of the armed forces. This is true today and was certainly true in World War I. Having a slight technical advantage over one's aerial foes could mean the difference between gaining and losing air superiority. The Germans could not hope to match the production capability or resources of the Allied powers; during the course of the war the French built 52,000 aircraft and the British 43,000 aircraft to Germany's 48,000 planes.[140] However, in most areas of aviation technology in World War I, the German air service maintained a lead over the Allies in developing and fielding equipment. This is one of the factors that accounts for the combat effectiveness of the Luftstreitkräfte in the face of consistent Allied numerical superiority.

The highly experienced Colonel Wilhelm Siegert was made the inspector for aviation in 1916 with the responsibility for aircraft development and procurement as well as the production of other related aircraft weaponry and equipment. Siegert ruthlessly and efficiently organized the aircraft manufacturing companies for war and centralized materiel procurement in January 1917.[141] Throughout the war, the Germans held an advantage over the Allies in superior aircraft design. The Germans were pioneers in the effective use of plywood construction with steel-tube airframes, which made their aircraft sturdy but light. Another major innovation in which the Germans took the lead was in the design and construction of all-metal aircraft. After the successful Junkers J 1 attack plane of 1917, the Junkers Company followed up with the production of the Junkers D 1 all-metal single-seat fighter and an all-metal two-seater ground attack plane, the Junkers CL I.[142]

In general, the German aircraft of World War I tended to be more stable and possessed better handling characteristics than did their Allied counterparts. Designing aircraft that were easy to fly was important when one's pilots would enter combat with a hundred or less total flying hours. Several of the most important Allied aircraft were notoriously difficult to fly—the most famous case being the British Sopwith Camel, which was light, fast, and maneuverable but deadly in the hands of an inexperienced pilot. The Sopwith Camel probably killed more British pilots in training than German pilots in combat.[143] On the other hand, the German Fokker D 7 fighter of 1918 was fast, maneuverable, and had the best climb rate of the time. It was also easy to fly. The D 7 is widely regarded as the finest single-seat fighter aircraft of World War I.[144] American Air Service General Billy Mitchell expressed his admiration for the D 7. The aircraft had been designed to be easily and rapidly dismantled for rail or road transport. Upon arriving, it could be reassembled in a few minutes. This design aspect gave the Fokker yet another advantage not possessed by Allied aircraft.[145]

The one area of technology in which the Germans consistently lagged behind the Allies was in aircraft engine manufacture and design. The French had led the world in engine design and production before World War I, and they continued to hold their edge during the war with 88,000 aircraft engines produced to Germany's 43,486.[146] Moreover, the French were able to manufacture much more powerful engines, which gave their aircraft an advantage in speed by the last year of the war. However, the advantage in engine power held by the French was offset to some degree by the reliability and durability of the Daimler, Benz, and BMW in-line engines that powered most of the German aircraft during the war.[147]

In the use of radio communication the Germans held a clear lead during the war with artillery spotting and attack aviation being coordinated with radio in Flanders in 1917. Radio use never became a feature of the Allied air tactics. With a lead in radio technology, the Germans also pioneered the use of navigation by radio beacon in 1915 when naval airships began to navigate by radio beacon. By 1918, several aerial direction finding (ADF) stations had been set up by the Luftstreitkräfte to help their bomber and airship crews.[148] The Germans also developed oxygen equipment for their aircrew, enabling them to operate at high altitudes. The Germans combined several technologies such as oxygen masks and a special high-compression Maybach engine and automatic cameras in designing the Rumpler C 7 high altitude reconnaissance plane of 1917–1918. The oxygen-equipped pilot could take the Rumpler to over 20,000 feet to photograph Allied ports, airfields, and military installations in relative safety as no Allied aircraft could climb that high to attack it.[149]

Finally, one simple piece of technology made an enormous difference to the fighting ability of the Luftstreitkräfte in the aerial battles of 1918. During the war, the Germans designed a light and practical parachute that could be comfortably worn by a pilot. In 1918, the Luftstreitkräfte made parachutes standard equipment for their aircrew. During the intense air battles of that year hundreds of German pilots, including top ace Ernst Udet, were able to bail out of disabled aircraft and live to fly and fight again.[150] Although the Allies also had parachutes, none of the Allied air forces made them standard pilot equipment. Thus, many Allied aircrew fell to their deaths who could easily have been saved to fight again.[151]

CONCLUSION

During the war the Luftstreitkräfte won tremendous prestige in the eyes of the German people and armed forces, because of the way it fought effectively to the very end. By early November 1918 the morale of the Imperial Navy had collapsed, and the High Seas Fleet had mutinied. Most divisions of the army were reporting that their soldiers were "fought out," no longer capable of combat. Only the Luftstreitkräfte remained as a cohesive combat force, capable of offering effective resistance. By any account, the Luftstreitkräfte had fought very well—usually better than its opponents. Although consistently outnumbered, it had often managed to gain air superiority, and during the course of the war the German pilots had shot down their opponents at a two or three to one ratio.[152] By the end of the war, the general view of the army's officer corps was that the Luftstreitkräfte had earned the right to take its place as an independent service, equal to the army and navy.

The Luftstreitkräfte provides an example of how superior doctrine and tactics can offset a lack of numbers and resources. During the war, the Luftstreitkräfte was consistently a step or two ahead of the Allies in developing new tactics and operational methods. The Germans pioneered modern fighter tactics and put together the first large fighter organizations. The Luftstreitkräfte developed the ground attack units as a specialized branch of the air force and employed them in mass with a significant effect on the battlefield. The Germans conducted the first true strategic bombing campaign in history. The Luftstreitkräfte combined the new technologies of aviation effectively and was the first air force to regularly use radios to coordinate artillery spotting and close air support. Throughout the war, the Luftstreitkräfte demonstrated greater skill at conducting joint operations than did the Allies.

The Luftstreitkräfte had benefited from good leadership and the general staff tradition. The Imperial Air Service had been established with a sound doctrinal and technical foundation before the war. One reason for the good performance in the war of the Luftstreitkräfte was the solid prewar tradition. The Luftstreitkräfte was especially fortunate in its leadership. In General Ernst Hoeppner and colonels Hermann Lieth-Thomsen and Wilhelm Siegert, the Germans had some first-rate air power thinkers and practitioners. It had an excellent officer corps, with a disproportionate number of its senior leaders drawn from the elite general staff. Because of good leadership, the Luftstreitkräfte was able to absorb lessons and adapt to new technologies and conditions more rapidly than their counterparts of the Allied air forces. The accomplishment of creating a large body of effective air doctrine is even more remarkable when one considers that the Luftstreitkräfte leaders were dealing with a brand-new technology and a form of warfare that was entirely new.

Although the form of warfare was largely new, many of the traditional principles of warfare were still applicable to air fighting. The principle of mass, the necessity of employing one's forces at the decisive point, the importance of surprise, and employing reserves to sustain a successful offensive were all important parts of the German army's tactical and operational tradition that were successfully adapted to aerial warfare. The Luftstreitkräfte leaders also stressed the German army's tradition of thorough training. For most of the war, the German pilots entered the battle with much better training and preparation than their opponents.

During the four years of war, the German military had developed its own comprehensive approach to air power. The German wartime experience included broad operational experience with most forms of aerial warfare from strategic bombing to air defense operations as well as developing the organization, technology, and logistics to support a modern air force.[153] This comprehensive vision of air power expressed by the German air force's first leaders and the broad experience of World War I air operations would shape the evolution of German air power theory and development in the years after World War I.

CHAPTER TWO

Response to Disarmament: Von Seeckt and Wilberg

The Allied powers were certainly impressed with the combat efficiency of the German Luftstreitkräfte of World War I, because at the conclusion of the war, the Allies made a concerted effort to completely eliminate Germany's capability to wage war in the air, and also to cripple Germany's civilian aviation capability.

As part of the Armistice of 11 November 1918, the Allies demanded the surrender of 2,000 German aircraft.[1] The rapid demobilization of the Luftstreitkräfte was demanded as well. Six months later, on 8 May 1919, the Allies first made public the terms that they would impose on Germany as part of the final Versailles Treaty provisions. Articles 198–202 of the treaty directly addressed German military aviation. The Allies required Germany to surrender a vast quantity of aviation materiel, including 17,000 aircraft and engines. Also, Germany was to be permanently forbidden from maintaining a military or naval air force. Furthermore, the German aviation industry was to be shut down completely for six months after the treaty went into effect. No aircraft or parts were to be imported during that period. Afterward, the German civilian aviation industry—which would be carefully restricted—was to build only aircraft with limited range, performance, speed, and engine power.[2] The final twist of the knife: The Germans were not even allowed to control their own airspace for several years. Allied aircraft were to be granted free passage over, and landing rights in, Germany.[3] On 23 June 1919, the German government reluctantly accepted the Versailles Treaty under strong protest. The formal demobilization of the Luftstreitkräfte was begun in 1919 and on 8 May 1920, the Luftstreitkräfte was officially disbanded.[4]

Other provisions of the Versailles Treaty were equally draconian. Germany's army was to be reduced to a lightly armed, 100,000-man force, which would be denied tanks, heavy artillery, poison gas, and other modern weaponry. The officer corps was to be restricted to 4,000 officers. The German navy was to be reduced to a 15,000-man force equipped with a few obsolete ships and some torpedo boats, and was denied submarines and aircraft. Germany was to be effectively disarmed, and to be made militarily helpless. To ensure compliance with the treaty, the Inter-Allied Control Commission was established, with officer representatives from all the Allied powers. The commission was given broad authority to inspect military and industrial installations throughout Germany.

At the same time that Germany was demobilizing its air arm, the organizational foundation and doctrine for a new air force was being laid under the direction of Colonel General Hans von Seeckt, Germany's chief of the general staff from 1919–1920, and commander in chief of the German army from 1920–1926.

Hans von Seeckt was one of the most influential military thinkers of the twentieth century. He rebuilt and reorganized the German army in the chaotic situation of postwar Germany, and imbued that force with his own vision of warfare. It is testimony to the German general staff tradition that, at a time when the German nation had been brought low, it put forward a man of genuine vision, with a first-rate strategic mind, and great tactical and operational competence, to command the army. Von Seeckt was considered by the officer corps to be a logical choice to be postwar chief of the general staff. During World War I, von Seeckt had earned a reputation as a superior tactician.

In 1915, von Seeckt served as chief of staff of the army group that conducted the Balkans campaign and crushed the Serbian army. In 1916 von Seeckt was in Romania as an army group chief of staff, under the nominal command of Austrian Archduke Karl. Von Seeckt played a major role in this mobile campaign, which, in a matter of weeks in late 1916, overran and then forced Romania out of the war. During 1918, von Seeckt served in Turkey as chief of staff of the Ottoman field armies. The experiences of von Seeckt on the eastern front in World War I had a great influence on his approach to military doctrine in the 1920s, for on the eastern front, maneuver and mobility played a far greater role than they did on the western front. Furthermore, on the eastern front, smaller but better-led, trained, and equipped German armies consistently outmaneuvered and defeated the larger but slower Russian mass army. Von Seeckt's performance in large-scale campaigns in Poland, the Balkans, and Romania showed his superb grasp of the operational level of war. Von Seeckt, moreover, proved to be extremely talented at the strategic level of war. On the eastern front, he worked with and commanded Austrians, Bulgarians, and Turks as well as Germans. In planning each campaign, he knew what could be realistically expected of the coalition partners and had a sound understanding of the political goals of each country in the German-led coalition on the eastern front.

In many respects, von Seeckt was the archetypal Prussian officer. Born in 1866 of a noble Pomeranian family, his father was a general in the Prussian army. In 1885, von Seeckt enrolled as an officer cadet in the Kaiser Alexander Guard Regiment, and was commissioned as a lieutenant in 1887. As a young officer, he showed great promise, and was accepted at the Kriegsakademie in 1893. In 1897, he joined the general staff, holding an array of staff jobs and also serving as a battalion commander.

Unlike many in the German officer corps, however, von Seeckt had a rather sophisticated worldview. He had not attended the Prussian cadet schools, but had instead attended the Strasbourg Gymnasium. Von Seeckt spoke English and French fluently, and also knew Latin and Greek. Prior to World War I, he traveled widely in Europe and India. He preferred to read English novels.[5] Von Seeckt was comfortable in a variety of political, academic, and intellectual circles. As commander in chief of the army in the 1920s, he even occasionally breakfasted with Berlin newspaper publishers.

VON SEECKT'S VISION

Most important, von Seeckt was a man of tremendous mental agility. Of all senior army commanders in the immediate postwar era, von Seeckt was the only one to have correctly analyzed the operational lessons of World War I, and who accurately predicted the direction that future wars would take. Such generals as Petain, Pershing, and Haig had done good service in 1918, yet in the postwar period, when their thinking tended to dominate their respective allied armies, the British, French, and American senior commanders seemed locked into the methods of 1918: emphasizing the importance of defensive firepower, and of overcoming the defense by a methodical offensive based on overwhelming firepower. Von Seeckt, in contrast, drew the lesson that maneuver and mobility would be the primary effective means of warfare and operations in the future, that mass armies were cannon fodder, and that the trench war of 1914–1918 was an anomaly not likely to be repeated in the future. Von Seeckt insisted that smaller but better-trained, more mobile, and technically superior forces would consistently defeat larger but more cumbersome mass armies.

Von Seeckt outlined his vision for the new army operational system, and for essentially a new army to conduct this type of war, in a memo presented to the army headquarters in February 1919.[6] Von Seeckt argued that the future German army should drop the German tradition of the large field army based on conscription. Instead, von Seeckt advocated a smaller, professional army of twenty-one divisions, manned by approximately 200,000 to 300,000 volunteers. This army would be highly trained and outfitted with the most modern weapons and reinforced by a conscripted militia. In war, the professional field army would engage in a mobile campaign, while the militia force would provide replacements and reinforcements to the field army. Von Seeckt believed that the mass army had operational value only in the defense. Unlike many other generals, even in the German army, von Seeckt by 1919 held that the defense was not the superior form of warfare.

VON SEECKT ON AIR POWER

Hans von Seeckt was a significant air power theorist in his own right. To a greater extent than the western army commanders of the 1920s, he recognized the importance of the air arm as an independent branch service, not just a support weapon for the ground forces. Throughout his tenure as commander in chief, von Seeckt made funding for the shadow Luftwaffe he had created within the Reichswehr a high priority.

Between February and May 1919, von Seeckt served in the delicate position of the general staff's representative to the Allied powers at the Versailles negotiations. As his air adviser, von Seeckt selected Captain Helmuth Wilberg, one of Germany's first aviators, a general staff officer who had served with great distinction as commander over 700 aircraft on the Flanders front in 1917. Wilberg was already well known to von Seeckt, as he had served as an air staff officer under von Seeckt during the Balkans campaign of 1915.[7]

In early 1919, Wilberg drew up a plan for an independent German air force for the postwar era. This force would consist of approximately 1,800 aircraft and 10,000 men. Wilberg's air force was a well-balanced force composed of fighters, observation planes, attack aircraft, and heavy bombers. Von Seeckt approved of Wilberg's plan wholeheartedly, presenting it as a German proposal for force levels to the Allied negotiators at Versailles.[8] In 1923, von Seeckt again repeated his position that the air arm should be a fully equal branch of the military service, along with the navy and army, presenting his ideas in a Denkschrift that year.[9] Von Seeckt was considered by the professional airmen to be one of the most air-minded of the army generals and a consistent supporter of aviation. General der Flieger Wilhelm Wimmer said of him, "Seeckt used all of his influence and authority to protect his group of flyers against attacks all the way up to cabinet level."[10]

In von Seeckt's concept of aerial warfare, the primary responsibility of a strong, independent air force in war would be, first, to gain air superiority. Af-

Colonel General Hans von Seeckt, commander in chief of the German army, 1920–1926, and significant air power thinker in his own right. (Photo from Friedrich von Rabenau, *Seeckt: Aus seinem Leben.* Leipzig: Hase und Koehler Verlag, 1941.)

ter control of the air had been obtained, the air force's operational and strategic mission would be serving in concert with the army to disrupt the enemy's mobilization and transportation systems. Von Seeckt firmly believed that the air force was primarily an offensive, not a defensive weapon. He described his vision of a future aerial war:

> The war will begin with a simultaneous attack of the air fleets—the weapon which is the most prepared and fastest means of attacking the enemy. Their enemy is, however, not the major cities or industrial power, but the enemy air force. Only after its suppression can the offensive arm be directed against other targets. If both sides have a roughly equal force, decision will not be reached quickly. Even if one side is pushed onto the defense, it will employ every means to destroy the attacker. The degree of material and moral success of the superior attacker against the enemy sources of power depends upon the passive and moral powers of resistance of the defenders. Thereby, it is stressed that all the major troop assembly points are worthwhile and easy targets. The disruption of the personnel and materiel mobilization is a primary mission of the aerial offensive.
>
> Alongside the air force–led attack will be the prepared field force, essentially the regular army, which will attack with all possible speed. The higher the quality of the army, the greater its mobility, the more competent its leadership, the greater its chances of driving the opposing forces quickly from the field, the more rapidly it can disrupt the development and deployment of further forces, and the faster the enemy can be pushed to sue for peace.[11]

While von Seeckt was familiar with the concept of strategic bombing, and believed that aerial attack did strongly affect enemy morale, he did not accept the more popular theories of the 1920s, with their primary emphasis on targeting enemy cities. Von Seeckt firmly believed that the primary target of the air force should always be the enemy's military, for the enemy's military power embodied his capability to resist:

> Whoever talks of modern military technology will first think of the air force, which was first admitted as a fully recognized sister service alongside the army and the navy during and largely immediately after the war, without changing the basic principles of war. Certainly, the soldiers and the technicians allied with them have an entirely new battlefield with its own requirements. Through aerial attack, one has the possibility of striking the centers of resistance of the enemy state. Not a new target, but one more easily reached by air, are the key elements [*sic*] of military strength, whose disruption degrades the land army's powers of endurance. The only difference is that, when before the decision was sought on land and sea, now it is also sought in the air.[12]

Von Seeckt worked unceasingly within the army and German society to encourage "airmindedness." Immediately after the war, Captain Kurt Student, the Luftwaffe's expert in the Weapons Office, sent von Seeckt a memorandum encouraging the promotion of the military sport of gliding as a means to foster airmindedness among German civilians. Von Seeckt took up this suggestion, even attending gliding competitions in the central German mountains, and awarding prizes.[13]

Although von Seeckt saw no direct purpose in strategic bombing of cities, he firmly believed that the next war would see city bombing, like the Germans had conducted against London in World War I, become a standard feature of war. Throughout the 1920s, he constantly urged the German government to make provisions for a national system of civil air defense:

> Some believe that, in many ways, the aerial battle will be redirected only against the civilians in the office and workplace. The fight against the homeland, the citizens, is not new, as we can see from the old examples of total wars. We need only think of the Thirty Years' War, the Turkish Wars, and on Heidelberg. It would be frivolous to minimize or gloss over the danger and terror of aerial attacks on the homeland, especially the use of gas. It brings to the new battlefield the same dangers and the same viewpoints. . . . The active defense falls to the air force, the best counterweapon to carry the fight to the enemy's country, or at least to destroy the attacker. A new requirement to meet this type of danger is the provision for the passive defense of the nation's population centers, which can be expensive and inconvenient. Still, for us in Germany, where an active air defense is forbidden, there are no provisions for passive defense, and no provision to create one, it is difficult to understand and even more difficult to answer.[14]

ORGANIZATION OF THE REICHSWEHR AIR STAFF

In the Treaty of Versailles, the Allied powers ordered Germany to disband the greater general staff. At the same time, the Luftstreitkräfte, with its own general staff, was also ordered dissolved. Therefore, von Seeckt was faced with the daunting task of organizing, in 1919, an army staff and headquarters.

In some respects, a completely new beginning was an advantage. The dissolution of the German imperial system also meant the elimination of various inefficiencies and redundancies in the old imperial military. The old German empire actually had been a federation of small monarchies under Prussian leadership. Small nations like Saxony and Bavaria had maintained their own war ministries and general staffs under the prewar system. Bavaria even had its own air service. The whole had come under the operational planning and control of the greater general staff in wartime. Procurement and budget issues were not, however, under the purview of the general staff, but were kept under the control of the Prussian war ministry, and the national war ministries.

The Revolution of 1918 swept all of this away. When a new republican government defeated the communist revolutionaries and, by mid-1919, had established some semblance of order, the foundation was laid to ensure a relatively smooth transition from the old Imperial army system to the provisional Reichswehr, and finally, in 1921, to the military command system agreed on by the Germans after accepting the Versailles Treaty—the Reichswehr. In its final form, after the two-year transition period, the Reichswehr consisted of the navy (Reichsmarine) and the army (Reichsheer, though the army was generally referred to as the Reichswehr). The small armies and war ministries were subsumed into one national army. The army and the navy each had a military commander in chief, who served under a single defense minister.

While no army can function without some form of a general staff, the old general staff would simply remain the "Troops' Office" (Truppenamt), which consisted of four sections: T-1, Operations and Planning; T-2, Army Organization; T-3, Intelligence (referred to as the "Statistical Office" as a sop to Allied sensibilities); and T-4, Training. The chief of the Truppenamt served, in effect, as chief of the general staff, with responsibility for war plans, training the military, and establishing service doctrine. Next to the Truppenamt, which contained approximately sixty officers in the 1920s, there stood small staffs for the army branch inspectorates that served to establish doctrine, training, and requirements for each branch of the army. The infantry, cavalry, artillery, engineers, communications troops, motor troops, medical service, and veterinary service all had their own branch inspectorates. Also both parallel to the Truppenamt and under the direct command of the army commander was the Waffenamt, or Weapons Office. The Waffenamt also contained approximately sixty officers and a much larger number of civilian civil servants and was responsible for the procurement, testing, and development of weapons and equipment for the army. Each of the army branch inspectorates had a corresponding office in the Waffenamt to deal with equipment and procurement for that branch.[15]

Above the Truppenamt, the Waffenamt, and the branch inspectorates was the commander in chief, with his own special staff for dealing with political matters and for economic planning. Above the army and navy commanders stood the Reichswehr minister, who had civilian command and authority over the defense forces, with his own small staff to deal with parliamentary questions, budget questions, and also an intelligence staff. For the first time in German military history, the entire army and most of the air force of the nation served under a unified control, answerable to the sole army commander, who had full command authority in wartime.[16] One advantage of the Reichswehr system was that the people who developed doctrine for the armed forces, and those who developed the weaponry in accordance with that doctrine, were now under one, central authority instead of the divided leadership of the old system.

Von Seeckt saw that an air staff was set up within the Truppenamt. The senior air staff officer for the army was known as the Luftschutzreferat, and served in the plans and operations office of the Truppenamt; his title was abbreviated as TA(L).

Helmuth Wilberg was representative of the bourgeois influence on the general staff and the Imperial officer corps in the years leading up to World War I. Wilberg was born in 1880 of a Jewish mother and a Prussian Protestant father.[17] His father was a prominent portrait painter. Normally, a man from this background would not have achieved a career as a general staff officer. Wilberg's father, however, gave art lessons to the crown princess, later Kaiserin for ninety-nine days. After the death of his father when Helmuth was four, the empress mother looked after Wilberg's family. For example, Wilberg was terribly flat-footed, a deficiency that might have kept him from his goal to become an army officer. However, the empress mother used her influence and arranged for Wilberg to join Infantry Regiment 80 after he completed his abitur in 1898. Accordingly, despite his Jewish ancestry and fallen arches, Wilberg entered the officer academy, performed well, and embarked on a successful career as an infantry officer. For a two-year period, he even served as a military tutor to some of the Kaiser's relatives, a prestigious assignment granted only to officers of solid academic and military ability. In 1910, Wilberg was selected for the General Staff Academy. He received permission to undergo flight training at the same time, becoming one of Germany's first pilots, known as Die Alten Adler, "The Old Eagles." Wilberg completed his flight training in the fall of 1910 and received Imperial pilot's license number 26. He was an enthusiastic aviator who took part in Germany's early air races—a very dangerous and even deadly pastime during this period.[18] After completing the General Staff Academy course in 1913, Wilberg was officially transferred to the Inspectorate of Flying Troops, where he served as adjutant before the war. During the latter part of the war, Wilberg gained considerable renown as an air unit commander.

Wilberg was a popular officer in the Luftstreitkräfte, and as senior air officer was an excellent choice for the Reichswehr. He was best known as an expert in ground attack aviation, but as the wartime Fourth Army air commander he also had experience directing large-scale bomber and fighter operations during the war.

As air staff officer, Wilberg was the senior officer for all aviation matters in the Reichswehr. Under his direct supervision were aviation officers assigned throughout the different branches of the Truppenamt and the Waffenamt. In the 1920s, each section of the Truppenamt contained one or two qualified aviators, who dealt with personnel, planning, doctrine, training, and intelligence issues—of the sixty officers in the Truppenamt during this period, approximately six were airmen. Of the sixty officers in the Waffenamt during this period, about six were pilots. A much larger number of former officer pilots and observers were, however, employed as civilians by the Waffenamt, as a means of getting around the strict limitations on the number of commissioned officers within the German army. In the postwar period, 180 qualified pilot and observer officers were retained within the Reichswehr, even though the Reichswehr possessed neither an air arm, nor aircraft. It was the responsibility of these 180 pilot officers, spread throughout the military, to serve as air staff officers for the various commands, to conduct theoretical and practical training in air war and doctrine.[19]

Another means of getting around the restrictions of the Versailles Treaty in employing airmen during the 1920s was the civilianization of former branches of the military and the general staff. For example, the old history section of the general staff was disbanded, and in its place, a military history office, staffed with former general staff officers—now civilian civil servants—was opened as part of the national archives. Their work functions remained fundamentally unchanged. Several former Luftstreitkräfte officers were engaged to write the history of air operations in the world war.

THE AIR DOCTRINE PROCESS

In 1919, during the revolution, while demobilizing the defunct army and creating a new army, the Reichswehr embarked on the process of conducting a comprehensive examination of wartime tactics and operational doctrine. This was the most comprehensive examination of military doctrine by any major combatant power of World War I. Although this might be explained as typical behavior, for the losing side in a war would have a greater incentive for learning and reforming, it is also consistent with the German general staff tradition. All operations were routinely carefully postmortemed, so that lessons could be learned and doctrine, methodology, and equipment revised.

On 1 December 1919, one week after officially dissolving the general staff and taking over the Truppenamt, von Seeckt issued a directive to the Truppenamt, the Waffenamt, the branch inspectorates, and the Air Service, outlining a program to create fifty-seven committees and subcommittees of officers. These groups were to put together studies of tactics, regulations, equipment, and doctrine.[20] Von Seeckt stated, "It is absolutely necessary to put the experience of the war in a broad light, and to collect this experience while the impressions won on the battlefield are still fresh, and the major proportion of the experienced officers are still in leading positions."[21]

The officers were to write "short, concise studies of the newly gained experiences of the war," considering the following points:

> A. What new situations arose in the war that had not been considered before the war?
>
> B. How effective were our prewar views in dealing with the above situation?
>
> C. What new guidelines have been developed from the use of new weaponry in the war?
>
> D. Which new problems, put forward by the war, have not yet found a solution?[22]

During 1920, more committees and study groups were set up, until virtually every section of the defense ministry was involved in this program. By mid-1920, over 400 officers had been put to work compiling Germany's war experience. At the same time that the Truppenamt embarked on this program, the Air Service conducted its own program in coordination with the Truppenamt to study the lessons of the war. On 13 November 1919, Helmuth Wilberg issued a directive outlining the plan to analyze war experiences to develop new manuals and new regulations for the air arm. The work flow was initially distributed among eighty-three officers, assigned to twenty-one subcommittees that would examine three major aspects of air war: air unit organization; combat tactics; and technical developments that affected air power.[23]

Most of the senior commanders of the Luftstreitkräfte were involved in doing studies for Seeckt and Wilberg's programs. Most of the eighty-three officers initially assigned to write reports had either served as aviation commanders for armies, like Hugo Sperrle, or as unit commanders, like Captain Ernst Brandenburg, who had commanded the strategic bombing wing of the Luftstreitkräfte. Erhard Milch, who had commanded a fighter squadron in 1918, was also put to work editing several studies. Several of Germany's leading combat pilots, such as Pour le Mérite aces First Lieutenant Ernst Udet and Lieutenant Karl Jacobs, were called on to help develop new tactics for fighter aircraft. Many of the officers who participated in the air staff studies of 1919 and 1920, such as captains Hugo Sperrle and Kurt Student, would become famous air commanders in World War II.

After von Seeckt's directive of 1 December was passed to the Air Service, additional committees were established. In many respects, the Air Service's effort surpassed the requirements set by von Seeckt for their comprehensiveness. Already the most technically oriented branch of the army, the Air Service appointed thirty-one officers, most of them with engineering experience, to study the technical and industrial aspects of air war.[24] Later in December, the Air Service formed another twenty-seven committees to study specific organizational and tactical questions.[25] By early 1920, over 130 experienced Air Service officers and engineers were busy writing study papers and serving on committees. The entire range of aerial warfare doctrine was examined. The tactical air support of the field army was a primary subject of study for most of the special study groups established on 24 December 1919. Five of these groups were devoted to aspects of reconnaissance and observation. Eight groups were formed to study aspects of the tactical support of ground troops and cooperation between air and ground units.[26] Three committees were formed to study aspects of air defense, including methods of combatting enemy fighters and gaining air superiority.[27] The remaining committees examined more specialized aspects of aerial warfare, including supply organization, air support in mountain operations, and air operations over the ocean.[28]

About two dozen of these reports still survive to this day. From them, one can form a fairly detailed picture of how the Reichswehr's shadow air staff conducted its doctrinal debates.[29] The studies and reports are examples of sound, terse, military writing. They are brief, usually two to four pages, and in accordance with von Seeckt's directive, are critical and straightforwardly address specific questions.

One of the more important topics to be examined was the organization of divisional air support. In a four-page study of this question, one officer recommended that each division possess an organic air group for its support. This group would consist of an observation/ground attack squadron of twelve planes, a liaison plane squadron, and a squadron of twelve heavy ground-attack aircraft—in all, forty-two aircraft, supported by a maintenance squadron, a fuel squadron, a headquarters squadron, a communications company, and a searchlight detachment.[30]

Major Streccius, one of the Luftstreitkräfte's most experienced commanders, wrote another study of divisional air support, largely in refutation of the aforementioned report. Wartime air commander for the Eighteenth Army, Streccius pointed out that divisional air squadrons had to be sufficiently small and mobile to move forward with the division over a limited road net, and to relocate quickly. In his view, a squadron consisting of a section of four observation/ attack planes, a section of four liaison planes, and a section of four artillery-spotting planes would suffice to fulfill the basic observation/liaison needs of the division. Streccius argued that the ground attack, or "infantry" planes ought not to be dispersed at division level, but rather organized en masse as attack groups under the direction of the army air commander.[31] Major Streccius's more realistic assessment was the one eventually adopted as Reichswehr air doctrine.

Another example of the tone of discussion and debate within the air staff comes from the committee to examine fighter group tactics. This committee, which released its report in October 1920, consisted of three Pour le Mérite aces and eight wartime senior tactical air leaders, including future Luftwaffe generals Sperrle, Student, and Wilberg.[32] The first question examined by this committee was the maximum strength of fighter groups. Ace lieutenants Bolle and Degelow argued for four squadrons; another ace, Lieutenant Jacobs, argued for six. All the former senior commanders came down on the side of six squadrons per group. The committee studied the question of whether fighter groups or wings should serve as tactical organizations, and unanimously agreed on fighter groups. A third question dealt with the deployment of one-seat and two-seat fighters. Two officers argued that fighter groups should possess only single-seat fighters, but other members opted for a mix of one-seat and two-seat aircraft in a group, though the committee also reported that no clear agreement had been reached as to what the mix should be. All members of the committee did state that the fighter group commander should command from the air with his pilots.

One half of the report deals with the question of whether more than one group of fighters could be employed together under one tactical commander. The three aces initially insisted that one commander could not successfully control more than one group. The debate went on for several committee sittings. After discussion and debate, the committee agreed that the operational leadership of several groups by one commander in the air might be possible, depending on the further development and deployment of aircraft radio. In the tactical case of several groups in combat, the wing commander would fly in the control role, above and behind his air groups. Fighter ace Lieutenant Bolle, it is noted, disagreed with these findings.[33]

In another study, the role of the heavy bomber in army support was examined. Captain Hoth (later, colonel general) was one of the officers to address this question. Hoth, who was involved in air staff planning throughout the 1920s, pointed out that by 1918, the enemy fighter planes had become such an effective opponent for the heavy bombers that their operations had to be restricted to night attacks, which decreased accuracy. Hoth scrutinized the German bombing campaign against the major Allied rail centers and supply depots during the 1918 spring offensive. He argued that bomber attacks against the more forward Allied depots and rail yards would have been more effective, because rerouting munitions and materiel to undamaged rail lines would then have been considerably more difficult for the Allies.[34]

Hoth made a number of additional recommendations. The technical development of heavy bombers should be continued. For the daytime protection of heavy bombers, each should have three to four machine guns and operate from high altitudes of at least 20,000 feet. Future bomber groups should consist of a mix of both day and night bombers. The squadron, however, should not consist of a mix of both types due to supply and logistics complications. Hoth argued that the bomber force's main objective should be the interdiction of enemy lines of supply and communications.[35]

Wilberg himself wrote a study of the effectiveness of the air service supply service during 1918. He stated that the problems of replacing obsolete aircraft had created aircraft shortages in 1917 and early 1918, but that by March 1918, the aircraft production replacement system was functioning well, so that some combat units went on the offensive with a surplus of modern aircraft. Wilberg asserted that the air service's supply and aircraft replacement system had worked well throughout all of 1918. The charge that the defeat of the German 1918 offensive was due to a lack of materiel was, according to Wilberg, not true—at least as far as the Air Service was concerned. Wilberg pointed out that the greatest supply problem of the Air Service in 1918 was the shortage of gasoline, and that the shortage might have had a decisive effect in 1919. According to Wilberg, the Luftstreitkräfte's primary wartime problem had been the severe shortage of trained pilots and personnel—not a shortage of machines. He argued that the Allies had gained air superiority, not only by fielding more aircraft, but also by having a far larger reserve of personnel.[36]

Some of the 1919 and 1920 studies, which are no longer extant in Luftwaffe files, seem to have found their way to German military journals. An article by Captain Seydel entitled "Flak," published in 1921 in the *Militär-wochenblatt,* conforms in its style, length, and critical approach to the other surviving Air Service studies. Captain Seydel mentions the success of the antiaircraft artillery, which from May to September 1918 alone shot down 420 Allied aircraft. His study mainly consists of a critical analysis of wartime flak organization and technology. According to Captain Seydel, equipment standardization was poor, which meant that, by the end of the war, there were twenty-five different flak gun models in use.

Seydel also asserted that the Air Service's wartime communications command was overburdened, and ought to have had many more trained soldiers assigned to it. He commented that, as aircraft performance increased, the range of flak guns needed to be improved correspondingly. At the end of the war, most flak targets were flying above 4,000 meters. Future flak defense would, accordingly, have to be oriented largely to high-altitude defense. In his conclusion, Captain Seydel argued for considering flak as a multipurpose weapon. Thanks to their mobility and rapidity of fire, flak guns would make superb antitank weapons. Seydel recommended that the flak artillery be assigned to antitank defense as a secondary mission, prefiguring the German use of antiaircraft guns in this role in Spain in the 1930s, and in World War II.[37]

The army and air service studies provided the basis for a new, comprehensive army war doctrine, emphasizing an elite, modern, and technically proficient military capable of winning through mobility and maneuver. The Truppenamt Training Section, or T-4, had the primary mission of editing and writing the tactical and operational regulations. The T-4 staff always contained some general staff officers who were aviators, and the abundant extant correspondence between Wilberg and the T-4 Section indicates a harmonious relationship.

POSTWAR AIR DOCTRINE: 1921–1923

The efforts of Wilberg and other aviation officers resulted in a considerable body of air doctrine being incorporated into the new operational doctrine of the Reichswehr, Army Regulation 487: *Leadership and Battle with Combined Arms.*[38] Part I of Army Regulation 487 was issued in 1921, Part II in 1923. Both parts of *Leadership and Battle with Combined Arms* contain extensive sections on operational air doctrine.

In most respects, the German air doctrine of the immediate postwar period was a codification of well-known German operational principles developed during the war. The principle of massing aircraft at the decisive point, and not dispersing them once aerial operations commenced, was emphasized as a primary rule of air operations:

> During operations the leadership has the responsibility for determining the most important objectives for reconnaissance, as well as the decision to assemble and deploy superior aerial forces, in coordination with the ground forces, over the most important sector of the ground battle. All possible force must be employed at this decisive point. Troop units who are not directly involved in combat at the decisive point cannot generally count upon receiving air support.[39]

The 1921 doctrine gives considerable importance to battle groups, ground attack aircraft, and their employment in mass, coordinated attacks against enemy ground troops.[40] The use of heavy bombers is also discussed in *Leadership and Battle,* which recommended their employment to attack targets far behind the front, beyond the range of artillery. Because bombers were not capable of effective defense against enemy fighters, their activity would generally be reduced to nighttime.[41] It was also recommended that bombers "should be primarily directed against enemy railyards and supply depots."[42] A large part of the 1921 regulations are devoted to flak defense and also include the requirement that each army unit be responsible for its own air defense, and set up an aircraft spotter system.

The greatest departure of the new air doctrine from wartime practice was the emphasis on air power in the offense. Based on the conclusions of von Seeckt's air staff, the defensive wartime air strategy was rejected, and the battle for air superiority was made the primary object of the air force in wartime:

> The battle for air superiority is an offensive one. The enemy aviation is to be sought out and attacked forward of the zone of troops. The opponent is to be pushed onto the defensive, and his power and aggressiveness broken by the destruction of numerous aircraft.
>
> Defensive screens or sector barriers are made essentially impossible by the nature of the air battle. Strong numerical superiority cannot permanently eliminate aerial activity—only hinder it, and restrict its periods of action. It is therefore recommended that measures to restrict enemy aerial observation be carried out on the ground.[43]

The air power section in Part II of Army Regulation 487 is a more detailed explanation of the offensive air doctrine outlined in the 1921 regula-

Colonel General von Seeckt, Army CIC, viewing maneuvers, ca. 1925, with Major Wilberg, his senior air officer. Seeckt regularly viewed maneuvers in the company of Wilberg to ensure that the army would become "air-minded." (Photo from the Wilberg family.)

tion. Fighter aircraft, for example, are advised to form themselves into squadron-abreast formations, to gain altitude, and to fire on the enemy at close range.[44] Single-seat fighter planes are recommended for air-to-air combat, while two-seat fighter planes are recommended as bomber escorts.[45] German army regulations of the 1920s provided army officers with detailed instructions on how to create an air tasking order, or how to provide an observer report. On the whole, the emphasis is given to the use of air power in a combined arms campaign in a war of maneuver.

The Renaissance of German Military Education

The era of Hans von Seeckt saw the most extensive reform of Germany's military education system since the days of General Scharnhorst in the Napoleonic era. With an officer corps of only 4,000 men allowed by the Versailles Treaty, von Seeckt had no choice but to opt for quality over quantity. The new German army officer corps would, as von Seeckt put it, become a Führerheer, or "Leaders' Army," wherein each officer would be capable of carrying out duties or commanding units at one, or even two ranks higher than his present one.

In the early 1920s, the old cadet schools of the Prussian army were eliminated, and the one-year course for cadet officers abolished. These were replaced with an entirely new officer training program, consisting of an intensive, three and a half year course. Although the majority of German officers had possessed the abitur (German university matriculation certificate) prior to World War I, after the war, the abitur was made mandatory for all officers. This restricted membership in the German officer corps to only the best-educated young men. Officer selection standards became stricter, in every sense, after World War I. In a letter to the branch schools, written in November 1924, von Seeckt pointed out that there were plenty of aspiring officer candidates for the army, so that tests needed to be more difficult, and the courses more demanding, to weed out marginal candidates.[46]

According to von Seeckt, the new Reichswehr officer corps would be much better educated in technology and combined arms than the old officer corps. Education in air power was made an important part of the curriculum in the officer corps. In 1920, the officer branch schools for the infantry, cavalry, artillery, and engineers were directed that "The importance of air defense is to be emphasized by all faculty in all military history subjects."[47] The newly established officers' courses would hire specialists on aviation, who would determine the curriculum on military aviation in all of the schools. The Truppenamt, however, directed that the following guidelines be met: that the officers' courses provide, first, a general introduction on air forces and the technical aspects of modern military aviation; second, the organization of aviation in wartime and the employment of observation, fighters, bombers, attack planes, and antiaircraft artillery. Furthermore, army tactical aspects of aviation would be stressed, such as cooperation and liaison with the air force while on the offensive, while in battle, while on the defense, and while crossing rivers.[48] In the first two years of the basic officer course of the Reichswehr, approximately one hour per week would be devoted specifically to military aviation.[49]

Because the general staff was officially abolished by the Treaty at Versailles, the Truppenamt created a revised model of the old General Staff Academy, with an intensive, three-year officer education program. The primary difference between the new system and the old is that the new system would conduct most of its course education in the seven military districts of Germany, at the district headquarters. The general staff officers were officially to be called "leadership assistants" (Führergehilfen), but the style and intellectual attitude of the old general staff corps remained. In 1922, the Truppenamt directed that "The most important goal is to create a full comprehension of the cooperation of all arms in successfully conducting operations."[50] The new general staff education would emphasize practical exercises as well as a considerable amount of private study. A new emphasis on the technologies introduced during the war was also evident. One of the sharpest criticisms of the army's comprehensive examination of wartime doctrine is that the General Staff Corps had not had a sound grounding in technology. Therefore, considerable weight was placed on the study of modern weaponry and technology in the Reichswehr's general staff curriculum. The Truppenamt directed that aviation would be studied as part of the curriculum on technology.[51]

In the first year of the general staff course, there was to be at least one hour of lectures a week on military aviation, and one written essay or paper every two months on military aviation. In the second year of the course, there were to be lectures on aviation for at least two hours per month, and in the third year, at least one and a half hours of seminars on aviation every other week.[52] Perhaps the most far-reaching reform of the general staff system was the requirement that every officer had to take the general staff entry examination, and pass this examination to be retained in the army. In the Imperial army, the decision to apply for the General Staff Academy was completely voluntary. However, in the Reichswehr all officers, either as senior first lieutenants or junior captains, were to meet a new set of high standards. For example, to be commissioned, all Reichswehr officers had to pass a competence examination in at least one foreign language. This requirement for military education meant that the officer corps in every regiment, battalion, and small garrison of the army spent a considerable amount of time in study groups as preparation for the general staff examination. It was the duty of regimental commanders to be the senior educators for their regiments, to see that the officers of their regiments performed well on the general staff examination. Thus, throughout the army, each regiment regularly arranged reading groups, seminars, and lectures on military subjects. The general staff examination itself included questions on technical matters, emphasizing military tactics and operations at the level of both the battalion and the reinforced regiment. To pass the examination, officers needed at least some knowledge of military aviation and its role in unit operations.

The desire to create an officer corps that was fully conversant with modern technology was spelled outside the realm of the officer cadets and those preparing for the general staff. In 1924, von Seeckt himself directed that the Weapons Office and the branch inspectorates needed to demonstrate a better grasp of the role of technology in modern military affairs. Thus, the section chiefs within the Weapons Office and branch inspectorates as well as the Truppenamt sections were required to hold two or more seminars on technology per month. All aspects of modern military technology were discussed, including aviation, foreign weaponry, engine technology, and industrial processes.[53]

Finally, one of the most dramatic departures from the general staff tradition of the Imperial army was the substitution of an engineering degree or technical education for the General Staff Academy as a means of admittance to the elite general staff. Throughout the 1920s and into the early 1930s, as many as twelve officers per year were detailed to attend civilian universities and complete engineering degrees, at which time they could return, normally to be employed in the Truppenamt, the Waffenamt, or the Reichswehr Ministry staff. Many of the generals of the Luftwaffe of World War II took part in this program, receiving engineering degrees in lieu of attending the general staff course.[54] The most famous officer who served on the general staff of the Luftwaffe to undertake this program was Field Marshal Wolfram von Richthofen. Von Richthofen, as a young officer, had flown in his famous cousin Manfred's Jagdgeschwader 1, and shortly after the war had been demobilized. At this time, he undertook an engineering course at the Technische Hochschule in Hannover, and dedicated himself to a career in engineering, since he had always been excited by mathematics and machinery. While visiting the family in 1922, von Seeckt, a personal friend of von Richthofen's father, told Wolfram von Richthofen that there would be a place for him in the Reichswehr officer corps as soon as he had completed his degree. When von Richthofen completed his degree in 1925, his first assignment was on the Reichswehr general staff in Berlin.[55]

THE STUDY OF FOREIGN AIR FORCES

No effective military organization can be without an intelligence staff, and the T-3 Section of the Truppenamt, called officially the Statistical Office, served that function for the Reichswehr. Throughout the 1920s, an experienced air officer was always part of the T-3 staff. The air intelligence officer specialized in collecting and disseminating information on the civil and military aviation establishments of the major powers. Although deprived of an official air force and modern army weaponry, the Reichswehr made it a primary goal to intensively study foreign armies and air forces to draw lessons for its own doctrine.

The tenure of Hans von Seeckt saw a renaissance of German military thinking and doctrine, and the results of innumerable studies being conducted for the military were published in a variety of German journals. The primary journal of the German army in this period was the *Militärwochenblatt.* This weekly journal published not only army news, but also lengthy articles concerning army and air force doctrine and technology. Under the editorship of retired General Konstantin von Altrock, the *Militärwochenblatt* encouraged study and debate within the German officer corps.[56] Von Altrock was one of the most progressive military thinkers of his day. Under his tenure from 1920 onward, virtually every issue of the *Militärwochenblatt* contained articles on air power, either relating wartime experiences, current military air power events, or analyzing emerging aviation technology. Throughout the 1920s, air activities of the foreign powers was given particular emphasis in the *Militärwochenblatt.*[57] For example, Red Air Force operations against the Polish army in 1920 and the campaign of the French Army Air Service against rebels in Morocco in the 1920s were examined, and reported in some detail. Most important, the *Militärwochenblatt* served as a means of transmitting the most up-to-date air power ideas to a large audience in Germany. In numerous instances, speeches and articles by the most important air power thinkers were translated and published in the *Militärwochenblatt.* U.S. Army Air Corps General Billy Mitchell's speeches were given extensive coverage in the *Militärwochenblatt* throughout the 1920s.[58] The Germans were particularly interested in Mitchell, not only because of his advocacy of modern air power, but because Mitchell himself had served as a senior American air commander in France in 1918, and was therefore a highly credible source for the Germans.[59] Another airman often featured in the *Militärwochenblatt* was RAF chief of staff, Air Marshall Hugh Trenchard. Trenchard's speeches to British military audiences were translated, and reported on in detail, in the *Militärwochenblatt.* From the early 1920s on, Trenchard was a staunch advocate of strategic bombing, and his views were followed with interest within the Reichswehr.

Helmuth Wilberg and the German air staff, particularly the air intelligence officer, made a considerable effort to keep abreast of foreign ideas and technology. Beginning in 1919, the Reichswehr air staff published a regular newsletter for Reichswehr officers entitled *Luftfahrt Nachrichten (Flight News)*. The first issue, published in August 1919, provided data on the major and minor air powers, particularly emphasizing technical information.[60] In 1920, another newsletter, the *Technical Air Report,* was published by the Truppenamt. This publication contained articles translated from foreign journals.[61] The Reichswehr air staff made a point of subscribing to all the major German and foreign aviation journals, including the American Air Service journal, *U.S. Air Services,* and the British journals.[62] German military journals and books of the von Seeckt era show an easy familiarity with foreign ideas on air power. For example, military commentator and former general staff officer Hans Ritter discussed Trenchard's air theories in his book, *The Air War,* published in 1926.[63] In his book, Ritter was able to comment with accuracy and perception on the views of General Billy Mitchell and British General J. F. C. Fuller. He even mentioned Professor Robert H. Goddard's rocket experiments—indicating just how closely foreign technological developments were studied in Germany. Ritter's 1924 book, *Der Zukunftskrieg und seine Waffen (The War of the Future and Its Weapons)* surveys the military theories of all the major powers, and discusses some of the strategic bombing concepts of the period.[64]

The air intelligence files from 1926 were several hundred pages long, contained up-to-date tables with textual summaries of the strength, organization, equipment, and deployment of all the major air forces in the world. Analyses of all the major military aircraft then in use were also kept by the air intelligence office.[65]

One of the more innovative programs in the 1920s for the education of the officer corps encouraged and financed Reichswehr officers to travel overseas in order to improve their foreign language capabilities, and also to observe foreign maneuvers and to visit foreign militaries. After returning to Germany from a one- to four-month trip overseas, Reichswehr officers would write extensive reports, which were then forwarded to the air intelligence office. All German officers traveling to foreign countries were expected to obtain the most recent military literature, and provide it to the Truppenamt staff. A favorite foreign destination for German officers from 1924 onward was the United States. The Reichswehr frankly admired American technology and industrial methods and found that when German officers visited the United States, they were very warmly received by the American officer corps. During 1925, for example, Helmuth Wilberg, accompanied by the Reichswehr's chief of aviation research, Adolf Baeumker, a former air service captain, and other officers, traveled extensively throughout the United States.

Reichswehr air officers (in civilian clothes) visiting the U.S. Army Air Corps installation at Crissy Field, Presidio of San Francisco, early 1925. Front left is Major Helmuth Wilberg, senior air officer of the Reichswehr. Directly behind him is captain Adolf Bauemker, chief of aviation research for the shadow Luftwaffe. Wilberg is talking to U.S. Air Corps Lieutenant Colonel Frank Lahm. Lahm had served as air commander for the Second U.S. Army in World War I and later that year would be promoted to be one of two generals in the Army Air Corps. (Photo from the Wilberg family.)

The Army Air Corps officers received Wilberg and their other former enemies graciously, and showed them the Army Air Corps' latest aircraft and installations.[66]

Under von Seeckt, the Reichswehr strove to become the best-educated army in the world. The language requirement was taken seriously within the Reichswehr, and officers were expected to be well-informed on foreign developments. This knowledge of foreign technology was emphasized even more strongly in the Shadow Luftwaffe, as a technically oriented service. Airmen realized they could not fall behind in their understanding of technological developments.

The Reichswehr air staff used its study of foreign air forces and foreign technology as a means of testing their own ideas and technical concepts. For example, the Germans were able to observe the French autumn maneuvers of 1923, and reported critically on the French air operations as unrealistic, and still mired in the concepts of 1918.[67] Often, the study of foreign armed forces provided a useful model for the Germans. For example, one report from 1925 provides a detailed analysis of the American mass production program of 1917–1918, and of American preparations for mass production in the case of a future war, and indicates the American mass production system and mobilization preparations that were developed from the American experience in the world war could be a useful model that ought to be followed by the Germans.[68]

THE EVOLUTION OF AIR DOCTRINE: 1923–1926

The comprehensive postwar study of 1919–1920 conducted by the Truppenamt, and which resulted in a new operational doctrine, was merely the first step in the process of creating a modern operational air doctrine. Military doctrine, and most especially, air doctrine is in a constant state of evolution and revision. Air doctrine is revised even more often than army doctrine, due to the greater dependence of air doctrine on technological factors. During the post-World War I period, moreover, aviation technology changed and improved very rapidly.

Because Germany was not authorized an air force by the Allies, the Truppenamt air staff resorted to several subterfuges to hide the fact that the Germans were active in creating an operational air doctrine. Pamphlets conveying the latest Truppenamt air doctrine were developed and distributed to Reichswehr officers under green covers—thus, nicknamed "green mail." They were usually entitled as "Compilations from the Publications of Foreign Air Forces." In reality, these documents were nothing of the sort, and were specifically intended to present the force Truppenamt air staff's view of air warfare.[69] One of the green mail documents, published around 1925, provides a glimpse of where Reichswehr air doctrine stood seven years after the end of the war. This 1925 pamphlet discussed air power at the operational level and specified that, in wartime, there would be essentially two air forces: one, allocated to army control for air support of the divisions, corps, and armies; and the other, the aerial fighting forces, consisting of the fighters and bombers. The aerial fighting forces would be under the control of the air staff and the armed forces high command. The primary mission of the air force allocated to the ground units would be reconnaissance and observation. The 1925 pamphlet outlined tables of organization and equipment for five specialized types of observation units that would be assigned to the army. Observation Squadron F was the long-distance reconnaissance squadron, which served under army control at army level. Observation Squadron A was the artillery observation squadron for the army headquarters; Observation Squadron N was the army's night observation squadron; Observation Squadron D was the divisional air squadron for short-range reconnaissance; and Observation Squadron K was the squadron devoted to liaison and support for army cavalry units. The 1925 pamphlet also outlined the difference between operational reconnaissance for the high command, which would be undertaken at up to 600 kilometers from the front lines, and the mission of the other squadrons: to conduct tactical reconnaissance, in this case no more than two or three days' corps march from the army's front lines—perhaps 100–120 kilometers. The army-level operational reconnaissance squadrons were expected to conduct surveillance of enemy logistics and transportation systems, as well as enemy air bases. The tactical observation units at corps and division command levels were basically assigned to monitoring enemy troop movements within 50 kilometers of the front.

The aerial fighting forces were, as a rule, to be organized into fighter and bomber groups. The fighters would be organized into groups by aircraft type—either single-seat fighters, two-seat fighters, or night fighters. Each group consisted of three squadrons, and two to four groups were organized into a fighter brigade. The bomber force was also organized into a brigade, with groups of day and night bombers with the day bombers predominating.[70] Several principles of operational employment were outlined, most specifically the principle that "careful organization of the mission is the prerequisite for successful completion of the task."[71] The appropriate aircraft were to be matched to the specific requirements of the battle. For this reason, the army ended up with five different reconnaissance squadron organizations. The principle of conservation of the force was also emphasized. Air force commanders were advised to ensure plenty of rest for aircrew during quiet periods, as well as a reduction in flying activity, so that aircraft and aircrew would be ready for periods of intense combat. Another principle stated the fighter planes' primary goal was the achievement and maintenance of air superiority in battle, thereby protecting their own bomber reconnaissance and attack aircraft, while hindering the operations of enemy aircraft near the front. The pamphlet strongly advised that air superiority could only be won if the fighter force was concentrated, and held under a single command.

These 1925 guidelines recommended sortie rates for the different aircraft types. Reconnaissance aircraft were normally assigned one sortie per day. Fighters were considered capable of three sorties a day, and night fighters, one sortie per day. Bombers could reasonably be expected to undertake two medium-range missions per day.[72]

After Germany's failure to conduct a successful strategic bombing campaign in World War I, the postwar studies carried out by the Truppenamt in 1919–1920 largely ignored strategic bombing operations deep into the enemy homeland. It was understood by the airmen that, even though the bomber force was the primary force of an air force, its attacks were to be primarily concentrated on the enemy military field units and armies, rather than on enemy industry. In the early 1920s, however, the viewpoint arose in all the western countries that the preferred target for a bomber force should be the enemy cities and industries, as the sources of enemy power, rather than the fielded forces. This viewpoint was expressed most eloquently by the Italian general and air minister, Giulio Douhet, in his 1921 work, *Command of the Air.* In this book, Douhet advocated direct attacks on the enemy homeland and cities, with the objective of breaking the morale of the enemy country.[73] Although Douhet voiced the best known expression of these views on strategic air war, and was the most adamant advocate of bombing an enemy to break the morale of the civilian population, the idea of bombing the sources of enemy power, particularly the industrial plant of an opposing force, was also popular in the early 1920s in the writings of such air power thinkers as Air Marshal Hugh Trenchard, chief of staff of the Royal Air Force, and General Billy Mitchell of the U.S. Army Air Corps. With the growing popularity of the concept of strategic bombing with the airmen of all the major western nations, it was natural that, as aircraft technology improved, and more efficient aircraft engines provided greater lifting capability, range, and speed, once-discredited concepts like strategic bombing would soon creep back into German air thought.

The first example of an outline for a strategic air campaign by the Reichswehr is from the 1924 air war games conducted by the Truppenamt air staff in Berlin. The 1924 war games postulated a German-French conflict, with the French air force being much stronger than the German. Due to the strength of the frontline French air forces, it was not considered practicable for the German air force to meet the French in head-on combat. Thus, the German war game players proposed a stratagem of attriting the French air force. As part of their plan, they drew up a target list of the eight most vital aircraft and aircraft motor factories in France, reasoning that if these were heavily bombed, the supply of parts and aircraft to the frontline forces would be sharply reduced.[74] This well-researched target list that had been carefully drawn up for the 1924 war games demonstrates that, for some time, the Truppenamt had been considering aspects of a strategic air campaign.

One of the detailed pictures of German air doctrine from the mid-1920s comes from the reports of Captain Martin Fiebig, a German air officer in World War I employed by the Reichswehr as an instructor and adviser to the Soviet air force General Staff Academy in the mid-1920s. In 1924, the small, poorly-trained Red Air Force had requested that General von Seeckt send a team of their "best" aviation officers. Fiebig was one of seven experienced German air officers sent as advisers and instructors to the Soviet air force between 1924 and 1926.[75] Fiebig eventually became the senior instructor at the Red Air Force Staff College. As such, it was his duty to lead the staff college war games. His extensive report on the 1926 Red Air Force war game tells us much about contemporary Russian and German air doctrine. The war game scenario for the Red Air Force was realistic: a defensive war pitting the Soviet Union against Romania and Poland.[76] Fiebig assailed the Russian officers for initiating strategic air bombardment of the enemy industrial centers. This was an air strategy, he argued, that could only be undertaken by a large, modern air force—and the weak and technologically deficient Soviet air force of 1926 was not realistically capable of such long-range bomber operations.[77] To the Russians, Fiebig identified the primary target of bombers and long-range reconnaissance aircraft as the enemy air force. The primary mission of the bomber force and reconnaissance assets should be to find and destroy the primary enemy airfields.[78] Only after the enemy air force was beaten down, should other bombing targets be considered.

GERMAN AIR BASE IN RUSSIA

One of the most important means by which von Seeckt and the Reichswehr's airmen were able to neutralize those provisions of the Versailles Treaty banning a German air force was the program of secret training and testing conducted in cooperation with the Soviet Union. Von Seeckt had first explored the possibilities for German/Russian cooperation as early as 1920. His quiet diplomacy had resulted in the German/Russian Rapallo Treaty of 1922. In a series of secret military provisions, the Soviets agreed to allow the Germans to establish air force and army training and testing centers in Russia, in return for German technological assistance and training for their own airmen and soldiers.

Colonel Lieth-Thomsen, the renowned wartime Luftstreitkräfte chief of staff, was sent to Moscow to serve as the Reichswehr's direct representative to the Soviet government. Lieth-Thomsen led a special Reichswehr staff instituted especially for the German/Russian operations, and as chief, reported directly to the army commander in chief. From the start, the German emphasis was on developing a "Shadow Luftwaffe."[79] The top priority was the establishment of a pilot training school, where Reichswehr officers could take a proper military combat aviation course using the latest aircraft. In addition, the Reichswehr could have a facility to test warplanes developed by German aviation firms, far from the eyes of the Interallied Control Commission that enforced Versailles Treaty provisions in Germany.

During 1924, the Reichswehr poured several million reichsmarks into the project. A modern air base was built at Lipetsk, about 220 miles from Moscow. There were two runways, as well as hangars and machine shops. Fifty new Fokker D XIII fighters were secretly obtained, and in 1925 the Lipetsk facility opened as a fighter school and testing station. During the base's existence (1925–1933), an average of two to three hundred Reichswehr officers, NCOs, and civilian employees were stationed at Lipetsk as students, instructors, ground staff, and test pilots.[80] At Lipetsk, an observer training program was soon established, and German airmen could now test tactics and doctrine by dropping live bombs on simulated targets.[81] At Lipetsk, the Reichswehr was even able to test the aerial delivery of poison gas.[82] The Reichswehr's program in Russia, conducted with the knowledge and approval of even Germany's democratic centrist political leaders, ensured the maintenance of a proficient cadre of fliers, and a thorough research and development program for aerial weaponry.

Post-World War I German civil aviation was completely dominated by former Luftstreitkräfte and naval aviation officers. This was to be expected, as the group in Germany with the most experience in aviation had come from the armed forces. These ex-officers tended to remain staunchly loyal to their former profession and to their colleagues within the military. While in the years immediately following World War I, the Interallied Military Control Commission was active in seeking out forbidden stockpiles of airframes and engines. The Reichswehr air staff, aircraft companies, members of the airlines, and former officers who belonged to the local aviation organizations made a sport of violating the Versailles Treaty, and hiding military aviation equipment from the Allies. During the immediate postwar period, some of the major German aircraft companies set up factories and operations overseas, so as to avoid the technical restrictions of the Allies. Junkers and Albatross set up aircraft factories in Russia, Dornier set up operations in Switzerland and Italy for a time, and Rohrbach relocated to Denmark.[83]

In most cases, the men at the top of the German civil aviation industry were former Luftstreitkräfte officers with talent, command experience, and a thorough knowledge of aviation. The best-known of these was former squadron commander and general staff officer, Erhard Milch, who left the German army for a position with Junkers Airline in 1920, and five years later played an instrumental role in consolidating Germany's two largest airlines, Aero-Lloyd and Junkers, into one large national airline: Lufthansa, of which he became director.[84]

In his position as the director of Lufthansa, Milch cooperated wholeheartedly with his former commander, Helmuth Wilberg, chief of the Reichswehr air staff, and with his other colleagues within the Reichswehr by providing extensive information on the latest developments in civil aviation technology, passing on information related to navigation, and in developing long-distance routes throughout the 1920s.[85] Milch's cooperation with the Reichswehr was typical of the German civil aviators of the 1920s.

Within the government, the most important person in German civil aviation was former Luftstreitkräfte Captain Ernst Brandenburg, who had commanded the German 1st Bomber Wing in its attacks on London in 1917, earning the Pour le Mérite. In 1922, Brandenburg went to work for the Ministry of Transportation as deputy state secretary for aviation. In 1924, thanks to General von Seeckt's energetic lobbying of the Reich's government, Brandenburg was appointed chief of the Reich Office of Civil Aviation, a department within the transportation ministry, with the rank of ministerial director.[86] It took considerable nerve, and used up some of von Seeckt's political capital for Brandenburg's appointment. Von Seeckt's insistence that Brandenburg—someone who had led a bombing campaign against British and French cities during the war—would be appointed chief of civil aviation gave rise to a political outcry from the western Allies. Brandenburg's appointment was, nevertheless, worth any temporary political outbursts. Until forced from office in 1933 for an unsympathetic attitude toward the Nazis, Brandenburg worked assiduously to build up civil aviation as a military reserve force.

Another important step in the creation of a civil aviation reserve force was the establishment of the Ring Deutscher Flieger, a society of German wartime aviators that was led by Colonel Wilhelm Siegert, formerly the inspector of aviation for the army. The Ring Deutscher Flieger was much more than a military veterans' organization. It kept careful records on wartime pilots and aviation officers, and served as the unofficial office for mobilization planning, in case Germany should need to recall men with Luftstreitkräfte experience.[87] The career of Wilhelm Haehnelt illustrates the domination of civil aviation in Germany by former military pilots. Haehnelt, commander of the Second Army's air group during the war, was one of the Luftstreitkräfte's senior airmen. He had served as Inspector of Flying Troops from 1918 to 1919 before retiring from the army in 1920. From 1919 to 1935, he served as vice president of the Aero Club of Germany. From 1926 to 1928, he was vice president of the German Air Sport League, a group involved in the Reichswehr's secret pilot training programs. From 1926 to 1933, he served on the board of the Reich Air Defense League (Reichs Luftschutz Bund), an organization that conducted research and civilian training for air defense in close cooperation with the Reichswehr air staff during the 1920s and 1930s.[88]

A considerable portion of the Reichswehr's aviation budget went to establishing an extensive program of pilot training. In 1924, a comprehensive training system was established, called "Sportflug GmBh," ostensibly a civilian company that provided sport aviation training through its ten flying schools. The curriculum of the Sportflug training program was actually geared to producing military pilots.[89] Other Reichswehr aviation programs were functioning by 1925. Under Wilberg's direction from 1923 on, German civil airfields, flight schools, aircraft factories and repair shops were carefully monitored, their equipment inventoried, and their capacity assessed to provide a planning base for the creation of an immediate reserve air force in the case of an invasion by France or Poland.[90]

The foundation for industrial planning of the future air force was laid in 1924 when a special section of the Weapons Office for industrial planning was created, and a military economics officer was assigned to each of the seven military districts in Germany, to serve as a liaison with industrialists, and to facilitate industrial mobilization and industrial military planning.[91] A further step in the creation of an industrial planning system for the Reichswehr was taken in 1925 when the Reichswehr sponsored the formation of a group called Stega, a council of industrial leaders, who could conduct liaison and planning between industry and the Reichswehr.[92]

GERMAN NAVAL AIR DOCTRINE

Unlike the army, the Reichsmarine did not conduct a comprehensive examination of the lessons of the war to create a new naval doctrine. There are several reasons for this. The German navy was in a worse position than the army in its ability to recover from the defeat of 1918. The German army could look back through its own history for examples of recovery from defeat by means of reforming the organization, doctrine, and strategy of the army and eventually gaining victory. In the historical example of Prussia's defeat by Napoleon, which was followed by the reform program of generals Gneisenau and Scharnhorst, the army had a model for reform. This period in German military history was a favorite theme of the German military writers of the 1920s. The army could also look back to a more impressive record of major battlefield victories such as Tannenberg, Gorlice, and Caporetto to draw lessons from. Although it had fought bravely during the war, the navy could not point to any major naval victories or victorious campaigns. Finally, the navy was more traumatized by the events of 1918 because the event that marked the beginning of the revolution and the fall of the Imperial government was the mutiny of the High Seas Fleet in October 1918 as the German seamen refused to sail their warships in one last sortie against the blockading Royal Navy. This was again in contrast to the army, whose frontline divisions had at least fought to the bitter end in 1918. The navy was not only sensitive about its wartime record, but also of its status as the junior military service of the nation.

All of this contributed to a genuine reluctance to make a comprehensive examination of the lessons of World War I. This was to be a detriment for certain departments of the navy, such as naval aviation, which had performed well in the war. By 1918, the German naval air arm had developed into an effective naval air striking force that could sink ships in the North Sea, and actually gain air superiority over much of the North Sea.

Finally, in the view of the senior leadership of the navy in the immediate postwar period, the mission of the naval air arm was to preserve a small naval reconnaissance force, along with the technology for maintaining naval seaplanes, float planes, and airships. Again in contrast to the army, of the 1,500 officers allowed in the German navy by the Versailles Treaty, only twenty (1.5 percent) had aviation experience, as opposed to nearly 5 percent of the officers of the postwar German army. While the army worked consciously to maintain a real air cadre, the navy's personnel office had little interest in retaining the services of an experienced aviation cadre so that by 1921 the navy had a total of only fifteen pilots.[93]

As of 1924, the German navy's aviation section consisted of a small air staff on the model of the army's air staff, with a group of five experienced naval air officers serving under Kapitänleutnant Faber.[94] As with the army, the navy's aviation department was responsible for establishing a naval air training program, and for coordinating the development and procurement of aircraft and equipment for the small secret naval air arm.

The German army and navy were able to cooperate on vital matters, but interservice rivalry was still the hallmark of army/navy relations in the interwar period. The naval general staff shared information with the Truppenamt in the 1920s, and also participated on war games and attended army maneuvers.[95] There was a reluctance on the part of the navy to get too closely involved with joint army-navy air operations and doctrine. For one thing, the wartime rivalry between the army and the navy was still very much on everyone's minds. The former Luftstreitkräfte officers knew that the navy had been the primary opponent of the creation of the air force as a separate and independent service. For its part, the navy had resented the control that the Luftstreitkräfte had had over airframe and engine production during the war, and the wartime reluctance of the army to adequately support naval aviation logistics requirements. Finally, under the command of Admiral Zenker in the 1920s, the navy was very much aware of its status as the junior service, and was reluctant to be placed in a situation in which they might come under army command. In the immediate postwar period, there was even some question in the Reichstag regarding the usefulness of the small German navy.[96] This made the navy's attitude even more reticent and defensive on issues of interservice cooperation.

The navy was able to successfully support a small naval aviation program under an ostensibly civilian firm, the Severa GmBh, founded as a commercial aviation firm in 1924, but in reality supported with secret funds from the navy budget. In the 1920s, over a million marks a year was spent to support Severa, which operated seaplane stations out of the former German naval aviation stations at Norderny and Holtenau.[97] The Severa Company allowed the navy to carry on a small pilot and observer training program, and served as a cover for the testing of naval reconnaissance aircraft. In 1923, Ernst Heinkel, who had recently founded his own aircraft company, and who was experienced in the building of seaplanes during World War I, undertook the construction and design of ten new reconnaissance seaplanes, named the He 1, which proved to be highly successful naval seaplanes.[98] Seaplane aircraft made considerable progress in terms of range, payload, and airworthiness in this era. The Dornier Company produced the famous Dornier Wal, one of the best seaplanes of the 1920s.

One advantage of the German navy was that it was allowed to maintain a moderately large antiaircraft arm, and to conduct antiaircraft training and testing during the 1920s. Because of their need for antiaircraft training, the navy was actually allowed to possess several float planes for target towing. Thus, the navy could operate an aviation program more openly than the army, and felt less need to get involved in the army's aviation program in Russia.[99]

While the navy was able to maintain a small training program and encourage technical advances for naval reconnaissance aircraft, in contrast to the Americans, British, French, and Japanese, the 1920s saw few advances in the development of naval air doctrine in Germany. Indeed, there seems to have been almost a regression, with naval aviation's strike role being deemphasized, and the reconnaissance role proffered as the primary use of that arm. With the Reichsmarine spending on aviation less than one-sixth of what the army was spending on its aviation program, it is clear that the navy, under Admiral Zenker, gave aviation a relatively low priority in the early 1920s.

A NEW STRATEGIC AIR DOCTRINE

While the doctrinal emphasis of the air staff in the early 1920s had been to develop a comprehensive doctrine for joint operations in cooperation with the army, in the mid-1920s the air staff was ready to return to the question of the strategic use of air power. Technologically much had happened since 1918 to change attitudes about the capability of air forces to conduct bombing campaigns in the enemy heartland. Long-range civilian air transports were proving their effectiveness. Lufthansa was conducting long-distance passenger flights throughout central Europe and flying in night and bad weather with an excellent safety record. The 1920 Rohrbach all-metal four-engine monoplane transport of 1920 showed the way for future aviation.[100] The result was an increase in interest in strategic bombing throughout Europe from Germans such as Hans Ritter to Italy's Douhet and Britain's Trenchard.

Already in the 1924 air war games, the air staff had created a plan for the strategic bombing of the French armaments industry. In 1926 Wilberg and his staff published a formal doctrine of strategic bombing under the title, *Directives for the Conduct of the Operational Air War,*[101] issued to the German airmen in May 1926. The *Directives* was a fairly long document of thirty-nine pages and laid out the organization, targeting strategy, and operational parameters for the conduct of strategic bombing.

The *Directives* is the first document to use the term "operational air war" to describe the German approach to strategic bombing. The air staff envisioned that there would be essentially two air forces in a future war. The first would be oriented toward providing tactical support and reconnaissance to army and navy units and operate under the direction of the theater commander. The second air force would be composed of long-range bombers and reconnaissance aircraft and would remain as a single unified force directly under the command of the high command.[102] This force would be oriented toward the destruction of targets in the enemy homeland as its primary mission.

The *Directives for the Conduct of the Operational Air War* is somewhat Douhetian in tone. The morale of the enemy population is seen as a primary target and a strategic bombing force is the only force that can directly attack the enemy population right from the outset of hostilities:

> The air force allows the supreme commander to carry the war simultaneously to the innermost political, moral, economic and military sources of the power of a state. The attack of the air force is directed against the population, industry, and transportation net as well as against the enemy armed forces and the facilities that sustain them. By attacks against the enemy's major cities and industrial centers, it will be attempted to crush the enemy's moral resistance and will to fight by targeting his armaments industry and food distribution.[103]

Because warfare was now dependent on the industrial capacity of a nation, it was argued that there was now little to separate the civilian part of the economy of a nation from the military part: "The requirements for civilian life are closely tied to the necessary requirements of the military. Civilian machinery that is brought to a standstill by attacks of the operational air force will also have a decisive effect upon the war industries and the total support of the armed forces."[104]

Much of the *Directives* is concerned with a discussion of the various targets that can be attacked in a strategic air campaign. The armament industries and transportation nets were seen as primary targets as were the seaports of the enemy.[105] The electricity generation plants of the enemy were listed as one of the most worthwhile targets as a means, with a few blows, to shut down war plants, civil life, and much of the train network (then being electrified in parts of Europe).[106] The impact of the bombing on the morale of the enemy civilian population is stressed throughout.

The strategic air force would be composed of bomber wings (called brigades here), and several bomber wings would constitute an air division. As the enemy could be expected to tenaciously defend his major industrial centers from attack, the air divisions of the strategic air force would also be equipped with long-range, heavily armed two-seat fighter aircraft wings to provide escort for the bombers.[107] The tactical requirements for intelligence, weather planning, and logistics are also discussed. The importance of escort fighters and maintaining a strong air defense system in one's home base set out in some detail in the German regulations[108] clearly illustrate that this doctrine is not a mere copy of Douhet. The German approach in stressing the capability of the air defense remained a trademark of German operational air doctrine.

The *Directives* also outline the conditions by which the strategic air force could be gainfully employed in joint operations with the army and navy. As a rule, the most effective use of the bomber force would be to strike targets in the homeland. However, when the ground campaign leads to a decisive battle in which the opportunity exists to annihilate the enemy armed forces, it was asserted that the best use of the strategic air force would be to conduct an interdiction campaign and cut the vulnerable enemy ground forces off from their sources of supply and rail transport.[109] Air and ground commanders were cautioned not to dissipate the effect of the bomber force in these circumstances but to wait and look for the "critical moment of decision" in which the massed air force would be thrown in quickly and decisively.[110]

The *Directives for the Conduct of the Operational Air War* read as something of a cross between Douhet and Clausewitz. Indeed, Wilberg and the air staff had taken the tradition of air war and adapted it to the traditional theory of war of the German army. In many respects, the *Directives* is not as radical an approach to air power as Douhet or Trenchard as the Truppenamt's airmen made no claim that a war could be won by air power alone or that anything but a truly joint war could be considered realistic. However, by holding out the possibility of decisively striking the enemy homeland and breaking the morale of the enemy population, the airmen were now arguing that, in a future war, the air force might not just be a junior partner to the other services but could become the primary instrument of victory.

CONCLUSION

In the years immediately following World War I, it looked to the world as if Germany had been completely disarmed as an air power. On the surface, this was so. Yet, in the long-term view, the Allied powers failed miserably in their effort to disarm Germany. Hans von Seeckt and his small group of airmen had succeeded in keeping air power as a central aspect of their view of warfare. Due to the effective militarization of the German civil aircraft industry, civilian airlines, and pilot training, the Reichswehr built up and maintained a secret reserve force. The German aircraft companies, with carefully applied subsidies from the Reichswehr, made great technological progress in aircraft and equipment design after World War I so that, by the mid-1920s, Germany was again one of the world's leading nations in aviation.

Just as important as building the industrial and technological base necessary for the creation of a future air force, the small air staff led by Helmuth Wilberg, an experienced and thoughtful airman, had conducted a thorough analysis of the air campaigns of the war and had developed a tactical and operational doctrine for a future air force that was equal to the air doctrine and theory of the major military powers in its detail and comprehensive nature. Moreover, through a program of training, war games, and exercises the Reichswehr was able to provide a sound education in the nature of modern military air power for both its air and ground officers. Despite Versailles, German officers of the 1920s were as well-informed—probably better informed—on the capabilities of military aviation than the army officers of other major powers. Certainly the ability to conduct combat training and flight testing with modern aircraft and equipment in Russia played a major role in keeping and maintaining the operational edge of the airmen.

The German airmen had found a superb mentor and spokesman in the person of Hans von Seeckt. Alone of the major military commanders of the 1920s, von Seeckt came to the conclusion that maneuver and mobility would dominate the battlefield of the next war. Von Seeckt's vision of future warfare was essentially the modern doctrine of maneuver warfare and the use of air power, in its tactical, strategic, and operational forms, was central to von Seeckt's vision. Von Seeckt provided an intellectual framework for the German ground and air officers to develop an effective and practical doctrine. The effort that the Germans made to remold their armed forces in the early 1920s provides an example of what a few individuals can accomplish in adversity. By the time that von Seeckt retired in 1926, he and the small corps of Reichswehr airmen had laid sound foundations for the eventual rebirth of a true German air force.

CHAPTER THREE

Preparation for Aerial Rearmament

IMPROVING THE ORGANIZATION

When Colonel General Hans von Seeckt was forced to resign as commander in chief of the army in October 1926, it did not signal any changes in attitude toward aviation on the part of the army high command of Reichswehr ministry.[1] Von Seeckt's successor as army commander, General Wilhelm Heye, army commander from 1926–1930, was handpicked by von Seeckt, and dedicated to carrying out von Seeckt's policies. Another protégé of von Seeckt, General Georg Wetzel, was chief of the Truppenamt at the time, thus not inclined to change von Seeckt's policies either. Wetzel's successor as Truppenamt chief from 1927–1929, General Werner von Blomberg, also favorably inclined to the role of air power.

From 1926 to 1932, several reorganizations of the Reichswehr's air staff and its subdivisions took place, which tended to increase the centralization of the Shadow Luftwaffe and its subordinate departments. In 1927, the Weapons Office was reorganized and its command structure simplified; the new Weapons Office consisted of four large departments. At the same time, the branch inspectorates, which until then had reported directly to the army commander in chief, were incorporated into the Weapons Office, so that after 1927, army headquarters in Berlin consisted primarily of two large staffs. The successive reorganizations, and the greater emphasis on the work of the Weapons Office in the late 1920s, resulted in a strengthening of the numbers and influence of the aviation branch officers working on that staff.

Under the strict Versailles Treaty provisions, the German army was allowed only 4,000 officers, so the number of officer aviators working in the Weapons Office was relatively small. The Reichswehr was, however, also authorized 3,040 civil service employees with officer rank, called "Beamte."[2] The majority of employees in the Weapons Office were such civil servants, and a disproportionate number of the Beamte within the defense ministry were former aviators who worked under the air staff—one means of getting around the Versailles restrictions. For example, in 1928 the Weapons Office aviation testing department was staffed by forty-eight people, the vast majority of them civilians, led by Captain Kurt Student. The testing department also employed Lieutenant Hans Jeschonnek as a section leader. In this department were three active, serving officers, eleven former officers, and fifteen engineer specialists with officer rank.[3]

A great deal of military talent was concentrated in the air staff of the Truppenamt and Waffenamt between 1926 and 1932. A high percentage of these officers and civil servants would attain high rank in the Luftwaffe. In 1927, after seven years' service as the senior air staff officer, Lieutenant Colonel Helmuth Wilberg was transferred. From 1927–1929, his place was taken by Major Hugo Sperrle, a highly qualified general staff officer and wartime observer. Sperrle, who had commanded the Seventh Army aviation force on the western front, was known to have an especially firm grasp of technical matters.[4] In 1929, Sperrle was followed by Lieutenant Colonel Helmuth Felmy, who served as senior air staff officer until 1932. Here was another experienced wartime aviator and commander, who had one of the best minds in the Luftwaffe.[5] Felmy had served as the staff officer for tactics and doctrine from 1924–1925, and was one of the officers behind the 1926 doctrine, *Directives for the Conduct of the Operational Air War.* Sperrle and Felmy were reputed to be knowledgeable, capable, experienced, and competent commanders. Both were highly respected within the army. Other very talented officers who were destined for senior rank, such as Captains Kurt Student and Wilhelm Wimmer, played leading roles in the Weapons Office during this period. In 1929, Captain Wilhelm Wimmer was made chief of development and testing for the aviation section of the Waffenamt.[6] Captain Walter Schwabedissen, a wartime pilot who had recently completed the general staff course, later to become a Luftwaffe lieutenant general, was made chief of the tactical manual section of the air staff in 1930.[7] Helmut Volkmann, a World War I squadron leader and later commander of the Condor Legion, served on the air staff from 1925 to 1929. Among the civil service airmen working in the Truppenamt and Waffenamt were: future Luftwaffe generals Martin Fiebig; Werner Junck, later Luftwaffe lieutenant general commander of the 2nd Fighter Corps in 1943–1944; and Rudolf Spies, a wartime aviator who earned an aeronautical engineering degree after the war, later to become a senior Luftwaffe engineer with general rank.

In 1929 the new reorganization of the staffs took place, primarily as a result of the commission led by Major Albert Kesselring, who served as Reichswehr commissioner for retrenchment and simplification.[8] Kesselring proposed that all of the aviation officers and agencies be openly consolidated into one inspectorate for aviation. For political reasons, the army could not establish an independent aviation inspectorate at this time. Instead, on 1 October 1929, a new training inspectorate was created under Major General Hilmar Ritter von Mittelberger. The new training inspectorate of the Reich defense ministry reported directly to the commander in chief of the army, instead of through the Truppenamt or Waffenamt chiefs. This inspectorate was primarily a cover: a means of consolidating all army aviation activities under the direct supervision of the senior air staff officer. Lieutenant Colonel Felmy, as chief of staff of the training inspectorate, was referred to de facto as the inspector of aviation.[9] The air office under Mittelberger's training inspectorate was organized into nine departments, seven of which belonged specifically to the aviation branch. Section I was the department for strategy and tactics; Section II was the officer personnel branch; Section III, the air technology office; Section IV, foreign air forces (intelligence office); Section VII, the air defense office; Section VIII, the air training office; and Section IX, the meteorological office.[10] At this time the term Luftwaffe came to be used in official correspondence, and the designation of the air activities as the Luftwaffe was encouraged by Lieutenant Colonel Felmy and his staff, although most of the army continued, in many cases, to use other terminology such as Luftstreitkräfte.[11] It was at this time that consolidation of other branches of the military associated with aviation also took place. In 1930, the army high command created a command staff and a special subinspectorate for flak artillery within the inspectorate of artillery and the Weapons Office.[12] In addition to these measures, some of the signals units of the army were specially identified as aviation signal units, and equipped and trained as such, although these units remained under the direction of the army signals inspectorate.[13]

From 1930 to 1932, however, there was some dissent from the top reaches of the army at strengthening the bureaucratic position of the air staff at that time. General von Hammerstein-Equord, chief of the Truppenamt and later commander in chief from 1930 to 1934, raised objections to the Luftwaffe's plans for semi-independence. In a letter to the branch schools dated 30 September 1929, von Hammerstein-Equord insisted that aviation training continue to stress the army support aspects of aviation.[14] In 1931, von Hammerstein-Equord, backed by the chief of the Truppenamt, proposed a wartime organization for military aviation. Under their plan, aviation would be divided into three branches, the greater part coming under the direct control of the army commander. This branch would be further subdivided into two groups: flying troops and air defense. A smaller aviation branch inspectorate would belong to the commander in chief of the navy. The remaining aviation

The Reichswehr's air staff, November 1930. Second row (standing left to right): Bruno Maass, Walter Schwabedissen, Fritz Loeb, Ulrich Grauert, Major General Hilmar von Mittelberger, Helmuth Felmy, Herr Gehrkens, Herr Hermann. Third and fourth rows (left to right): Herr Pank, Herr Stich, von Buelow, Herr Morrell, Herr Giesler, von Hollwede, Karl Drum, Werner Kneipe, Rudolf Bogatsch, von Lebedour, von Karmainsky. The majority of officers here—mostly majors and captains—became generals of the Luftwaffe and held senior commands during World War I. (Photo from USAF HRA.)

forces would be grouped together under their own commander in chief, commander of the Reich air defense, who would report directly to the chief of the Wehrmacht.[15] The position of von Hammerstein-Equord represented the army's last major effort to control all aspects of aviation. Von Hammerstein-Equord's opposition to a unified Luftwaffe office was answered in a paper written in 1932 by General Staff Captain Hans Jeschonnek, which advocated the centralization of all aviation assets—army, navy, and civilian—under one office, placing that office either under the aviation department of the Reich transportation ministry or under the defense ministry. The final outcome of the debates on air force organization would quickly be resolved once the Nazi party came to power on 30 January 1933.

THE INFLUENCE OF DOUHET

Central to the air power debates in the 1920s and 1930s was the thought of Italian general and air minister Giulio Douhet. In 1921, Douhet had written *The Command of the Air,* a book that would become the primary theoretical work of modern air power theorists.

Giulio Douhet was not the first to speak of strategic bombing. Even before World War I, the concept of strategic bombardment had been discussed. In 1908, H. G. Wells wrote *The War in the Air,* which featured the use of airship bombing to cripple enemy cities at the start of a war and to create panic in the enemy capital.[16] In 1909, Englishman R. P. Hearne theorized that airship bombers could terrorize London and cripple Britain's fleet by bombing Britain's cities and ports at the outset of a future war.[17]

By the end of World War I, the vision of strategic bombing as a decisive weapon of war already existed in the minds of many airmen. During the war, the Italian manufacturer of heavy bombers, Giovanni Caproni, had discussed strategic bombing ideas with the American army mission in Italy, even writing reports and publishing pamphlets advocating long-range bombing deep in the enemy heartland.[18] U.S. Colonel Edgar S. Gorrell, assistant chief of staff of the American Air Service in 1918, had spent time with Caproni during the war, and advocated that the U.S. Air Service acquire and manufacture a large number of heavy bombers. At the end of World War I, Gorrell conducted an extensive study of the strategic bombing campaigns of the war for the chief of the American air service Major General Mason Patrick. In this study, Gorrell criticized the aerial bombing methods of the British, and advocated tighter formations and more precise bombing. Gorrell argued that bombing enemy industrial areas could have a major impact on the course of future war.[19] In Britain, Air Marshall Hugh Trenchard, who had commanded the Royal Air Force's independent bomber force in 1918, became chief of staff of the Royal Air Force at the end of the war, whereupon he began speaking about the potential of air power and advocated a strong bomber force for the RAF.

Though Douhet was not the only theorist of strategic bombing, his *Command of the Air* remains the most eloquent, elaborate, and comprehensive theory of air power in the interwar period. While Douhet, like many theorists, tended toward extreme positions, he is also a reflection of many of the most common views of his era. In Douhet, these 1920s' and earlier theories on air power were brought together into a unified theory, so that Douhet became for airmen what Mahan and Corbett became for naval theorists. In the

1920s and 1930s, virtually all the major nations with air forces were influenced, to some degree, by the thought of Giulio Douhet.

The best exposition and analysis of Douhet's thought remains Edward Warner's essay on Douhet in the 1943 edition of *Makers of Modern Strategy.* As Warner explains, Douhet based his theory of air power on two assumptions: first, that aircraft were powerful offensive weapons, against which an effective defense cannot be made; and second, that civilian morale would be broken if cities were bombed. Douhet's theory has five major elements:

1. It is necessary to gain command of the air—in other words, to gain air superiority—in time of war. This requirement is the sine qua non for successfully conducting a decisive campaign.
2. The prime objective of a strategic air attack should be the cities and industries of the enemy nation, not their fielded military forces.
3. The enemy air force is not likely to be defeated in air to air battle, but can be defeated by attacking its installations, and the aircraft industry that supports it.
4. The surface forces, the army and navy, are defensive forces designed to hold fronts while air forces can paralyze the enemy's capability to maintain an army and navy.
5. The best airplane to conduct the war of the future will be the "battle plane," a heavily armed bomber capable of striking targets deep in the enemy hinterland with heavy bombloads, and also capable of defending itself against fighter planes.[20]

Douhet and his supporters provided a vision of conducting, and decisively winning a war in a matter of weeks, by attacking and paralyzing the enemy heartland with concurrently few military and civilian casualties. Douhet pointed out that all trained troops can stand up to intensive bombardment, while—he assumed—civilians could not. The factory workers "will melt away after the first losses."[21] With the civilian population panicked and fleeing the cities, and the shutdown of the enemy's industries, the paralysis of his government would quickly ensue. This was a very heady vision to nations that had endured the months-long, yet indecisive, bloodbaths of Verdun, the Somme, Flanders, and the Meuse Argonne.

Douhet made a number of assumptions regarding the power, accuracy, and effectiveness of bombers against cities. Douhet argued that twenty tons of bombs carried by ten aircraft could destroy everything within a 500-meter-diameter circle. According to such mathematics, 500 or 1,000 bombers could literally destroy any major city. To guarantee the effective destruction of the target, an aerial offensive would rely on three kinds of bombs: high-explosive, to break up the buildings and sever utility lines; incendiary bombs, to set fire to the ruins; and poison-gas bombs, to demoralize the population and prevent an effective response to the destruction and fires.[22] Douhet argued that the morale effect of bombing on a population was even more important than the material effect of the damage. "The complete breakdown of the social structure cannot but take place when the country is subjected this kind of merciless pounding from the air. The time would come when, to put an end to the horror and suffering, the people themselves, driven by the instinct of self-preservation, would rise up and demand an end to the war—just before their army and navy had time to mobilize at all!"[23] At the heart of Douhet's thought was a kind of Victorian-era Social Darwinism: the view that the lower classes did not possess "the right stuff," and would be unable to stand up to the hardship that modern war would bring.

Although Douhet's vision of future war would bring considerable material damage and losses and hardship to the civilian population for a short period, it was argued that such an approach to war was actually more humanitarian. Such a means of waging war would end wars very quickly so that future wars would result in tens of thousands of air-inflicted casualties, instead of the millions of ground-inflicted casualties that soldiers of World War I had seen. By the end of World War I, air power had shown that it had the nascent ability to strike deep into the enemy homeland. It was concluded that this new capability of warfare required a new approach to warfare and military doctrine. Although few military or air power theorists accepted Douhet's views completely, the trauma of World War I and the desire to avoid another attrition war in the trenches almost necessarily led to a theorist like Giulio Douhet, who could promise a quick, decisive, and relatively bloodless outcome to warfare.

STRATEGIC BOMBING CONCEPTS OF THE MAJOR POWERS, 1919–1932

Professional airmen and military theorists of every major power developed variations of the strategic bombing theory during the 1920s and early 1930s. In Britain, airmen and military theorists came to propose a Douhetian doctrine of strategic bombing, even before Douhet's work was known in Britain. Air Chief Marshal Hugh Trenchard, RAF chief of staff through the 1920s, insisted in numerous speeches and reports to the government that the Royal

Air Force should be bomber-heavy. Trenchard consistently maintained that the primary purpose of the air force was to conduct the offense. To Trenchard, accordingly, attempting to defend against an aerial offensive by acquiring fighters and antiaircraft guns was a virtual waste of resources.[24] In contradiction to Douhet, however, Trenchard argued that the primary target of the aerial offensive was not the enemy's civilian population, but its war industries and transportation network. Civilian morale was important, but it would be broken by the destruction of the enemy nation's military capability. Trenchard stated that "The army policy is to defeat the enemy army—ours to defeat the enemy nation."[25] Although Trenchard carefully avoided offending the sensibilities of civilian politicians by discussing the targeting of the civilian population, the targets that Trenchard proposed hitting—the factories and the transport system—all were located in cities, and the question of avoiding large-scale civilian casualties by strategic bombing was left unanswered. Time and again, however, Trenchard returned to the theme of assailing morale by bombing. In a 1928 memo, Trenchard argued that the dislocation of civilian morale was the true object of war.[26]

Trenchard's fears of another war of attrition like World War I, which reflected the majority view in the RAF staff, were taken several steps further by the civilian theorist, Basil Liddell Hart, one of the leading military theorists of the interwar period. In *Paris, or the Future of War,*[27] a small volume published in 1925, Liddell Hart argued that air power had become the dominant form of military power, and would prove to be the decisive weapon in any future conflict. Laying enemy cities in ruins, Liddell Hart argued, would result in "The slum districts maddened with the impulse to break loose and maraud, the railways cut, factories destroyed. Would not the general will to resist vanish, and what use would be the still-determined factions of the nation, without organization and central direction?"[28] Such a use of air power would decide the fate of a nation within days or weeks of the outbreak of a war. In a 1927 book, *The Remaking of Modern Armies,* Liddell Hart argued for the extensive use of poison gas in future wars, as being a more humane method of fighting, as gas tended to incapacitate rather than kill.[29]

Trenchard's concept of strategic air war provided the Royal Air Force with a justification for maintaining its service independence during a period in which budget cutbacks and retrenchments threatened the very independence of the RAF. Trenchard's views, although probably supported by a majority of the RAF officers, are not, however, representative of the unanimous position of British airmen in the 1920s and 1930s. Between 1931 and 1934, squadron leader J. C. Slessor gave a series of lectures at the army's staff college at Camberley in which he asserted that the most decisive use of an air force in wartime is in coordination with, and support of, the battle of the ground forces. Slessor published his lectures as a book, *Airpower and Armies*, in 1936.[30] Slessor went on to become an air marshal, and had a distinguished career in World War II. Other RAF officers challenged the Trenchard vision of strategic air war. In an article in the *RUSI Journal* in November 1931, squadron leader J. O. Andrews, a specialist in armaments, argued that the fighter arm ought not to be ignored, and that the capability of the fighter against the bomber had been underestimated.[31]

Unlike the RAF, the French air force was a subordinate branch of the army until 1933. French army doctrine and requirements tended to dictate the content of French air service doctrine. Although France had the largest, most powerful air force in the world in the early 1920s, and was a world leader in aviation technology, there was little mention of strategic bombing or independent air operations in French doctrine or French military literature of the early 1920s. Prior to 1925, the primary activity of the French air force was supporting the army's large-scale ground campaigns in Morocco.[32] By the mid- and late-1920s, however, French airmen were chafing at their subordinate role to the army. By the late 1920s, they were turning to the thought of Douhet as a means of arguing for an independent air force.[33]

In 1928, the first real steps were taken orienting France toward a strategic bombing doctrine. That year, an air ministry was created, and the air minister accorded cabinet rank and the responsibility for developing aircraft and technology for the French air service. That same year, the French began the development of what Douhet described as a battle plane: a well armed, heavy aircraft that could carry out a variety of roles, but with the primary mission of bombing. The BCR Aircraft (*B*ombing, *C*ombat, *R*econnaissance) would be able to carry out reconnaissance and ground attacks for the army, yet would have the range, armament, and capability to carry out strategic bombing attacks deep in the enemy homeland. Indeed, some of the French air force officers at the time openly acknowledged that designating the BCR units as "reconnaissance" units was merely a means of building up a French bomber force.[34] France was the only nation that seriously put this aspect of Douhet's theory into practice. As it turned out, the BCR aircraft, while designed for several missions, was not particularly effective at any of them. The result was a series of thoroughly mediocre aircraft.[35]

By the early 1930s, especially with the establishment of the air force as an independent service in 1933, Douhet's tenets became the predominant view among French air force officers. This led to considerable doctrinal tension among army officers, who predominated in the French high command, and continued to view the air force as a subordinate, supporting force for the infantry. This debate would not be resolved in the interwar period.[36] In Italy, home of Giulio Douhet, the ideas of the prophet of air power were not accepted uncritically. Although Douhet's book was very popular in Italy, and strategic bombing doctrine became part of the official doctrine of the Italian air force in the early 1920s, by the mid-1920s, a school of Italian airmen arose to directly challenge Douhet's assumptions and theses. Amadeo Mecozzi, a captain in the Italian air force in the 1920s, became Douhet's strongest opponent in print, and the leader of the school that argued for the primacy of assault aviation—the idea that air power is inherently joint, and performs at its best in close air support and interdiction campaigns. The best operational use of the Italian air force would be as a support arm, rather than a strategic bombing arm.

General Amadeo Mecozzi (1892–1971) was a decorated airman of World War I.[37] In dozens of articles written in the 1920s and 1930s in the Italian air force journal, the *Rivista Aeronautica,* Mecozzi systematically refuted the Douhetian concept of air war. Since the *Rivista Aeronautica* featured Douhet as its primary author—he wrote dozens of long articles on air power, until his death in 1930—the Italian air force was able to witness an informed debate between two leading air power experts. The differences in personality between the two air power theorists are evident in their writing styles. While Douhet constantly theorizes about what the future might look like, Mecozzi preferred to remain rooted in hard data, and regularly referred back to the war, recent air campaigns, and historical evidence to bolster his position. For example, Douhet argued that air reserve forces were unnecessary, and that the entire operational strength of an air force ought to be used immediately and wholeheartedly at the beginning of a war. Mecozzi, however, stressed the importance of maintaining an air reserve, to be held back and employed at the critical moments of the ground battle. He illustrated these principles with examples taken from World War I.[38] Mecozzi also disagreed with Douhet's assertion that it was impossible to defend against strategic air bombardment. He illustrated his position by proposing, in detail, a coordinated defense plan for Italy, with fighter groups covering specific geographical zones.[39] At the heart of Mecozzi's air theories was his concept of the organization of the air force as three different forces: (1) a strategic bomber force, to directly oppose the enemy nation; (2) naval air force, to attack the enemy navy; and (3) a third force to oppose the enemy's ground army. Mecozzi argued that the force created to oppose the enemy army, and to support the Italian army, should be the primary branch of the air force, and accordingly receive the largest share of aircraft and personnel.[40]

From the 1920s to World War II, Mecozzi's ideas gained ever greater popularity within the Italian air force and military high command. Air Marshal Italo Balbo, Italian air minister from 1926 to 1933, claimed to be a follower of Douhet and regularly praised him. In reality, however, Balbo tended to support the concepts of assault aviation as propounded by Amadeo Mecozzi. In 1929 under Balbo's direction, the Italian air force organized tactical ground attack units, and practiced maneuvers based on Mecozzi's theories.[41] By 1931, the Italian air force had established its first ground assault group, under the command of then-Colonel Mecozzi.[42] Mecozzi opposed Douhet's concepts on both moral and practical grounds. Mecozzi referred to Douhet's theories as "War against the unarmed." On a practical level, Mecozzi viewed Douhet's strategic bombing concepts as inappropriate to the kind of wars that Italy would probably have to fight.

In the Soviet Union, there was considerable enthusiasm for strategic concepts of air warfare. The ferment of Russia's early revolutionary period and the formation of the Red Army resulted in the Soviet military leaders' attempt to create a new and specifically Communist concept of war. The Red Army, formed in the revolution, produced numerous, well-informed, and thoughtful theorists and military leaders in the 1920s and 1930s. Concepts of strategic bombing appealed to the revolutionary instincts of the Bolsheviks, because such doctrines were modern and scientific, and the Bolsheviks pictured themselves on the cutting edge of modern and scientific thought.

Douhet was known relatively early in Russia, and was translated and well-known in that country by the late 1920s. As mentioned in chapter two, Captain Martin Fiebig, who taught Russian air force officers in the mid-1920s, reported their enthusiasm for strategic bombing campaigns. Russian military chiefs saw tremendous interest in the potential of air power. General Mikhail Frunze (1885–1925) was a highly successful Russian civil war commander who became a leading theorist of the Soviet military after the civil war. In January 1925, Frunze became commissar for national defense, but his tenure was cut short in late 1925 when he was assassinated by Stalin, who feared his popularity and prestige. Frunze argued consistently for the importance of the offense in warfare, and in his theory of the offense, air power played a primary role. In an article in 1923, Frunze claimed that air warfare would decide the outcome of future conflicts.[43]

Marshall Mikhail Tukhachevskii (1893–1937) succeeded Frunze as chief of staff of the army in 1925. Tukhachevskii is recognized as one of the most original and influential military theorists of the twentieth century. Like Frunze, Tukhachevskii was a believer in the offense, and air power was an important part of his conception of modern warfare. Through the 1920s and 1930s, Tukhachevskii restated his theory of the "Deep Battle." In the Deep Battle doctrine, air power played an important role, but as part of a combined arms offensive rather than an independent campaign. In 1932, Tukhachevskii stated that the light bomber in ground attack air units supported the army, prepared the battlefield, then interdicted enemy reserves. Air units belonging to the army group would then isolate the breakthrough sector and interdict the enemy's strategic reserves. Finally, airborne forces would be dropped behind enemy lines to seize their headquarters and supply bases.[44] Tukhachevskii did not, however, relegate the air force bomber to an army support role. In 1932, he declared that, in the future, independent air operations would be decisive in warfare. Tukhachevskii predicted that, in the near future, improved aerodynamic design would enable aircraft to fly fast, with great range, at high altitude. He foresaw that, in a decade or so, strategic bombing coupled with airborne drops could seize the enemy's transport systems, paralyze the mobilization enemy forces, thus "turning previous operational concepts inside out."[45]

One of the most notable early theorists of Soviet aviation, later chief of staff of the air force, was General A. N. Lapchinsky, who in 1920 wrote a book and a series of articles outlining how strategic bombing would be a major weapon of modern warfare.[46] Lapchinsky declared that "The airplane enters the field of military equipment as a new, independent factor of war—and not just as a support weapon."[47] In the early 1920s, Lapchinsky laid theoretical groundwork for the creation of what would, by the early 1930s, become the world's largest strategic bomber force. Lapchinsky's arguments in the early 1920s were supported by A. W. Sergejew in his book, *The Strategy and Tactics of the Red Air Force.*[48] Air power enthusiasts, however, were challenged by other Soviet military leaders and theorists, who saw the role of the aircraft and the bomber as part of an army support force. Soviet Air Commander W. W. Chripin argued that the air force should be closely aligned with ground operations.[49]

Another important Soviet theorist, General V. K. Triandafrillov, deputy chief of the general staff in the late 1920s, outlined his vision of air power in one of the most important of the Soviet military theory books, *The Nature of the Operations of Modern Armies,* published in 1929.[50] Triandafrillov argued in favor of Tukhachevskii's Deep Battle concept. However, Triandafrillov's own vision of air power was primarily of a support force for the strategic ground offensive, and the only mention of air power in his book is of a supporting force for the ground battle.[51]

As the Soviet military doctrine matured, the early enthusiasm for strategic bombing concepts was modified. In 1932, Lapchinsky himself attacked Douhetism, and denied that air power would be the sole arbiter in wartime. He argued that the role of aviation was in the interaction of all arms, and that while there was still room in doctrine for independent strategic bombing operations, most aircraft of the Red Air Force would be committed to supporting the ground battle.[52] In the United States, the enthusiasm of air officers for strategic bombing concepts could be traced back to a commission led by Army Colonel R. C. Bolling. Colonel Bolling led an American study group to Europe during World War I, visiting the British, French, and Italians. During his return to Washington, D.C., he formally reported that the United States should acquire a large number of bombers of the Caproni heavy bomber model.[53] American Secretary of War Newton D. Baker, however, set the tone for much of the discussion of strategic bombing when in 1919 he argued strongly against the concept of bombing cities.[54] Under the command of chief of staff, General John G. Pershing, the army saw little value in the concept of strategic bombing, and insisted that the air service role was that of an army support weapon.[55] The official army doctrine of this era was published in manuals in the early 1920s.[56]

Official disapproval at the top did not, however, keep the officers of the Army Air Corps from consistently supporting and developing concepts of strategic bombing. Giulio Douhet thus had considerable impact on American airmen at a fairly early date. A short extract of *Command of the Air* was received by the War Department Military Intelligence Division in March 1922, less than a year after its initial publication. A typed translation of the first hundred pages of *Command of the Air* was received at the Air Service Field Officers' School in 1923.[57] Although Douhet's theories were not accepted uncritically by American officers, they did provide additional ammunition in the argument for an independent air force.

In the 1920s and early 1930s, the leading American airmen, particularly the officers teaching at the Air Corps Tactical School, developed some specifically American concepts of strategic bombing. American officers tended to view the bombing of cities, and the targeting of civilians as advocated by Douhet, as fundamentally immoral. The Air Corps Tactical School started studying the enemy as an organic industrial system, and by the early 1930s were searching for the most vulnerable targets whose destruction could paralyze the enemy system. By studying the United States economy, the Air

Corps Tactical School faculty came to the conclusion that the heart of any modern industrial system was the electrical power system, because virtually the entire economy was dependent on it. Therefore, destruction of a few key generating centers and power transmission lines could actually result in the breakdown of the enemy's war industry and economy, without the massive loss of life incurred when cities and civilians were targeted. The vulnerabilities of other systems, such as the transportation system, food distribution system, and certain industries such as the steel industry, were examined and analyzed in the search for the most vulnerable targets.[58] By the early 1930s, the Air Corps Tactical School's views on strategic bombing as a decisive means of quickly winning a war had been fleshed out in some detail, and were probably supported by the majority of officers in the U.S. Army Air Corps.[59] Thus, the airmen's view of air war, and the doctrine taught at the Air Corps Tactical School existed in parallel with the official army operational doctrine, which insisted that air power was a subordinate arm of the ground forces.

The doctrine of precision strategic bombing was not, however, the monolithic view among air corps officers. In the 1920s and 1930s, the Air Corps maintained an attack group that specialized in close air support aviation, and there were some advocates of attack aviation in the Army Air Corps in the 1920s.[60] The contention of American bomber enthusiasts, and the Douhetian belief that the bomber would get through, was challenged by Air Corps Captain Claire Chennault, who taught fighter doctrine at the Air Corps Tactical School between 1931 and 1936. As a leading member of the aircraft development board in the early 1930s, Chennault argued for fighters could do more than point interception of bombers, but that could also serve as long-range escort aircraft in an offensive role.[61] Chennault did not deny the efficacy of strategic bombing or the importance of gaining an independent air force, but at every step he did challenge the assumptions of the strategic bombing enthusiasts on the capability of bombers to accomplish their mission.

THE STUDY OF FOREIGN AIR POWER CONCEPTS

Throughout the late 1920s, the German military took an increasing interest in foreign theories of strategic air power. Basil Liddell Hart's book on air power, *Paris or the Future of War,* was reviewed by the *Militärwochenblatt* in 1926, and by the late 1920s, Douhet was referred to regularly. During this period, the Germans demonstrated a fairly comprehensive knowledge of foreign military and civil aviation. For example, an article published in the *Militärwochenblatt* in 1928 discussed Italian air control of the Mediterranean, and the geographical advantages that air bases in Italian colonies gave to Italy, quoting the ideas of Italian air force commander Italo Balbo in detail, and providing a chart of all the Italian air force bases and units in the Mediterranean.[62] Another article featured in 1928 concerned Colonel J. F. C. Fuller, a leading British theorist, and his ideas on the problems of aerial warfare.[63] Between 1927 and 1933, the air power doctrines and theories of all the major air powers were discussed in some detail in the *Militärwochenblatt.* Von Altrock, the *Militärwochenblatt* editor, demonstrated considerable interest in, and support for, ideas of strategic bombing. For example, in an article featured in the 25 September 1929 issue, von Altrock described the French prototype of the Douhetian, heavily armed, long-range battle plane, the Bleriot 127. A wartime German fighter pilot was quoted in the article as stating that such a plane could mean the end of the old pursuit craft, and that this concept could be the means of gaining aerial superiority.[64] British concepts of defense against strategic bombing were also examined in the *Militärwochenblatt.*[65] Italian aviation activity was covered in some detail, for in the late 1920s and early 1930s, Italy was considered to be on the cutting edge as an air power. Douhet was not, however, the only Italian air power thinker covered in the *Militärwochenblatt.* The concepts of Major Amadeo Mecozzi, Douhet's opponent in the air power debates, were discussed as well.[66] Most important, each issue of the *Militärwochenblatt* contained reviews, summaries, and translations of foreign military literature on important aviation debates taking place overseas.[67]

Von Seeckt's insistence that all German officers were to be fluent in a foreign language paid off handsomely by ensuring a better-educated officer corps with a broad, international perspective. The primary foreign language in German schools of the 1920s and 1930s was English, and English was the most common second language for Reichswehr officers. An officer corps with a broad fluency in English, combined with subsidies and encouragement to travel overseas, made the United States and the American military a favored study tour destination for German officers of the 1920s and early 1930s. To be sure, the U.S. military had few qualms about allowing active German officers to visit their military installations, and to speak with American officers, virtually without restriction. Active American involvement in World War I had been limited to only a few months of ground combat, and America had chosen not to participate in the extreme provisions of the Versailles Treaty, or to demand any reparations from Germany in the peace settlement. Indeed,

American policy toward Germany in the era before the Nazi takeover was quite friendly, and German prosperity was derived to a large extent from large-scale loans by American banks. This friendliness and lack of hard feelings toward the Germans, combined with the fact that America was seen as the most technologically advanced nation in the world, attracted German officers, who wrote detailed reports after returning concerning American theory, doctrine, and technology, as well as obtaining up-to-date copies of American military books and manuals.

Major von dem Hagen, senior air officer in the Truppenamt's intelligence section, visited the United States in 1928, and wrote an extensive report on the U.S. Army Air Corps for the Truppenamt.[68] German officers were generally impressed with many aspects of U.S. military training and military technology. Captain Kurt Hesse, who traveled to America in 1925, visited numerous military installations and war industries. Hesse reported that the U.S. Army Industrial College was doing an excellent job of studying military economics and economic mobilization.[69] Various other Reichswehr officers were able to visit American factories in the late 1920s, and provided extensive reports on U.S. technological developments and industrial capacity.[70] Colonel von Boetticher, who later became military attaché to the United States in the 1930s, made several visits to the United States in the 1920s and commented favorably on the American concepts of personnel and economic wartime mobilization.[71]

The Reichswehr was somewhat limited in acquiring information on foreign armed forces by the Versailles Treaty provision that forbade Germany from having accredited military attachés. In the late 1920s, however, the Reichswehr initiated a program of attaching its officers to foreign armed forces, whereby the attached officers became, in effect, military attachés. Like any other military attaché, the primary duty of the attached officer was to collect information and report back to army headquarters. In 1929, the Reichswehr air branch arranged for Captain Wilhelm Speidel, later a Luftwaffe general, to be attached to the U.S. Army Air Corps and to attend Air Corps service schools. He was the first German since the war to be attached to the U.S. Army.[72] Captain Speidel was able to spend two to six weeks at the Air Corps Tactical School, Air Corps Engineering School, and Air Corps Technical School, also visiting the primary and advanced flying schools. He was able to briefly serve with attack observation bomber and fighter squadrons, and the Army Air Corps allowed him to fly several of its latest aircraft.[73] Speidel sent several boxes of current books and manuals of U.S. Army Air Corps doctrine to the Reichswehr's air intelligence officer. In 1929 Captain

Wolfram Freiherr von Richthofen was given the opportunity to serve as an attached officer with the Italian air force for six months. His instruction from the Reichswehr staff was to report back on the state of the Italian air force: its technology, training, and most important, its doctrine and theories.[74] Von Richthofen, who had to learn Italian for this mission, got along quite well with the Italian air force. After his initial attachment, he stayed in Italy for two years as the formal air attaché to the Italian air force.[75] Von Richthofen was specifically instructed by Major Helmuth Felmy, chief of the Reichswehr air office, to report on the ideas of Giulio Douhet, whom Felmy described as "well-known and followed carefully in the magazines."[76]

The Reichswehr's most important foreign connection was the Russian army. Throughout the 1920s and early 1930s, Russian officers were attached to the German army, and several Russian officers attended German general staff instruction.[77] German instructors commented very favorably on the enthusiasm and competence of the Russian general staff officers.[78] At the same time, German army officers and airmen were active in the Russian staff colleges as instructors. From 1925 on, Russian officers took part in the courses taught by the Germans at the Reichswehr's aviation school in Lipetsk and armor school at Kazan. Most important, numerous high-ranking German officers were able to freely visit Russia in the 1920s and 1930s, observe Russian maneuvers, and discuss military affairs with their counterparts. As a result, Russian thought and doctrine was well-known in the Reichswehr, and many of the Russian theorists, Tukhachevskii in particular, were frankly admired, and their ideas carefully studied.[79]

AIR WAR IN THE POPULAR LITERATURE

In the 1920s and early 1930s, the United States, Britain, and Germany witnessed a flood of popular books and films on aviation, primarily providing glorified accounts of the air war of World War I. The public was treated to dozens of books about famous aces of the war. In Germany, books about air heroes Richthofen, Boelcke, and Immelmann were published. Britain saw an entire series on the aces of the war,[80] and America witnessed books such as *Falcons of France* by Charles Nordhoff and James Norman Hall,[81] which depicted the wartime struggle of France's Foreign Legion air squadrons. The turn of the decade saw two of the classic air war films, *Wings* and *Dawn Patrol.* These popular books, magazine stories, and films shared a common theme: invariably, they centered on the aviator as the "lone eagle" fighter pilot, and presented an image of chivalry and adventure in warfare that certainly did not exist in the trenches of the Great War.

In *The Great War in the Air,* Domenick Pisano posits that these stories of the intrepid fighter-pilot/airman became popular public myth in the war period: "These myths have influenced the planning and use of air power during World War II, and are still with us today."[82] In reality, however, these popular depictions of air warfare had absolutely no effect on the development of air war doctrine. If the fighter pilot was glorified as the chivalrous personality of the last war, by the time of the heyday of popular aviation books and films, every major air force was relegating the romantic and individualistic fighter pilot to a secondary role. Every major air force—including Germany's Shadow Luftwaffe—concentrated its efforts on developing corps of unglamorous, less individualistic bomber pilots.

The popular literature common to the United States, Britain, and Germany did, however, have some long-term effects on the future of military aviation. First of all, the popular press accorded aviation greater prestige than the other military services. German, British, French, and American boys, brought up on such films and books, preferred to become aviators if given the chance. Thus, in no country was recruitment of aviators from the best and brightest of the nation's young men ever any difficulty. Secondly, the genre of popular books and films encouraged and ensured continued public support for aviation, particularly military aviation. The glamorous vision of aviation ensured public support for higher levels of funding that armies and navies, with more mundane missions of a less glorious and glamorous nature, could not equal politically.

In the late 1920s and early 1930s, however, there was an attempt to bring the concept of strategic air war to the public in the guise of popular fiction. The best-known work of this nature, *The Air War of 19—,* was written as an article by Giulio Douhet and published by the *Rivista Aeronautica* in 1930.[83] *The Air War of 19—*is a fictional account of describing what would happen if a nation actually put the doctrine described in his *Command of the Air* into practice. *The Air War of 19—*postulates a future air war of Germany against France in which, despite heavy losses, the German bomber fleet gains control of the air. Within days, as French cities are heavily bombed, the French urban populations flee, and the French government is forced to sue for peace. Another book of the Douhet genre was written in 1932 by Dr. Robert Knauss, the director of Lufthansa, an aviator and World War I German officer. In *Luftkrieg 1936: Die Zertrümmerung von Paris* (*Air War 1936: The Destruction of Paris*),[84] Knauss, writing under the pseudonym of Major Holders, postulated a war between Britain and France in which the RAF had secretly developed a large force of high-speed, long-range bombers. In Knauss's fictional account, the mission of the RAF was to "break the will of France by destroying war industry, and by terror attacks on the population."[85] Knauss even described doctrinal debates within the RAF in which the bomber advocates won by convincing the air staff that the day fighters ruled the air was long gone.[86]

Knauss, a much more knowledgeable airman than General Douhet, described some aspects of strategic air attacks far more realistically than Douhet's accounts. Knauss describes the RAF as using 1,000-kilogram bombs on Paris in an attack, using several hundred tons of high explosives, 3,000 incendiary bombs, and ten tons of mustard gas. Some aspects of Knauss's envisioned war, however, belie the extreme optimism of the bomber theorists. The close bomber formation of the RAF proves invulnerable against French fighter attack, and the attack on Paris proves completely successful, with no RAF bombers lost.[87] RAF attacks on Paris bring chaos to the French economy, and the civilian population goes out of control, with thousands fleeing the cities and many others looting Paris. In Knauss's fictional account, the French surrender after only two weeks of bombardment by the Royal Air Force.

Still, the Douhetians did not have it all their own way in the fictional air wars of the future. In 1933, German Axel Alexander wrote a novel, *Die Schlacht über Berlin (The Battle over Berlin),*[88] in which an aggressive Bolshevik Russia has invaded and conquered Poland, and has set out to conquer Germany. When the Russians institute a strategic bombing campaign against German cities, the West unites to stave off the Bolshevik menace, and the Germans receive assistance from the British and Italian air forces. In Alexander's air war of the future, the German civilian population has been well trained in civil defense. Shelters are available, as well as gas masks. After the initial attacks by Russian heavy bombers, civilian losses actually decrease, and the public becomes calmer, more careful, and more determined.[89] Other forms of passive air defense make the Douhetian bombing attack less effective. For example, the Germans defend their vital industries and reduce Soviet bomber accuracy by the extensive use of artificial fog generators on the ground. Alexander further postulates a strong antiaircraft gun defense, as well as night fighters, which take a heavy toll on the attackers.[90] Finally, a large force of modern fighters is assembled, which meets the Soviet bombers head-on in a dramatic air battle in which the Russian bomber squadrons lose 50 percent of their aircraft.[91] The attempt to defeat Germany and the West by strategic air power is foiled by strong defensive measures, and the West is saved.

THE DEBATE ON STRATEGIC BOMBING

By the early 1920s, the German professional soldiers fully accepted that strategic bombing campaigns would become an integral part of a future conflict. Former German general staff Captain Hans Ritter, one of the most important writers on military air power in the interwar period, expressed what was most probably the standard general staff viewpoint in his 1924 book, *The Future War and Its Weapons,* when he stated that modern war was "a pure economic war," and that modern industry makes the entire homeland "a giant depot." In such a condition, the former difference between the warfighters and civilians had become obsolete.[92] Under such conditions, according to Ritter, it was now morally acceptable to use the full array of weapons available to a nation to break the will in the enemy homeland.[93]

The primary question, however, was not whether Germany would experience strategic bombing in the next war, but the degree to which Germany was vulnerable to strategic bombing. Many German writers of the interwar period emphasized the vulnerability of the defenseless Germany to bombardment by its enemies. Numerous articles appeared, typically showing a map of Germany with radii depicting the ranges of enemy bombers, demonstrating that almost three-quarters of Germany was within easy range of enemy air power based in France, Czechoslovakia, or Poland.[94] Lieutenant General (ret.) Max Schwarte, a prolific military writer and one of the many retired generals who turned their hands to military commentary and history after the Great War, was fairly typical of the strategic bombing alarmists of the late 1920s and early 1930s. Impressed by the claims of foreign strategic bombing enthusiasts, Schwarte lectured on strategic bombing theory in 1928, asserting that the German population and industries were helpless against the air forces of France, Belgium, Czechoslovakia, and Poland. Schwarte insisted that these enemy nations possessed 14,000 new aircraft, 60 percent of them large bombers, each having a bomb capacity of 2,000 kilograms.[95] The Truppenamt air staff conducted a study of Schwarte's assertions, probably in response to alarmed politicians who had heard Schwarte's lectures, and concluded that Schwarte had grossly overestimated Germany's vulnerability to strategic bombing. Indeed, the Reichswehr air intelligence assessment of the French, Belgian, Czech, and Polish air forces was that, at best, they might total approximately 6,300 aircraft, including obsolete planes and trainers. Even this number was suspected to be too high. The air staff provided several corrections to the record. For example, they noted that, of the bombers possessed by Germany's enemies, the overwhelming majority were light bombers. Only a handful of modern bombers were available with the capability of carrying 1,000- to 1,500-kilogram bombs. In short, while the threat was potentially there, Germany would not face serious danger from strategic bombing attack until considerable strides were made in aircraft technology.[96]

While the Reichswehr air staff generally favored the theories of strategic bombing, they were sufficiently professional to maintain a healthy skepticism regarding many of the assumptions made by the strategic bombing enthusiasts. Numerous studies on the ballistics and accuracy of bomb patterns were made on the initiative of the air staff and the Truppenamt throughout the 1920s, and extensive data were collected on foreign bombs.[97] The Technical College of Berlin was also contracted to carry out studies and collect data on bombing patterns and accuracy.[98]

One positive aspect of Germany's lack of an air force in the 1920s was to push German military personnel and civilians to seriously consider how one might conduct a passive defense that would minimize the effect of a strategic bombing campaign against Germany. In the early 1920s, the Luftschutzliga (Air Defense League) was established in Germany. By the early 1930s, the league had tens of thousands of members, subscribing to its journals, taking part in lectures on air defense, and even participating in voluntary air defense exercises. Several journals on the subject of civil air defense were published in the interwar period, and received wide circulation. Some of the best-known of these include the *Luftschutznachrichtenblatt (Air Defense Newsletter),* established in 1923 and published as a journal of the flak veterans. Another contemporary journal was *Die Luftwacht,* and finally the journal of the Luftschutzliga itself, *Die Sirene (The Siren).* The Luftschutzliga became a large and very effective organization for training the public in civil defense. The Air Defense League worked in close cooperation with the Ring Deutscher Flieger, the Flakverein (organization of flak veterans), and the interior ministry of the national government. A large correspondence file of the period indicates that there was constant and close cooperation between the military, the civilian government, and the civilian air defense organizations.[99] Many of Germany's leading military figures were roped into the air defense movement of the 1920s and 1930s. For instance, General von Stülpnagel was elected chairman of the Ring Deutscher Flieger Committee for Air Defense in January 1932.[100] Another was Hans von Seeckt, who after his election to the Reichstag after retiring from the army made numerous speeches on the theme of creating an effective civil defense system against enemy air attack.[101]

As Peter Fritzsche has pointed out in *A Nation of Fliers,* the air defense propagandists and the civil defense organizations played a major role in the militarization of Germany, by giving the German public the impression that Germany was in a desperate and embattled state.[102] On the other hand, the civil defense organizations and their literature also provided considerable impetus to carrying out some solid, academic study regarding the nature of air war and air defense. Several themes on methods of air defense are examined in detail in the military literature of this era. In 1929, an article in the *Militärwochenblatt* discussed various methods of defending civilian targets against air attack, including producing chemical fog to cover the target, camouflage, and the creation of gas-proof installations. It was practical to consider placing electricity plants, power transfer stations, radio stations, and telephone centers underground to minimize their vulnerability to air attack.[103] German army industrial planning also took into account the problem of vulnerability to air attack. In 1925 and 1926, when the Weapons Office was developing plans and estimates for the establishment of emergency weapons production facilities in case of war, it was planned that most of these facilities would be sited in Germany's interior, at extreme range for any enemy bomber force.[104]

The use of flak artillery against strategic bombing attacks was given more coverage in German military literature of the 1920s and 1930s than that of any other nation. The *Militärwochenblatt* devoted a great deal of space to articles on flak gun developments in foreign countries, as well as direction-finding equipment and calculators.[105] Lieutenant Colonel von Keller (retired), wartime commander of the home air defense, made a strong argument in favor of flak defenses in his 1929 book, *The Present Defenselessness of Germany in Light of Her Defense Against Air Attacks in the War of 1914–1918.* Citing numerous statistics, he discussed the effectiveness of German passive and active defense in the latter period of the war, and particularly through the use of barrage balloon belts and gun batteries for the protection of various targets.[106]

One of the assumptions of the air war theorists and commentators of the 1920s and 1930s was that poison gas would be used as part of the strategic campaign against cities in a future war. The German military and civil defense literature of the period argued that the gas attack against civilians need not have the dramatic effects foreseen by Douhet if the civilian population were well trained in civil defense procedures, and were provided with gas masks.[107] A conference between von Seeckt, Chancellor Luther, Foreign Minister Stresemann, and Interior Minister Schiele on the vulnerability of the German population to gas attack led to the military's establishment of the Institute of Gas Analysis in the Technische Hochschule Berlin in Charlottenburg. This institute was given the mission of conducting research to assist an effective civil defense against gas warfare.[108] There was some debate, however, as to whether the Germans would consider using air-dropped poison gas against civilian targets in a future war. In 1924 von Seeckt instructed the general staff officers involved in writing doctrine that, in a future war, only nondeadly gas, such as irritants (tear gas), would be employed against enemy civilians. This led to a letter to von Seeckt from Helmuth Wilberg, questioning this pronouncement. Lieutenant Colonel Joachim von Stülpnagel also protested von Seeckt's position in letters to Wilberg and to Major Albert Kesselring, in which he provided the unique argument that if Germany used nonlethal gas, "Enemy propaganda will always say the Germans have employed gas bombs against civilians, and no difference will be made between tear gas and deadly gas, so that Germany might as well consider using deadly gas."[109] Despite such debates, the Reichswehr proceeded to conduct several tests in the mid- and late-1920s on the air-dropping of poison gas at secret testing sites in Russia,[110] and considerable effort was devoted by the Reichswehr in the 1920s and 1930s to the development of new, improved poison gases as well as bomb and artillery delivery systems.[111]

TRAINING THE ARMY IN AIR POWER

The German army of the interwar period took air power more seriously than other armies. Under von Seeckt in the early 1920s, it became the goal of the Reichswehr to have the ground soldiers understand the role that air power would play in future war, and methods of defense against opposing air power including camouflage, deception, and ground-based antiaircraft defense. Officers were to have a thorough understanding of how air forces cooperated with the armies, how to employ aerial reconnaissance assets on the offense and defense, and how to employ air defense units.

Aviation officers played a major role in all Reichswehr unit maneuvers, and aviation was portrayed in virtually all Reichswehr maneuvers beyond the regimental level. In 1923 General von Seeckt directed that modern weaponry, specifically aircraft, were to be portrayed and practiced more often in Reichswehr maneuvers.[112] This directive was followed by the army through the 1920s and 1930s. The American military attaché to Germany commented regarding Reichswehr training in 1926, "The assumption of the presence of both friendly and hostile air forces was made in every maneuver witnessed during the year, which assumption the umpire has never failed to bring home to the commanders of every grade by constantly giving them an assumed air situation—the presence of friendly or hostile observation, combat, artillery or bombing planes in the air overhead. These were sometimes represented by balloons, various colors representing different types of planes, but often merely assumed and not represented. In any case, the first consideration of every officer and man throughout was concealment from overhead observation by cover, camouflage and, when this was not possible, by the dispersion of men and materiel in such a manner as not to offer an effective target either for air bombing or for artillery fire directed by air observers."[113] To add realism to maneuvers, civilian airplanes were sometimes employed on Reichswehr maneuvers to simulate aerial bombing and reconnaissance.[114] Foreign military observers who attended Reichswehr maneuvers repeatedly commented on how carefully the Reichswehr practiced camouflage and other passive air defense.[115]

Air power and its defensive and offensive aspects as it affected the operations of ground forces, was given considerable emphasis in the numerous tactical handbooks published for German soldiers in the 1920s and 1930s.[116] Officers attending the general staff course were required to study air doctrine, theory, and technology, and at the divisional level numerous courses and exercises were created to educate the midlevel staff officers of the army in air power. Every year, each division of the Reichswehr was required to conduct a yearly air defense study.[117] Every Reichswehr division contained a divisional air defense office, manned by officer aviators. These officers ensured that division-level training plans included training in aviation employment. In the late 1920s, one feature of Reichswehr division training was for a division air officer to lead a tactical staff ride emphasizing aviation for the officers.[118] To maintain a corps of effective, well trained air defense artillery officers, approximately thirty to forty officers a year were sent to special courses at the Königsberg Fortress, where they underwent flak training and exercises.[119]

The Reichswehr general staff and the defense ministry conducted a major war game every winter at the operational and strategic level of war, in which several dozen aviator officers drawn from the Truppenamt and throughout the army were employed to play the role of a proper air force staff. From

January to March, two series of war games were played in Berlin: one, an operational-level war game played over several days in January, primarily for the aviation officers; and another series, played in February–March for the entire Truppenamt. The latter series incorporated a considerable degree of military air participation.[120] Normally, several of the leading ground officers from the Truppenamt would play roles in the aviation winter war games with the air staffs. In the January 1927 war games Lieutenant Colonel von Fritsch, chief of operations of the Truppenamt, played the commander in chief of the blue forces.[121] This 1927 war game was not limited to employing air power in the tactical sphere. The war game scenario, which postulated a German defense and counterattack against Poland as the enemy, featured tactical air power employed operationally, as well as the bombardment of German towns and cities from the air by the Polish air force.[122] The defense ministry invited members of the foreign ministry to participate, both to lend strategic realism to the exercise, and to critique it.[123]

By means of such a comprehensive program of educating the soldier in doctrine—depicting air power in small and large-unit exercises, employing aircraft and simulated flak guns in divisional and army maneuvers, providing special courses in military aviation, and stressing military air power in general staff education and war games—even the least intellectual of the Reichswehr officers were bound to come away with a sound understanding of the role played by aviation in German military doctrine, a firm grounding in how to defend against aviation, and how to use one's own air force in time of war.

THE DEVELOPMENT OF NAVAL AIR DOCTRINE 1926–1932

Unlike the army, the German navy in this period was not especially air-minded. Under the leadership of Admiral Hans Zenker, the commander in chief of the navy from 1924 to 1928, and Admiral Erich Raeder, navy commander from 1928 to 1943, the primary goal of the Reichsmarine was to regain its place as one of the world's major navies. To both admirals, this meant the construction of a surface battleship and cruiser fleet. In the late 1920s, Zenker and Raeder and their staffs consistently lobbied the defense ministry regarding the need for a battleship surface fleet. In a navy staff document of April 1928, *Guidelines for the Use of Our Sea-Striking Force in a Future War,* the naval staff argued that there were four primary missions of the navy: first of all, to protect German commerce, and to attack enemy commerce; second, to protect militarily essential sea transport; third, to protect the German coast against an enemy amphibious landing; and finally, to support amphibious operations of the German forces. All four of these missions depended on "gaining control of the sea." Furthermore, sea control could only be obtained if the Reichstag approved the funds for the building of new surface pocket battleships.[124]

Another report by the navy staff in 1929 reinforced the argument for a heavy surface fleet. In a paper entitled "Does Germany Need Large Warships?" the role of air power is brushed off with the sentence, "The influence of the air force on the conduct of future war is difficult to determine because this weapon and defensive measures against it is still in the state of constant development and flux."[125] Indeed, while the paper makes the argument that the large battleships still dominate the sea, the only mention of the aircraft carrier is of a ship that can support the commerce raider with aerial reconnaissance.[126] Throughout the period, any mention of naval aviation, or military aviation in general, was relatively rare in German naval doctrine. This is not to say that the Germans were unaware of major aviation developments being carried on in the United States, Japan, France, and Britain, and in the development of naval aviation as a true striking force. All these themes were reported on and covered extensively in German military journals of the 1920s and 1930s. The naval staff in this period, however, exhibited a single-minded determination to see the creation of a surface battleship fleet. To this end, the Reichstag in 1928 began the appropriation of hundreds of millions of reichsmarks for building pocket battleships: 10,000-ton, heavily gunned, fast ships that were capable of both commerce-raiding and direct ship-to-ship engagements.

In this period, aviation was not completely ignored by the Reichsmarine. The navy staff maintained a small air staff and its own naval aviation training schools, ensuring a small force of pilots and observers was maintained and kept proficient.[127] The naval staff also had a small technical development office under command of a naval aviator, set up in the naval transport office. The German naval aviators were funded at approximately a tenth of what the army aviation branch received. Considering the large appropriations that the Reichstag voted to the German navy in this period, the level of aviation activity indicates more a lack of interest than a lack of funds.

Several aircraft were developed under German navy contract between 1926 and 1933, primarily by the Heinkel and Dornier companies. Under the prevailing naval doctrine, the primary development goal was light seaplanes for short-range reconnaissance that could be flown off the new battle cruisers, and heavier flying boats that would be capable of long-range naval reconnaissance. In 1930 the Heinkel Company began development of the He 59, a twin-engine, general purpose float seaplane that was tested in 1931 and 1932, found to be satisfactory, and was ready for serial production in 1933. The He 59 was a sturdy but fairly slow aircraft, built to take four crew members and armed with three machine guns, which could carry a ton of bombs.[128] A long-range naval flying boat was contracted by the naval staff from the Dornier Company, and the military version of the Dornier "Wal" was in production by 1932. Known as the Do 15, it was a fairly successful flying boat, capable of moderately long range as a patrol craft, but armed with only three machine guns and 400 pounds of bombs.[129] Further evidence of the lack of interest in a naval air strike force was the inability of the naval air staff to develop an effective air-dropped torpedo in this period.[130]

A primary reason for the lack of development of naval aviation technology was the old problem of interservice rivalry. The German naval staff feared—and rightly so, as later events would prove—that a specialized naval air arm would become absorbed by the army's air arm if the navy cooperated too heartily with the army, or merely became the junior partner in the army programs. Before 1933, the navy tended to reject any close cooperation with the army aviators. In 1927 the Truppenamt air staff proposed a program for joint army-navy development of aviation technology. The air staff outlined a 30-million reichsmark program of aircraft research and development. The navy replied with the vague answer that it would like to be active in such a program, but could not take a direct part in concert with the army. The navy, which was about to get enormous appropriations for shipbuilding, claimed that lack of funds made it impossible to coordinate aviation technology programs with the army.[131]

In contrast to the army, German naval maneuvers and war games of the late 1920s minimized the role of naval aviation. In naval maneuvers, all the primary action was based on surface operations.[132] Occasionally, air power was mentioned in connection with naval surface operations. For example, in a German navy operational study of 1930 in which a Polish war scenario was examined, concern was expressed regarding the possibility of Polish air attacks on German ships in the confined waters of the Baltic near Poland. From this, the German navy understood that it needed its own fighter arm to protect the fleet.[133] Thus, a version of the Heinkel 51 fighter, developed between 1931 and 1933, was fitted with floats and tested as a German navy fighter plane.[134]

Another example of the deficient doctrinal thinking on air power within the German navy was the lack of interest in the dive bomber. In the 1920s, the American, French, and Japanese navies were all working on the development of a naval dive bomber that could be flown off a carrier and used as an antiship weapon. In 1931 the Japanese navy placed an order with Heinkel for a two-seat dive bomber capable of carrying a bombload of at least 550 pounds. Heinkel's response was to develop a prototype dive bomber known as the He 50. Later, in 1932, it was demonstrated to German army airmen. The Heinkel 50 was accepted as dive bomber by both the German army and the Japanese navy in 1933. There is no record, however, of the Reichsmarine expressing interest in either the He 50, or dive bombers in general.[135]

Admiral Raeder, as navy commander, expressed some interest in naval aviation. In a paper addressed to the defense ministry, which outlined his ideal program for the navy of the future, Raeder specified that he wanted a force of several battleships, several battle cruisers, eight light cruisers, forty-four destroyers, numerous U-boats, and one aircraft carrier. In addition to the carrier, he wanted a bomber force of 244 aircraft plus ninety-six trainers and 220 reserve aircraft.[136] When pressed by the defense ministry in 1930 to modify this extremely ambitious and expensive program, Raeder responded by outlining the minimal requirements for the German fleet of the 1930s. Raeder's minimal navy consisted of two large battleships, three pocket battleships, four cruisers, two light cruisers, fourteen destroyers, twelve U-boats, and one 10,000-ton aircraft carrier/seaplane tender. In the 1930 report, there is no mention of a land-based naval air arm.[137]

AVIATION TECHNOLOGY AND ITS EFFECT ON AIR DOCTRINE

The German aviators of the interwar period believed that the operational doctrine of military aviation was dependent on the state of technology. Although Germany was denied an air force, it was not denied civil aviation or aviation technology by the Versailles Treaty. This gave the Germans an inherent advantage in the air, for Germany in the interwar period was a world leader in aircraft design and technology.

By the lifting of the final restrictions on German aviation technology by the Paris Air Accords of 1926, the Germans already had one of the largest, most progressive, and most profitable civil aviation systems in the world. By 1926 Lufthansa alone flew more kilometers, and carried considerably more passengers, than all the French airlines combined.[138] In the following years, the disparity between French and German civil aviation would grow even greater. Although the French airlines were, on paper, possibly the most heavily subsidized in Europe, they were also commercially inefficient, receiving only 10.6 percent of their income from purely commercial activities in 1928. Lufthansa, which received a somewhat smaller subsidy than the French airlines, earned greater passenger and cargo profits, obtaining approximately 30 percent of its income from commercial sources.[139] The estimated 20 million reichsmarks per year that Lufthansa received in subsidies from the German government in the late 1920s, however, was not the only subsidy that German civil aviation received from the government. Unlike France, where the administration of civil aviation was centralized in the French air ministry after 1928, each of the German states maintained its own civil aviation offices and programs for supporting aviation. In addition, individual German cities and communities established their own aviation offices, and put up money for the establishment of modern airports. Thus, when direct subsidies from the national government are added together with the state and local government support given to civil aviation, public funding of the German civil aviation industry was probably surpassed only by the United States.

The German aircraft industry had enjoyed a strong technical and academic base since before World War I. The Aeronautical Research Institute at the University of Göttingen was a world-class institution in the 1920s and 1930s. This institute led the world in research in fields such as high-speed aerodynamics. As early as the 1920s and 1930s, aeronautical engineers at Göttingen discovered that the swept-back wing would be more efficient at higher speeds by reducing drag. At Göttingen, German engineers were on the world's cutting edge, working on projects including the all-wing aircraft, the tailless airplane, and even rocket-propelled aircraft at an early date.[140] In many aspects of airframe design, the Germans had clearly established their superiority as far back as World War I, when Junkers Aircraft produced the first effective all-metal combat airplanes. Beyond that, Hugo Junkers also pioneered the thick-wing cantilevered monoplane.[141] Another German designer, Dr. Adolf Rohrbach, carried the all-metal aircraft a step further in 1919, when he designed the smooth-skin, all-metal aircraft in his four-engined, eighteen-passenger Zeppelin-Staaken transport monoplane. Rohrbach's stressed-skinned metal aircraft was a milestone in the development of the modern airliner.[142]

Throughout the 1920s and 1930s, German companies were generally well ahead of their European competition in aircraft design. In 1919, Junkers developed the F 13, an all-metal, enclosed-cabin monoplane, which remained for a decade one of the most popular civilian passenger planes in the world, with about 350 in service.[143] Junkers led the way, in 1922, with the development of the three-motor passenger aircraft, the G 24. By 1929 Junkers had developed the G 38, the world's largest commercial passenger plane, a four-motor aircraft with 3200 horsepower that could carry thirty-eight passengers.[144] The Dornier Company also came out with some original designs, the most important of which was to be the largest aircraft of the period, the Dornier 10. This twelve-engine flying boat, designed for transatlantic operations, was flown for the first time in 1929.[145]

The design of effective instruments, including radios and navigation aids, was almost as important as aircraft design for the development of a comprehensive and effective aviation program, capable of providing the basis for future rearmament. In many respects, the Germans had been ahead in radio development during World War I. Both the German military and civilian aviation industry continued to put considerable effort into the development of effective radios. During the 1920s, German military and civilian aviation industry made great strides in producing effective high-frequency radio equipment.[146] Ultra-high-frequency radio was also employed extensively by the German armed forces.[147] While it was important for German commercial aviators to have effective radios, the creation of effective radio direction-finding and navigation aids for aircraft in the 1920s was almost as important. Regarding effective radio navigation systems, German technology of the interwar period could only be matched by American technology. By 1931 eighteen German civil airports were equipped with Lorenz navigation systems, which enabled pilots to fly by following a radio signal under zero-visibility conditions, and navigate safely.[148] The Lorenz navigation system, as well as an extensive system of lighted airways and a national system of aerial direction-finding transmitters meant that, by the late 1920s, German civilian pilots could fly and navigate effectively at night, in bad weather, and under poor visibility conditions, with a superb safety record.[149] In addition to being world leaders in aircraft and navigation equipment, the German aircraft companies were also on the cutting edge, in the 1920s, in the development of accurate instruments essential for safe and exact long-distance flying. In the 1920s, German companies pioneered gyroscopic artificial horizons, more accurate aircraft compasses, and altitude indicators, putting them into mass production early on.[150]

While Germany led the world in areas such as pressurized flight at high altitude, and was ahead of the other European powers in airframe design and navigation instruments, the German aviation industry tended to lag behind the other European nations in the development and production of large piston aircraft engines. This disadvantage in piston engine development would have a major impact on the future development of the Luftwaffe.[151] The Germans lagged behind in the development of their own aircraft engines to the point that, in the 1920s, BMW took out a license to produce the American Pratt-Whitney Hornet engine.[152]

TRAINING AND AIRCRAFT TESTING IN RUSSIA

At the Reichswehr base in Lipetsk, Russia, from 1925 to 1933, German airmen had the opportunity to undergo a thorough course of military flight training in up-to-date military aircraft. They were able to fly prototype reconnaissance, fighter, and bombing aircraft, and to test bombsights, weaponry, and navigation equipment. The first commandant at Lipetsk was former general staff officer and aviator, Major Stahr. From 1924 to 1930, he commanded a staff of up to 300 Germans, who were engaged as instructors, test pilots, aircraft technicians, and airfield staff. All were secret employees of the Reichswehr.[153]

From its inception, the core of the Lipetsk center's operation was a fighter school. This school was equipped with fifty Fokker D XIII fighter planes, surreptitiously acquired from the German military's old friend, Dutchman Anthony Fokker. The D XIII was a single-seat biplane fighter, one of the best combat aircraft of its day. It first flew in 1924, and in 1925 it gained four world speed records.[154] The fighter pilot course provided advanced training to pilots who already possessed a pilot's license. The course emphasized basic fighter tactics; ground attack operations with bombing practice against simulated enemy columns, bridges, airfields, and ground troops; squadron operations; and instrument navigation.[155] In the first year of the Lipetsk operation, the first students were wartime fighter pilots brought to Russia for refresher training. All subsequent courses at Lipetsk, however, concentrated on training younger, less experienced pilots who had undergone their basic flight training in Germany before coming to Russia. This was a recognition that service as a fighter pilot was essentially a young man's game, and thus it made more sense for Germany to build a corps of younger, new pilots than to retrain older pilots. In addition to the fighter school, there was a one-year aerial observer course at Lipetsk. This was offered to selected officers who had already undergone a six-month training course in Germany. The observer course included not only training in aerial observation, but also emphasized navigation, and even included some bombardier training.[156] By 1933 the Lipetsk program had trained 120 fighter pilots, and 100 observers.[157] The

Fokker D XIII practicing attacks against ground targets at the secret Reichswehr base in Lipetsk, Russia, ca. 1925. (Photo from USAF HRA.)

Lipetsk course was an elite program. Officers were carefully selected for training in Russia, and many of the young officers that underwent training in Lipetsk in the 1920s and 1930s went on to become senior commanders in the Luftwaffe. In 1928 the Lipetsk course graduated four future generals der flieger: Paul Deichmann, Rudolf Meister, Kurt Pflugbeil, and Hans Seidemann; nine future lieutenant generals of the Luftwaffe; and ten future major generals. Similar statistics and results can be found for the Lipetsk course of other years.[158]

Lipetsk was especially important as a testing base. As the decade wore on, and the restrictions on flight training in Germany eased with the departure of the Interallied Military Control Commission, the testing aspect of the Lipetsk installation grew in importance. The Dornier Do P, the Dornier Do 11, and the Rohrbach Roland bombers were all tested at Lipetsk in the early 1930s. The Arado 64 and the Heinkel He 38 prototype fighters underwent extensive frontline testing at Lipetsk.[159] Other aircraft later adopted by the Luftwaffe were also tested at Lipetsk, including the Heinkel He 46, a short-range reconnaissance aircraft; the Heinkel He 45, a reconnaissance aircraft and light bomber; and the Arado Ar 65, a single-seat fighter.[160] Particularly noteworthy in the further development of Luftwaffe doctrine and equipment was the testing at Lipetsk of the Junkers K 47, a two-seater, all-metal fighter first produced in Sweden in 1928. The K 47 was a very strong and stable aircraft, well liked by the pilots. It was fairly fast, for its day, with a 168-mph speed, and had an effective range of 404 miles. In testing, the K 47 did not compare favorably, in air-to-air combat with the single-seat biplanes. The K 47, however, was capable of carrying a 250-pound bombload, and performed well in dive bombing and ground attack tests.[161]

By 1931 the political situation in Germany was such that it was no longer as necessary as before to hide the military buildup and training. It was difficult and expensive to get equipment and personnel to and from Lipetsk, and though the cost of maintaining the installation itself was only 2 million reichsmarks a year ($500,000),[162] the German military—under pressure to save money by a government wracked by the Great Depression—decided to close the schools at Lipetsk, and move all operations back to Germany. During its heyday, the German installation and schools at Lipetsk enabled the Reichswehr to conduct aviation training that would have been impossible in Germany: live-fire practice, dive bombing, fighter bomber operations, as well as bombing experiments with high-explosive and poison-gas bombs. At Lipetsk, the Germans were able to keep up with the western nations in the development of aircraft weaponry and bombs, as well as in the development of the ancillary equipment, such as bombsights.

The German installation at Lipetsk also played an extremely important role in the development of German air doctrine. As the home of German fighter training in 1929, the fighter school instructors at Lipetsk were directed to write fighter operational doctrine for the Shadow Luftwaffe. The Lipetsk instructors completed an extensive manual, which provided a comprehensive doctrine for fighter forces, including formation flying, squadron attacks, aerobatics, air-to-air combat, and tactics for ground attack and close air support. While the fighter pilots' primary job continued to be engagement of the enemy air force in the air, the school at Lipetsk reinforced the notion of the secondary job of the fighter pilot as ground attack and support of the army. This was further reinforced by some of the joint operations with the Russian military.[163] The fighter manual was not just purely tactical and operational; it also included principles and guidelines for the fighter commander.[164] The fighter school staff at Lipetsk also developed a comprehensive training program outline and curriculum. In 1929, the Lipetsk fighter pilot curriculum contained several very progressive features, including the use of gun cameras to facilitate the training of pilots in air-to-air combat.[165]

THE EVOLUTION OF AIR DOCTRINE

The years immediately preceding the Nazi takeover of the German government in January 1933 were very fruitful for the Reichswehr air staff for broadening and deepening their concepts of aerial warfare. The study of air power history in the Great War, as well as a study of foreign military aviation and the Germans' own experience with maneuvers and testing in Russia, considerably affected the development of operational, and especially tactical doctrine. Numerous historical studies emphasizing tactical applications and practical lessons found their way into the air staff's doctrine section. In 1928 a former night-fighter pilot who had helped defend Germany against Allied night bombing attacks in 1918 wrote a historical account of the experience, also including a "lessons learned" section in which he outlined what the current tactics and organization of night-fighting units ought to be.[166] In October 1931, Colonel (ret.) Lieth-Thomsen, former commander of the field aviation force, wrote an extensive study of his war experience, again as a "lessons learned" thesis, which emphasized the operational use of bombers in the latter part of the war.[167] Thomsen's essay combined world war history with current events. Lieth-Thomsen berated the current French military leadership for their ultraconservatism, and for having emphasized the army support operations of the air force while ignoring the development of a strong operational bomber fleet.[168] In his essay, Lieth-Thomsen also praised the German strategic air attacks against England in 1917 and 1918,[169] proffering as his model the strong bomber force concentrated in Flanders in 1917, which conducted large-scale attacks against rear airfields and depots of the British army.[170]

The army continued to play a major role in shaping Reichswehr air doctrine. In the 1930 Reichswehr air staff document, *Principles for Employment of the Air Force,* the first thirty pages were devoted to an operational doctrine for the employment of reconnaissance/observation aircraft in support of the army.[171] The army's doctrine of a rapid, mobile war of maneuver required that the air force provide considerable short-range reconnaissance assets for the army. In addition, the fighter force was largely oriented toward conducting short-range ground attack operations. Due to the expectation that the ground forces would move quickly, the Reichswehr air staff devoted considerable effort to thinking through the organization and establishment of highly mobile air force engineer, supply, and support units capable of traveling behind the leading formations of the ground forces and setting up mobile airfields for fighters and reconnaissance aircraft close behind the lines.[172] Considerable effort was also expended, during this period, in the development of tactics for employing close air support and dive bombing aircraft, as well as the need to defend against such attacks by the enemy. A substantial literature on these subjects appeared in the late 1920s and early 1930s.[173] Leading aviation writers, such as Captain Hans Ritter, also wrote extensively on air operations in support of the army's maneuver war.[174] The forward air battle played such a large role in army doctrine that, when drawing up the outline for proposed motorized division in 1926, the Truppenamt Training Section proposed that each of a division's three motorized infantry regiments should have a flak battery, and that the artillery regiment should have an additional flak battalion. In the late 1920s, the army ground forces were thinking in terms of forty to fifty flak guns for every ground division.[175]

Some very original and provocative new ideas were being circulated among air power thinkers of this period. In the December 1929 issue of the journal *Wissen und Wehr,* Friedrich Wilhelm Borgemann proposed the view that a future war would likely become a trench war. As posited by Borgemann, one way out of this dilemma was "vertical strategic envelopment," in which a large force of paratroops and air-transported units of up to a division in size could be brought over the enemy trenches and dropped in strategic locations deep behind enemy lines to outflank and outmaneuver the enemy.[176] This was one of the first detailed discussions of the use of paratroops in large-scale operations in military literature.

The Reichswehr's senior air officers at this time, Helmuth Felmy, air staff officer for the Truppenamt, and Wilhelm Wimmer in the Waffenamt, both staunchly supported the view that the strategic bomber would play the primary role in any future air war, and the development of heavy bombers ought therefore to be the primary mission of the air staff. At a 1932 Waffenamt conference on air force development plans, Major Wimmer summarized the Waffenamt's staff study with an eloquent argument for the primacy of a strong bomber fleet in German air plans.[177] In the 1930 *Principles for the Employment of Air Forces,* Felmy and the air staff argued that "the mass of the bombers should be united under a 'commander of the Bomber Force,' and should be employed in the conduct of the operational air war under the direction of the high command."[178] The mission of the bomber force was to "battle for the air against the military and economic sources of power of the enemy."[179] Although Germany's senior airmen were largely bomber force advocates, a healthy skepticism toward Douhetian notions was also exhibited by 1930. The concept of the Douhetian multipurpose battle plane was rejected. "The numerous missions of the air force require different types of airplanes. If an aircraft is not used for the mission for which it was designed, it is not likely to succeed, and more likely to be shot down."[180] The fighter force was seen as having an important role, but subordinate to the bombers, with their primary mission being the achievement of aerial superiority. The fighters were to accomplish this in combination with a strong ground antiaircraft force.[181] The secondary mission of the fighter force was to conduct low-level attacks and direct support of the ground troops.[182] The greatest departure from the Douhetian ideal was a rejection of the concept of gas and terror bombing attacks against civilians. "The bombardment of undefended cities, as well as the use of poison gas, are forbidden by international treaty."[183]

PREPARING TO REARM

One of the advantages enjoyed by the Reichswehr's Shadow Luftwaffe was the close and effective cooperation between those who developed doctrine for the aerial war; the army and the defense ministry staffs that made military plans within the greater strategic context; with those who developed and built weapons and prototypes in the Weapons Office; and finally, with the actual producers of the weaponry. From the early 1920s on, the Reichswehr air staff conducted extensive planning and data collection in coordination with the defense ministry and civilian producers, to lay the groundwork for a rapid and effective rearmament program for the future. From 1923 to 1925, the Truppenamt and the air staff developed an army enlargement and rearmament plan for a future army of thirty-five divisions. This study, covering several hundred pages, included detailed plans for the creation of an air force, complete with tables of organization and equipment for every type of air unit possibly required for a future air force.[184] From 1923 to 1925, rearmament plans became the foundation for future Shadow Luftwaffe planning. Heavy bomber squadrons would have six aircraft. Reconnaissance/observation squadrons would also have six aircraft. Fighter squadrons would have fifteen aircraft. Three or more squadrons would constitute a *Geschwader* (Wing), and wings had units to maintain reserve aircraft. The future air force was expected to be highly mobile, and completely motorized, with every flying unit normally equipped with fifteen or more trucks. Plans for airfield support units were drawn up, as well as for the mobile air force engineers who would build and maintain forward airfields.[185] The creation of these plans required extensive research by the air staff into the state of the aircraft and armaments industry planning for the mass production of the materiel and aircraft necessary to support such a plan.

Even though emergency mobilization was never required, the planning process compelled the air staff and the Civil Aviation Department to draw up and maintain tables of organization and equipment, and to establish detailed training plans for the training of ground personnel, mechanics, aerial photo interpreters, and communications troops, as well as pilots and observers. Economics officers of the military districts and officers of the war economics staff attached to the defense ministry had to research issues and compile data on subjects such as the aviation fuel requirements for the future air force. In the course of the decade before the Nazi accession to power, a small corps of officers and civil servants with a sound understanding of the economics of aviation planning and procurement was assembled within the army, the defense ministry, and the civil aviation department.[186]

In 1928–1929, the Reichswehr air staff initiated its first limited rearmament program, the "A Program," which would provide a small and secret air force station within Germany by 1932–1933. Part of the program to build up equipment for a twenty-one-division army would entail creating a force of approximately 150 combat aircraft, comprising eight reconnaissance squadrons, three fighter squadrons, and three heavy bomber squadrons.[187] In 1930, the government provided the army with 484 million reichsmarks to provide equipment for an enhanced, twenty-one–division army. It is noteworthy that approximately a quarter of the total rearmament program budget went to aerial rearmament, with 110 million reichsmarks set aside for airplane and equipment procurement, and additional millions set aside for air defense and for subsidizing passive air defense for armament firms.[188] Considerable funds were also allocated for the creation of a large flak force with twenty-eight light flak batteries, each battery having six 20- or 37-mm guns, and twenty-seven heavy flak batteries, each battery having four 75- or 88-mm guns.[189] In

Dornier Do 11 bomber. Developed by the Reichswehr's shadow Luftwaffe in 1932 and produced as one of the Luftwaffe's first bombers. (Photo from USAF HRA.)

the seven years before the Nazis assumed power, the German government made available 170 million reichsmarks for secret aerial rearmament programs.[190] This was not enough money to provide for the establishment of a real air force, but it did at least help keep some of the German aviation companies solvent during the business downturn of the Great Depression.

In 1932, taking into account the rapid demise of the Versailles Treaty system, Helmuth Felmy submitted a plan to develop an eighty-squadron air force of 720 aircraft, 240 in reserve, by 1938. Felmy's proposed air force would consist of six long-range reconnaissance squadrons, fourteen short-range reconnaissance squadrons, eighteen fighter squadrons, and forty-two bomber squadrons. The bomber squadrons would have 370 aircraft, and 126 reserves. Along with the acquisition of ninety-six trainers, Felmy was proposing an air force of over 1,000 aircraft.[191] During 1931–1932, the aircraft for the 1,000-plane force were in development. Prototype models of aircraft were built and tested during this period for the Reichswehr staff and were ready for serial production by 1932–1933.[192] In addition, the German naval air staff had two aircraft models developed and ready for production.[193]

The five aircraft models for the air force were the Heinkel 45 long-distance reconnaissance aircraft, which doubled as a light bomber; the Heinkel

46 short-range reconnaissance aircraft; the Heinkel 51 fighter; the Arado Ar 64 fighter; and the Dornier 11 bomber. These aircraft, which were to constitute the first generation of the reborn Luftwaffe's aircraft, were roughly equal in performance and capability to their counterpart aircraft of the European and American air forces of the period. The Heinkel He 45 reconnaissance aircraft, a sturdy biplane with a 600-horsepower BMW VI twelve-cylinder engine that could achieve a maximum speed of 180 miles per hour, could double as a light bomber with its armament of two machine guns and 440-pound bombload.[194] The Heinkel He 46 was a parasol-winged monoplane, slightly underpowered, with the 450-horsepower Bristol Jupiter engine, and had a maximum speed of 155 miles per hour. The He 46, which first flew in 1931, was known as a stable, easy-to-fly aircraft.[195] The Heinkel He 51 was a derivative of the Heinkel He 49A, which first flew in 1932. The He 51 was powered by a BMW VI engine, carried two machine guns, and had a maximum speed of 205 miles per hour.[196] The Dornier Do 11 bomber, which would come to be seen as the backbone of the new Luftwaffe, was first flown in March 1932. The Do 11 was also somewhat underpowered, with two 600-horsepower Siemens engines. It carried three machine guns, and a 2,200-pound bombload. Its flying characteristics were mediocre, and its maximum speed was 155 miles per hour. It did, however, incorporate several up-to-date design features. For example, it was the first European bomber with retractable landing gear. Generally, it compared favorably with other standard European bombers of the period.[197] The French heavy bomber of this period, the Bloch 200 Bbn 4, had similar characteristics to the Do 11, but with a slightly lower speed, and slightly larger bombload.[198]

In 1931, Heinkel had also developed the He 50 biplane dive bomber, powered by a Bramo 650-horsepower engine, which was capable of carrying two machine guns and a 1,100-pound bombload. The prototype He 50 was tested and demonstrated to the air staff in 1932, and was ready for serial production soon after that.[199] Heinkel had also developed two good aircraft for the German naval air arm, the He 38 seaplane fighter and the multipurpose He 59 seaplane, a large craft capable of carrying a four-person crew and of being armed with three machine guns, and 2,000 pounds of bombs.[200] In addition, Junkers' superb and innovative Ju 52 transport was developed as a prototype in 1930, underwent trials in 1931, and was already in production by 1932. This sturdy, all-metal, trimotor monoplane was to become one of the most important aircraft of the Luftwaffe.[201]

CHAPTER FOUR

Theory and Air Doctrine in the Wever Era, 1933–1936

When Adolf Hitler came to power as German chancellor on 30 January 1933, the Reichswehr air staff was ready to begin a limited rearmament program. The German military airmen could look back on a relatively successful fourteen years of service. During the Weimar Republic, the airmen had developed air doctrine, air force plans, an effective air training program, kept up with new modern technology, and had helped the civil aviation industry to build a solid infrastructure. German airmen were, however, unprepared for the scale of rearmament envisioned by the Hitler government. Reichswehr air officers immediately found themselves in the middle of a crash program to make Germany a major air power within three years.

Leaders of what would become the Luftwaffe had one of the most challenging tasks that airmen have faced in the twentieth century: building a major air force in a short time from a minimal foundation. The task the Luftwaffe faced included organizing a large air force, developing modern weaponry, revitalizing and building up the aircraft industry, and instituting a comprehensive training program. Moreover, early in the process, it had to develop a coherent air doctrine that would guide the process of rearmament and of building a new organization.

The years 1933–1936 were of foundation-building. Several major personalities dominated the Luftwaffe organization and played vital roles in creating new concepts of air power for a reborn German air force. Germany's air minister, World War I fighter ace Hermann Göring, who was simultaneously commander in chief of the Luftwaffe, played a central role in building up the Luftwaffe during 1933–1936. As a member of the cabinet and Hitler's inner circle, Göring was able to ensure that the German Luftwaffe and the aviation industry would receive unprecedented and massive amounts of funding for rearmament. At the same time, Göring interfered very little with the related technical decisions or the revision of air doctrine. Even though Göring was proud of his rank as commander in chief of the Luftwaffe, he had in fact very little knowledge of current aviation. Göring had last flown an aircraft in 1922, had done relatively little to keep himself informed on aviation matters, and was known to visit his office in the air ministry headquarters only rarely.[1] Outside of formal staff meetings, which Göring rarely attended in the early years of the Luftwaffe, he was notorious for showing a lack of interest in modern aviation thought or technology. Wolfram von Richthofen recollected that, outside of staff meetings, the only time that Göring would talk about aviation was when he would get together with Ernst Udet or one of his World War Jagdgeschwader 1 flying comrades to talk about the good old days of aviation.[2] In these early years, however, Göring's lack of interest in the details of the Luftwaffe actually worked positively for the Luftwaffe. Göring's cronies, including his World War I wingman, Bruno Loerzer, were given prestige posts within the new Luftwaffe. None of them was in a major doctrine or policy-making position prior to 1936. As long as an impressive Luftwaffe was being built, Göring refrained from interfering with decisions on production or planning, or even with the content of air doctrine. In the early years, Göring let the seasoned air professionals do their job, while he provided an inexhaustible supply of funds.

The next major personality of the Luftwaffe, one of the dominant figures of Luftwaffe history, was Erhard Milch, who served as state secretary for aviation. In effect, Milch ran the air ministry and coordinated the vast program of building up the German aviation industry and its production capability as well as creating a Luftwaffe organization and infrastructure. Erhard Milch was probably the best man in Germany, at this time, to take over this position.[3] As director of Lufthansa, he had proven himself to be a brilliant administrator, organizer, and planner. Milch had the business acumen to take what were essentially dreams of a large air force, and translate them into the reality of aircraft and military organization. Erhard Milch was seen, throughout his career in the Luftwaffe, as an administrator and organizer, but not as an air leader, nor an air power theorist. While Milch was admired throughout the Luftwaffe for his managerial competence, he was also generally disliked by most of the senior airmen. Milch, who had developed a close relationship with the Nazi leadership prior to the Nazi takeover in January 1933,[4] was seen as a politician and an intriguer. In short, while admired, he was not trusted.

As a major general during the early years of the Luftwaffe as well as the most senior officer in the air ministry when it was created in 1933, Helmuth Wilberg would play a major role in the development of Luftwaffe operational doctrine. Wilberg, who had headed the Reichswehr shadow air staff for eight years in the 1920s, and had a proven record of combat leadership, was

Hermann Göring as Reichsmarschall and commander in chief of the Luftwaffe. (Photo from USAF HRA.)

seen by many within the German aviation community as the logical choice for chief of staff of a reborn Luftwaffe. Wilberg, however, did have one impediment: a Jewish mother. Although Wilberg could not for that reason be considered for chief of staff of the Third Reich's Luftwaffe, Göring was not about to lose the services of a talented officer no matter how ardent the Luftwaffe's official commitment was to the ideology of National Socialism. From Hitler, Göring obtained a signed order ensuring the aryan laws of the Third Reich would not apply to Wilberg or to his family. Thus, Wilberg was kept on as a senior officer of the new Luftwaffe, and would play a central role in the creation of a comprehensive air doctrine as the committee chief and editor of Luftwaffe Regulation 16, *The Conduct of the Aerial War,* which was published in 1935.[5]

In creating an air doctrine and organization, the Luftwaffe and air ministry also had the services of several very talented and experienced air staff officers including Helmuth Felmy, a staunch proponent of building a strong heavy-bomber force who served as an operations officer during this period.[6] As chief of the Technical Office, Wilhelm Wimmer had the arduous task of organizing all the Luftwaffe's technological planning, production, and research and development facilities into one organization, while the air staffs, planners, and operations officers, like Wilberg and Felmy, would develop air doctrine, organizational concepts, and outline future equipment requirements. It was Wilhelm Wimmer's task to translate general requirements into detailed specifications for aircraft and technology for the aviation industry, and to supervise the development of the weapons that the planning staff and operations officers envisioned. It was largely up to Wilhelm Wimmer to determine what was, and was not, technologically feasible. Placing Wimmer in charge of the Luftwaffe's technical development was another example of the right man in the right place. Wimmer had already successfully proven this capability as the planner and organizer in the Reichswehr's air staff since the 1920s. He was known as a staunch supporter of bomber aviation,[7] and was highly respected among the officers of the new Luftwaffe. Field Marshal von Richthofen said of Wimmer that he had "the best technical understanding in the Luftwaffe."[8] In addition to the Reichswehr professionals, outsiders—most notably, Dr. Robert Knauss of Lufthansa—would also have an important effect on the development of air doctrine concepts in the early years of the Luftwaffe.

From 1933–1936, however, the dominant figure of the Luftwaffe was Lieutenant General Walter Wever, who served as the Luftwaffe's first chief of the general staff from September 1933 until his death in an airplane accident on 3 June 1936. It was Wever who had the job of not only organizing a large air force, but also of understanding the many strands of air power technology and theory, and developing a coherent and comprehensive doctrine of air power from several competing positions.

THE STATE OF AIR POWER THEORY, 1933–1934

In January 1933, when the Nazis came to power, there was a wide range of competing concepts within military circles in Germany. Within the army, there were still many officers—most notably, army commander in chief General Freiherr von Hammerstein-Equord, who still thought of the air force as a force with the primary mission of supporting the ground armies. General Hammerstein-Equord led the opposition within the army general staff to the idea of removing aviation from army control and transferring all army aviators and aviation assets to the Reich air ministry.[9]

General Ludwig Beck (later commander in chief of the army), one of the most highly regarded minds in the German military, was one of the most articulate voices in the army who argued that the primary mission of air power was to support the ground forces. Ludwig Beck, in 1932–1933, was assigned the task of revising and updating the army operational doctrine, which had last been published under von Seeckt's tenure in 1921–1923 as *Leadership and Battle with Combined Arms.* Beck's work resulted in Army Regulation 300, *Truppenführung* (Troop Leadership), which remained, through World War II, the primary expression of operational doctrine within the German army.

Truppenführung was, in many respects, a brilliant expression of the operational art of war. Regulation 300 provided a sound outline of the art of leadership and command in modern maneuver warfare.[10] Seeckt's concepts of air power as expressed in 1932 were still, however, essentially those of World War I and the early 1920s. *Truppenführung* viewed air power as being important, arguing that air superiority was necessary "in order to successfully carry out major ground operations."[11] The regulation also insisted that the fundamental military principle of mass was also necessary for air power.[12] In most respects, however, the army doctrine viewed the aviation force, not as a separate service, but as a force subordinate to the ground commander. *Truppenführung* referred to a single air commander,[13] but also spoke of air units attached to the ground forces commander.[14] Under the army doctrine, the fighter force was to be organized into groups and regiments (wings), and normally attached to the army headquarters—exactly as in World War I.[15]

Truppenführung viewed the primary mission of the air force as direct support, like the World War I model. Air power was to be dispersed throughout the army, with each army containing an aviation headquarters and an air commander: "Reconnaissance squadrons generally support headquarters down to the corps level."[16] This was little different from the 1918 system. Direct support of the army in the vicinity of the front was seen as the primary mission of the air force. The fighter force was expected to participate in ground attacks to support the army. *Truppenführung* further argued that "these attacks can be especially effective in cooperation with the actions of our own ground troops."[17] The army doctrine also said the dive bomber was an important new weapon in the army support role. *Truppenführung* contained an entire section on the dive bomber, which described the stuka as especially useful in conducting attacking on point targets.[18] The stuka (dive bomber)—which was the closest thing to a long-range precision weapon available to the army—was seen as important for the destruction of enemy artillery, headquarters, rail lines, bridges, and depots.

Throughout the 1920s and early 1930s, the Reichswehr air staff had looked at the eventual rearmament development of a small air force, capable of a variety of missions. Since the *Directives for the Conduct of Operational Air War* of 1926, the air staff had not concentrated on developing any grand theories of air operations, but rather had devoted its effort to developing doctrine at the operational and tactical levels of war. Former air operational doctrine was carefully monitored and examined in the German military literature, with an emphasis on the conduct of limited air operations, namely the protection of specific areas, and the support of an army in combat.[19] A special interest in monitoring new foreign aviation technology was shown by the German airmen.[20] The tactical/operational emphasis of the air staff, as well as the careful monitoring of foreign aviation, tended to push many of the air staff intellectuals toward army support operations. A typical view was expressed in the *Militärwochenblatt* of 1934, which gave a favorable assessment of the French air force's army support tactics.[21]

The air doctrine manuals produced by the air staff in the early 1930s had a tactical orientation. Luftwaffe Regulation 10, *The Bomber* (Luftwaffe Dienstvorschrift 10: *Der Kampfflugzeug*), published in 1934, outlined how bomber units might make attacks, and covered the types of approaches, formations, size of bombs recommended, as well as night attack tactics. Manuals recommended that day attacks were only likely to be successful if air superiority was obtained.[22] The modern fighter plane was seen as the most dangerous opponent of the bomber, and much of the manual deals with tactics of fighting and avoiding fighters, for instance using low-level approaches and varying approach routes.[23] At the same time that modern bomber tactics were being developed, modern fighter tactics were also being published by the air staff. The fighter tactics manuals produced at this time were based on the experiences of foreign air forces, and the work of the fighter training school in Russia between 1925 and 1933. A 1934 fighter operations manual produced by the air staff was thoroughly up to date, and as comprehensive as any other major air force's fighter doctrine.[24] The primary mission of the fighter unit was seen as home defense, and its secondary mission, the destruction of the enemy air force—would largely be accomplished by offensive fighter sweeps. A third mission of the fighter was low-level ground attack.[25] The weaponry of the fighter was to be the machine gun and the aircraft cannon. Single-seat fighters would also be equipped with bomb racks for shrapnel bombs and ordered to carry out the ground attack mission.[26] The fifty-seven-page fighter manual outlined large-unit, small-unit, and individual fighter formations and tactics. General principles of fighter operations were outlined, and at this time the basis of squadron tactics was the three-aircraft flight, flying normally in a V formation.[27] Small flights were organized into squadrons, and three squadrons constituted a wing, or *Geschwader*.[28] Fighters were to fly normally in squadron or wing formations. The manual also outlined a suggested training program for fighter squadrons, and devoted a section to the tactics of attacking ground troops.[29]

In 1933–1934, the air staff had produced an effective operational doctrine for a small to medium-sized air force. In the tactical sphere, the air staff's doctrine was fairly effective for the era, and in many cases very innovative. In 1933 a regular commentator on air power affairs, Lieutenant Feuchter, discussed the operational use of transport aircraft in fighter warfare with military units landed behind the front by transport, and resupplied by transport.[30]

When the Nazis took power and Erhard Milch became the state secretary for aviation, his former deputy at Lufthansa, Robert Knauss, preached to his former superior on his vision of German air power. Robert Knauss was one of the best qualified in Germany to comment on air power in 1933. Knauss had served as an officer in the Luftstreitkräfte during World War I.[31] After the war, he had studied in Berlin and earned a doctorate in economics; his dissertation had discussed the financing of the British war effort during World War I. Knauss was a highly cultured man who spoke fluent English and French, and whose worldviews were influenced by foreign contacts, foreign travel, and foreign journals and books. Knauss had joined Lufthansa in the 1920s, where he soon became an accomplished pilot (he had not undergone pilot training during the war). Knauss was the pilot in command of the record-breaking Berlin-to-Peking flight in 1927. He had risen swiftly within the Lufthansa hierarchy, and by 1933 was in charge of developing foreign air routes.[32] In May 1933, Knauss delivered to Milch a long and detailed idea paper, providing arguments that Germany's first military priority should be the creation of a large bomber fleet along the lines of the theory of Italian General Douhet.[33]

Besides his superior Erhard Milch and other leading civil aviation experts in Germany, Knauss maintained a close and frequent correspondence with the Reichswehr air staff. For example, after the 1927 Berlin-to-Peking flight, he turned his log books and data on the problems of long-distance navigation over to his close friend on the air staff, Lieutenant Colonel Helmuth Wilberg.[34] As Knauss turned his intellect and experience to questions of air theory, he soon became an enthusiastic admirer of the views of General Giulio Douhet. So enthusiastic was Knauss on the subject, in 1932 he published a fictional account of a war which described Douhet's principles in action.

The heart of the argument in Knauss's 1933 memo was that a virtually disarmed Germany, threatened by France and Poland with a two-front war, required a powerful military strike force that could be built quickly, and that could also serve as an effective deterrent to Germany's enemies. Knauss argued that a powerful force of 400 well-armed bombers, possessing great range and heavy bombloads, could be built faster and more cheaply than any other military force.[35] Heavy bombers had become the most effective and decisive weapon in war due to the nature of the European economy, Knauss insisted. Drawing on his Ph.D. in economics, Knauss further argued that modern industrial nations and armed forces required a complicated production and transportation system, and such a system was vulnerable to attacks on electric power, transport, and fuel systems. Modern armies had become mechanized, and thereby dependent on a complex armaments industry. The heavy bomber could cripple a modern industrial nation and its armed forces by a few, carefully chosen attacks on its industrial base.[36]

Knauss stated that Germany needed to immediately build a "risk air force," whose existence would so threaten Germany's enemies, they would be deterred from attack: "Even an air fleet of two hundred heavy bombers becomes a major military/political factor and reduces the aggressive instincts of the enemy."[37] The risk of attack by her enemies would be reduced due to the capability of Germany to immediately attack her enemies' homelands. The economics of a bomber force also made sense to Knauss. A bomber fleet might cost as much as two pocket battleships of the navy, or five divisions of the army, but would have far more strategic value.[38] Since the armaments ca-

Air theorist Robert Knauss as colonel and commander of a bomber wing in 1938. (Photo from the Knauss family.)

pability of any nation was limited by its financial resources, each nation had to set priorities. Knauss argued that air forces ought to have a high priority regarding financial resources, because they gave Germany more military potential in return for the expenditure: "an armored cruiser like the Deutschland costs eighty million Reichsmarks. For the expense of building two armored cruisers, an air fleet of four hundred heavy bombers can be built."[39] Germany, moreover, could build a significant heavy bomber force within a year or two—much less time than it would take to build some of the armored cruisers envisioned by the navy.

Well-informed on foreign air theories, Knauss argued that under the present command of Air Minister Italo Balbo, inspired by Douhet, a very capable bomber force had been created within the Italian air force. France, which had seen the dynamic new air minister, Pierre Cot, appointed in the previous year, was also building up a bomber fleet.[40] If it did come to war with France and Poland, Knauss outlined in detail on paper the organization and mission of his "risk" air force. First of all, the air force would need to become primarily a bomber force, and fighter production was to have a low priority: "Single-seat fighters cannot support (escort) the operations of the air fleet, as they are incapable of bad-weather operations—unlike the bombers."[41] Also, fighters were unlikely to be needed as escorts, because the heavy bombers could protect themselves: "A well-trained bomber wing can keep the enemy fighters at bay through the use of the powerful and long-range fire of its moveable machine guns and machine cannons, without having to divert its course. This is the situation any light fighters will meet when they have to engage a bomber fleet."[42] The missions of the bomber fleet were to destroy the enemy air forces and air bases—with enemy bombers a top priority target—and to disrupt the enemy mobilization and operational movement of enemy ground armies by targeting the assembly centers and railroad centers. The disruption and destruction of the enemy armaments industry was also seen as a primary mission. Another mission of the bomber forces, as set out by Knauss, was pure Douhet: "The crippling of the enemy government and administration system, terrorizing the population of the major cities."[43] Knauss left the prioritization of the missions at the discretion of the commander in chief. He firmly believed, however, in the value of terror attacks, if necessary. It is also interesting to note that, aside from the attacks on mobilization and transport centers advocated by Knauss, there was no mention of using air power in the support of ground or naval forces.

Arguments such as Knauss's in favor of Douhetian theory provoked some strong disagreement in army circles. Colonel von Gosslar, chief of operations in the army general staff, argued that adoption of the Douhetian idea would lead to eliminating the distinction between the homeland and the front, and would make civilians the primary targets in any warfare. An approach in which the Germans targeted the enemy civilians would also mean that German civilians would become the primary target of any enemy. Colonel von Gosslar argued that Douhetism was a dangerous theory because targeting civilians could soon lead to an increase in pacifistic views among the general population. Von Gosslar also argued that the supporters of Douhet, like Knauss, were simply blinded by enthusiasm: history showed that every time a new weapon was created, older weapons and older forms of war were all declared obsolete by enthusiasts. However, this had rarely been the case.[44] Yet, despite open opposition from army officers, Knauss's argument was generally well received by professional airmen.[45]

Thus, at the commencement of rearmament, some very strong and contradictory positions on air power had been staked out within the German military. The challenge for the Luftwaffe senior commanders would be the synthesis and integration of prevailing air theories into a guiding air doctrine that would prove not only useful but acceptable to the majority of army and navy, as well as air force officers.

AIR POWER THOUGHT OF WALTER WEVER

Lieutenant General Walter Wever served as chief of staff of the Luftwaffe from 1933 to 1936. In those years, Wever played an important, even a central role in the development of air power thought in Germany, and his work would significantly impact the development of the Luftwaffe.

Wever was an outstanding choice for Luftwaffe chief of staff. He had an impressive record as a general staff officer and was highly regarded by the senior officers of the army, such as generals von Fritsch and von Blomberg.[46] Wever had begun his career as an infantry officer in the Prussian army, and during World War I served as a general staff officer at the front. Wever's competence was such that, by 1917, he had been selected as a captain to serve on the general staff of the high command under General Ludendorff. During the 1920s, Wever had held a number of general staff appointments, also serving as a very successful company and battalion commander. By 1931 Wever had risen to section chief in the Truppenamt, and was regarded by his superiors as good material for a future commander in chief of the army.[47] General Blomberg remarked that he was giving up his best officer when Wever was transferred to the air ministry.[48] Wever had an especially solid reputation in the army as a good troop leader.[49] Prior to his assignment to the air ministry on 1 September 1933, Wever served as chief of training in the Truppenamt, one of the most important of the Truppenamt branches.[50] Major General Walter von Brauchitsch, later army commander in chief, had been Wever's immediate predecessor as chief of the training branch.[51] Prior to his selection as Luftwaffe chief of staff, Wever had opposed granting the Luftwaffe status as a separate service.[52] By all accounts, Wever had a formidable mind and a tremendous capacity for work. He spent much of his first year in the air ministry reading voraciously about air power, and learning from the experienced airmen. Starting at age forty-six, he also learned to fly.

Wever was known as a strict and demanding commander, but he tempered his role as a taskmaster with a serious concern for the well-being of his troops, and an ability to listen carefully to his subordinates. He possessed considerable charm, and was able to get along with many difficult personalities such as Göring and Milch. After his appointment, Wever quickly took firm control of the nascent Luftwaffe, and came to be regarded as the dominant personality of that service.[53]

Wever acquired a decided preference for strategic bombing as the primary mission of the air force, a view shared by the majority of the professional airmen who formed the core of the Reichswehr air staff, and who were being transferred to the Reichs air ministry in 1933–1934. Much has been made of Wever's preference for strategic bombing, as if Wever attempted to impose this doctrine on the air force. This image of Wever is, however, greatly exaggerated. At no time did Wever express any especially radical views on air power. For example, Wever did not argue that a war could be won by bombing alone, or that the army or navy did not have vital missions. Although Douhet was well-known at this time within German air circles, Wever easily rejected many of Douhet's propositions concerning strategic bombing, instead developing his own theories.[54]

Even though Wever was not a pilot when he joined the Luftwaffe, his mind and personality won him the loyalty of the senior officers in the air ministry headquarters. Erhard Milch said that Wever was the "most significant of the officers taken over from the army. If he had remained in the army, he would have reached the highest positions there, as well. He possessed not only tremendous professional ability, but also great personal qualities."[55] Ministerialdirektor Willi Frisch, a leading official of the air ministry at this time, said that "Wever was one of the most highly qualified and, I would say, one of the most farsighted general staff officers Germany had. . . . Wever ra-

Lieutenant General Walter Wever, first chief of staff of the Luftwaffe, 1935. (Photo from USAF HRA.)

diated calmness and assurance. His decisions were always well-founded. He never tried to do things in a hurry."[56]

What Wever provided the Luftwaffe was a sense of enthusiasm for the study of air doctrine. When he took over as Luftwaffe chief of staff, he had energy—as a relatively young forty-six-year-old commander—and a searching intellectual attitude. He was willing to apply himself to intensive study, and to learn. He was also open to intellectual growth, evolving from someone opposed to air force independence to an advocate for air power and its capabilities among the senior Wehrmacht officers. By directive and his own personal example, Wever pushed the Luftwaffe officer corps into a similar intensive study of air power. This was especially important for the somewhat eclectic body of officers that the Luftwaffe contained in its early years. With so many officers coming into the air force from the ground troops, the police, and the navy, encouraging an intensive study of air doctrine, and creating such a doctrine, would provide important newfound principles for what was essentially a new officer corps.

Wever outlined his own theory of air warfare in a lecture given at the opening of the Luftwaffe's Air Technical Academy in Berlin-Gatow in November 1935.[57] Wever's lecture theme was his vision of the role of air power in a future war. First of all, he argued that air power, by its ability to strike the enemy homeland and rear areas, would help prevent the occurrence of another trench war: "We hope and believe that a modern army, cooperating with the air force, will find a means of preventing the positional warfare of massed armies. In the air force, we have a weapon which knows no boundaries: its operations cannot be impeded by natural formations of a country or by concrete fortifications."[58]

Wever stated that the air force had two primary tasks: "One, home defense, to which all the services and the whole population will contribute, and two—the second, more important and decisive task—the defeat of the enemy threatening us. Command of the air is the condition upon which both of these tasks depend if they are to be carried out with complete success."[59] As to the first task, General Wever had great confidence in the effect of an air defense, including the use of flak and civil defense to protect Germany from attack by enemy bombers: "Air warfare is based upon cooperation. The antiaircraft artillery, the air reporting organizations, and all the measures with which we are forming for civil air defense offer just as great a contribution to the command of the air as the air force itself. . . . To the antiaircraft artilleryman, in particular, it seems self-evident that, thanks to the extensive technical development of his branch of the service, he can protect any target entrusted to him, provided that sufficiently strong forces are made available for its defense."[60]

Although air power had the capability to overcome the restrictions of terrain and distance, Wever asserted that some traditional principles of warfare, as had been elucidated by Clausewitz, still applied to aerial war. "The objective of any war is to destroy the morale of the enemy. The morale of a leader and of a nation is reflected, to a great extent, in the armed forces of that nation. Thus, in a war of the future, the destruction of the armed forces will be of primary importance."[61] Wever, however, defined "armed forces" broadly, and meant much more than just the fielded armies and navies: "This can mean the destruction of the enemy air force, army, and navy, and the source of supply of the enemy's forces, the armament industry." Of these, however, Wever identified no single or priority target, which, by itself, would normally cripple the enemy: "The point at which the concentrated use will be made of the air force at any given time will be decided by the situation as a whole."[62]

To achieve the objective of defeating the enemy armed forces, Wever set five operational tasks for the air force:

1. To destroy the enemy air force by bombing its bases and aircraft factories, and defeating enemy air forces attacking German targets;
2. To prevent the movement of large enemy ground forces to the decisive areas by destroying railways and roads, particularly bridges and tunnels, which are indispensible for the movement and supply of such forces;
3. To support the operations of the army formations, independent of railways—i.e., armored forces and motorized forces, by impeding the enemy advance and participating directly in ground operations[63];
4. To support naval operations by attacking enemy naval bases, protecting Germany's naval bases and participating directly in naval battles;
5. To paralyze the enemy armed forces by stopping production in the armaments factories.[64]

Wever insisted that, if the army carried out its mission correctly and suitably concentrated its forces in decisive situations, "the air force will enable our army to achieve a modern Tannenburg by keeping enemy reserves, even reserve armies, away from the battlefield."[65] Note that, while endorsing the use of air power directly in the ground battle, Wever by no means wanted to see the Luftwaffe as an army tactical support force. Direct Luftwaffe intervention was not promised to the whole army, but to the elite and decisive striking arm of the army: the motorized and armored divisions. As Wever built up a doctrine of army support operations, the special emphasis on armor/air cooperation was made a central principle.

Regaining control of the air by defeating the enemy air force was the primary objective. Wever said it could be attained partly by the application of traditional principles of warfare: "The element of surprise and the opportunity of rapidly concentrating forces in the air is achieved in a manner quite distinct from that known in ground operations, but the old principles of warfare are true—even for the air force."[66] Gaining control of the air in the face of a competent enemy defender was, for Wever, a matter of developing superior tactics. Gaining surprise, dispersing the enemy defenders, using deception against already predictable behavior by the attacker, are all to be used in the air superiority battle.[67]

While a modern system of air defense consisting of civil defense, flak, and fighters was formidable, Wever believed that a defense could be overcome. Indeed, Wever argued that the best defense against enemy air power was to go on the offense: "It is not sufficient to build up defense on the basis of defensive weapons. Instead, the evil should be attacked at its root, i.e., the enemy bomber formation should be caught at the most vulnerable moment—when they are on the ground, taking on fresh fuel and ammunition, and reservicing."[68] Building a national system of air defense seemed restricted by Germany's limited financial resources, which necessitated a trade-off between defensive and offensive weapons spending: "It is not possible to create an unlimited number of areas adequately defended against air attack and at the same time build up a strong air force."[69] Wever went on to draw an analogy between air power and ground and naval forces: "Just as the great leaders of the past had to strike a balance between infantry and cavalry and artillery, it is the modern army's most formal ratio between armored and non-armored formations, or navies, between large and small warships, the relationship between offensive and defensive power must also be considered in the air force. When, at some later time, you are called upon to participate in these matters, never forget that the bomber is the decisive factor in aerial warfare."[70] "Only the nation with strong bomber forces at its disposal can expect decisive action by its air force."[71]

In attack and defense, a modern air force requires "a ground organization that will not fail, even if one base after another falls victim to the enemy air attack: a ground organization that will guarantee that the fuel, ammunition, and the countless spare parts for the deplorably large number of different types of aircraft are at the right place at the right time. . . . Do not say 'that is no work for a general staff officer.' You know that the proper control of ammunition and fuel is an essential task of a commander and his general staff."[72]

Throughout the three years of his tenure, Wever would regularly elucidate these basic principles in numerous speeches, and in the yearly remarks of the commander in chief circulated throughout the air force. The most enduring example of Wever's thought exists in Luftwaffe Regulation 16: *The Conduct of the Aerial War,* which set out in detail a broad vision of the use of air power.

LUFTWAFFE REGULATION 16: THE CONDUCT OF THE AERIAL WAR

After becoming Luftwaffe chief of staff, having ensured that the expansion of the Luftwaffe staff and the air rearmament program were under way, General Wever turned his attention to operational air doctrine. Just as the army expressed its conception of ground operations in Army Regulation 487 in the 1920s, and in the new Army Regulation 300: *Troop Leadership,* the air force clearly needed a straightforward and comprehensive expression of operational doctrine, and of its concept of warfare. Accordingly, in 1934 Wever directed the air ministry's most experienced general staff officer, Major General Helmuth Wilberg, to head a committee to create and publish a comprehensive air doctrine for the Luftwaffe. The result was published in 1935 as Luftwaffe Regulation 16: *Luftkriegführung (The Conduct of the Aerial War).*

Regulation 16 was a treatise focusing on the operational side of air war. Numerous subsections dealt with virtually all aspects of air operations, including the operations order, day attacks, night attacks, and naval support. A long document with over a hundred pages and nearly 300 sections, it was divided into an introduction, and five parts: (1) the air war; (2) leadership: the principles of leadership; (3) reconnaissance; (4) employment: battle against the air force; and (5) execution. The vital issues of supply and ground organization were covered by later regulations.

Like any proper expression of military doctrine, *The Conduct of the Aerial War* began by elucidating the principles of war that would guide the air force. The air force was defined as the flying forces, flak artillery, air communications force, air reporting service, and civil air defense.[73] The primarily offensive nature of air power was stressed: "From the start of the conflict, the air forces bring the war to the enemy."[74] Regulation 16, however, outlined a traditional view of war in its focus on the enemy armed forces as the primary objective in war: "The mission of the armed forces in war is to break down

Helmuth Wilberg. The author/editor of the Luftwaffe's operational doctrine, Regulation 16. As colonel, Commandant Breslau, 1930. (Photo from the Wilberg family.)

the will of the enemy. The will of the nation finds its greatest embodiment in its armed forces. Thus, the enemy armed forces is the primary goal in war."[75]

As with army operational doctrine, the role of personal leadership was emphasized:

> One can only be an air force leader who fully understands the demands of air warfare. True leadership demonstrates trust, and gives the troops an irresistible power to achieve goals that seem unreachable. Personal example; the presence of the leader at the point of gravest danger; outstanding knowledge; a strong will; calm, perseverance, and confidence in troop-handling and decision-making; flexibility, joy in responsibility, a spirit of fellowship, and untiring care for the well-being of the soldier—all these create in misery and death an unbreakable fighting fellowship.[76]

Joint operations and the ability to operate willingly with the other branches of the armed forces was emphasized in Regulation 16. The central role of joint operations was elevated to the status of a primary principle of modern warfare: "The mission of the Luftwaffe is to serve these goals by (destruction of the enemy armed forces) by commanding the war in the air within the framework of combined operations. . . . By taking part in operations and conflict on land and at sea, the Luftwaffe directly supports the army and navy."[77] While stating that a strategic campaign against enemy sources of power supported the army and navy by disrupting enemy logistics, *Conduct of the Aerial War* also emphasized that the target priorities of the air force would be decided with the framework of a strategy decided by a high command comprised of representatives from all the services: "In determining which mission has priority. . . . in other words, which will have the greatest contribution towards a decisive victory, one must look within the framework of combined warfighting. The most decisive targets will be decided under the most careful consideration of all military, political, and economic factors."[78]

While endorsing joint operations and strategy, however, *Conduct of the Aerial War* also argued that the Luftwaffe should not be considered merely a support force for the army and navy. Support operations should only be conducted when decisive results could be obtained. Otherwise, the power of the air force would be dissipated: "The use of the air force in direct support of the army or navy is required under the circumstances of decisive operations, if recommended by the combined war leadership. . . . the air force, working in close cooperation with the army and navy, is often diverted from using its most effective forces, especially the bomber forces, against the most important targets."[79]

Despite the Luftwaffe's preference for independent and strategic operations, Luftwaffe Regulation 16 firmly insisted that an unhealthy spirit of interservice rivalry had no place in the Luftwaffe: "Wide separations between the various parts of the Luftwaffe and their various roles must never lead to a breakdown of the feeling of common purpose and camaraderie of all the branches. The Luftwaffe, therefore, even if it is not in direct proximity to the army and navy, must remember that it is part of the whole Wehrmacht. The Luftwaffe must remain aware of the unity of all parts of the Wehrmacht in the common struggle."[80]

The first and most vital mission of the air force was to be destruction of the enemy air force. This was a basic defensive measure to ensure the security of the German military and homeland from air attack.[81] Defensive forces alone could not defend against enemy bombers. The enemy air force had to be destroyed in its bases, and its infrastructure wrecked: "The battle in the enemy territory will be carried out not only against the mobile air units and their bases. It should be also directed against the support and production of the enemy air force, as well as the sources of enemy power."[82] Moreover, the attacks on the enemy air force must be sustained, lest the enemy recover his strength.[83]

The heart of *Conduct of the Aerial War* was a doctrine of strategic air warfare, termed "the attack on the sources of enemy power." The bulk of the text was devoted to a discussion on the whole variety of targets that an industrial nation would require to wage war. The regulation listed the sources of enemy military power as production, food production, import facilities, power stations, railroads and rail yards, military barracks, and centers of government administration.[84] The significance of each target for the enemy's war effort was discussed. In each case, the advantages and disadvantages of the target were also discussed. At all times, the enemy was expected to put up a strong and capable defense. In many cases, specific guidelines for targeting were given. In a campaign against enemy commerce, for example, fuel unloading and storage facilities in ports were recommended as especially lucrative targets. Most countries imported fuel, and fuel was a primary requirement for modern war: "The fuel tanks and off-loading pipelines in the ports are especially vulnerable targets. In some cases, these port facilities are protected, but in most cases they are easy to identify, and their most sensitive sections easy to put out of action."[85] In another case, the strategy of attacking the enemy rail net was discussed. Rail systems were seen as difficult targets due to the size and redundancy of modern rail systems, and the capacity of the enemy to repair them. Due to their difficulty to repair, however, bridges, viaducts, and tunnels were held to be the best targets for cutting or disrupting rail traffic.[86]

No series of panacea targets was recommended by Regulation 16 as the best targets in war. Targeting an enemy nation required extensive intelligence, and a careful understanding of all the military, social, and economic factors relating to the enemy war effort: "The enemy, the weather, the season, the infrastructure of the land, national character, and one's own fighting power are all aspects to be considered in determining the capabilities and limitations of the Luftwaffe."[87]

Regulation 16 discusses the operational side of air warfare in some detail. Examples of standard operations orders are given.[88] Methods of reconnaissance[89] and of air force/navy cooperation[90] are discussed. Tactics for the conduct of day and night strategic attacks are outlined, as is the organization and tactics of mounting an air defense.[91]

In *The Conduct of the Aerial War*, the Luftwaffe rejected that theory of Italian General Douhet which made the primary goal of strategic bombing to bomb the enemy cities, inducing terror into the civilian population with the expectation that they would arise and force an early end to the conflict: "Attacks against cities made for the purpose of inducing terror in the civilian populace are to be avoided on principle."[92] The regulation's authors did, however, reserve the right to retaliate in kind if the enemy initiated strategic attacks directed against the German civilian population: "If the enemy should initiate terror attacks against defenseless and open cities, however, the retaliation attacks may be the only means of stopping the enemy from continuing this brutal method of aerial warfare. The timing of the retaliation attack depends upon the timing of the enemy terror attack. In every case, the attack must clearly be recognized as a retaliation."[93]

While the regulation's authors couched their opposition to terror attacks in the language of moral principle, there were also sound military and operational reasons to reject Douhetian theory. The primary objection to terror bombing of civilians was that it was likely to prove counterproductive, actually increasing the will of the enemy population rather than breaking it: "The retaliation attack requires exact knowledge and understanding of the thought patterns and moral attitudes of the enemy population. Selection of the wrong time, combined with a poor estimate of the desired effect upon the enemy, can in some circumstances result in an increase in the enemy's will to resist, rather than a reduction of that will."[94]

Bombing the enemy seat of government was also discussed by Regulation 16. A strike against the government and its administration and communications system might pay off handsomely by disrupting the functioning of the enemy government.[95] If conducted at the right moment, national morale might be affected by a strike against the government and its communications.[96] The regulation also cautions against conducting such an attack, for the enemy capital would surely be well defended, and attackers could face heavy losses.[97] For such an attack to succeed, the regulation recommended conducting it at the start of a war, "when the internal or foreign situation is most unfavorable for the enemy."[98]

The Conduct of the Aerial War was a synthesis of the views of General Wever, the air staff, and existing doctrine. It expressed no revolutionary, new theories of air warfare. It did, however, provide the Luftwaffe with a broad vision of air warfare. As Edward Homze has stated, Regulation 16 was "a fundamentally conservative concept of aerial warfare."[99] It served as an effective framework to guide the Luftwaffe over the next years. According to Edward Homze, Regulation 16 was a practical document, "intended not as the unalterable dogma of aerial warfare, but as a convenient summary and guideline, to be revised and modified in the light of subsequent developments in weaponry, further experiences in combat and new theorizing at home and abroad."[100]

THE NAZI CONCEPT OF WARFARE

A fundamental weakness of the Third Reich, in creating a military policy, was that the military and civilian leadership of the nation held opposing conceptions of warfare. Indeed, the military and civilian leadership were regularly at cross-purposes, resulting in a dysfunctional system of establishing military strategy. Up to the start of World War II, the military essentially did not understand the aims, methods, or objectives of warfare set by Hitler and the inner Nazi leadership.

The Nazi concept of war can be found in Hitler's writings, especially *Mein Kampf,* and in the writings of General Ludendorff, one of Hitler's earliest followers, a prolific author who continued to expound theories of strategy, warfare, and race until his death in 1936.

Probably the most radical difference between the Nazi ideology and the strategic vision held by the senior military officers was their disparate objectives of warfare. Hitler and Nazi theorists explicitly rejected limits on warfare. Under Nazi ideology, war was viewed as a life-or-death struggle between nations, with total defeat or overthrow of the enemy nation as the only acceptable outcome. In *Mein Kampf,* Hitler referred to the "final, decisive battle" with France, and France's destruction as a "means of subsequently and finally giving our nation a chance to expand elsewhere."[101]

In his numerous books and articles, General Ludendorff outlined his horrific vision of what modern conflict between nations would become in the future. In his fictional work, *The Coming War* (1931), Ludendorff envisioned Germany's participation in a general European war. In Ludendorff's war, set in the not-too-distant future, guerrilla warfare, the suppression and impressment of civilians, and the regular use of airborne gas against civilians were common features.[102] Ludendorff developed his theories further in *Total War (Der Totaler Krieg),* written in 1935. This work begins with an attack on Clausewitz's theory. According to Ludendorff, warfare no longer merely served the purpose of the state. The state now carried out a "total politics" to prepare the nation for the inevitable, total war.[103] Hitler's concept of war was evolving into one of total conflict between peoples and races—wars of total annihilation. Hitler was decidedly popular with the German military leadership in the early years of his rule, but not because of his theories of warfare. Hitler won the admiration and gratitude of the military for instituting rearmament on a scale beyond the military's wildest dreams, providing the resources to quickly restore Germany to its status as a major military power. In their operational doctrines, however, the general staff of the Luftwaffe and the army remained true to the traditional, Clausewitzian notions of war. The army's primary operational regulations of the interwar period, Regulation 487: *Leadership in Battle with Combined Arms* (1921–1923) and Regulation 300: *Troop Leadership* (1933), as well as Luftwaffe Regulation 16, all emphasized defeating the opponent's armed forces in a decisive battle. Although Douhet's concepts found great favor in Nazi circles, the Luftwaffe specifically rejected the policy of targeting the enemy will by attacking its population centers. Such attacks on the enemy population were discounted for pragmatic reasons, for they might harden the enemy will.[104] Even more important, terror attacks were seen as a diversion and dilution of the Luftwaffe's effort to establish superiority in the air for a decisive battle against the enemy armed forces. While the operational concepts of the Wehrmacht employed new methods of strategic bombing, motorized maneuver warfare, and combined arms operations, the general understanding behind the aims of military operations was still in the spirit of Clausewitz, Moltke, and Bismarck.

The Luftwaffe is often said to have been the most National Socialist of the armed forces, because it owed a special debt of gratitude to the Nazi regime for having brought it into existence. Wever is said to have been a staunch Nazi. Samuel Mitcham argues that Wever used Hitler's *Mein Kampf* as his military bible, and used strategic principles from *Mein Kampf*.[105] Certainly, Wever made numerous public protestations of loyalty to the National Socialist regime, and its ideology. How much of this was heartfelt, however, and how much the typical lip-service given by the senior military to the leadership of any fascist state, is unclear. There is no evidence that Wever ever took *Mein Kampf* seriously, or drew principles of war from it. The evidence mainly lies in the other direction, for Luftwaffe Regulation 16 would have looked considerably different if it had been inspired by Nazi ideology. One must also account for the many senior military leaders who, though definitely not Nazis, regularly expressed support for the Nazi party, such as army commander Freiherr von Fritsch.[106]

There are numerous instances of differences between words and actions in the Luftwaffe concerning the loyalty of the officer corps to Nazi ideology. Luftwaffe Regulation 7: *Directives for the Training of the Luftwaffe* specified that "the officer must set an example of the National Socialist conception of the state and way of life. Those officers involved in pre-military training, in the officer academies, and serving with troops, must have a foundation in National Socialist thought, and must seek to deepen their understanding."[107] The reading of *Mein Kampf* and of Hitler's speeches was recommended in the regulation.[108] Yet, despite numerous directives from the high command regarding the importance of propaganda and training in Nazi ideology, the military in actuality was largely uninterested in establishing a Nazi propaganda program within the armed forces. Political education remained firmly in the hands of professional officers, and not until December 1939 did the Wehrmacht agree to create an office for military propaganda to oversee the political education of the soldiers. Even then, the military insisted that its own officers, not Nazi officials, would direct military education efforts.[109] Another example of the discrepancy between words and actions is seen in the curriculum of the Luftwaffe's general staff college, the Luftkriegsakademie. Lectures on National Socialism in 1937–1938 shared the 2 percent of the curriculum devoted to military law, administration, and public relations.[110]

Within the Third Reich, one of the few places one could find a refuge from the party propaganda and Nazi influence so prevalent within the business community and the state administration was the military. By regulation, Wehrmacht officers were forbidden to belong to political parties until 1944, and overt political activity was banned in the armed forces. Those who quietly disliked Naziism could find a home in the military. Horst Boog describes this process as "inner exile," and uses the example of Dr. Robert Knauss, the well educated senior Lufthansa executive known for his friendships within antiparty circles, who joined the Luftwaffe in 1935 with a considerable cut in pay, to escape the politicization of daily life.[111] There is also the example of Helmuth Wilberg, the Luftwaffe general who, despite his Jewish mother, was well liked within the Luftwaffe officer corps, and who enjoyed the close confidence of Walter Wever.

In short, Hitler was quite popular with the senior military and Luftwaffe leadership, especially in the early years of the Third Reich, and there were certainly many confirmed Nazis within Germany's senior military leadership, but Naziism failed to provide anything resembling a coherent strategic framework or philosophy for warfare. Given this major limitation of Nazi ideology, and its lack of coherence, the military officers in the service before World War II generally felt far more comfortable with traditional theories of warfare.

CIVIL DEFENSE DOCTRINE

The concept of civil defense played a central role in German air doctrine. For one thing, the concept of civil defense in Germany was fairly comprehensive. It included planning for limiting the vulnerability of industrial installations to damage by strategic bombers. It also included measures for camouflaging military/industrial centers, training the population to deal with enemy air attack, and organizing local governmental authorities, such as the police, fire departments, and health authorities, to deal effectively with the damage likely to be caused by enemy air attack. The Germans believed that a comprehensive and effective program of civil defense could limit the nation's vulnerability to air attack, minimize damage, complicate the enemy air force's mission, and maintain civilian morale by giving them a means to deal with enemy bombing. A major civil defense program had the additional advantage of making the public "air-minded," and educated about air power.[112]

The Luftwaffe and air ministry were given the responsibility for coordinating all civil defense programs and training. They took this mission very seriously. Luftwaffe officers were assigned to the headquarters of the air districts, and civil defense staffs were created for monitoring training programs and coordinating local civil defense planning. The numerous studies on bomb ballistics and civil defense that had been undertaken in the 1920s and early 1930s, by the Reichswehr air staff and by organizations such as the Reich Air Defense League, paid off handsomely when rearmament began in 1933. There was a large body of German technical literature in the 1920s and early 1930s on bomb ballistics and effects, and on erecting buildings and shelters to minimize bomb damage. One example is Hans Schoszberger's *Bautechnischer Luftschutz (Air Defense in Building Design),* which contains dozens of equations, diagrams, tables on bomb effect, and an extensive bibliography on passive air defense systems.[113] The air ministry plan for aircraft factories and air force installations to be built with passive defense from strategic air attack was a primary concern. The new aircraft factories were located mostly in Brandenburg, central Germany, or Bavaria—as deep as possible into Germany. This put vital industrial sites at the maximum range from French bombers, increasing the difficulty of enemy air forces, which would have to carry more fuel to reach these targets, and consequently carry a smaller bombload. The new factory buildings were dispersed so that a single bomb could not destroy an entire installation. Buildings were hardened, fire-fighting equipment was first-rate, and workers were provided with good shelters.[114] Due to the Luftwaffe's foresight, the Allied air forces in World War II would find Germany's aviation industry to be an especially difficult target to destroy by strategic air attack. The defense ministry also took care of the bulk of civil defense while planning for Germany's rearmament. In April 1934 the Defense Ministry War Economics Committee began developing plans to shift industry away from the Ruhr district—which was too close to Germany's western border, and consequently vulnerable to air attack.[115]

Under the guidance of the air ministry, a national civil defense doctrine was developed, and in 1934 a series of small air defense exercises were held to test the rudimentary civil defense plans in effect. It was determined that, in many small cities, police and civil defense cooperation was poor, and the police, civil defense organizations, fire departments, and other municipal services required fairly basic training on how to coordinate their planning and efforts.[116] Based on the experience of the 1934 exercises, the Air Defense Law of 26 June 1935 was passed, setting up a comprehensive Wehrmachtlike civil defense system. The new law required the creation of civil defense regional command centers, and gave civil authorities the responsibility for creating local civil defense stations. A system of medical stations was outlined, and local authorities were required to set up transport sections using local resources. Police were given jurisdiction over coordinating the medical plans for civil defense. A large part of each local population was expected to be included in civil defense training, and women—though not allowed to serve actively in the military—were allowed to hold responsible positions in the civil defense organizations.[117] Civil defense law was thorough. For example, an air defense veterinary service was established, with plans to treat injured animals and, in case of gas attack, to decontaminate animals.[118] The German economy still used large numbers of horses for local transport, and ignoring civil defense provisions for animals would have a detrimental effect on the local economy, should Germany experience bombing.

The year 1935 saw a civil defense exercise in Berlin; the year 1936 saw a series of major civil defense exercises in other cities. Communications and the coordination of agencies was tested. A civil defense observer network had been organized, and was tried out on a larger scale. Local authorities practiced camouflage measures, and gas decontamination. In general, the exercises proved that Germany had made great progress since the small exercise of 1934. Detailed local plans had been made, and the Luftwaffe was generally satisfied with the civil defense planning and training system.[119] By 1936 a complex civil defense command system was in place. At the local level, civil defense was organized around the police and fire departments and used their communications networks. Local and regional civil defense commands included city officials, the Luftwaffe reserve personnel, Luftwaffe specialist units, and decontamination units. Regional command staffs included the police chief, air defense officer, an adjutant, and a communications officer. Staff specialists included the fire department commander, an advising chemist, an industrial defense specialist, and a personal defense specialist.[120] Three years into the air rearmament program, Germany possessed the largest and most

Civil defense exercise, ca. 1936. (Photo from *Jahrbuch des deutschen Heeres,* 1938.)

effective civil defense system in the world. This was possible due to the emphasis placed by senior Luftwaffe commanders on air defense.

STRATEGY, WAR GAMES, AND DOCTRINE

War games and exercises played a central role in the development of air doctrine. Within the German general staff tradition, strategic guidance was provided by the government and senior military officers. This strategic guidance formed the basis for war planning. This, in turn, was carefully examined through the use of war games and large-scale maneuvers. The results of war games and maneuvers were carefully analyzed, and plans and doctrine adapted accordingly. Because their armed forces had more experience in war gaming and the conducting of exercises, the Germans enjoyed a decided advantage when it came to developing operational doctrine for the air force.

In the first four years of the Nazi regime, the strategic guidance provided both by the government and the high command was essentially the same as it had been under the Weimar Republic. Werner von Blomberg, as war minister, provided general strategic guidance to the military services for the development of war plans. In May 1935 Blomberg provided a general strategic overview that covered the case of a possible war on Germany's western border. The primary enemy of Germany throughout this entire period was France, and Blomberg's strategic directive was that for the time being, Germany would remain on the strategic defensive, and orient its armed forces and war plans toward that mission.[121] The most feared war situation to the Germans—also, the most probable—was the development of a two-front war, with France on the western border and France's eastern allies, Czechoslovakia and Poland, attacking Germany in the east.[122] Until the late 1930s, the combination of enemies comprising France, Poland, and Czechoslovakia formed the basis for all German war planning and war gaming.

Prior to every major war game, staff studies were drawn up discussing various possible enemy courses of action, and means for the Germans to deal with them. Within a short time of its establishment, the air staff initiated its own studies concerning the development of air war plans. One 1934 study discussed the possible use of air power to delay and disrupt enemy movements during a hypothetical French and Polish invasion. The Luftwaffe air staff discussed the possibility of interdicting and cutting the French rail net but concluded, due to the redundancy of rail yards and rail lines in France, that attacks against large- and medium-sized rail yards would have relatively little effect.[123] Mobility studies done on the French army determined that attacks against French rail lines were not likely to be very successful. It was also noted that, as the French army became more motorized, its vulnerability to interdiction by air attack was further reduced.[124] It was predicted that air attacks against bridges and mobilization centers could have some effect in delaying the French, but in the case of a war with France, making the center of gravity the destruction of the enemy air force was the preferred course, due to the difficulty of hindering the French mobilization, the difficulty of blocking French movement west of the Rhine, and the greater vulnerability of German mobilization.[125] The Germans noted, however, that the Polish rail and transportation system was much less developed than the French, and estimated that a well trained air force, well equipped with dive bombers (to hit point targets) could "sever most of the Polish rail transport lines in a relatively short amount of time."[126] The inferior Polish rail system made the Polish military vulnerable to paralysis, and their lack of motor vehicles increased that vulnerability. The Luftwaffe predicted that a properly conducted air campaign against Polish transportation could delay the mobilization of the Polish military by eight to fourteen days.[127] Thus, the Luftwaffe argued that, in the case of a strategic defensive war, the Luftwaffe was especially valuable as Germany's first line of defense, and could serve to paralyze the mobilization and movement of its enemies at the very outbreak of the war.

German war games and maneuvers were useful for much more than simply developing war plans. They also played an important role in pointing out the need for new concepts and equipment. In 1933 and early 1934, the Luftwaffe conducted a winter war game, concluding that a small but very fast bomber in the form of a battle plane, equipped with cannons, machine guns, and a small bombload, would be a sound means of hitting point targets deep behind enemy lines, and of conducting interdiction and close air support attacks without putting larger, more expensive heavy bombers at risk for relatively minor targets. From the war game after-action report came a Luftwaffe general request for the development of a destroyer aircraft or a multipurpose fighter bomber that would have long-range, heavy armaments, fast speed, and all-weather capability. This in turn would become the program for the Me 110 twin-engine fighter plane, referred to by the Germans as a "destroyer aircraft."[128] The specifications were drawn up in 1934, when the program began. The destroyer aircraft program received a high priority for funding and development.[129]

In the winter war games of late 1934 and early 1935, General Wever developed his concepts for a strategic/operational air campaign. As set out by Wever, the scenario was based on defending against a French invasion of southwest Germany.[130] In the very realistic scenario outlined by Wever, the French air force served largely as an army support force, but part of the French air force attacked Germany's Ruhr industrial area with some success, and inflicted damage on Stuttgart and Munich with incendiary raids.[131] In response to the French invasion, Wever—who personally led the war games—created a campaign plan in several phases. In the first phase, after the war began, the French air force would be the number one target for the Luftwaffe.[132] Wever saw the French air force as relatively vulnerable, as it had moved to forward airfields early in the campaign. From the start, therefore, the Luftwaffe directed its attacks against French airfields, particularly the ground facilities, and against the French aircraft industry.[133] The purpose of this campaign was to force the French to pull their airfields back out of range of the Germans, and to allow the Germans to gain air superiority in the battle area.[134] Once the Germans had gained air superiority over the front, the second phase of the air campaign kicked in, wherein the dive bombers would support the ground troops by attacking French communications over the Rhine River bridges. The French rail lines in the army front area were also attacked, while German medium bombers attacked the French bomber airfields, to protect the movement of the German army.[135] In the third phase, as the Germans prepared to counterattack French forces across the Rhine, the air region commander for the southwest would use his bombers and available aircraft to support the army by attacking French army logistics in rear areas, with French vehicle columns being a primary target.[136] Wever was very pleased with the planning that went into the war game, and invited the commander in chief of the army and his staff to participate in the war game, which began on 6 November and ended in December 1934.[137]

It is impressive to note that in these late 1934 war games by Wever, virtually all aspects of aerial warfare are included, from strategic bomber attacks against the enemy aircraft industry and transportation net by Germany's longest-range and heaviest bombers, to the use of dive bombers as an interdiction weapon, to fighter planes operating in the close interdiction and air support roles, attacking the enemy army directly. The war game plan itself was well conceived, with the use of considerable intelligence information on the French road and rail system, as well as the French air force and airfield system.[138]

Wever used the 1934 war games partly as a means of testing out his own ideas on strategic bombing. At that time, most of Germany's bomber force was equipped with the provisionally armed Junkers Ju 52 transports, which were slow and not especially capable as long-range bombers. The maneuver umpires, noting that Ju 52s would be easy prey to the French fighter force, wished to assume a loss of 80 percent of the German bomber force. Wever, however, refused: "That would deprive me of my confidence in strategic air operations."[139] In several instances, Wever personally led the air staff on staff visits, and put his senior commanders to work developing plans and war games under his supervision. In spring 1936, Wever took a number of officers—who had little experience with fighters—from the operational and organizational branches of the general staff. He had these officers study, in some detail, the fighter operations for a proposed war against Czechoslovakia. Wever invited Hermann Göring and the commanders in chief of the army and navy to the final discussion session at the conclusion of the exercise.

The future Luftwaffe strategy for the subjugation of Czechoslovakia was to use part of the bomber force to support the army in breaking through the Czech border fortifications while using most of Germany's air power in hard, relentless blows to destroy the Czech air force. In the case of a war against

Czechoslovakia, Wever had developed plans to include large-scale attacks by Luftwaffe bombers against the primary political and military targets in and around Prague.[140] Wever believed that Czechoslovakia, ethnically divided and politically unstable, offered one instance in which the Douhetian use of air power—that is, the use of air power to break the morale of an enemy nation—would be appropriate.[141] Throughout Wever's tenure, during the different war games and maneuvers, the air staff practiced developing target intelligence and targeting strategies against Germany's primary enemies: France, Poland, and Czechoslovakia. Other exercises led directly to the development of air doctrine. In autumn 1936, quartermaster exercises for the Luftwaffe were held by the senior quartermaster of the Luftwaffe. The final discussion sessions were attended by State Secretary Milch and the new chief of the Luftwaffe general staff, Lieutenant General Albert Kesselring. The presence of the senior officers of the Luftwaffe at a logistics war game was meant to underline how important the Luftwaffe leadership believed effective mobile logistics were to the Luftwaffe. Out of this 1936 maneuver, the Luftwaffe developed its primary logistics doctrine, *On Supplying the Luftwaffe in War.*[142]

Numerous lessons concerning the equipment of the Luftwaffe were learned in war games and maneuvers. For example, the Germans learned the importance of developing a heavy fighter bomber/destroyer aircraft and effective fighter escort for the bomber force, the requirement for Stukas in conducting interdiction campaigns, and for flak and fighters to defend German cities and industrial centers. On the side of pure doctrine, the maneuvers emphasized the importance of jointness, planning, and working together closely with the army, and of developing an effective forward logistics system, and different strategies for targeting the enemy. The Luftwaffe would be used in nearly parallel campaigns, first to suppress the enemy air force, then to devote part of its forces to support the army by interdiction and close air support, and another part of its force to suppress the enemy air force by bombing its home industries and its airfields.

CHAPTER FIVE

Air Organization and Technology in the Wever Era, 1933-1936

ORGANIZATION OF THE LUFTWAFFE

After Hitler's assumption to power in January 1933, the process of creating an air force organization proceeded very rapidly. In the first week of the Hitler government, Göring was named as the Reichskommissar for aviation, and assumed authority for all German civil aviation departments, with Erhard Milch as state secretary for aviation.[1] Meanwhile, the Reichswehr ministry was organizing the Luftschutzamt, the Air Defense Office, which came into being on 1 April 1933. All army and navy aviation activities and resources were consolidated into this one headquarters, which reported directly to the defense minister. The Luftschutzamt took over all training activities, technological development programs, official aviation functions such as the weather service, and was also responsible for developing air doctrine. This was the forerunner of the true Luftwaffe general staff, and contained staff sections for tactics, training, and Luftwaffe organization.[2]

The Reich aviation ministry came into being on 1 May 1933, with Göring as aviation minister, and on 15 May 1933 the Reichswehr's Air Defense Office was transferred from the defense ministry to the air ministry.[3] The Air Defense Office was renamed the Air Command Office (Luftkommandoamt) on 1 September 1933. By this time, it had been expanded into a recognizable air force general staff, with branches for operations, organization, training, flak, logistics, signals, and all staffed with general staff officers transferred from the army and navy.[4] Also, during the summer of 1933, offices were established within the air ministry as part of the Luftwaffe staff. This included the Administration Office, the Personnel Office headed by Colonel Hans-Jürgen Stumpf, and the Technical Office headed by Wilhelm Wimmer.

At the same time, the air ministry was creating a general staff and headquarters organization. Aviation and technician training programs were consolidated and expanded. In spring 1933, a flying school command was set up within the aviation ministry. Now all commercial flying activities, including the basic flight schools and the seven commercial flying schools that had been run by the Deutschen Luftsportverbandes (German Air Sport Organization) and the Deutschen Verkehrsfliegerschule (German Transport Aviation School), were absorbed by the air ministry. This amounted to nineteen different aviation schools.[5] The five secret air training installations maintained by the army and navy in Braunschweig, Schleisheim, Würzburg, Jüteburg, and Warnemünde also came under the control of the new flying school command, which by 1 April 1934 had been formed into an inspectorate of flying schools and of reserve fliers.[6] By summer 1934, the inspectorate of flying schools controlled a significant infrastructure for pilot, navigator, observer, and technician training, including two reconnaissance schools, one fighter school, four bomber schools, one air armament school, two instrument schools, and twenty basic pilot training schools.[7]

The first combat air units of the Luftwaffe came into being in October 1933, when a seaplane squadron for naval operations, a bomber wing, and a dive bomber squadron were officially established.[8] The Luftwaffe activated military units as fast as equipment could be acquired. By May 1934, the Luftwaffe possessed two bomber wings, and one fighter wing.[9] In April 1934, to provide intermediate command authority within the Luftwaffe, Germany was divided into six air districts. Each district had a senior air commander who was responsible for all aviation units and infrastructure in his district. Each air district also possessed a full staff, with a senior flak commander, a signals officer, procurement, supply, and medical officers. The air district commands would evolve into the headquarters and staffs of the air fleets and air divisions, and would provide the cadre for the operational commands that the Luftwaffe envisioned.[10] In April 1934, along with the air district system, the Luftwaffe created the headquarters for the First Air Division, placing Colonel Hugo Sperrle in command. The First Air Division was given responsibility for coordinating army support aviation.[11] In July 1934, a similar naval air command was established, with responsibility for specialist support for the German navy.[12]

By 1 March 1935 when Hermann Göring officially announced the existence of the German Luftwaffe to the world, the Luftwaffe possessed a fully fledged organization, complete with twenty land and seaplane squadrons, as well as intermediate command headquarters, logistics organization, and an extensive pilot and specialist training infrastructure. The years 1934 through 1936 would see several additions to the basic Luftwaffe structure. Flak artillery, which had been an army responsibility, was transferred to the Luftwaffe on 18 March 1935. The Luftwaffe supply and logistics structure would undergo changes in 1936. On 1 April 1936, the Luftgau commands were created in nine regions to serve as logistics and airfield support headquarters.[13]

The general staff also saw several major changes take place after the official establishment of the Luftwaffe in 1935. They moved quickly to reestablish a program of air force attachés, accredited to foreign countries, to provide information to the recently enlarged Luftwaffe military intelligence section of the general staff.[14] In late 1935, the Luftwaffe General Staff Academy and the Air Technical Academy for higher Luftwaffe officer education were established. In April 1936, an air warfare history section became part of the air staff.[15] The Luftwaffe organization had in only three years reached a fairly mature level, with an adequate infrastructure and organization to ensure their further rapid expansion.

BUILDING THE LUFTWAFFE OFFICER CORPS

The first great difficulty to be met by Göring's air ministry was the task of creating an officer corps for the large air force envisioned for Germany. Since the heart and soul of any military force is its officer corps—and a large Luftwaffe would need a lot of officers—the air ministry had to develop a program to ensure the Luftwaffe would have effective, competent officer leadership at every level. The dilemma was that, in 1933, the German army and navy had no more than 550 officers who had undergone recent pilot or observer training.[16] This small cadre of aviation officers was as knowledgeable and capable a group of air officers as could be found in any air force in the world. The problem was that there were simply not enough experienced aviators to provide more than a cadre for a small air force.

Creating a Luftwaffe officer corps virtually from scratch was the job handed to army Colonel Hans-Jürgen Stumpf, a highly experienced and well regarded army general staff officer—but not an aviator—who was transferred from the Reichswehr to handle the Personnel Office of the air ministry in July 1933. Stumpf possessed considerable vision and administrative ability, and had the advantage of support from Reichswehr Minister Werner von Blomberg and Air Minister Göring in requesting and transferring promising nonaviators from the Reichswehr and navy to join the cadre for rapid expansion of the Luftwaffe. Between 1933 and 1936, by which time the Luftwaffe had set up its own officer training schools, the Luftwaffe built and recruited its officer corps from eleven different sources:

1. Experienced army aviators
2. Army ground officers
3. Army and navy flak and signals specialists
4. Civil Service employees from the Reichswehr air ministry and Reichs aviation office
5. The police force
6. Germany's civil aviation industry
7. Retired officers
8. Army and navy officer cadets
9. Army and navy NCOs
10. Specialists drawn directly from civilian life
11. Civilian flight instructors

The first contingent of officers to be transferred to the air ministry were mostly army officers with a general staff background, men such as Helmuth Wilberg, Helmuth Felmy, Hugo Sperrle, Paul Deichmann, Wilhelm Speidel, Gunther Korten, Rudolf Meister, and Andreas Nielsen. Due to the shortage of airmen with a general staff background, however, General Blomberg authorized the transfer of army general staff officers such as Stumpf, Wolfgang Martini of the signals corps, and Colonel Albert Kesselring. Colonel Walter Wever was selected to become the first chief of the Luftwaffe general staff, to the disappointment of many in the army, including General Blomberg, who saw Wever as a probable future chief of staff of the army. The army officers transferred to the air ministry often undertook flight training. Kesselring and Wever accordingly became qualified pilots, holding to the traditional view of German officers: that it was best to lead by example, and not to order men to do what you yourself were unwilling to do. A small group of army communications specialists under the leadership of Wolfgang Martini and a small group of army flak specialists including Gothard Seidel and Heinrich Aschenbrenner provided a leadership cadre for building up the Luftwaffe's flak and communications branches.

During the Weimar Republic, the army and Reichswehr ministry, as well as the Reich Civil Aviation Office, had employed a considerable number of former officer aviators as civilian employees and specialists. Some, like Franz Mahnke and Ernst Marquard, both of whom worked for the Reichswehr Weapons Office, were former officers with engineering degrees. Over one hundred such civil servants were quickly transferred from the Reichswehr ministry and the Reichs Civil Aviation Office over to the air ministry. Once transferred, they were quickly given officer ranks and put back into uniform. This was scarcely a change for many of these men, as they had already been working in military jobs, shouldering the responsibilities, and carrying out the duties of officers.

The police forces of the Weimar Republic, and especially the security police, had been trained and organized after World War I along paramilitary lines. During the 1920s, the Prussian and Bavarian state police forces had been given considerable military training. Police forces had been equipped with rifles, machine guns, and armored cars, and organized into military-type companies and battalions. Turning the security police into a reserve force for the Reichswehr had been an intentional means of circumventing the Versailles Treaty's ban on the creation of an army reserve force in Germany. By the late 1920s, there were an estimated 70,000 security police with full military training in the German states.[17] A large proportion of the police officers were former army officers who had seen action during World War I. It became a fairly simple task to take entire police units and to retrain and reequip them, usually as Luftwaffe flak units. A high percentage of the Luftwaffe officer corps came from the German police. One former police officer, Karl Koller, eventually became chief of the staff of the Luftwaffe.[18] Prussian and Bavarian police also had the advantage of maintaining a corps of trained aviators. Future Luftwaffe General Veit Fischer belonged in 1933 to the Bavarian air police, essentially a military pilot reserve force of the Weimar era that was officially justified as policing the airfields and civil aviation facilities in Bavaria. One future Luftwaffe general, Walter Grobmann, came from the air police and had actually received his pilot training as a police officer.[19]

The most lucrative sources of officer recruitment for the Luftwaffe were the former officers and pilots of the wartime air service who had served in civil aviation from 1919 to 1934. When rearmament came in 1933–1935, there were several hundred wartime officers with combat experience working for Lufthansa, the aircraft companies, the Aviation Department of the Transportation Ministry, and in civilian flight schools. Many of these former officers were eager to reenter the military and join the new Luftwaffe. Hundreds of the former Luftstreitkräfte officers had also maintained their status as reserve officers. Just how important these officers were to aerial rearmament in Germany is demonstrated by the number of senior leaders of the Luftwaffe who came from the interwar civil aviation. Of the 600-plus Luftwaffe generals who served between 1935 and 1945, approximately 150 had been involved with civil aviation between 1920 and 1934. Many of the Luftwaffe's top officers came from the ranks of civil aviation, including Erhard Milch, state secretary for aviation and later field marshal, who served as the director of Lufthansa before rejoining the Luftwaffe. Robert Knauss, later General der

Flieger and commander of the Luftwaffe General Staff Academy, also came from the Lufthansa's senior management. Alfred Keller, later colonel general and commander of the First Air Fleet from 1940 to 1943, worked for Junkers and ran a flight school before 1934. Werner Junck, later lieutenant general and wartime commander of Jagdkorps II, worked for Heinkel before joining the Luftwaffe. Theodor Osterkamp, a World War I Pour le Mérite holder, managed a seaplane station before returning to the Luftwaffe. Osterkamp would become air commander for North Africa in 1941–1942.

A small number of people were brought in directly from civilian life, and given officer rank in the Luftwaffe. Dr. Rudolf Benkendorff had a Ph.D. in meteorology, and worked as chief meteorologist for the transportation ministry. Transferred to the air ministry, he became the Luftwaffe's chief meteorological officer. Hans Neuber, MD, had run the psychological laboratory of the Reichswehr ministry from 1930–1933, and was transferred to the air ministry to become chief psychologist of the Luftwaffe. One of the more notable civilians brought into the Luftwaffe was Dr. Heinrich Steinmann, an engineering professor who specialized in teaching courses on airfield design and construction. As Germany's leading civilian specialist in airfield construction, Steinmann was given an officer's rank. He soon rose to the rank of general, and was placed in charge of designing and building airfields for the Luftwaffe.

A number of retired army officers who had had distinguished careers were invited to receive commissions in the Luftwaffe. Those officers who were not aviators were at least knowledgeable and capable in areas of military administration and logistics. Retired and former officers soon found their way to administrative and logistics jobs in the air districts and the Luftgaus. Retired Army General Otto von Stülpnagel was asked to assume a general's commission in the Luftwaffe, and served as the first commandant of the Luftwaffe's General Staff Academy, the Luftkriegsakademie.

Young men undergoing training as officer cadets for the army between 1933 and 1936 were given the opportunity to transfer to the Luftwaffe after completing their officer training. An exciting new service, the Luftwaffe attracted a significant number of the army and navy officer cadet corps.[20] Both the army and the navy were in the process of rapid expansion at this time, and both services initiated programs to give considerable numbers of senior NCOs officer commissions. A number of these army and navy NCOs transferred to the Luftwaffe, generally ending up in logistics administration services or in the flak artillery. Several dozen of the top aviation instructors coming from the flight schools that had been maintained by the transportation ministry were given a crash course of military training for several months, and became Luftwaffe officers, at which time they returned to their duties staffing thc Luftwaffe's training command.

From all these sources, Hans Jürgen Stumpf managed to create an officer corps of several thousand fully qualified officers for the Luftwaffe by 1936–1938. Some historians, including Richard Overy, have suggested that the Luftwaffe later suffered from serious leadership problems because a large proportion of the Luftwaffe officers had come from civil aviation and the army ground forces.[21] Another historian writing about the hundreds of officers transferred from the army in 1934–1935—officers such as Wever, Kesselring, and Stumpf—refers to the senior leadership of the Luftwaffe as "amteur aviators."[22] Richard Overy avers there was a clash between the "Prussians," the regular officers who had remained with the Reichswehr, and the "outsiders," who had reentered the military in 1934–1935. He argues that this clash of cultures and viewpoints seriously damaged the Luftwaffe.[23]

Such comments may make for colorful leadership theories, but there is actually no evidence of animosity among the senior officers of the Luftwaffe on the basis of "Prussian" or "outsider" status. There were, of course, serious personality clashes between the senior officers of the Luftwaffe—as one would find within any military service. Milch, for example, was disliked by many because of his personality and his penchant for political intrigue, rather than his service with Lufthansa. Even those who disliked him, moreover, regarded him as highly competent. Walter Wever came from the army, but was nonetheless revered by the professional airmen of the Luftwaffe. Rather than being a disadvantage to the Luftwaffe, the influx of hundreds of reserve officers, particularly from civilian aviation, during the first stages of rearmament was one of the great advantages enjoyed by the Luftwaffe at this timc. The officers who came from Lufthansa and Junkers and Heinkel were probably better informed regarding the nature of modern aircraft technology and conditions of long-distance flight than many of the regular officers of the French or British air forces, who had led an air force garrison life. Considering the small cadre he had to begin with, General Hans Jürgen Stumpf did a superior job of building up a sound foundation for the Luftwaffe's officer corps. Much of the later success of the Luftwaffe can be directly attributed to Stumpf's early efforts at creating an officer corps.

AERIAL REARMAMENT, 1933–1936

Perhaps the greatest contribution made by Erhard Milch to the Luftwaffe was organizing the massive program of aerial rearmament begun by the

Luftwaffe in 1933. The first major difficulty faced by the Luftwaffe in creating an air force was the state of the German aviation industry. Badly battered by the worldwide depression at the end of 1932, the eight German airframe manufacturers had declined to a total of only 3,200 employees.[24] Working night and day, by May 1933 Milch and the air staff had developed the plans for the implementation of an immediate program to produce 1,000 aircraft that would pump enough investment into the aircraft industry to build it up for further production of advanced aircraft at a later time. The first thousand aircraft for the Luftwaffe were to be completed within a year, mostly light training aircraft, but also including 244 military planes.[25]

The policy of the air ministry in developing the first generation of Luftwaffe aircraft was to take aircraft models that had already been developed, or well along in the development process, and put them into production immediately. This generation of Luftwaffe aircraft included the already developed Heinkel He 45 long-range reconnaissance aircraft and the Heinkel He 46 short-range reconnaissance aircraft. The He 45, which was also able to serve as a light bomber, entered serial production in late 1933.[26] The Heinkel 46 entered production in 1934.[27] Due to the lack of manufacturing capacity at this time, even at large German airplane companies like Junkers and Heinkel, many aircraft were built under license by other firms such as Focke Wulf. For example, the He 45 and many of the He 46 airplanes were built by Gothaer Waggonfabrik.[28]

The Luftwaffe's first dive bomber was the Heinkel He 50, which was already in production to fulfill a contract with the Japanese military. A robust airplane, it could carry a 550-pound bombload. Like many of the early Luftwaffe aircraft, it was accepted as an interim model.[29] The Luftwaffe's first fighters were the Arado 65, already in production, and the 200-mph Heinkel 51, which was being tested in 1933, and entered production in 1934.[30] As the Junkers Ju 52 trimotor transport was already in production, the Luftwaffe wanted a large number of them, after requiring the model's conversion into a bomber aircraft.[31] The Luftwaffe's purpose-built bombers were the Dornier Do 11s, which the Luftwaffe started receiving in 1934.[32]

The capabilities of the first generation of Luftwaffe aircraft produced between 1933 and 1935 were not particularly impressive. The Dornier Do 11 and Do 23 bombers had poor handling characteristics, and a high accident rate.[33] The Heinkel He 51 fighter was fast, but also difficult to handle.[34] In general, however, German military aircraft of the early 1930s were roughly equivalent to that of the other major powers. For example, the Arado 65 and Heinkel 51 biplane fighters had similar speed and firepower characteristics

The improvised Ju 52 bombers first used by the Luftwaffe until modern bombers could be built, ca. 1935. (Photo from *Jahrbuch der deutschen Luftwaffe,* 1936.)

to the American Air Corps' Curtiss P-6 Hawk, introduced in 1932, or the RAF's Hawker Fury Mark 1, the main RAF fighter of this period.[35]

The first production programs of the Luftwaffe succeeded in their objective of rapidly expanding the aircraft industry. By the end of 1933, the German aircraft industry employed 11,000, and the engine plants were employing over 5,700 workers.[36] The Luftwaffe's early production programs also served as the means for rapidly equipping newly formed Luftwaffe units with fairly modern equipment. Once truly modern, high-performance fighters and bombers became available, beginning in 1936, the first-generation aircraft were mostly either relegated to training units, or were sold for export. For instance, some of the Dornier Do 11s went to Bulgaria,[37] and most Heinkel He 50s were sold to China.[38]

The Luftwaffe's next major production plan, the Rhineland program, was issued in January 1934. It called for 4,021 aircraft to be produced for the Luftwaffe in 1934–1935. As the Luftwaffe was still in the process of building up, the largest category of aircraft ordered was trainers, with 1,760 on order. The operational military aircraft ordered under the Rhineland program showed the long-held belief in the bomber as the primary air weapon, a view supported by Milch and the air staff. The Rhineland program planned for a

Flight of Do 23 bombers in training, ca. 1934–1935. (Photo from USAF HRA.)

force of 822 bombers and 590 reconnaissance planes, 246 fighters, and 51 dive bombers. The relatively low priority accorded to naval aircraft is belied by the mere 149 aircraft planned for production to equip the naval air arm.[39] The Rhineland program was quickly expanded to demand yet more production of the rapidly expanding German aircraft industry, so that by the end of 1935, production figures for the industry totalled over 5,000 aircraft—more than a thousand of which had been planned for under the Rhineland program in 1934.[40]

The production programs of 1933 and 1934 meant that, when the Luftwaffe's existence was officially announced on 1 March 1935, it already possessed a significant force of 800 operational aircraft.[41] These ambitious production programs were continually expanded by the Luftwaffe. Under the revised production program of October 1935, Milch and the air staff planned for the acquisition of 1,221 medium bombers. The next year, they included the development of three heavy-bomber prototypes.[42] The additional program of October 1935 called for 3,820 combat aircraft for the Luftwaffe, as well as 462 combat aircraft for the naval support arm. Although a fighter production increase to 970 fighters was planned for 1936, the bombing doctrine emphasis within the air staff was still evident. Also included in the revised production plan was a call for the manufacture of nearly 500 dive bombers of the Henschel 123, Heinkel 50, and new Ju 87 types.[43] The rapid expansion of the German aviation industry was, in many respects, inefficient and wasteful.[44] However, despite all the inefficiencies, in the space of three years Milch had pushed the German aircraft industry to a point of world leadership in capacity and technical excellence. By mid-1935, the labor force working in the aircraft industry had grown to 60,894 employees, and by 1936, this had doubled again, to a labor force of 124,878.[45]

While Milch and the air staff coordinated the program for planning the production of new aircraft for the Luftwaffe, the actual development of aircraft models was in the hands of Wilhelm Wimmer, then chief of the Technical Office, who had a corps of highly capable assistants, including Major Wolfram von Richthofen. In the process of development, the Technical Office, in coordination with the air staff, would draw up performance specifications for the types of aircraft that the air staff believed the Luftwaffe would need. Wimmer and his corps of aviation engineers would develop general specifications into very detailed guidelines, then invite two to four aircraft manufacturers to develop prototype aircraft. These aircraft would then be carefully tested, and the winning design would be selected for serial production.

During 1934, the Luftwaffe general staff developed the specifications and production priority requirements for an entire second generation of aircraft, which were to be high-performance aircraft, superior to contemporaneous foreign models. In May 1934, the Technical Office of the Luftwaffe issued new primary development priorities. The first priority went to a heavy, long-range bomber. The second priority went to a heavy dive bomber. The third priority was for medium bombers, and the fourth priority went to a heavy fighter. Dornier and Junkers began work on a heavy bomber project. Four firms began development of the heavy dive bomber, which would become the Ju 87. The medium bomber program would lead to production of the Dornier Do 17, Junkers Ju 86, and the Heinkel He 111 bombers. The heavy fighter plane project initiated the development of the Me 110 twin-engine fighter. In the second group of priorities were a single-seat fighter/interceptor, a light dive bomber, a long-distance seaplane, and a multipurpose seaplane for the naval air arm.[46]

For the most part, Wimmer's direction in developing the second generation of Luftwaffe aircraft was remarkably successful. The development of the Me 109 single-seat fighter is a testimony to the effectiveness of the Technical Office between 1933 and 1936. In 1934, the Technical Office called for the development of an all-metal, low-wing, single-seat fighter plane, armed with cannon and machine guns, with a top speed of not less than 450 kilometers per hour. The Messerschmitt 109 design was ready for testing and fly-off competition by October 1935, and fulfilled all the Technical Office requirements, and more. By 1936 the first serial production of the Me 109 had begun. This superior fighter plane represented an enormous leap in technological capability for the era. The total time from specifications to serial production of the Me 109 was only two and a half years.[47] Development of other aircraft followed a similar course. The Ju 87 dive bomber development program began in 1933. It was ready for testing in 1935, and production began in 1936. The Ju 87 provided the Luftwaffe with an aircraft capable of putting a 500-kilogram bomb within 100 meters of the target.[48] Development of the Heinkel 111 medium bomber began in 1934; it was in production by 1936. The Heinkel 111 was a very impressive medium bomber for the period, with a 217-mph maximum speed, a range of over 900 miles, and a maximum bomb-load of over 3,300 pounds.[49] In addition to the bombers and fighters, a series of very effective light aircraft for army support were rapidly developed. The Technical Office developed the Henschel 126 two-seater light reconnaissance plane in rapid time, and in two years oversaw the development of the Fiesler 156 Storch, a light observation and liaison aircraft that had superb capabilities for short takeoffs and landings.[50]

The creation of the Messerschmitt Me 110 heavy fighter illustrates the interesting and innovative approach to operational doctrine shown by the Technical Office. In 1934, the Technical Office called for the development of a twin-engine fighter that would be fast, heavily armed, and possess great range. It was to be a multipurpose aircraft, capable of serving as a reconnaissance plane, a fighter-bomber, and most important, as a long-range escort to bombers. Due to the lack of adequate engines, the development of the Me 110 was somewhat slower, but by 1936 there were prototypes ready for testing.[51] The early models of the Me 110 had impressive characteristics: long range, a maximum speed of 283 mph, and heavy armament of two 20-mm cannons and five machine guns.[52] In the words of aircraft expert Eric Brown, the Me 110 was a well-designed aircraft that "placed Germany out in front in strategic fighter development."[53]

ARMY SUPPORT, FLAK, AND PARATROOPS

Although in Luftwaffe Regulation 16, Wever and the air staff argued that strategic air war was the primary mission of the Luftwaffe, the creation of an effective doctrine and organization for army support was not ignored. The army's most vital requirement for Luftwaffe support was for short- and medium-range air reconnaissance. To meet this need, the Luftwaffe structure contained a large number—both existing, and planned—of squadrons of light reconnaissance and observation planes. Yet, while the Luftwaffe gladly agreed to provide significant resources to fulfill the army's reconnaissance needs, Wever also insisted that reconnaissance units remain within the Luftwaffe chain of command. This meant that, although specific air units would be assigned to support specific ground units, the army would still have to request air missions through the Luftwaffe. This ensured that only experienced airmen would decide the manner in which the mission was flown. Thus, the operational misuse of air power and the employment of poor tactics were avoided, both likely to occur if ground officers lacking aviation experience were to actually command the air reconnaissance units. To facilitate army/Luftwaffe operations by coordinating air force support for the army, a special command for army cooperation was set up within the Luftwaffe in 1934.[54]

The Luftwaffe agreed that air units would be ordered to support army units during operations to facilitate the close air support mission. General Wever placed a high priority on the training of air liaison officers: pilot officers who would be detached from operational squadrons or air groups, and attached to supported army corps. These liaison officers were directed to keep the supporting Luftwaffe units informed of the combat situation on the ground. Wever directed that the air liaison officers, or *Flivos* (*Fli*eger *V*erbindungs *O*ffiziere) were to be provided with a Luftwaffe communications team with "appropriate equipment, so that they can maintain liaison with headquarters and the squadron—even at a great distance."[55] Wever strongly supported the mission of training the Luftwaffe in ground support operations, and encouraged Luftwaffe units to conduct local, small-scale training exercises with nearby army units, commenting that Luftwaffe commanders need not coordinate with the headquarters in Berlin to arrange such training: "Army training exercises should be used as much as possible as Luftwaffe exercises in order to deepen our understanding of interservice cooperation. . . . The participation of the Luftwaffe should be considered from the start of the exercise planning. It must be made clear that independent missions in the larger operational framework can assist army operations, or that sometimes a situation calls for direct army support. . . . Direct coordination of air unit commanders with the army saves unnecessary paperwork, and is useful for the units that take part in exercises."[56]

Wever clearly had a further agenda in fostering Luftwaffe/army cooperation. The participation of Luftwaffe officers in army units and army training was also meant to educate the army in the capabilities and missions of the Luftwaffe, thus maintaining an "air-minded" army, the ethic emphasized by von Seeckt.

The army, especially the armored and motorized troops, appreciated the importance of air/ground cooperation. More than any other branch of the army, the panzer and motorized units developed training programs with the Luftwaffe to coordinate reconnaissance and attack aviation, understanding, and operations. In 1936 the first commander of the panzer troops, General Oswald Lutz, ordered the panzer units to train with the nearby Luftwaffe units, and to include them on radio and reconnaissance exercises. Lutz realized that the observation pilots needed to understand ground operations to make effective tactical reports during a campaign. Lutz also believed that well trained army cooperation pilots would make good ground attack pilots once capable attack aircraft were developed. General Lutz also requested that each of the air district headquarters set up special army cooperation staffs.[57]

Flak artillery played a major role in the Luftwaffe's conception of air power. From the beginning of rearmament, the flak artillery force was planned to grow to a large size. Until 1935 the flak troops remained part of the army, even though as early as 1933 it was known that the Luftwaffe would eventually control all flak forces. The army served as the developing and training agency for flak, because it already had a cadre of flak units and antiaircraft specialists capable of rapidly training and expanding the force for the Luftwaffe. By the first of April 1935, when the army flak forces were formally transferred to Luftwaffe control, they comprised a significant force of twelve battalions.[58] The defense ministry had provided an impressive level of funding for the development of the flak arm. All flak units were motorized, and the units that came online in 1935 were equipped with the new, very effective 20-mm and 37-mm light flak cannon, and the heavy 88-mm flak gun produced by Krupp and Rheinmetall. By 1936 the flak force had nearly doubled again.[59]

For all practical purposes, the flak artillery was divided into three forces, designed for different missions: heavy flak, light flak, and mixed battalions with both heavy and light batteries. As the system developed, the battalions were formed into regiments in 1936.[60] By the end of 1936 the number of flak units had grown to seven regiments, with thirty-two mixed, and nine light battalions. Two battalions were assigned to a specialized naval flak command.[61] In 1935 a senior commander of flak artillery, complete with staff, was organized in each air district to coordinate training and operations for flak units.[62]

Regulation 16 placed considerable stress on the importance of flak in air defense.[63] The Germans had found flak to be extremely effective during the war. By late 1918, flak guns had improved dramatically in mobility, rate of fire, range and destructive power, and mechanical time fuses, effective searchlights, and better range finders had all increased the lethality of flak against aircraft.[64] Flak would become the core of German homeland defense. By the mid-1930s, air defense doctrine emphasized the creation of air defense zones around vital industrial and military facilities. The tactics for emplacing flak batteries for all-around defense and coordinating with the attached searchlights and ground observer system were well established by this period.[65] In the air defense zones in the homeland, fighter squadrons would cooperate with the flak artillery for area defense.[66] Essentially, however, fighter aircraft were seen as auxiliary weapons to support the flak for home air defense.[67] In developing this doctrine, the Germans were relying on studies conducted in the mid-1930s that greatly overestimated the ability of flak artillery to hit enemy aircraft.[68]

Outside the German homeland, in the area of army operations, the army maintained effective operational control of Luftwaffe air defense units and assets. Indeed, until 1937 German doctrine allowed fighter units to be attached to the ground armies for air defense against enemy aircraft.[69] The army leadership regarded flak artillery as an essential element of modern warfare, and basically envisioned that the Luftwaffe would oversee all air defense operations in the homeland while the army would control air operations in its own zone of operations. In 1936 the army general staff recommended that the army form its own flak troops for defense of the army, and that every army and Panzer corps should have one light flak battalion and two heavy flak battalions, for a total of fifteen light flak battalions and thirty heavy flak battalions for the army.[70]

One of the most innovative aspects of air doctrine to be developed under the tenure of General Wever was the establishment of a Luftwaffe paratroop force. Since 1933 the German military had carefully followed the development of the Soviet airborne force, including the Soviet use of small airborne units in maneuvers.[71] In 1933 the Soviets had made a small unit airborne drop, and in 1934 had made company- and battalion-sized parachute drops.[72] In 1935 the Soviets had carried out a relatively large airborne exercise, using two regiments on maneuvers northwest of Kiev. The German press covered this maneuver, and commented favorably on it.[73] Thus in April 1935 when Reichsmarschall Göring decided to create his own Luftwaffe guards regiment out of a unit of the Prussian state police, Wever, looking for a practical use for Luftwaffe infantry, ordered that the Regiment General Göring would be trained as a parachute unit. In fall 1935 Wever ordered paratroop training to be begun in 1936.[74]

Even before 1935, the Luftwaffe had the infrastructure and training program for the development of an airborne force. From 1930 onward, the Reichswehr had carried out extensive parachute testing and research.[75] By 1933 modern and efficient parachute research facilities were available to the air ministry, complete with effective parachute designs and research data on parachuting.[76] When Wever ordered the creation of a Luftwaffe airborne force, the initial doctrine for the force was to use small paratroop units of platoon size to drop behind enemy lines and act as commando troops, raiding and destroying vital targets and enemy installations.[77]

DOCTRINE AND TECHNOLOGY

The development of air war doctrine is more sensitive to the state of technology, and the development of technology, than that of the other military services. In many instances, doctrine drives technology. For example, the Luftwaffe's emphasis on flak artillery for air defense helped push the rapid development of modern antiaircraft artillery. In other cases, however, technology acted as a limitation on doctrine. The best example of this is the German long-range bomber program in effect between 1934 and 1936.

The Luftwaffe initiated a program for a four-engine, heavy bomber in 1934. This bomber was to have the ability to carry a heavy bombload over a long range. The Luftwaffe gave the development of the heavy bomber its top priority in May 1934.[78] A considerable mythology has built up around the Luftwaffe's heavy bomber program of the early 1930s. General Wever was a staunch supporter of the program. According to some, the bomber program was a result of Wever's understanding of *Mein Kampf,* from which Wever learned that Germany's primary enemy was not France, but Russia. He thus concluded that Germany needed a heavy bomber capable of reaching targets deep in the industrial heartland of Russia. As the story goes, the heavy bomber was primarily Wever's project. Accordingly, when he died, interest in the heavy bomber program quickly died away as well.[79]

The actual story is much more mundane. There is no evidence that

Hitler's turgid book, or the strategic views of the Nazi leaders, provided any impetus for the development of the long-range bomber. Wever was most certainly not the only senior officer advocating such a weapon. Wever's advocacy of the long-range bomber program actually reflected the majority view of the officers on the air staff. General Wilhelm Wimmer, head of the Technical Office, who was charged with developing the heavy bomber, had long been an advocate of the strategic bomber force. His assistant in the Technical Office, Wolfram von Richthofen, had long been a staunch believer in the primacy of the heavy bomber force within the Luftwaffe force structure.[80] Even Luftwaffe airmen such as Robert Knauss, of whom it can clearly be said found no inspiration either in *Mein Kampf* or in the Nazi party, were excited by the concept of developing a four-engine, heavy bomber.

In many respects, these senior airmen of the Luftwaffe reflected the opinions and conventional wisdom of their contemporary military air power leaders. For military airmen of all the major powers, the heavy bomber was the ultimate symbol of air power in the era. For air force officers in the early 1930s, the heavy bomber had the same symbolism as battleships did for naval officers: a "real" air force had to have them. Heavy bombers were truly prestigious symbols of service independence and equality with the other services, due to their ability to strike at long range with heavy bombloads. The Soviet air force was first off the mark in developing heavy bombers with the fielding of the Tupolev TB-3 in 1931. The Tupolev TB-3 had a range of 1,350 miles and a bombload of slightly over two tons. Though it was a slow and ungainly aircraft, by summer 1934 over 250 TB-3s had entered service, giving the Soviet Union the largest heavy bomber force in the world at that time.[81] In 1934 the Russians began development of a more modern heavy bomber, which would become the PE-8.[82] The American Army Air Corps, fighting doggedly at this time to gain the status of an independent service, was next off the mark in the race to develop a heavy bomber. In August 1934 the U.S. Army Air Corps set specifications for a fast, long-range, four-engine heavy bomber that would become the B-17. A prototype would fly in 1935, and was quickly adopted by Air Corps leadership as the symbol of modern air power.[83] The British, and even the Italians, initiated heavy bomber programs in the mid-1930s.[84]

The difficulty faced by the Luftwaffe and the Technical Office in the development of the heavy strategic bomber was the weakness of the German aircraft engine industry in the early 1930s. While German airframe design and aerodynamic research in 1933–1934 was very advanced, the Germans lagged behind both Britain and the United States in the design and production of powerful aircraft engines.[85] When German rearmament began, the

Luftwaffe had only a few aircraft engine models available, and these were not in quantity production. Germany's major aircraft engine manufacturers: Junkers, Daimler-Benz, and BMW, initiated research and development programs for aircraft piston engines. By the outbreak of the war, these programs would result in such excellent engines as the Daimler-Benz DB-601 and the Junkers Jumo 211. These liquid-cooled engines, when introduced into Luftwaffe service, would have the advantages of direct fuel injection, and would prove their reliability in combat.[86]

German manufacturers began crash programs to develop larger, more efficient aircraft engines. In 1933 BMW began development of large, modern, radial air-cooled engines, which would evolve into the BMW 801 engine that would later power the FW 190 fighter and the Ju 88 bomber.[87] Large, efficient engines were, however, still years away when the first heavy bomber prototype, the Dornier Do 19, was completed and first flown in 1936. The Do 19 was grossly underpowered with Bramo nine-cylinder, radial air-cooled engines that were only rated at 600 horsepower each, giving the Dornier Do 19 a maximum speed of less than 200 miles per hour, and a cruising speed of 155 miles per hour. The very impressive-looking Do 19 bomber was a tremendous disappointment.[88] The Junkers contribution to the heavy-bomber program was the prototype Ju 89 bomber, an improvement over the Dornier design. When the prototype Ju 89 first flew at the end of 1936, it was powered by four Daimler-Benz DB-600 A engines. This gave the Ju 89 a maximum speed of 242 miles per hour, and a cruising speed of 196 miles per hour, plus a slightly better range and bombload than the Do 19.[89]

Even before the two heavy bomber prototypes were finished, it was clear that neither would have adequate speed, range, or bombload. Neither of these mid-1930s aircraft came close to the American Boeing B-17 in performance. Disappointed by the design and development work on the heavy-bomber program, Wilhelm Wimmer issued entirely new specifications for a heavy bomber program on 17 April 1936, calling for completely new designs and prototypes. The new requirements for a heavy bomber were personally endorsed by General Wever, who argued that range, speed, and defensive capability were the most important attributes of a heavy bomber. It was at this point, with General Wever's full approval, that Germany's initial heavy bomber was essentially terminated.[90]

In 1936, due to the limitations of engine technology, it became the policy of the Luftwaffe air staff to simply skip the entire first generation development of bombers and begin research and development of a future heavy bomber, which would be deployed when the German aircraft engine industry

Dornier Do 19 heavy bomber prototype. First flew in 1936. (Photo from USAF HRA.)

and aircrew training had caught up technologically. In the meantime, the excellent family of medium bombers then coming into production, the Heinkel He 111 and the Dornier Do 17, would provide Germany with an adequate bomber force until acceptable heavy bombers could be developed a few years later. This decision was the most rational and sensible decision for the Luftwaffe to make, and represented the best use of available technological capabilities.

The Luftwaffe's mid-1930s emphasis on the development of bombers also led to the development of numerous technologies for long-range navigation, which would be vital for a future strategic bomber force. Under the Luftwaffe's direction, the Lorenz Firm, manufacturer of Europe's best radio navigation and landing systems, began in 1933 to adapt its radio navigation technology to an automatic bombing device that would give Luftwaffe bombers a very low center of probable error when bomb-dropping in night or poor weather conditions. The result was the Lorenz X-Gerät. A pilot equipped with this device would fly along a radio beam, and after reaching the target a signal would automatically initiate the bomb-dropping sequence. In only two years, the Luftwaffe had an operational automatic bombing device, with a range of 300 to 400 kilometers, which could ensure a stick of bombs would hit within 400 meters of the intended target.[91] Germany may not have had a four-engine long-range bomber, but due to advanced navigation aids and technology, by the end of the decade the Luftwaffe bomber force would be the only one able to fly at night or in bad weather and conduct bombing raids with some reasonable degree of accuracy.

The Luftwaffe's emphasis on flak led to the development of a variety of excellent, new antiaircraft equipment. One of the most lethal pieces to be developed in the era was certainly the Luftwaffe's four-barreled, 20-mm light flak gun.[92] With an 88-mm flak gun already developed, and the excellent fire control computer, the Kommando Gerät 36, the Luftwaffe had the most lethal system of flak weaponry for the era.[93]

Under Wilhelm Wimmer, the Luftwaffe Technical Office also ensured that the Luftwaffe established a base of scientific research for the development of future weaponry. From 1933 on, the Luftwaffe was involved in funding cruise missile research, and the development of rockets and ram jets. According to Michael Neufeld in *The Rocket and the Reich,* Wimmer and the Technical Office were "receptive to radical new technologies like the jet. . . . The Luftwaffe was unusually open to revolutionary ideas."[94] As early as the mid-1930s, the foundation was laid for jet engine research and the development of jet aircraft.[95] By 1936 Germany had also taken the lead in other areas of aircraft development that would have military applications. That year, the world's first effective military helicopter, the Focke Wulf FA 61, was produced under Luftwaffe contract.[96]

Under Wilhelm Wimmer, and assisted by Wolfram von Richthofen, the Luftwaffe's chief of research Adolf Baeumker,[97] and such officers as Wolfgang Martini and Heinrich Aschenbrenner of the Luftwaffe signal troops, the Luftwaffe Technical Office between 1933 and 1936 was generally successful in coordinating the development of technology, and linking contemporary technology, and future technology under development, to German operational doctrine. A lack of effective aircraft engines was a serious difficulty that the Luftwaffe would strive mightily to overcome. By 1936, however, the Germans actually had the lead in many of the technologies required for modern air war. The Germans developed superior flak weaponry and control systems. Luftwaffe ballistics specialists were producing some excellent machine cannon and effective aerial bombs, and most important, the Luftwaffe had

General der Flieger Wilhelm Wimmer, chief of the Luftwaffe Technical Office, 1933–1936. Wimmer was known as "the best technical mind in the Luftwaffe." Under Wimmer's direction, the Me 109 fighter, the He 111, Do 17, Ju 86 bombers, and Ju 87 stuka werc developed. (Photo from the Von Richthofen family.)

taken the lead in air force radio navigation technologies, and technologies required for accurate bombing.

NAVAL AIR DOCTRINE

In 1932 when it appeared that all army and naval aviation would be consolidated into one command under the direct responsibility of the defense minister, Admiral Raeder, commander in chief of the navy, put up a stout resistance to the idea of losing control of naval aviation.[98] There is little chance that Admiral Raeder's proposal for the navy to keep a separate naval air arm would be accepted by either the army or the defense ministry. Unlike the army, until it became a matter of losing control of their aviation arm, the navy had shown relatively little interest in the capabilities of naval aviation. In negotiations with the army and the defense ministry, the navy had very few pilots, aircraft facilities, or aviation programs to bring to the table.[99] After the Nazi seizure of power, it was quickly decided that the naval aviation arm would be under the control of the new Luftwaffe, in the spirit that "if it flies, it belongs to the Luftwaffe."[100]

What the navy would get from the Luftwaffe would be operational control of a naval aviation corps, to be called the "Marineluftstreitkräfte." This corps would consist of a commander and staff, which, in turn, would control reconnaissance, fighter, and composite squadrons that would serve under fleet direction.[101] The training facilities for aviation already possessed by the navy as of June 1934 were transferred to the director of the Luftwaffe's training command. The Luftwaffe's air training commander was, in turn, directed to closely cooperate with the naval commanders to develop an appropriate training program for naval aviators, as well as a system of common doctrine and procedures for the naval aviation branch, and the rest of the Luftwaffe.[102]

During the early rearmament period of the Nazi government, the navy under Admiral Raeder developed a plan for the rapid increase in the size of the German navy. Raeder's fleet-building plan became, in turn, the foundation for planning a naval aviation force to support the fleet. The first naval rearmament plan aimed to build up a German fleet equal to the French fleet. The 1934 plan included the completion of five pocket battleships called Panzerschiffe and seven cruisers by 1938.[103] To support this force, there would be a need for at least thirty-six fleet seaplanes, which could be carried aboard ships and used for fleet reconnaissance.[104] The initial fleet plan of 1934 also included the building of two medium-sized aircraft carriers. The fleet carriers, tentatively entitled "Carrier A" and "Carrier B," would be between 18,000 and 20,000 tons, and would carry fifty to sixty aircraft. It was expected that the first carrier, which would be named the "Graf Zeppelin," would be ready for the fleet by fall 1939. At that time the navy would need, from the Luftwaffe, three reconnaissance squadrons, three general-purpose squadrons, and three dive bomber squadrons to operate from the carrier.[105]

The Graf Zeppelin aircraft carrier was a relatively modest ship. According to its final plans, it was to be 19,250 tons, contain a 240-meter-long armored flight deck, and carry a very heavy, shipboard flak battery consisting of twelve 105-mm guns, twenty-two 37-mm guns, and twenty-eight 20-mm guns. The initial plans for the ship included a requirement for only forty-two aircraft, including fighters and dive bombers, but later plans called for an increase to fifty aircraft, and catapult launching.[106] It was expected that Carrier B, which would be ready a year or two after the Graf Zeppelin, would be a virtual twin of the Graf Zeppelin.[107]

The German navy, like the air force and the army, constantly increased the scope of its rearmament plans. In 1935, the navy gave the Luftwaffe a planning document outlining its projected aircraft requirements for 1938. By 1938 the navy expected the Luftwaffe to provide one air district commander, aircraft, and personnel for three seaplane tenders, a commander for the naval aviation corps, commanders and staffs for eighteen airfields for the group headquarters, and staffs for command and control of coastal naval air units, and a total of twenty-three small naval air squadrons, to be apportioned as follows: three coastal reconnaissance squadrons for close reconnaissance; three coastal reconnaissance squadrons for long-range reconnaissance; three general purpose seaplane/float plane squadrons; three fighter squadrons; and two fleet air squadrons. In addition, nine squadrons of aircraft were expected to staff the Graf Zeppelin carrier. This was not an especially large naval aviation force.

How did the Reichsmarine expect to use its air arm? Certainly, the emphasis on aircraft in the procurement program requested by the navy was for reconnaissance and patrol aircraft. In early 1936, in the journal *Militärwissenschaftliche Rundschau,* one navy captain outlined the doctrinal ideas behind the German naval aviation concept. Captain Metzner saw the primary purpose of the naval air arm as support of the heavy ships, especially the battleships. Consequently, the primary aircraft of the navy was to be the multipurpose seaplane.[108] Metzner saw strategic reconnaissance as a primary duty of the German navy, and saw other possibilities for the naval air arm, including using multipurpose aircraft to sow mines, an intriguing idea that had not yet been tested.[109] Captain Metzner's article on naval aviation provides some insights into how the Reichsmarine viewed the aircraft prior to the war. For example, Metzner was aware that the U.S. Navy had been successful in developing dive-bombing and torpedo aircraft operating from carriers.[110] Metzner, and the naval officers, were also aware of the aircraft carrier construction being carried out by the U.S., British, Japanese, and French navies.[111] There is, however, little understanding apparent of exactly how an aircraft carrier might operate. To Metzner, it was clearly an auxiliary naval weapon, albeit a useful one.[112] The stress on navy aviation would remain essentially defensive, and not offensive, with coastal patrol aircraft being the most useful mission of the naval aviation arm.[113]

The initial rearmament plans of the Luftwaffe included the production of several aircraft specifically designed for naval use. One of these was the Heinkel He 59, a twin-engine biplane/seaplane designed for use as a torpedo bomber, and for fleet reconnaissance. The Heinkel He 59 was a sturdy, but relatively slow aircraft, with a maximum speed of 137 miles per hour. It was designed to carry either two machine guns or a bombload of 2,000 pounds or one 1,543-pound, or one 2,205-pound naval torpedo.[114] A somewhat smaller, two-seat Heinkel seaplane, the Heinkel He 60, was also developed. The single-engine He 60 was envisioned solely as a short-range, coastal reconnaissance aircraft. Both the He 59 and the He 60 quickly entered service with the naval squadrons. The Dornier Company, which had long built some excellent flying boats, began a program in 1934 for the development of what would become the Dornier Do 18 flying boat. The Do 18 was a twin-engine aircraft, powered by Junkers 205 diesel aircraft engines. Tests were conducted in 1935 and 1936. In 1936 the Do 18 flying boat commenced service with the Luftwaffe naval air arm as a long-range patrol aircraft.[115] The Do 18 carried little armament—only two machine guns and two 110-pound bombs—but it was a reliable aircraft and set a long-distance seaplane record of 5,242 miles in March 1938.[116]

It is clear from the models and types of aircraft produced by the Luftwaffe for the naval air service that naval air doctrine in Germany had scarcely progressed beyond the earliest concept of the naval seaplane as an aircraft for fleet reconnaissance. Indeed, in this period there is only moderate interest, within the navy, in developing aircraft as a true, naval strike weapon. The obvious question arises: If naval aviation were only seen as an auxiliary arm, and not an offensive strike weapon, why did Germany's early naval plans include the construction of two aircraft carriers? The answer seems to be that the Graf Zeppelin was designed primarily as a prestige ship, symbol of German naval status rather than an integral and effective part of a combined fleet. Admiral Raeder himself, and his senior staff, were primarily battleship men, men who believed in the primacy of the heavy-gun ship, and who saw naval warfare in terms of the battle of Jutland—in other words, grand battles between heavily armed fleets. The carrier would support the fleet, but even more important, the German naval officers, like the officers of the other services, dreamed of the time that Germany would be acknowledged again as a world-class military power. Of course, any world-class military power required a large and powerful fleet. Because the fleets of the major naval powers of the era, the Royal Navy, U.S. Navy, and Japanese navy, all had aircraft carriers, Germany too would acquire an aircraft carrier—even if it wasn't sure exactly what to do with it.

CONCLUSION

On 3 June 1936 Lieutenant General Walter Wever was conducting an inspection tour of Luftwaffe installations at Dresden. Wever had flown himself to Dresden in a Heinkel He 70, one of the hottest airplanes the Luftwaffe had at that time. He was in a hurry to complete his tour and return to Berlin, for he had to attend the funeral of a World War I hero. Wever was in such a hurry that, arriving at the airfield, he violated a basic rule of flying: He did not conduct a routine pilot's check of the aircraft, using the standard checklist to ensure the aircraft was ready to fly. The checklist included releasing the switch that locked the aileron controls; this was not done. He climbed in, started the engine, and took off. Moments later, the He 70 crashed at the end of the Dresden airfield, killing General Wever and the flight mechanic accompanying him. With this simple oversight, the Luftwaffe had lost its first chief of the general staff.

Looking back at the whole history of the Luftwaffe, one can see in perspective that the loss of General Wever was a genuine disaster for the service. Wever had been an extremely effective chief of staff. During his three-year tenure, he had won the respect, even the reverence, of the Luftwaffe's officers and men. Wever had possessed both political acumen and considerable charm. He had managed to work well with both Hermann Göring and Erhard Milch—a feat demonstrating his extraordinary talent at conducting personal relationships. Although Wever had come to the Luftwaffe from the army, he had quickly won the admiration, and the cooperation, of the longtime professional airmen who constituted the core of the air staff. As a result, the vital years of early growth of the Luftwaffe were conducted in a fairly harmonious manner, with the willing cooperation of many strong personalities, coordinated effectively by Wever.

Wever had other leadership qualities. He was a general who was willing and prepared to listen and learn from his more experienced subordinates. As a military and air power thinker, Wever ranks as one of the most influential air power theorists of the twentieth century. Wever's ideas were not, for the most part, necessarily new, but he had a singular talent for assimilating ideas from many different sources, modifying and adapting those ideas into a broad and comprehensive theory of air power.

Wever stands out from most of the air power thinkers of the 1920s and 1930s. He did not take any narrow view of the role and mission of air power. For most of the officers and senior leaders in both Britain's Royal Air Force and the U.S. Army Air Corps, air power meant the strategic bomber, and theories of strategic bombing. While Wever was an enthusiastic advocate of strategic bombing, and did see the strategic bombing campaign as a primary purpose for the Luftwaffe, he was also able to view air power in a broad and comprehensive manner. To Wever, air power meant civil defense and the employment of flak artillery as well as strategic bombing. At no time did Wever forget the importance of joint operations, or of cooperating in campaigns with the other services. Luftwaffe Regulation 16, *The Conduct of the Aerial War,* stands as one of Wever's most significant contributions to air power theory and doctrine. Although Helmuth Wilberg actually wrote Regulation 16, it was Wever who provided direction for the authors, and approved the final document.

Regulation 16 is not a simple document to understand. It does not provide a simple list of panacea targets to hit in time of war. Rather, *The Conduct of the Aerial War* provides a sophisticated, rational discussion on the meaning of strategic air war, somewhat Clausewitzian in tone, concerning the advantages and disadvantages of each type of strategic target, and the circumstances by which an air campaign might be influenced. In the three years that Walter Wever served as Luftwaffe chief of staff, the Luftwaffe grew from a tiny cadre to an effective air force. By March 1935, when the Luftwaffe's existence was officially acknowledged, the Luftwaffe contained a total of 18,200 members, with 10,000 men in the flying troops, 7,200 men in the flak artillery, and 1,000 men in the air signals corps.[117] By 1936, when Wever died, this force had grown fourfold, and by the middle of 1937, the Luftwaffe had a total of 178,000 personnel, with 109,000 belonging to the flying troops, 46,000 belonging to the flak artillery, and almost 23,000 belonging to the air signals corps.[118]

Under the leadership of Erhard Milch, after Wever's death, the German air industry had become a first-class organization, and the rearmament program was in high gear with a generation of highly effective aircraft beginning to reach the Luftwaffe flying units and flak units. The German flak corps at this time was the largest and most effective in the world. In many areas of military organization and doctrine, for instance, civil defense, the Germans led the world.

In many respects, Walter Wever demonstrated considerable innovation in his ideas of air doctrine and of organization within the Luftwaffe. His 1935 decision to create an airborne corps within the Luftwaffe would have tremendous strategic implications at the beginning of World War II.

Finally, the role of Wilhelm Wimmer, who took Erhardt Milch's rearmament program and translated plans into prototype aircraft, deserves recognition for his role in the buildup of the Luftwaffe in its early years. When Wever died, materielly the Luftwaffe was in excellent shape, thanks to Wimmer, with an effective development program, and could look forward to a future of receiving some of the finest aircraft in the world of that era. In short, under Wever's direction, the Luftwaffe was in an excellent position, in 1936, to grow from a moderate-sized air force into a world-class air force with first-rate equipment, equipped with an effective doctrine for battlefield and strategic operations.

The Luftwaffe, so carefully built up by Erhard Milch, equipped by Wilhelm Wimmer and his staff, and given a doctrine and organization by Walter Wever, would undergo a severe military test of its readiness doctrine and capabilities, within a few weeks of Walter Wever's death. Unforeseen by anyone in Germany, the situation in Spain was rapidly building up to a civil war. By July 1936, the Luftwaffe, with no plans or preparations, would find itself engaged in an aerial war against tough aerial opposition. This war would, moreover, not be fought in or near Germany, but rather in Spain, at the end of a long logistics pipeline in thoroughly unfamiliar surroundings.

CHAPTER SIX

The Luftwaffe in the Spanish Civil War, 1936–1939

By 1936 Spain was effectively divided into two nations. One nation was conservative, Catholic, and nationalist. There were strong factions arguing for the return of the monarchy, and the 1930s had also seen the rise of a large fascist party, the Falange. The other nation was a coalition of forces that held the majority in the Spanish parliament. These included socialists, radical socialists, anarchists, progressives, and assorted liberals supported strongly by the labor unions and the poor tenant farmers of Spain. Since the defeat of the attempted right-wing coup d'etat in 1932, the situation between the two Spains became ever more polarized. By summer of 1936 right-wing forces led by a coalition of army generals were deep in planning for a national uprising. The uprising itself was triggered 13 July 1936 when Calvo Sotelo, the leader of right-wing opposition in Spanish parliament, was arrested and then assassinated by the government police. A few days later, on 17 July 1936, much of the Spanish army, backed by an assortment of monarchists, conservatives, and Fascists, went into open revolt against the republic. After several days of confused fighting, much of Spain had declared itself for the Nationalist coalition. However, attempts by the Nationalists to seize control of Madrid and Barcelona were soundly defeated as a large part of the army and police, supported by most of the air force and navy and backed by an assortment of workers militias, declared itself for the defense of the Spanish republic.

One of the most decisive events in the early days of the rising of Spain was the success of the Nationalist rebellion in Spanish Morocco. General Francisco Franco, the most decorated officer in the Spanish army and hero of the colonial wars in North Africa, flew from the Canary Islands to assume command of the rebellion in Spanish Morocco. Morocco was vital for the Nationalists' cause because it had a large military garrison with the best-trained and equipped troops of the Spanish army. The approximately 30,000 troops of the Morocco garrison included the tough Spanish Foreign Legion veterans and a large number of Moorish troops. These forces, the best troops in the Spanish army, could have a decisive effect in defeating the forces of the Republic who were generally poorly trained and equipped. However, because the Spanish navy had, for the most part, opted in favor of the Republic, Franco's forces were effectively marooned in North Africa. They were unable to cross the short distance of the Mediterranean into Spain due to the Republican naval blockade. General Franco's first requirement was to obtain aircraft so that he could fly his North African troops directly to the Nationalist stronghold of Seville in southern Spain and thus bypass the Republican naval blockade.[1]

With the Nationalist cause faltering a week into the initial rising, General Franco dispatched two German businessmen who were residents of Spanish North Africa to Germany to plead his cause with the German chancellor. Adolf Langenheim and Johannes Bernhardt were members of the Nazi party and believers in the Spanish Nationalist cause. Bernhardt and Langenheim flew to Germany on 25 July in a civilian German Ju 52 passenger transport. Due to their Nazi party connections, they were able to meet with Rudolf Hess, who quickly arranged for them to meet with Hitler—who that night was attending the Wagnerfest at Bayreuth. On the night of 25/26 July, the two German businessmen met with Hitler and related General Franco's message with its request for aircraft and military equipment for the Nationalist cause. Hitler immediately agreed to provide aircraft and military equipment to Franco and told Hermann Göring, who was attending to Hitler in Bayreuth that day, to make arrangements. Göring, who initially had no enthusiasm for the operation, was capable of moving quickly and decisively when it pleased the Führer. Göring got on the phone to the Luftwaffe headquarters in Berlin and the next morning, 26 July, Lt. General Helmuth Wilberg was ordered to form a special staff to organize Luftwaffe assistance to the Spanish Nationalists. Within two days, Wilberg had created Special Staff W (for Wilberg). Plans were made and orders quickly issued. By 31 July, Germany aircraft and personnel were on their way to Spanish Morocco.[2]

THE AIRLIFT FROM NORTH AFRICA

The first Luftwaffe force to be committed to the Nationalist cause was a group of twenty Ju-52 transports, which were deployed by flying them directly from Germany, refueling in Italy, and then on to Spanish Morocco. The first German transports arrived in North Africa at the end of July, and the Luftwaffe pilots began airlifting troops of the Nationalist army into Spain.

At the same time that the transport aircraft were being deployed, a force of Luftwaffe fighter pilots, flak gunners, and support personnel was quickly assembled and embarked with aircraft, antiaircraft guns, munitions, and other equipment by ship to Spain. It was decided the German air transport force would need protection in the form of fighter aircraft and antiaircraft guns so the first ship carrying aircraft and guns, the *Usaramo,* left Hamburg on 31 July.[3] This hastily assembled Luftwaffe detachment included six Heinkel He 51 fighters, twenty antiaircraft guns, and personnel to man both the aircraft and the guns. The Usaramo arrived in Spanish waters on 6 August. More ships with guns, planes, men, and munitions were already sailing from Germany to Spain. It is a testimony to the competence of General Wilberg and his Luftwaffe staff that within four days of the decision being made to support the Spanish Nationalist rebellion a significant force of German aircraft and personnel were already deployed on their way to Spain.[4]

During the 1920s, the RAF had occasionally flown small company-sized units by air transports around the Middle East to conduct imperial policing duties. The U.S. Army Air Corps in the early 1930s had also practiced moving squadron support personnel around the country on maneuvers by air transport. However, up to this time, there had never been a major airlift carried out. Nevertheless, at the end of July, the Luftwaffe transport force assisted by a small number of the Italian bombers and an assortment of Nationalist aircraft, began airlifting troops of the Nationalist army to the Spanish mainland.[5] When the airlift began the Luftwaffe transports were carrying over 1,200 men per week from North Africa to Seville accompanied by their equipment.[6] By the week of 10–16 August 1936, the Luftwaffe was able to airlift 2,853 soldiers along with 7,985 kilos of equipment.[7] On 11 October 1936, the airlift ended as, by this time, the Nationalists had gained control of the air over the Straits of Gibraltar and were now able to begin shipping men and material into Spain by sea transports protected by air cover. Between the end of July and mid-October 1936, over 20,000 Nationalist soldiers were airlifted into Spain.[8] Of this total over approximately two-thirds, or 13,000 troops, had been airlifted by the Luftwaffe along with a total of 270,199 kilos of equipment including machine guns, artillery pieces, and ammunitions. The entire operation was carried out under extremely arduous conditions with the loss of only one aircraft.[9]

The airlift of the North African army to mainland Spain was one of the decisive military operations of the Spanish Civil War. Indeed, the German-organized airlift probably saved the Nationalist cause from defeat in summer of 1936. The airlift itself demonstrated that an entirely new factor could be added to the primary attributes of military air power, for the airlift of 1936 proved that air power was something much more than just strategic bombing.

Condor Legion Ju 52 transporting Moroccan troops to Spain in 1936 in the first major airlift in history. (Photo from Heinz Bongartz, *Luftmacht Deutschland.* Essen: Essener Verlagsansalt, 1939.)

An airlift of over 20,000 men along with their equipment demonstrated that a new factor of mobility had been added to warfare. At the time, the airlift was recognized as a great success and a major innovation in air doctrine. Brigadier Hap Arnold, of the U.S. Army Air Corps, wrote in 1937 that the Luftwaffe airlift in Spain had been one of the most important developments in military air power in recent years.[10]

EARLY GERMAN OPERATIONS

As soon as the airlift operations were functioning smoothly it was decided that some of the Ju 52 transports could be converted into bombers and used to support the Nationalist forces then engaged in desperate fighting on their way to relieve the garrison of the Alcazar in Toledo and then in their advance on Madrid. In late August 1936 German airmen began flying a few small bombing missions against the Republicans. These were usually in the form of harassment raids against enemy airfields.[11] By September, several hundred

Luftwaffe personnel were in Spain and by the end of September a total of twenty Ju 52 transport/bombers, twenty-four Heinkel He 51 fighters, and twenty-nine He 46 reconnaissance aircraft/light bombers had arrived as a part of the German contingent.[12] With fighter escorts now available, the German aircraft started conducting more bombing missions.

In September 1936, the Germans started taking their first battle losses. In addition to bombing Republican logistics targets, the primary target of Luftwaffe aircraft in Spain was enemy troop concentrations.[13] In September 1936, the first low-level attacks in support of the Nationalist infantry were made by the Luftwaffe.[14] With German air support, the Nationalist cause was faring well and by October 1936, Nationalist units were closing in on the capital of Madrid. By the end of October 1936 the Nationalists began conducting some air raids against Madrid itself.[15]

However, the Germans and Italians were not the only major power intervening in the Spanish Civil War. In September 1936 the Soviet government decided to send significant military aid to the Republic to include not only equipment but military advisers and military pilots as well.[16] Soviet arms shipments to the Republic began in September 1936 and by October significant aid was on the way.[17] In October 1936 alone, the Soviets dispatched 311 trucks, sixty-five tanks, numerous aircraft, and large quantities of munitions. In that same month over 300 Soviet pilots and military advisers also departed for the war in Spain.[18]

By the end of October 1936, when the Nationalist forces reached Madrid, Soviet tanks and aircraft had arrived in Spain and were available to counter the Nationalist thrust.[19] On 29 October, a strong force of Russian T-26 tanks, an armored force that outclassed anything the Nationalists had on the battlefield, as well as Russian SB-2 bombers appeared over the Madrid front.[20] At the same time Soviet-supplied modern Republican aircraft began a campaign against the Nationalist airfields.[21] The Russian-supported counterattack at the end of October provided a major shock to the Nationalist leaders. Not only were the Russian tanks the best armored vehicles on the battlefields of Spain but the Russian-provided and often piloted SB-2 bombers were superior to the improvised Ju 52 bombers of the Germans. The Soviet I-15 and I-16 fighter planes were superior to the Heinkel 51 and Fiat biplane fighters of the Nationalists. By November 1936 the Republicans had gained air superiority over the vital Madrid front.[22] Before the end of 1936, the war had obviously bogged down, and the tide had turned in favor of the Republicans—primarily because of the arrival of modern Russian equipment.[23]

In an attempt to break the stalemate on the Madrid front, the German,

Italian, and Nationalist air units began a bombing campaign against Madrid between 18 and 22 November.[24] This was not the first attempt to bring strategic bombing into the conflict in Spain. In the early months of the war both sides had carried out some relatively minor raids on each others' cities. However, the raids against Madrid in 1936 were the most significant example of strategic bombing in that war to date. On 30 November 1936 the Nationalist bombing of Madrid inflicted a total of 244 civilian dead and 875 wounded.[25] Yet, the strategic bombing raids conducted during the first half year of the Spanish Civil War, including the Madrid raids, had very little effect on the war or on the morale of either side. The bombing of Madrid was soon called off partly because night bombing was inaccurate and day bombing was far too dangerous for the Nationalist bombers in the face of Republican/Soviet air superiority. By December 1936 on the Madrid front, Nationalists found themselves unable to fly except in large formations and under heavy fighter escort.[26]

GERMAN STRATEGY IN SPAIN

The initial German decision to intervene in the Spanish conflict was based on the belief that a relatively small force of aircraft and support troops combined with guns, munitions, and military advisers could quickly turn the tide for the Nationalist cause and enable a quick victory in Spain. Soviet intervention and large-scale support for the Republic had foiled the German strategy and by October it was clear to all the intervening governments that the war was becoming a stalemate. At the end of October 1936 the Wehrmacht high command decided to dramatically increase the air force support to the Nationalist cause. The German force of a few hundred men and a handful of aircraft would be expanded to a force of approximately 5,000 mostly Luftwaffe personnel to be equipped with over 100 of the most modern aircraft the Luftwaffe could provide.[27]

This expanded force in Spain would be called the Condor Legion and as it was envisioned, would consist of a staff, a bomber group of three to four squadrons, a fighter group of three to four squadrons, a reconnaissance group of two squadrons, a seaplane squadron, a communications battalion, a logistics supply battalion, a medical detachment, and a flak battalion that would consist of eight batteries (five batteries of 88-mm guns, two batteries of light 20- and 37-mm antiaircraft guns, one battery for training Spanish personnel). The Condor Legion would also include experimental flight, which would include the latest preproduction models of German aircraft for combat testing.[28] In addition to the large Luftwaffe commitment to Spain, the army would provide a small tank battalion and a couple hundred military advisers who would run training schools for the Nationalist officers and army units. The army units would be, in turn, supported by logistics elements of the Condor Legion. Colonel Warlimont, who had commanded the Germans in Spain since August 1936, was replaced by Major General Hugo Sperrle, who would serve as commander in chief of all German forces in Spain. Sperrle arrived in Spain on 1 November 1936 and he was soon followed by Lieutenant Colonel Wolfram Freiherr von Richthofen who was initially slated to command the experimental aircraft squadron but, after his arrival in Spain, was assigned to be chief of staff of the Condor Legion.

Aside from the initial decision made to commit German forces and aid to the Nationalists in Spain in July 1936, neither Hitler nor senior members of the Nazi leadership ever showed any particular interest in the German military operations in Spain. Thus, somewhat by default, the Luftwaffe and the Wehrmacht high command came to bear the primary responsibility for the execution of the German war effort in Spain. This also included the political and strategic as well as the operational decisions. From the Wehrmacht point of view, Spain and the Mediterranean were not important areas of German interest, but there were still significant advantages that Germany could gain by supporting the Nationalists. First of all, Germany's primary enemy, France, would be discomforted and distracted by a pro-German government on her southern border. Because Italy was also competing with French interests in the Mediterranean, this now meant that France would have to face three unfriendly nations on her borders.[29] Second, because the Soviet Union was providing equipment and personnel to Republican Spain, a defeat for the Republic would be a defeat for Soviet prestige. At a time when Germany was making a strong diplomatic effort to turn central and southern European states into its client states and allies against the Soviets, the high command did not want to see a Soviet political victory in the Mediterranean.[30] The German military was also deeply concerned about raw materials for its massive rearmament program. Spain was a mineral-rich country, and a friendly Spanish government could provide plentiful and stable supplies of high-grade iron ore, mercury, wolfram, pyrites, and other necessities for the arms industry.[31] Finally, a limited commitment of German forces in Spain would serve as effective live fire exercises in which the Luftwaffe in particular could try out its newest equipment and a cadre of the German military could gain experience in combat operations.

Major General Hugo Sperrle, ca. 1937. Sperrle was the commander of the Condor Legion, November 1936–November 1937. (Photo from the von Richthofen family.)

All these factors taken together provided a reasonable justification for sending equipment, aircraft, and the 5,000 troops of the Condor Legion to Spain. From the beginning, the German military operations in Spain were kept to a modest level. While a Nationalist Spain would be useful to the conduct of German strategy, Germany could also not justify risking a general European war or even the commitment of major ground forces. Germany was at this time in the midst of a major rearmament program and could not spare the men or equipment for a large-scale intervention. Indeed, the German military negotiated carefully with Franco as to the amount and type of German military assistance that he required. In 1936, when Franco requested an increase in German assistance, he argued that he needed modern equipment and training for his ground forces and air units. Franco never requested the commitment of German ground units.[32] It was established that German forces in Spain would operate under the strategic direction of General Franco and the Spanish high command yet would operate as a single force under German tactical command. The chain of command for the Germans went directly from the Spanish high command to the commander of the Condor Legion. The Condor Legion, in turn, had a fairly simple chain of command in which the Condor Legion chief reported to Special Staff W in Berlin and to the Wehrmacht high command.

The Luftwaffe and the Wehrmacht worked incessantly to keep the German commitment to Spain to a limited level and Franco and the Spanish approved of this policy. However, the German ambassador to Franco, Wilhelm Faupel, a World War I general and staunch Nazi, opposed the military's strategy for Spain. When Faupel arrived in Spain in November 1936, he began to lobby Berlin to send German divisions to Spain.[33] In a meeting in Berlin of Hitler, Faupel, and the senior leaders of the Wehrmacht, including Field Marshal Werner von Blomberg (war minister) and Colonel General Werner von Fritsch, army commander in chief, on 22 December 1936, the German military leaders unanimously opposed Faupel and his ideas of sending German divisions to Spain and increasing the level of aid to Nationalists.[34] Blomberg, Fritsch, and Colonel General Ludwig Beck, chief of the army general staff, pointed out that Germany was in the midst of a major rearmament program and the shipment of a large ground force to Spain would strip the military of the equipment and officers required to build a new army for the Third Reich.[35] The military high command was also concerned about provoking French intervention on the side of the Spanish Loyalists, which would have the potential of igniting a general European war—a war that the Wehrmacht was not ready to fight in 1936–1937.[36] During the entire course of the war, the

Wehrmacht staff monitored the political situation and was careful not to commit so much force to Nationalist Spain that it would push France into the conflict.[37] For example, during the war the Wehrmacht high command issued instructions that no German aircraft were to fly within 50 kilometers of the French border. Although General Keitel, chief of the high command, thought the danger of French intervention was minimal, nevertheless he directed that Condor Legion aircraft avoid combat near the border unless the Spanish were to request otherwise.[38]

When Faupel arrived in Spain in November 1936 as German ambassador to Franco, he immediately came into conflict with General Sperrle and senior Luftwaffe officers. Faupel's instructions were explicit in denying him any military authority.[39] However, Faupel immediately tried to set himself up as Franco's military adviser.[40] Indeed, Ambassador Faupel provides an interesting example of the Nazi party's incompetence in dealing with the complex matters of foreign policy. On the surface, Faupel seemed an acceptable choice for ambassador due to his fluency in Spanish and his directorship of the German Iberian-American Institute. However, Faupel's primary qualification for the job was his long membership to the Nazi party and his commitment to Nazi ideology. Although Germany had career diplomats who were fluent in Spanish and experienced in Spanish affairs, Faupel received his appointment partly to increase Nazi influence within the senior ranks of the foreign service bureaucracy.

Faupel soon alienated Franco and the Spanish high command by his attempts to meddle in internal Spanish politics. Faupel argued with Franco that Spain needed to remodel the Falange party on the image of the Nazi party, a policy that ran counter to Franco's position of building a Nationalist coalition of businessmen, monarchists, and conservative Catholics as well as the Falangists.[41] While irritating Franco, Faupel also upset the Condor Legion senior officers by his attempts to provide Franco with military advice. The relationship between the ambassador and the Luftwaffe was soon so strained that the Condor Legion installations were directed to refuse gasoline for the ambassador's car.[42] By July 1937, Faupel, who continued to argue that a much larger German contingent should be committed to Spain, demanded that General Sperrle be reprimanded by the high command.[43] This was too much for the German military. Faupel was finally relieved of his ambassadorship and summarily returned to Germany. His replacement was an experienced career diplomat who followed his instructions and stayed out of military affairs.

Both the professional officers of the Wehrmacht high command and the

Luftwaffe did an effective job in providing strategic direction for the German military intervention in Spain. In most respects, senior Luftwaffe officers in Spain possessed a sound grasp of the politics of war and of coalition operations. Von Richthofen, for example, had served as the air attaché to Italy from 1929–1932. He spoke Italian fluently and quickly learned Spanish.[44] Von Richthofen sized up the situation when he arrived in Spain and recommended that Berlin not commit too much aid to the Nationalists. "The Spanish have to win this war for themselves."[45] Both von Richthofen and Sperrle were convinced that Franco would never have been seen as a legitimate ruler in Spain if the primary burden of the Nationalist war effort were borne by foreign powers. Although the Condor Legion commander often disagreed with Franco on strategic matters, he never committed Faupel's faux pas of trying to interfere with Nationalist internal politics.[46] The Condor Legion commanders throughout the war provided sound strategic advice to Franco. Yet, even when German advice was not taken, the strategic/operational dialogue was appreciated by the Spanish. From the early days of German intervention in Spain, the Luftwaffe officers formed a good professional partnership with the Nationalist high command.

COMBAT OPERATIONS IN NORTHERN SPAIN, 1937

During the winter of 1936/1937 the Condor Legion underwent a period of reequipping and reorganizing. Conditions in poor and war-battered Spain were such that to conduct operations, the Germans had to set up a logistics network as well as create a modern meteorological service.[47] While flying a few minor missions, the major activity for the Condor Legion during this period was rearming with the latest German aircraft straight from the factory. The Ju 52 bombers were either turned over to the Spanish or reverted to their original status as transport aircraft while the Condor Legion bomber group was equipped with brand-new Heinkel 111, Dornier Do 17, and Junkers Ju 86 bombers—some of the most modern medium bombers available in the world at that time.[48] In early 1937, the Condor Legion began to receive some of the first production models of the Me 109 fighters. The Me 109 fighter that was sent to Spain was the B-1 production model. It had a maximum speed of 292 miles per hour and an operational ceiling of 30,000 feet.[49] Some of the Heinkel 51 fighters were transferred to the Nationalist air force but the Condor Legion retained a couple of squadrons of He 51s, which, although ineffective as fighter planes in air-to-air combat, had proven themselves useful as ground attack aircraft.

While the Luftwaffe in Spain was reorganizing, the Republican air force, now well equipped with modern Russian aircraft and Soviet pilots and instructors as well as support personnel, provided a demonstration of the decisive effect that air power could have on the battlefield. In March 1937, the Republicans counterattacked a motorized corps of Italian troops at Guadalajara. The Republican air force used a force 125, mostly Russian-piloted, new fighter aircraft, which interdicted the Italian columns strung along the roads. The corps of approximately 50,000 troops was quickly routed—primarily by the effect of Republican air power. The Italian army had 500 killed, 2,000 wounded, and 500 taken prisoner. Another estimated 1,000 vehicles and twenty-five artillery pieces were destroyed, again primarily by air power.[50] The impressive Republican victory at Guadalajara was one of the most dramatic examples of the era of what air power could accomplish on the battlefield. The results of that battle were extensively analyzed by the world military press.

While the Republican side was showing what air power was capable of in central Spain, the Condor Legion began to redeploy to airfields in northern Spain in March 1937. Northern Spain, where Republican enclaves existed in the Basque and Asturias regions, was seen by the Nationalists and the Luftwaffe as being extremely vulnerable to an offensive campaign. In the fall of 1936 the Nationalist army capture of San Sebastian cut off the Basque region from the rest of Loyalist Spain. The Basque forces could get military equipment and reinforcements only with great difficulty through the Nationalist naval blockade. With a superiority of ground forces and logistics as well as possessing a far larger air force than the Basques, the Nationalist junta saw the opportunity to overrun all of northern Spain and deal a severe blow to the Spanish Republic.

The primary mission of the Condor Legion headquarters and staff in the northern campaign of 1937 was to coordinate the air war against the Basque forces. The entire Condor Legion deployed to northern Spain to the airfields in the Vitoria area and General Franco gave the Condor Legion responsibility for all air operations in the theater—which meant that Spanish Nationalist squadrons and Italian squadrons came under German control. When the Condor Legion deployed to the north it had approximately 100 operational aircraft supported by two to three Nationalist Spanish air squadrons. This gave the Nationalist coalition forces over 150 aircraft in the northern sector.[51] To oppose the Nationalist air force and the Condor Legion, the Basques had a mere handful of aircraft. During the spring campaign the Republican government sent a force of ten fighter planes to fly across Nationalist Spain to reinforce the Basques. Of these, only seven arrived and the Republic gave up further attempts to reinforce the Basques by air.[52] Thus, the Nationalist forces were assured overwhelming air superiority both in quantity and quality of aircraft. The northern campaign would be the Luftwaffe's first major opportunity to show what a modern air force could achieve in combat.

The Nationalist offensive against the Basque region began at the end of March 1937, spearheaded by a force of several infantry divisions under the command of General Mola, the northern theater commander. The Basque army had dug in deeply into the mountainous terrain and, at the start, the Nationalist offensive progressed slowly. At this point in the war, the conflict had been going on for less than a year and both armies were still relatively poorly trained. The officer corps of the Spanish army, with the exception of the officers who had field experience in Morocco, were not particularly well trained nor did they have much troop-leading experience. The Nationalist forces were also weak in their artillery arm, with only a handful of batteries of World War I era guns. Given this situation, the Condor Legion was generally deployed throughout the campaign in direct support of the army, as flying artillery operating at the front lines or close behind the front lines. Indeed, due to the lack of Nationalist artillery, it was repeatedly necessary to use the Condor Legion's firepower to blast through the Basque defenses. In addition to the use of aircraft in the close support role, approximately half of the Condor Legion's flak force was brought up to the front lines and the 88-mm flak guns used as direct fire artillery.

As the Nationalist offensive in the north kicked off there was considerable friction between the Condor Legion and the Nationalist army. Many Condor Legion reports indicate German irritation with the Nationalists' inability to coordinate ground attacks with air support. The Condor Legion would carefully plan and execute air attacks against the Basque front line, but the Nationalists seemed incapable of following up their air attacks with ground attacks which took advantage of the shock effect of heavy aerial bombardment.[53] Thus, the Basque army was repeatedly given the opportunity to recover, reorganize, and to conduct an orderly retreat.

The Luftwaffe had to work hard to overcome the problems of coordinating an air/ground offensive. Each operation had to be carefully planned with German airmen coordinating with the Nationalist staff at the top level. At lower levels the Luftwaffe assigned liaison and communications teams to the front lines to ensure that there were good communications between the Nationalist army units and the supporting Luftwaffe units.[54] The coordination of the air and ground forces improved markedly during the course of the campaign.[55] However, despite improved communications and better signals to

Northern Spain, spring 1937. Major General Sperrle (standing center in Spanish uniform) with Spanish and German officers observing air strikes on Basque positions to their front. Major Siebert, Condor Legion communications officer, is standing on left. (Photo from the Von Richthofen family.)

prevent friendly fire, there were still several instances of German and Italian aircraft dropping bombs on Nationalist infantry in April 1937.[56]

Although the Luftwaffe doctrine emphasized use of air power in mass, one tactic employed regularly by the Luftwaffe in Spain that was found to be very successful was the tactic of shuttle attacks; that is, sending one flight at a time down to drop bombs on enemy positions and then returning to base to rearm and refuel while the next flight in the squadron took over the attack. Because the Condor Legion bases were close to the Basque front lines, it was possible for the Condor Legion to fly three or more sorties per day on the same objective by May 1937.[57] The tactic of shuttle attacks meant that the enemy could be kept under pressure for hours at a time, which increased the stress and psychological pressure on an enemy defender.[58] Air power was soon to show some impressive results. On 4 April heavy air attack preceded the Nationalists' ground attack against Basque positions at Ochandiano. After heavy aerial saturation bombardment, the Nationalist ground forces were able to overrun Basque positions with little resistance—finding over 200

Basque soldiers killed by air attack and taking 400 prisoners too dazed to retreat.[59] By employing all of the bombers of the Condor Legion in mass at Ochandiano, the Germans were able to rain down 60 tons of bombs within two minutes on one position. As von Richthofen put it "there were many dead and the target was clearly destroyed."[60]

Good communications remained the primary problem in conducting the support operations for the ground forces in Spain. Direct ground-to-air communications was not possible with the radios available, so each ground attack mission had to be preplanned and carefully coordinated by signals in the form of smoke, flares, panels, and lights. General Sperrle and Colonel von Richthofen made a point of personally observing and coordinating major ground strikes from forward command posts where they could observe Luftwaffe aircraft attacking Basque positions, which were usually on the neighboring hills.[61]

With strong and effective air support from the Condor Legion, the Nationalist forces relentlessly pushed the Basque army back toward Bilbao. The campaign in the north for the Condor Legion remained essentially a tactical air campaign, although some missions were flown against transportation targets near Bilbao. Although the Basque air defense was weak, the Condor Legion found it necessary to escort the Legion bombers with the new Me 109 fighter planes that quickly proved to be the best fighters in Spain—more than a match for any fighters the Loyalist forces could send against them. However, it is interesting to note even in circumstances of general air superiority the Luftwaffe learned the lesson that bombers need to be escorted by fighters.[62]

During April and early May 1937 the Nationalist army, with an impressive level of air support, pushed the Basques out of one position after another. A considerable effort was made by the Condor Legion to conduct interdiction campaigns to target Basque reserve forces and supplies to the rear of the front lines. During the northern campaign it became a standard Luftwaffe practice to attack the villages close behind the front, which normally contained the Basque troop reserves. In this manner Durango and Guernica were both bombed by the Condor Legion in April 1937.

During the spring of 1937 the Basque army built an impressive line of fortifications around the major Basque city of Bilbao. The fortifications, called the "Iron Belt," were actually two lines of fortifications built by engineers and architects, which consisted of bunkers and well-made strong points, some made of reinforced concrete, and connected by trench lines with machine gun nests sited every 500 meters. The line was 35 kilometers long and extended from northwest of Bilbao completely around the city to the east. Held by large a Basque force, it was in every way as strong a defense line as had been seen during much of the World War I.[63] By early June the Basque army had retreated behind the Iron Belt. Because its flanks rested on the sea it could only be neutralized by frontal assault. Because the Nationalist army was deficient in artillery and possessed no significant numerical advantage over the Basque army on the ground, the Condor Legion was put to work planning an air campaign that could breech the Iron Belt and open the way for the Nationalists to seize Bilbao. Once Bilbao was taken, the Basque resistance would collapse due to loss of supplies and armaments production. The Condor Legion thus put all of its resources toward the saturation bombing of vital sectors of the Iron Belt with its heaviest bombs. By this time, coordination of the ground and air forces had improved to the point where air attacks were quickly followed up by ground attacks and the air forces could react to any ground forces' requirements for additional support. Heavy bombing proved devastatingly effective against the Iron Belt and between 12 and 14 June the Condor Legion and the Nationalist army broke through the Basque defenses near the town of Fica.[64] The Condor Legion and Nationalist air force were effective not only in shattering the Basque fortifications, but were also used to prevent the Basques from bringing reserves up to the threatened parts of the line. The air forces assisted the Nationalist divisions in conducting a pursuit campaign against the Basque army once the breech in the lines was effected.[65]

Five days later, on 19 June 1937, Bilbao surrendered leaving a small enclave in the Asturias region to be mopped up by Nationalist forces during the summer. With the fall of Bilbao, the Republic lost one of its major industrial centers and the Nationalists proved that they could inflict decisive military defeats on the Republican government. The Condor Legion had proved that it could adapt to the circumstances of the Spanish War and could effectively coordinate an air ground campaign and overcome powerful defensive positions. It is no exaggeration to say that the Condor Legion made the Nationalist victory in the north possible. Not only did the Condor Legion and Nationalist aircraft inflict heavy casualties on the Basques and managed to blow defending troops out of carefully prepared positions, but air power in the interdiction role made it extremely difficult for the defenders to reinforce threatened points and react quickly and in strength to Nationalist ground movements. In short, air power in northern Spain in 1937 not only proved that it had great shock and destructive effects, but also proved that the side possessing air superiority would hold the initiative on the battlefield.

THE GUERNICA MYTH

The Condor Legion played the lead role in the single most famous incident of the Spanish Civil War. The air attack on Guernica, a small Basque town located close behind the Republican army lines, on 26 April 1937 became the most written about single battle action of the Spanish Civil War. Indeed, the bombing of Guernica by the Luftwaffe became, through the image of Pablo Picasso's most famous painting and extensive contemporary coverage in the world press, the symbol of the nature of the air war in Spain.

Guernica had a population of 5,000 and was located at the site of an important crossroad and bridge in the Basque mountains. The town had great emotional significance to the Basques because it contained the Basque parliament building as well as the sacred oak tree of the Basque people. On 26 April, a force of 43 Condor Legion bombers and fighters (the bombers being mostly the Ju 52 converted transports) dropped a total of approximately 50 tons of high explosive, shrapnel, and incendiary bombs on the town, leveling about half the town and causing heavy casualties.[66] Foreign correspondents writing for the *Times* of London and the *New York Times* as well as representatives of the Basque government, labeled the attack on Guernica as a "terror attack." One correspondent wrote "the raid on Guernica is unparalleled in military history. Guernica was not a military objective. The factory producing war material lay outside of town . . . the object of the bombardment was seemingly the demoralization of the civil population and the destruction of the cradle of the Basque race."[67] This was the story that went out to the world with numerous embellishments as Guernica became synonymous with the deliberate bombing of innocent civilians. A New York editorial said "none of the other atrocities of this sanguinary civil war has been more conclusively attested than this latest example of ruthlessness . . . against the terrorism of fire and destruction from the skies were pitted in the deep courage and deep faith of the people and their priests."[68] The *New York Post* printed a cartoon of Guernica showing mountains of civilian dead labeled "the Holy City of Guernica" with Hitler standing over with his bloody sword, which was captioned "air raids."[69] The U.S. Congressional Record even referred to poison gas used at Guernica[70]—an event that never occurred. The official civilian casualty statistics from numbers presented by the Basque government were 1,654 dead and 889 wounded.[71]

To this day, the German bombing of Guernica has maintained an almost mythical significance as a symbol of deliberate terror bombing carried out to break civilian morale. Even in fairly recent works of military history the bombing of Guernica is referred to as a "terror bombing" or "horror bombing." The total of over 2,500 casualties—fully half the town's population—has been commonly accepted by many historians.[72]

There is no evidence to indicate that the German air attack on Guernica was a "terror bombing" or that Guernica was carefully targeted to break the morale of the Basque populace. None of the German officers involved in planning and conducting the raid was familiar with the Basque culture and language. Wolfram von Richthofen, who planned the raid, seems to have been unaware that Guernica contained the Basque parliament building or the holy oak tree of the Basque nation while he studied the target. Von Richthofen only mentioned these facts when he visited Guernica for the first time on 30 April, shortly after the town fell to the Nationalists. He made some tourist-like remarks in his diary about the part of the town not bombed by the Condor Legion.[73] Von Richthofen's lack of knowledge about the Basques is further attested to his consistent references to the Basque as "Reds" in his reports to Berlin—although the Basques were capitalists—the only major group that fought for the Republic that could make that claim.[74] The Condor Legion bombed Guernica because of the simple fact that it was a significant military target. The two major roads needed for the retreat of much of the twenty-three Basque battalions east of Bilbao intersected at Guernica. At least two Basque battalions, the 18th Loyala Battalion and the Saseta Battalion, were stationed in the town. If fortified, Guernica would have made a powerful strong point for the Basque army. which would further delay the Nationalist advance.[75] If Guernica were leveled, the roads and bridge would be closed and the retreating Basque forces would be unable to bring out their vehicles and heavy equipment. This aspect of the attack was a military success because the bombing and firing of Guernica closed the area to traffic for about twenty-four hours.[76] While von Richthofen commented that the raid on Guernica was a "technical success" he was disappointed that the Nationalist army had not followed up the raid quickly enough and seized the town, and by doing so, cut off the retreat of much of the Basque army.[77]

More recent studies of the Guernica raid have come up with a realistic casualty figure of about 300 civilian dead instead of the well-known figure of over 1,600 dead.[78] As in so many wars, the 300 dead civilians of Guernica had not been deliberately targeted, but had unfortunately found themselves in the way of a military operation.

There is no evidence that Wolfram von Richthofen, who served as a senior Luftwaffe commander in Spain, Poland, the low countries, France, against Britain, and in Russia, ever carried out the policy of terror bombing or the deliberate targeting of civilians. On the other hand, von Richthofen was a ruthless commander who never expressed any sympathy or concern for civilians who might be located in the vicinity of the military target. Von Richthofen's actions at Guernica and throughout the Spanish War and World War II showed consistency in this attitude toward targeting.

The operational rationale of the Luftwaffe in bombing towns like Guernica is set out in a report of the Condor Legion commander made to Berlin on 11 February 1938. "We have notable results in hitting the targets near the front, especially in bombing villages which hold enemy reserves and headquarters. We have had great success because these targets are easy to find and can be thoroughly destroyed by carpet bombing." In the report it was noted that attacks on point targets, such as bridges, roads, and rail lines, were more difficult and generally less successful.[79] Essentially, the Germans could not hit the most vital point target in Guernica: the Rentaria Bridge, because the improvised Ju 52 bombers and the bombsights available in 1937 were simply not capable of delivering ordnance on target. The Nationalist high command was sanguine about the tactic of carpet bombing villages close to the front lines. Even the official Spanish histories of the Civil War contain photographs of Spanish towns under aerial bombardment by the Nationalist air force.[80]

In many respects, the press's sensationalized reporting of the bombing of Guernica worked to the advantage of Hitler's regime prior to the outbreak of World War II. People throughout the world received the impression that the Germans had created a fearsome air force that could obliterate entire cities—forgetting that Guernica was not a city but a small town. In reality, the Luftwaffe of 1937 was incapable of leveling a large city, nor had the Germans incorporated city-busting into their doctrine. However, the British and French governments saw the example of Guernica and assumed that the Germans were looking toward a city-bombing strategy in future war.[81] The German bombing of Guernica had a tremendous psychological effect on the population of western Europe. As Harold Macmillan remarked, "We thought of air warfare in 1938 rather as people think of nuclear warfare today."[82] The inflated image of German aerial capabilities, as depicted by the popular accounts of Guernica, played an important role in helping Adolph Hitler bluff his way through the Munich agreements and forcibly annex a major German enemy, Czechoslovakia, without any resistance from the British or French, or even a shot being fired by the Czechs themselves. The British, French, and the Czechs were all terrified by the idea of Prague, London, or Paris becoming another Guernica.

THE BRUNETE AND ARAGON CAMPAIGNS

After the Nationalist victory over the Basques, the government of the Republic realized that it was necessary to gain a major victory to restore the initiative that had been forfeited to the Nationalists. In late June and early July 1937, the Republicans massed large forces to the north and south of Madrid with the intention of a grand pincer attack that would cut off Nationalist army lines of communication and surround the Nationalist army before Madrid. To the north of the Nationalist salient, the Republicans massed fifteen infantry brigades supported by 130 pieces of artillery, seventy tanks, and twenty armored cars. In the southeastern suburbs of Madrid, on the southern front of the Nationalist line, the Republican offensive would consist of two divisions supported by thirty tanks and twenty armored cars. In addition, there was a reserve force of twenty-four guns, forty tanks, additional armored cars, and eight infantry brigades. The Republican force included the best troops of the Republican army, such as five of the international brigades.[83] The Republican high command had a sound plan and had carefully selected two relatively thinly defended portions of the front for the attack. To gain air superiority, Soviet General Schmouskievich, who commanded the Republican air force for the offensive, assembled approximately 400 aircraft. These included mostly new Russian fighter airplanes, as well as two groups of close-support aircraft and two bomber groups. In addition to this aerial force, the Republicans had also concentrated at least five antiaircraft batteries in the area of the offensive.[84] On 6 July 1937, the Republic began its grand offensive, with the road junction at Grenada as the immediate objective and the goal of linking the two pincers at the town of Brunete. At the start of the offensive, the Republic gained air superiority. Relying on its superiority in the air and large tank force, the Republic made progress in breaking the Nationalist lines. The Nationalist commanders, however, reacted quickly by rushing reinforcements to the threatened sectors, and managed to stall the Republican advance.[85]

With the crisis looming on the Madrid front, the Condor Legion was pulled out of operations in Asturias and redeployed quickly to the Madrid area with two of the Condor Legion squadrons redeployed on the second day of the offensive, 2 July, and the rest following quickly.[86] Because of the crisis, the Condor Legion headquarters took command of all the Nationalist air forces on the Madrid front, which included some squadrons of Italian aircraft and several squadrons of Nationalist air force planes. The first objective of the Condor Legion was to regain air superiority in the Madrid theater. Thus, the primary target of the Condor Legion became the Republican airfields. As early as 9 July, the Condor Legion bombers began bombing airfields in the rear of the Republican forces.[87] Throughout the summer of 1937 campaign, the Nationalist air force and the Condor Legion would continue pounding the airfields. It was a difficult mission because the Soviet advisers to the Republican government had established a policy of laying numerous airfields in the Madrid area and using dispersal and camouflage extensively, as well as constantly transferring aircraft to new airfields to limit the vulnerability of their air force.[88] However, the sustained attacks against the Republican airfields by the Condor Legion paid off and played an important part in helping the Nationalist air force and the Condor Legion regain superiority in the air. However, it was not only the attacks on the Republican airfields that turned the tide for the Nationalists, but also the superiority of the approximately twenty Me 109s of the Condor Legion. The Me 109 proved to be far more capable than the best Republican aircraft, the Soviet-made I-16 fighter. The Condor Legion's flak battalion also proved its worth, and Republican air units soon became cautious about flying over the Nationalist front. The Brunete campaign would prove to be one of the largest air campaigns of the war, and was concluded with a clear victory for the Condor Legion and the Nationalist air force. By the end of the campaign, the Republican air force had lost 160 aircraft for a loss of twenty-three Condor Legion and Nationalist aircraft.[89]

In addition to conducting the air superiority battle, the primary employment of the Condor Legion after the first days of the battle was to carry out close air strikes and interdiction attacks to blunt the Republican offensive. On the ground and in the air, the campaign, which centered on Brunete, became a war of attrition, with Condor Legion bombers and fighters normally flying several sorties a day in support of the ground troops.[90] On 18 July, as the momentum of the Republican advance slowed and the Nationalists gained air superiority over the front, the Nationalists were able to launch a counteroffensive under the cover of waves of German fighters and bombers conducting close support strikes. After a brief pause, the Nationalist counterattack resumed on 24 July, and the Condor Legion was able to win a Guadalajara-like aerial victory over the Republic's ground troops. A large Republican ground force of eight infantry battalions and numerous tanks, which had assembled to conduct a counterattack, was caught in the open by the Condor Legion. The entire Condor Legion was redirected to this target. During the day, the Republican counterattack was not only halted, but literally routed by German aircraft, which inflicted heavy losses. In flying several

Condor Legion Me 109 fighters in Spain, ca. 1938. The Me 109 outclassed the Republic's Russian-supplied fighters and won air superiority for the Nationalists. (Photo from *Jahrbuch der deutschen Luftwaffe,* 1940.)

sorties that day, the Condor Legion was able to destroy a large number of Republican guns and vehicles and instill panic in many of the Republican troops.[91] Lieutenant Colonel von Richthofen was able to boast in his report that a major Red attack was halted by the full use of German air power.[92]

The campaign at Brunete, which lasted from 6 July to early August 1937, became a major turning point for the air war in Spain. The Republic lost its last real chance to gain air superiority and from this time on the Nationalist side would enjoy general superiority in the air. The Condor Legion was able to prove the flexibility of air power by withdrawing forces from one end of the country and redirecting them into an attack in the central part of Spain—virtually without breaking stride. The German flak force proved that it could redeploy over a long distance in a matter of days. The Condor Legion reports complained of problems in coordinating infantry, artillery, and air power, but it is also clear that the Nationalist ground force and the air forces were getting better at carrying out army support missions.

Before the end of 1937, the Condor Legion would prove again that it could quickly redeploy to another front during major combat operations.

While the Nationalists were preparing for an offensive in the Madrid area, ten Republican divisions carried out a surprise attack against the Nationalist front in Aragon at the town of Teruel on 15 December 1937. With a Republican force of 80 bombers, 100 fighters and reconnaissance planes, as well as numerous Russian-supplied flak guns, the Republicans were able to gain local air superiority for the first couple of days of the campaign.[93] The Condor Legion, now under the command of General Helmuth Volkmann (General Sperrle had returned to Germany on 30 October 1937), directed the redeployment of the Condor Legion to the mountainous Teruel front in the middle of the Spanish winter. By this time, the weather was a far more dangerous enemy than the Republican air force. Flying in mountainous terrain with heavy blizzards and icing, the Condor Legion had to learn to conduct cold weather operations. The maintenance officers and NCOs improvised numerous methods to keep the German aircraft flying, such as putting special warming hoods around the engines and heating oil before flying.[94] The Nationalists soon won air superiority along the Teruel front and, by 29 December the Nationalist ground forces were ready for a major ground attack.

Within a year the Condor Legion had become a superb force for close air support operations. This was shown at Teruel when, on 29 December, the Nationalist counterattack was led by Condor Legion and all available Nationalist air force aircraft. The German and Nationalist air forces conducted saturation bombing of the Republican front lines and paved the way for a Nationalist infantry to break through. Once the Republican lines were broken, the Condor Legion switched its attention from the front lines to interdicting Republican reinforcements.[95] The Nationalist counterattack made limited gains until blizzards grounded all air operations and enabled the Republican forces to hold the line and even make limited gains.[96] Both the air and the ground fighting around Teruel became an attrition battle. During January and early February 1938, the Nationalist counteroffensive, which finally overran the city of Teruel on 17 February, witnessed the baptism of fire for the newly arrived Ju 87 stukas, which carried out dive-bombing attacks in support of the Nationalist army.[97] By the end of the Teruel campaign in February 1938, the Republican fighter force was largely destroyed—falling prey to the Condor Legion's Me 109 fighters.

THE 1938 CAMPAIGN

Because the Nationalist forces had decisively defeated the Republican army at Teruel and the Nationalist coalition now held air superiority over the front in Aragon, the Nationalist coalition put together a strategy to go on the offensive from Aragon and launch its forces through the middle of the Spanish Republic straight through to the Mediterranean. It was hoped that this campaign might deal the Republic a mortal blow. If conditions were right, a Nationalist offensive could lead to the rapid conquest of Catalonia. By this time, the Nationalist air force had been built up and trained by the Germans and Italians and constituted a significant force. In support of the Nationalist offensive would be the German Condor Legion, the Nationalist air force, and the Italian Air Force. The Italians would be supporting their own ground troops in the campaign, and the Condor Legion was assigned to support the Nationalist army's elite troops—its Moroccan and Naverese divisions—which would advance on the northern flank in the drive to the sea.[98] Although the Nationalist coalition held air superiority, the intense battles around Madrid and Teruel had given the Nationalists considerable respect for the Republic's air force. Thus, the Nationalist drive to the sea began with a German campaign, and Condor Legion's Heinkel 111 bombers were successful in destroying numerous aircraft on the ground.[99]

The Nationalist offensive began on 9 March 1938. The Condor Legion's primary activities in the first days of the campaign were to conduct saturation bombing of the Republican front lines and provide close support for the Moroccan/Naverese Corps.[100] In addition to these missions, the Condor Legion conducted a broad campaign against Republican strategic targets, primarily the Republican logistics system. The large suspension bridge over the Ebro River at Amposta, which was vital for the movement of supplies from Barcelona to the Republican army, was bombed and damaged by the Condor Legion on 10 March.[101] The Republican munitions factory at La Puebla de Hijar was also among the many logistics and strategic targets struck by the Condor Legion in the first days of the Nationalist offensive.[102]

The Condor Legion saturation bombing, as well as a larger and more effective Nationalist artillery force, quickly broke the Republican army's lines on the Aragon front. With the Republican lines finally shattered along a wide front, the Nationalists were able to move into open country and engage in mobile warfare. In the early stages of the offensive, the German aircraft began to shift their targets from saturation bombing at the front to attacking the rear of the Republican forces to pin down reserves and to prevent Republican attempts to counterattack and close the quickly widening breech in their lines. The Condor Legion's operational strategy was effective and played a major role in preventing the Republican army from restoring its front.[103]

After the Republican front was broken, the Nationalist offensive entered the phase of maneuver warfare. Up to this time, most of the Nationalist operations on the ground had resembled the limited offensives of World War I rather than modern mobile warfare. The Condor Legion had, up to the spring of 1938, operated in an environment in which the front was not likely to move more than a couple of miles per day. Now that the war had become one of more open maneuver, the Luftwaffe had to adapt its operational methods. First of all, in maneuver warfare good reconnaissance is essential and the Condor Legion had a good long- and short-range reconnaissance force that accurately monitored the locations and movement of the Republican army and air force. Air superiority coupled with effective reconnaissance was a great help to the Nationalist forces.[104] The Condor Legion continued to fly a large number of sorties, but the interdiction sorties that were intended to paralyze Republican movement took priority over the close air support strikes under these new conditions. The Nationalist army was fairly well motorized by this time and also possessed a significant armor force reinforced by a German armor battalion. In what is seen as one of the first true Blitzkrieg operations, the Nationalist armor force was able to make a breakthrough and advance 36 kilometers in one day, 12 March 1938.[105] The Condor Legion staff and logistics elements had to deploy forward several times during the March offensive.[106]

Despite stiffening Republican resistance, the Nationalist forces succeeded in reaching the Mediterranean on 14 April 1938, thereby splitting Republican Spain into two halves. With Republican Spain and its armed forces and industry divided, the Nationalists now had the advantage of attacking each sector in turn and defeating each in detail. Unless the Republican government could restore road and rail transportation between its two halves, it had no long-term chance for military or political survival. The Republic was lucky that the Nationalist forces were fairly exhausted by the drive to the sea and not in a position to quickly follow up their offensive. In the spring of 1938, bolstered by increased supplies from the Soviet Union, the Republican government prepared its army in Catalonia for an offensive intended to drive south and reunite the two halves of Republican Spain.

On 24–25 July 1938, the Republican army launched a surprise offensive from Catalonia south across the Ebro River. The Republicans had amassed an impressive force of 100,000 men and were well supported by tanks, artillery, and aircraft. The assault across the Ebro River was initially successful and drove in part of the Nationalist defense line. The Condor Legion at this time was carrying out air operations against the southern half of Republican Spain but, as soon as it was clear that a major offensive was under way, the

Germans began to redeploy their force to meet the new Republican threat. The Condor Legion again showed its flexibility for, within two days of the start of the Republican offensive, the Luftwaffe began a massive interdiction campaign against the Republican lines of communication, which were especially vulnerable because they relied on supply by boat and bridges across the Ebro River.[107] As with so many battles of the Spanish Civil War, the Republic's army gained an initial advantage and then bogged down. The campaign soon became a war of attrition. For the airmen, it also became an attrition war as the Republicans threw their best engineers into keeping the bridges and roads in repair and restoring the Republican logistics lines as quickly as the German and Nationalist air forces could damage them.[108]

The first mission of the Condor Legion was to gain air superiority over the Ebro front. This would entail some difficult fighting as the Republican air force had detailed ten fighter squadrons, equipped with new Russian fighter planes, to support the offensive.[109] The Condor Legion countered the Republican air force by using its Me 109 fighter group in large fighter sweeps over the front.[110] By this point in the war, the Condor Legion fighter force had developed a new system of fighter tactics instituted by a young lieutenant, Werner Mölders. Instead of flying in a three-plane "V" formation—which was standard in all major air forces of the time—the Condor Legion fighters began to fly in pairs. Each pair, called a Rotte, would consist of a pilot and wingman flying abreast about 200 yards apart. By flying abreast, each wingman was able to see and cover the other pilot's blind spots and, if one plane made an attack, the other would cover his rear. The Rotte could become a larger formation with the addition of other pairs of aircraft. A formation with more than one Rotte would be called a Schwarm. These fairly simple changes to the fighter tactics greatly increased the combat effectiveness of the fighter units and gave the Germans, who were already flying faster fighters, a tremendous advantage over the Republican fighter force.[111] During the intensive air battles over the Ebro front during late July and August 1938, the Condor Legion fighters alone shot down twenty-nine Republican aircraft.[112]

While the Condor Legion fighters were decimating the Republican fighter force, the German bombers and stukas conducted an intensive interdiction campaign against Republican bridges, logistics lines, reserve units, and artillery batteries. By this time, the Condor Legion had received eight early model Ju 87 dive bombers and six Henschel Hs 123 ground attack aircraft.[113] The Ju 87 dive bomber was used extensively by the Condor Legion in its interdiction campaign along the Ebro. The stukas proved to be more accu-

A flight of Ju 87 stukas of the Condor Legion over Spain in 1938. Note the Nationalist Air Force markings. (Photo from *Jahrbuch der deutschen Luftwaffe*, 1940.)

rate in hitting point targets than the conventional bombers, and the Condor Legion reported to Berlin that they were pleased with the stuka's performance. The Ju 87s became a favorite weapon of the Condor Legion with the stukas often ordered to fly two to four sorties per day.[114] Before the war in Spain it was believed that the dive bombers could expect very high attrition rates from ground fire. Yet, in Spain, even though the Republicans had covered their front with a force of Russian 20-mm and 45-mm antiaircraft guns, the attrition rate of the stukas and other close support aircraft was much lower than had been expected by the Luftwaffe staff.[115] The Condor Legion reckoned that its rapid redeployment to the Ebro front and its ability to conduct an extensive interdiction campaign had played a central role in slowing and eventually halting the Republican offensive by the end of July.[116]

By August 1938 the Condor Legion turned its attention to a close air support campaign to blast Republican front lines, artillery positions, and troop reserves in support of the Nationalist counterattack.[117] By November the Republicans had been pushed back across the Ebro. By this time the Republicans had few troop reserves and aircraft left while the Nationalist coalition was daily becoming stronger and better equipped. The final campaign of the war began with a Nationalist ground drive against Catalonia, which began 24 December 1938. With the Condor Legion in support, the Nationalist forces advanced rapidly and overran all of Catalonia by 10 February 1939. Within a month, all Republican resistance across Spain collapsed and the Republicans surrendered Madrid in March.

STRATEGIC BOMBING IN THE SPANISH CIVIL WAR

Contrary to popular belief, air power in the Spanish Civil War was not restricted to army support aviation. Early in the conflict, between August and September 1936, the small air forces of both sides carried out strategic bombing campaigns with the goal of demoralizing the enemy populace. In July and August 1936 the Nationalists bombed the cities of Malaga and Badajoz. At the same time, the Loyalists bombed Seville, Saragossa, Cordova, and Oviedo.[118] A few civilians were killed and moderate damage inflicted and the local populations were temporarily demoralized. However, both sides quickly concluded that bombing cities was having little effect on the outcome of the war as civilian morale proved to be far more resilient under bombing than many of the interwar air theorists had believed. The bomber forces of both sides were soon redirected against more vital military targets such as shipping, railroads, airfields, and the enemy ground forces.

The German involvement in any strategic bombing was carefully restricted from the time the Condor Legion arrived in Spain. The Condor Legion operated under Spanish strategic direction, and German bombing plans were always cleared through the Spanish high command. In November 1936 it appeared that Madrid might quickly be captured with just one more push by the Nationalist forces. Franco ordered a series of bombing raids on the city, which he hoped would break the defenders' morale.[119] The Spanish, however, insisted that the bombing was not to be indiscriminate. Franco ordered a bomb safety zone established to limit civilian casualties. The strategic bombing experiment proved to be fruitless; indeed, in a civil war situation the bombing of cities could even be considered counterproductive. Madrid contained many supports of the Nationalist cause and many of Madrid's civilian casualties were probably supporters of Franco.[120]

The Luftwaffe officers in Spain understood the limitations of a strategic bombing campaign in a civil war. As one Condor Legion officer put it, "It would be simple for the Nationalist air force to bomb Valencia, Barcelona, or Madrid into ashes with incendiary bombs but politically would that be unacceptable? . . . What would be the purpose of destroying the valuable industries of Bilbao or the weapons factory in Reinosa if they would be occupied in a short time? Fighting in one's own land is an example of a two-sided

Spanish ground crew loading bombs into Condor Legion He 111s in Spain in 1937. (Photo from *Jahrbuch der deutschen Luftwaffe,* 1940.)

sword."[121] However, while the Condor Legion refrained from a city-busting strategy, numerous strategic targets were bombed by the Germans. On 19 January 1938 Condor Legion bombers as well as Italian and Nationalist air units carried out a coordinated attack on the power stations near Tremp, which supplied power to the industries of Catalonia. This attempt to shut down Barcelona's arms manufacturing was repeated again later that month.[122] By 1938 the Legion bomber force had been reequipped with modern medium bombers such as the He 111 and Do 17. The German airmen became more ambitious in targeting the Republic's vital industrial installations. In March 1938 most of the Condor Legion bombers attacked the Puebla de Hijar rail yard and a munitions factory located nearby. Although the bomb pattern was poor, the factory was still destroyed.[123] Throughout 1938 and 1939, the Republic's rail system was one of the preferred targets of the German bombers. Along with rail centers, the Republican port facilities were seen as primary strategic targets throughout the war, because the Republic depended on importing most of its modern weapons and war materials by sea. Even when the Condor Legion was heavily involved in supporting ground operations, it could often find enough bombers to carry out attacks on the Republic's ports and munitions factories.[124] While the Condor Legion and the Nationalist air force conducted a limited strategic bombing campaign and avoided indiscriminate city bombing, the Italian air force refused to accept any limitations on bombing. In March 1938, while the Republican army on the Aragon front was in headlong retreat, the Reggia Aeronautica launched a three-day series of massive bombing attacks against Barcelona. From 16–18 March, a large Italian bomber force under the direct orders of Benito Mussolini conducted several raids targeting Barcelona's population. The raids caused approximately 1,300 deaths and wounded another 2,000.[125] Considerable damage was caused throughout the city, for the Italians had made no attempt to hit purely military objectives.[126] The Italian campaign was conducted without Franco's approval. As with Guernica, the bombing of Barcelona brought about widespread condemnation of the Italians and the Nationalists.[127]

The Italian bombing of Barcelona was the one attempt during the Spanish Civil War to apply Giulio Douhet's theory of air warfare. In reality, the Douhetian approach proved to be counterproductive. The bombing of Barcelona caused considerable demoralization of the population at first but aerial bombing also seemed to anger more people than it terrified. There are accounts of wounded civilians in Barcelona who extended their arm in the Communist clenched-fist salute as they were carried to the hospital and exhorted the other civilians to fight on.[128] The Condor Legion leaders described the Italian bombing as senseless. The German ambassador to Nationalist Spain reported the Condor Legion's assessment of the Barcelona bombing in a message on 23 March 1938: "Destructive bombardments without clear military targets are, in a civil war like Spain's, not likely to bring about the desired moral results—instead, it makes for a far more dangerous future."[129] The German officers believed that the bombing of Barcelona would cause political problems with the international community as well. In any case, the Germans realized that strategic bombing worked to increase the will and the morale of the enemy forces and population.[130] After the bombing of Barcelona, Republican morale indeed stiffened, and resistance to the Nationalist offensive increased. Rather than collapse—as Douhet predicted—the Catalonians fought on for another year.

If, at the start of the war, the Luftwaffe officers were not especially inclined toward Douhet's theory of breaking enemy morale by strategic bombing, the opportunity to observe the bombardment of Madrid and the civilian population's ability to adjust to aerial bombardment taught the Germans some important lessons about air warfare. The fact that civilian morale was surprisingly resilient and able to deal with air attack was not only noted by the Luftwaffe, but also by foreign military experts observing the war.[131] Finally, in addition to learning some important lessons about the veracity of Douhet's theory, the Luftwaffe learned the lesson that even with air superiority, strategic bombing is an extremely difficult enterprise. Prewar assumptions about the accuracy of high-altitude horizontal bombing and about the destructive power of bombs had been greatly exaggerated. Even under the best of conditions, the accuracy of the most modern Luftwaffe bombers and equipment was generally rated by the Luftwaffe as only fair. While the Luftwaffe officer corps did not discard the concept of strategic bombing during or after Spain, there was certainly considerably more skepticism about the claims made for strategic bombing after the Spanish War.

NAVAL AIR OPERATIONS IN SPAIN

As part of the initial German commitment to Nationalist Spain, in the fall of 1936 the Luftwaffe deployed a small reconnaissance flight of He 59 and He 60 seaplanes. The Luftwaffe seaplanes were to cooperate with the Nationalist air force and provide long-range overwater reconnaissance as well as serving as light bombers. Because Republican Spain depended on importing military supplies from the Soviet Union through the ports of Barcelona, Cartegena, and Valencia as well as many smaller ports, the German naval aircraft were given the mission of interdicting shipping and attacking ships inside the Republican harbors.

By July 1937 nine He 59 and eight He 60 seaplanes had arrived to give the Germans a full squadron-sized force.[132] Both the He 59 and He 60 were considered obsolete at the time. The He 59 was a four-seat, twin-engine seaplane and, although slow, it could carry 1,000 kilograms of bombs or torpedoes and was fairly well armed with two machine guns and a 20-mm Rheinmetall aircraft cannon.[133] The He 60 was a two-seat, single-engine seaplane, which was primarily a reconnaissance aircraft as it could carry no more than 120 kilograms of bombs.[134] Approximately fifteen He 59s and eight He 60 aircraft were deployed in the service of the Condor Legion in Spain between 1936 and 1939.[135]

In the summer of 1937 the German seaplane unit, which operated mostly out of Mallorca in conjunction with Spanish and Italian naval aviation units that operated from bases on the Mediterranean coast, formed a combined staff to coordinate the campaign against Republican shipping and ports.[136]

Heinkel He 59 seaplanes. Although obsolete, these aircraft served very successfully as bombers and coastal patrol planes in Spain. (Photo from *Jahrbuch der deutschen Luftwaffe,* 1940.)

The seaplane force of the Nationalist coalition, although equipped with obsolete equipment, proved to be remarkably successful. During the war, the Republicans lost 554 ships, 144 of these to the Germans and Italians. A further 106 foreign ships carrying supplies to the Republic were also sunk.[137] Although naval forces were also involved in blockading Republican Spain, air action sank a major proportion of the Republican ships.[138]

During the war the Condor Legion's naval air arm progressed from a fairly simple reconnaissance mission to port bombing and antishipping attacks.[139] By 1938 the naval aircraft had become proficient at attacking shipping inside Republican ports. Attacks were carried out by day and by night, but given the slow speed of the He 59s, the night attack came to be the preferred method. The He 59 pilots developed the tactic of flying to the ports at medium altitudes and then cutting their engines and gliding in to attack in silence. After the bombs were released the pilot would give the plane full throttle and fly back to sea.[140] Republican merchant ships were attacked and sunk at sea by He 59s, which normally used 250-kilogram bombs and made their attack approaches at low altitude.[141] A Nationalist air force officer who visited the harbor of Barcelona shortly after the fall of that city to the Nationalists in 1939 described "great devastation" in the harbor, with thirty ships sunk at their berths and many others damaged.[142]

COALITION ASPECTS OF THE SPANISH WAR

One notable feature of the senior German military leadership during World War II was its mediocre performance in conducting coalition warfare. Many of the problems that the Germans would have in World War II in the Mediterranean theater would be foreshadowed by their experience in Spain in which the Germans had to operate as a partner in a Nationalist/Italian/German coalition.

When the Spanish Civil War began and the Germans and Italians found themselves fighting side by side, the German military thought this to be a favorable development. The Germans had long admired the Fascist Italian system and the Luftwaffe, in particular, had carefully studied the Italian Air Force and the writings of Giulio Douhet. However, within months of the Germans' arrival in the country, the German relationship with the Italians had soured. General Franco and the Nationalist government had requested aid from Italy in the form of supplies, equipment, and air units. However, Italy had its own agenda to become the premier power in the Mediterranean and the Italians viewed the Spanish War as an opportunity to increase their influence in Spain and also to negotiate the rights to Spanish air and naval bases and thus dominate the western Mediterranean.[143] The Mussolini government, to foster Italy's pretensions to be accepted as a major military power, sent over 70,000 troops and over 5,000 airmen to Spain.[144] While the Nationalists appreciated the Italian aid and support in the desperate first months of the war, the Nationalist attitude soon turned to resentment as the Italian ground troops arrived in Spain. When General Franco was told on 14 December 1936 that Italian Fascist militia divisions would soon be arriving in Spain, he commented "Who asked for them?"[145] As soon as they arrived, the Italians insisted on carrying out their own independent offensive at Malaga in February 1937. General Roatta, the commander of the Italian forces, declined to fully brief the Spanish or German senior commanders on Italian plans—which considerably frustrated Italy's coalition partners.[146]

While the Italians were victorious at Malaga, their defeat at Guadalajara in March 1937 proved to be a humiliation that the Italians would not be able to live down for the rest of the war. While the Italian air units continued to do good work and cooperate with their allies, the Italian army gained a reputation for military incompetence. This perception carried over into the relationship between the coalition partners at the top level. Prior to the battle of Guadalajara, the campaign around Madrid had a combined nature. German and Italian air units flew missions together on the Madrid front throughout late 1936. However, after the Guadalajara debacle, the Germans and the Spanish were reluctant to conduct operations with the Italians. Von Richthofen came to the conclusion that his former friends were blithering incompetents.[147]

In contrast to the Italians, Condor Legion commanders and senior officers proved adept at operating and planning with their Spanish Nationalist counterparts. Major General Hugo Sperrle and his chief of staff von Richthofen made an effective command team in Spain and set forth policies and conditions for coalition warfare that would remain in place for the entire war. Both Sperrle and von Richthofen were professional soldiers, and neither could be said to have had a diplomatic personality. Hugo Sperrle was a highly experienced officer who had seen considerable combat in World War I. He was an officer who was considered smart by the other Luftwaffe officers but not brilliant. He was blunt, humorous, and had a reputation for enjoying good living. Sperrle was somewhat famous throughout the German armed forces for being the first Luftwaffe general to have a refrigerator installed on his Ju 52 personal transport. Sperrle had a tendency to be impatient and was tough and demanding of his subordinates. But no one doubted the wisdom of sending Sperrle to Spain as Condor Legion commander as he had an excellent reputation throughout the Luftwaffe officer corps.[148] Wolfram von Richthofen was younger than Sperrle, and his experience in war was limited to that of a fighter pilot late in World War I. Like Sperrle, von Richthofen has a reputation for being a good troop leader. Von Richthofen was also known to be very tough and demanding to his subordinates. Von Richthofen had a reputation of being not just smart but brilliant. However, his brilliance was combined with a strong streak of ruthlessness and an intolerance for slowness and excuses. Both Sperrle and von Richthofen regularly disagreed with Franco and the Spanish high command and the discussions could become fairly heated. However, there is much more to military leadership than diplomatic skills. Franco himself could speak with German senior military officers as one military professional to another. He does not seem to have personally liked the Germans but he accorded them due respect. For their part, the German records indicate irritation with Franco on the slow pace of the Nationalist's military effort, but they relate genuine respect for Franco's qualities as a leader. The officers of the Spanish high command came to respect Sperrle and von Richthofen for their professionalism. The German senior officers met with the Nationalist high command and the staff of the field army being supported by the Condor Legion on a daily basis, and they quickly developed an effective working relationship.

One of the primary problems with the Nationalist high command was the low level of military skills and knowledge possessed by so many of the senior Nationalist military officers. Aside from a few officers such as Franco, who had served extensively in North Africa, many of the senior Spanish officers were overage, possessed mediocre military educations and, in general, had no concept of modern warfare. Sperrle and von Richthofen found many of the senior Spanish officers to be outright incompetent. For example, von Richthofen found General Kindelan, chief of the Nationalist air force, to be an "old used up fellow."[149] However, the Germans found many midranking and some of the senior Spanish staff officers to be competent, so, in dealing with Spaniards, they quickly learned to identify the most capable officers and work through them, regardless of their rank. In planning strategy and operations, Major Sierra of General Kindelan's staff was regarded as being especially effective.[150] The Germans' favorite Spanish officer was Colonel, later General Juan Suero diaz Vigón. Vigón was capable, intelligent, energetic, and a first-rate general staff officer. Vigón and the Germans served together for much of the war. Vigón was General Mola's chief of staff for the northern campaign of 1937 and from July 1938 onward Vigón served as Franco's chief of staff. Vigón was very friendly with the Germans and developed a close personal relationship with the German senior officers.[151]

In contrast to the Hollywood version of the arrogant Nazi officer, the officers and men assigned to the Condor Legion seemed to have worked hard to demonstrate political sensitivity, understanding, and goodwill toward the Nationalist soldiers and airmen. The Condor Legion commanders set a Luftwaffe tradition by regularly visiting the Spanish units at the front to observe close air support operations. Junior officers of the Condor Legion attempted to learn Spanish and would also visit the Spanish units at the front.[152] The Germans developed a special affinity for several of the units of the Nationalist army, in particular, the Navarese and Moroccan divisions that they regularly flew support for. Luftwaffe personnel also developed a good working relationship with the Nationalist air force. Combined missions were common events. For example, Captain Jose Larios, duke of Lerma, and Nationalist fighter ace, regularly flew mission with the Condor Legion.[153] Luftwaffe reports often praised the combat performance of the Nationalist air force units.[154]

Even though Von Richthofen was not famous for his diplomatic sensibilities, his knowledge of Italian and his ability to learn Spanish was appreciated by the senior Spanish officers. Von Richthofen also showed considerably more understanding than his Italian counterparts when he was commander of the Condor Legion when Barcelona fell to the Nationalists on 26 January

1939. Von Richthofen ordered the Condor Legion troops to stay out of the city, and the Nationalists were given full credit for the victory even though the Condor Legion had played a major role in supporting the Nationalist advance. The Italians, on the other hand, irritated the Spanish by trying to claim a major share of the glory and demanding that Italian troops enter the city with the first battalions.[155]

In late 1937, Benito Mussolini made a blatant attempt to gain greater Italian influence over the strategic direction of the Nationalist war effort. Mussolini floated the idea of creating combined Spanish/Italian/German headquarters to direct the war effort. The Germans protested against the Italian proposal and argued to retain the command system that had already been developed. At this point of the war, the chain of command extended from Franco and his staff directly to the field armies and army groups. This system allowed the Germans direct access to Franco and the Nationalist war council. Fortunately for the Condor Legion and the Nationalist war effort, the Nationalists rebuffed the Italian proposal, which would have interfered with the direct access to Franco that the German commanders enjoyed.[156]

Yet, the Nationalist coalition was not dysfunctional. In several campaigns, particularly in Aragon and the April battles of 1938, the three ground and air forces cooperated fairly effectively.[157] While reporting on the success of the Nationalist interdiction campaign, General Volkmann remarked that despite every effort, a system of full command authority for the three coalition air forces through the Spanish air force chief was not to be achieved. Nor was it truly necessary. At the operational level of war, senior commanders generally agreed to cooperate and jointly coordinate the battle action. Yet, Mussolini and the Italian High Command continued throughout the war to disturb the cohesion of the Nationalist coalition. During the Teruel campaign in 1938 Mussolini actually ordered the Italian military to withhold Italian air support until Italian ground forces were allowed into the battle.[158]

It has been often remarked that the senior officers of the German military in World War II showed a superb understanding of the tactical and operational levels of war but lacked a sense of strategic understanding. Horst Boog points to von Richthofen, who later became a field marshal, as an example of someone who did not try to understand World War II within its whole context.[159] Historian Michael Geyer cites General Beck as remarking that the younger generation of military leaders "never learn to evaluate operations within the context of a coherent strategy."[160] However, the performance of senior Luftwaffe officers such as Sperrle, Wilberg, von Richthofen, and the senior leadership of the German high command during the Spanish Civil War provide some sound grounds for revising this image. Operating

Major General Wolfram von Richthofen in Spanish uniform as commander of the Condor Legion in 1939. (Photo from the von Richthofen family.)

with little strategic direction from their political masters, the German military leadership worked hard to ensure that the war in Spain remained limited and that the Wehrmacht was not overcommitted. For a relatively modest investment, the German high command reaped some substantial strategic gains from its involvement in Spain. The Russians were foiled in their attempts to gain strategic influence in the Mediterranean, the French were discomfited by the Nationalist victory, and Germany gained access to considerable amounts of vital minerals necessary for rearmament.[161] While Spain wisely refrained from joining Germany as an ally in World War II, it did provide the German navy secret submarine bases and, in addition, Spain provided an all-volunteer infantry division and air squadron to serve on the Russian front. Between August 1941 and mid-1944, 47,000 Spaniards fought in Russia and 4,500 were killed there. The Wehrmacht estimated that the Spaniards inflicted 49,300 casualties on the Soviets.[162] It is ironic that while Italy sent far more men than Germany did and provided more tanks, guns, airplanes, and money to the Nationalist cause, after the war the Franco government denied the Italians any economic or strategic benefits from their military intervention.[163] From 1936–1939 Italy provided Spain with 150 tanks, 700-plus planes, and 1,800 artillery pieces. Germany provided 150 tanks, 600–700 aircraft, and 400–700 guns.[164] For all their trouble, the Italians never did get the bases on Spanish soil that they so ardently desired.

The German intervention in Spain begin as a purely ad hoc affair with no prior planning or preparation whatsoever. It is a reminder of the efficiency of the Luftwaffe general staff that Helmuth Wilberg, given only vague instructions from the Third Reich's leaders, within two days had created a functioning staff and was rushing material and men to Spain. The Luftwaffe general staff along with the Wehrmacht high command created an effective and realistic strategy for dealing with the Spanish intervention. The Luftwaffe officers such as Sperrle, von Richthofen, Volkmann, and Wilberg proved themselves to be capable strategists and worked effectively within a coalition framework that tasked their political and diplomatical skills to the utmost. Given the situation, they performed admirably.

LESSONS OF THE SPANISH CIVIL WAR

The Luftwaffe experience in the Spanish Civil War had an enormous impact on Luftwaffe doctrine, tactics, and technology. From 1936 to 1939 over 19,000 Luftwaffe personnel served in Spain.[165] In Spain, the Luftwaffe had the opportunity to conduct virtually every type of air campaign. The Spanish war featured strategic bombing, interdiction campaigns, naval antishipping campaigns, close air support, and air superiority campaigns. The Luftwaffe had fought the war under conditions of a static front similar to World War I and, later in the war, under conditions of modern maneuver warfare with German aircraft flying in support of rapidly moving armored and motorized formations.

Basically, the Luftwaffe had done very well. From the beginning of the war and the German airlift campaign from North Africa to the air campaign to the north and the campaign in Aragon in 1938, the Luftwaffe intervention had proven decisive and provided the margin of victory to the Nationalists. A relatively small Condor Legion of 5,000 men and 100 aircraft had played a disproportionate role in the war and had demonstrated that air power now played a central role in modern warfare. The combat record of the Condor Legion was impressive. The Luftwaffe had shot down 327 Spanish Republican aircraft. In addition, the Luftwaffe flak battalion had proven its worth by shooting down an additional fifty-nine Republican aircraft.[166] Against this toll of 386 Republican aircraft the Condor Legion had lost only seventy-two aircraft in combat.[167] The Luftwaffe seaplane squadron claimed a total of fifty-two Republican ships destroyed and many other ships damaged. The stuka detachment of the Condor Legion claimed eight enemy ships.[168] German casualties in Spain totaled 298 Germans dead. Of these, only 131 were killed in combat. Another 167 German personnel died in accidents or by sickness. A further 139 Germans were wounded in action and 439 injured due to other causes.[169] Given the long period of combat and the high sortie rates of the aircraft, the high command in Berlin was surprised at the low losses suffered by the Condor Legion—which were far lower than had been estimated at the start of the conflict.[170]

Due to the Spanish Civil War, by 1939 the Luftwaffe had more veterans who had participated in a modern air war than any other air force in western Europe. The Luftwaffe officers and men who served nine- to twelve-month tours in Spain returned to their units and the lessons learned in Spain were quickly disseminated throughout the entire Luftwaffe. By the end of the Spanish War, many senior Luftwaffe officers, including generals Sperrle, von Richthofen, and future generals Drum, Plocher, and Seidemann, had all gained recent command experience in a major war. Adolf Galland, later Luftwaffe general and commander of the Reich fighter defenses, saw his first combat as a ground attack pilot in Spain. The staff of the Condor Legion had gained experience in planning and conducting combat operations in a diffi-

Condor Legion heavy 88-mm flak gun in action in Spain. (Photo from *Jahrbuch der deutschen Luftwaffe,* 1940.)

cult environment. When the Luftwaffe left Spain, it left as a confident and experienced air force. When World War II began in September 1939, the Luftwaffe was better prepared for war than any other major air force.

Several historians have argued that the Luftwaffe's experience in Spain was counterproductive because the Germans learned the wrong lessons from the war. Samuel Mitcham, in *Men of the Luftwaffe,* argues that the success of the close air support operations in Spain "was to result in the Luftwaffe's greatest victory in the years 1939–1942; it also contributed to the neglect of the strategic warfare, which was to lead (indirectly) to its greatest defeats."[171] Raymond Proctor makes essentially the same argument. "German officers . . . still view the Luftwaffe's lack of consideration for the strategic application of air power as a gross mistake."[172] These statements explain more about the influence of the traditional U.S. Air Force bias in favor of strategic warfare as "proper air warfare" than it relates to the actual facts of the Spanish Civil War. In Spain the Luftwaffe learned a great deal about strategic bombing. The city bombing of Madrid and Barcelona confirmed the suspicion of many in the Luftwaffe about the true vulnerability of civilian morale. At the end of the war the Luftwaffe conducted a study of the extensive civil defense procedures enacted by the heavily bombed Republicans. The German study of the Spanish experience convinced the Luftwaffe that a large-scale civil defense program could be effective in maintaining civilian morale.[173] From the strategic bombing that was conducted by the Condor Legion the Luftwaffe learned a great deal about the accuracy of high-altitude horizontal bombing. The Luftwaffe also learned a great deal about the vulnerability of bombers to modern fighter planes. From the early days of the war the Luftwaffe found it was necessary to provide fighter escort to even the fastest and most modern bomber aircraft. Largely because of the Spanish War experience, the Luftwaffe increased its requirements for the production of fighter planes. The experience of the Spanish Civil War did not at any time deter senior Luftwaffe officers from advocating strategic bombing theories. Even after planning close air support campaigns for the Condor Legion, Wolfram von Richthofen maintained a firm belief in the importance of the heavy strategic bomber. The Germans did not discard a strategic bombing doctrine in Spain; the German commanders simply realized that conducting a major strategic bombing campaign in Spain would not be appropriate under those conditions.

One of the primary lessons of Spain was the importance of aerial navigation and night flying. Over the course of the war the Luftwaffe lost more pilots and aircraft to operational accidents than they did to combat. While losing seventy-two planes in combat, the Condor Legion had lost 160 aircraft in operational accidents.[174] In most cases, the accidents had occurred at night or in poor weather. German pilots trained to fly in day conditions were prone to fly their aircraft into Spanish mountainsides at night. These problems provoked some immediate changes in the Luftwaffe training program. When General Sperrle returned to Germany in the fall of 1937 and took over the Luftwaffe forces, which would become the Third Air Fleet, he immediately told his new command that bad weather flying had not been pushed energetically enough and that every unit in his command would conduct winter exercises to practice bad weather operations and night flying.[175] Thanks to the experience in Spain, the Luftwaffe became better trained in the fundamental navigation and flying skills required for strategic bombing and by the start of World War II was the only air force in Europe that was even moderately competent at night flying and bad weather navigation. Ironically, this is in contrast to other air forces such as the Royal Air Force, which made strategic bombing the virtually exclusive focus of its doctrine while at the same time creating an air force training program that ensured a bomber force that could only fly by daylight and in good weather.[176]

The Luftwaffe's doctrine of close air support and joint air/army operations did not become part of Luftwaffe doctrine because of the Spanish War. As has been noted, close air support operations had long been part of Luftwaffe doctrine. Since the 1920s the Luftwaffe's fighter pilots had been training for this mission. However, the Luftwaffe in Spain was able to work out and perfect many of the tactics and techniques necessary for coordinating close air support operations. Because of the Spanish War experience, the Luftwaffe in 1939 was the best-trained force for close air support operations in the world. After the Spanish experience, close air support was given a higher priority by the Luftwaffe general staff although strategic bombing and interdiction operations remained the primary missions. The lessons of close air support in Spain were studied intensively by the air staff. Major General Jeschonnek, the chief of the Luftwaffe general staff, stated in June 1939 that close air support is "the most difficult mission that could be given to the air force" and that such mission required "the closest liaison between Luftwaffe commanders and the supported army units."[177] The success of the Luftwaffe close air support operations in Spain directly influenced the plans for the Polish campaign of 1939. The Luftwaffe consolidated more than half of the rapidly growing stuka force into a "close battle division" and placed it under the command of Wolfram von Richthofen. Its mission would be to replicate the effect that close air support operations had demonstrated in Spain on the Polish army in a few months.

CHAPTER SEVEN

The Luftwaffe Prepares for War: Problems with Leadership and Organization

When Walter Wever died in 1936, the Luftwaffe lost a commander who had the ability to provide clear guidance and leadership, which the rapidly growing organization sorely needed. Wever had developed a comprehensive vision of air power, and by the time of his death, had gained the stature and respect within the Luftwaffe to become its dominant figure. This vision of the role of air power was, to a large degree, lost with Wever. Even more troublesome, Wever's death kicked off a long series of power struggles within the Luftwaffe's top command, which would hinder its development and effectiveness.

Lieutenant General Albert Kesselring was selected to be the Luftwaffe's chief of staff after Wever's death. By any standard Kesselring was a good choice for the post, in his early fifties at the time, a hard-working and dynamic personality. Like Wever, Kesselring had been transferred to the air ministry from the army in the early period of the Luftwaffe's rearmament. Kesselring, like Wever and others, was no pilot, nor was he an expert on air power before transferring to the Luftwaffe. He was, however, a highly intelligent officer with a superb record as a general staff officer and troop leader.[1] Kesselring studied hard to learn the details of his new service. A quick study, he soon learned to fly. He quickly learned a great deal about aviation, and was especially interested in technology. By 1936 Kesselring could certainly no longer be called an amateur aviator.

Kesselring was nicknamed "Smiling Albert" because of his friendly demeanor. Most photos of Kesselring show him smiling and relaxed around his fellow officers. Kesselring was, after all, not of the Prussian nobility but a Bavarian from a middle-class background. Yet, behind his friendly Bavarian demeanor, he was as demanding a commander and as strict a disciplinarian as the toughest Prussian aristocrat. Although he tolerated considerable debate within staff meetings, when conducting operations, Kesselring expected immediate and complete obedience from his officers, and subordinates who dawdled or did not meet his high standards of performance soon found their careers terminated. Kesselring, like Wolfram von Richthofen, knew how to wage war ruthlessly. It is interesting that Kesselring and von Richthofen—two of the most talented senior officers of the Luftwaffe—did not get along well with each other. It was probably because they were too much alike.

One important talent that Wever possessed—getting along with both Erhard Milch and Hermann Göring—was lacking in Kesselring. It seems that Kesselring got along well enough with Göring but his relationship with Milch was a stormy one.[2] As a new chief of staff, Kesselring lacked the authority to put Milch in his place in a subordinate role. The year that Kesselring served as the Luftwaffe chief of staff (1936–1937) saw the start of a power struggle in which Milch attempted to expand his role as state secretary of aviation to become the de facto chief of the Luftwaffe. Kesselring also had to contend with Hermann Göring's desire to have a greater direct say in the operations of the Luftwaffe. Prior to Wever's death, Göring had enjoyed the title (and pay and fancy uniforms) of the commander in chief of the Luftwaffe. He had interfered relatively little in the day-to-day management of the organization. He had insisted on the appointment of some friends to high Luftwaffe rank and position, but these men had been sidetracked into prestigious positions with little impact over policy. For example, Karl Bodenschatz, Göring's World War I adjutant, was appointed adjutant of the state secretary for aviation. Göring's old wingman, Bruno Loerzer, was brought into the Luftwaffe and given the directorship of German Sport Fliers *(Deutsche Luftsportverband),* a Nazi organization created to control private aviation groups.[3] Ernst Udet, Germany's highest-ranking surviving World War I ace (with over sixty kills) was regarded as something of a darling of the Nazi party. When the Nazis took over, Udet was brought into the Luftwaffe and rapidly promoted. By 1935 he was named inspector of fighters and dive bombers. Actually, this was an appropriate position for Udet, as he was a brilliant test and stunt pilot. Testing planes and developing fighter tactics was certainly a job he could handle.[4]

After Wever's death, Göring started to take a more direct hand in the appointment of senior Luftwaffe officials—with disastrous results. With Wever dead only a month, Göring appointed Udet as the chief of the Luftwaffe's Technical Office—a position so capably held by Wilhelm Wimmer. While Wimmer had done his work well, he was certainly no "yes man" to Göring, and Göring preferred "yes men" to competence. Wimmer was thereafter relegated to minor commands in the Luftwaffe. The competent and experienced officers such as von Richthofen viewed Göring's demotion of competent officers such as Wimmer to be absurd.[5] It would not be Göring's last attempt to interfere with the appointment of the senior Luftwaffe leadership. As with most of Göring's decisions, this one would prove to be disastrous for the

Field Marshal Albert Kesselring, Luftwaffe chief of staff, 1936–1937. (Photo from the von Richthofen family.)

Luftwaffe. Udet himself realized that he was not qualified for a job that demanded extensive technical knowledge as well as superb administrative skills. He was, however, thrust into a very difficult job for which he was completely unsuited and unqualified. Ernst Udet would be in charge of the development and selection of Luftwaffe aircraft from 1936 to his death by suicide in 1941. He would, along the way, be given the additional responsibility for overseeing the production of aircraft for the Luftwaffe. The effect of Udet on the Luftwaffe in these roles will be discussed later in the chapter.

The atmosphere of harmony and cooperation in the top reaches of the Luftwaffe that existed at the time of Wever's death was quickly lost. Göring's appointment of Udet to the top ranks of Luftwaffe responsibility had much to do with it. Wilhelm Wimmer had put together a capable team to help guide the technological development of the Luftwaffe. In three years this group had done wonders in quickly building the Luftwaffe into a credible force. With Udet at the helm of technical development, some of the most capable officers who had worked with Wimmer asked for reassignment. One of Wimmer's top assistants and section chiefs, Lieutenant Colonel Wolfram von Richthofen—who possessed a Ph.D. in engineering and a first-rate technical mind—looked for another post. For him, the war in Spain was a godsend. After only a few weeks working for Udet, von Richthofen went to General Helmuth Wilberg, who was in charge of the German support for Nationalist Spain in the civil war that had just begun. Von Richthofen volunteered for the enterprise and soon found himself away from Udet and Berlin as chief of staff of the Condor Legion.

Kesselring held on to his post as chief of staff for a year until he finally asked to be relieved and given another assignment. He was given the air district in Dresden to command and was later named chief of staff of the First Air Fleet. Kesselring, like many others, found it impossible to work with Milch. Milch, for his part, instituted a campaign at Wever's death to put most of the functions and commands of the Luftwaffe under his jurisdiction and thus become the de facto chief of the Luftwaffe. On 1 June 1937 Lieutenant General Hans-Jürgen Stumpf, who had served as the chief of the Personnel Office since 1933, took over as the Luftwaffe chief of staff.[6] As with Kesselring, Stumpf objected strenuously to Milch's machinations and power grabbing. On 6 December 1937 he sent a memo to Göring pointing out that both the Luftwaffe general staff and the office of the state secretary were issuing orders and directives—often without consulting each other. He called the Luftwaffe's lack of a clearly demarcated chain of command "damaging for the Luftwaffe and unacceptable."[7] Stumpf sensibly recommended that there be a clear separation of responsibility in the Luftwaffe with Milch and the state secretary's office responsible for technical development, procurement, and production while the Luftwaffe chief of staff would be responsible for field command and operations, war planning, and training. The Luftwaffe chief of staff would serve as the Luftwaffe's representative in the high command of the Wehrmacht.[8]

While Stumpf had proposed a practical arrangement that would have worked to eliminate much of the top-level confusion in the Luftwaffe, Milch proposed making the command arrangements even more complicated. In a memo to Göring in September 1937, Milch proposed the creation of two new offices that would be equal in status to that of the chief of staff. The first would be the chief of air defense (Chef der Luftwehr) who would serve as a war ministry staff of the Luftwaffe,[9] and the other would be the general inspector of the Luftwaffe who would serve as the "eyes and ears" of the commander in chief of the Luftwaffe (Göring) and report directly to Göring.[10] Stumpf quite rightly saw these proposals as moves to diminish the authority of the Luftwaffe chief of staff. At this time the Luftwaffe had inspectorates for the various branches of the force (inspectorate of bombers, inspectorate for safety, inspectorate for fighters and dive bombers, and so forth). Stumpf wanted the inspectorates to be led by general staff specialists who would report to the Luftwaffe general staff and serve as the point of communication between the troops and the general staff.[11]

Colonel Hans Jeschonnek, chief of the operations staff of the Luftwaffe general staff, argued against Stumpf in a memo that he sent to Göring in January 1938. Jeschonnek argued that the general staff of the Luftwaffe should be "free of ballast" and should be kept small and serve as a purely operational staff concerned with only planning and operations.[12] Göring ignored Stumpf's arguments and in February 1938 created the post of general inspector of the Luftwaffe, which would supervise the ten inspectorates of the Luftwaffe and report to Göring. However, the inspectorates would still also report to the general staff on matters of training and personnel and equipment requirements.[13] Such an approach to the responsibilities of the general staff was anathema to General Wever who cautioned the Luftwaffe general staff that, on matters of supply, maintenance, and provision of spare parts, "Do not say—That is not the General Staff's work."[14] In 1935 Wever had insisted that the organization of supply from the factory to the units and the organization of ground support facilities as well as setting up communications nets was one of the primary missions of the general staff.[15]

On 1 February 1939 Stumpf, battered by the infighting at the top levels of

General Hans-Jürgen Stumpf, Luftwaffe chief of staff, 1937–1939. (Photo from USAF HRA.)

the Luftwaffe, gave up his post and was replaced by the forty-year-old Colonel Hans Jeschonnek. The young chief of staff had an impressive record as a staff officer but limited experience as a commander (Jeschonnek commanded a bomber wing from 1935 to 1937). Jeschonnek had seen service in World War I as a fighter pilot toward the end of the conflict and had even shot down two Allied planes. After the war he was sent to the Reichswehr air staff and then to the general staff training where he had graduated at the top of his class. From the late 1920s to 1935, he had held responsible positions as a section leader in the Truppenamt and Weapons Office.[16] He was clearly energetic and intelligent. He had a reputation for brilliance and was considered to be the "wunderkind" of the Luftwaffe general staff. Walter Wever saw in Jeschonnek an eventual chief of staff of the Luftwaffe.[17]

Jeschonnek assumed his post with numerous disadvantages as well. His youth and relative lack of command experience and low rank put him at a disadvantage in convincing older and much more experienced officers—men such as Sperrle, Kesselring, von Richthofen, and Felmy—that his own vision of air power was the right one. Jeschonnek also suffered from an attitude toward Hitler that was frank hero worship. In January 1939 a new production program, the Kammhuber program, was proposed by the Nazi leadership in which the Luftwaffe was expected to grow fivefold in three years. Most of the Luftwaffe's top leadership, including Milch, thought the proposal was ludicrous and that such an expansion was impossible given the scarcity of raw materials, resources, and finance. Yet, Jeschonnek, then the Luftwaffe chief of operations, argued for assuming an attitude of blind trust and obedience to the whims of the Führer: "I take the view that it is our duty not to let down the Führer. If he has ordered this program he also knows the means by which it can be carried out."[18]

The influence of Jeschonnek on the Luftwaffe during his tenure as chief of staff from 1939 to his death by suicide in 1943 was overwhelmingly negative. Despite his reputation for brilliance, Jeschonnek's vision of air power was deeply flawed. As commander of the bomber wing at Greifswald in the mid-1930s he had direct experience of the problems of hitting ground targets when flying horizontal bombers at high altitude. Along with Udet, he came to believe that the dive bomber was the only answer to improving bomber accuracy and so he accepted Udet's policy of turning virtually all bombers into dive bombers. The overemphasis of the dive bomber at the expense of delaying the development and production of some very good conventional bomber designs hurt the Luftwaffe greatly as World War II progressed. Jeschonnek is not alone in the responsibility for this policy, but he does carry much of the blame.[19]

Even more damaging to the Luftwaffe was Jeschonnek's overemphasis on the concept of blitzkrieg. Jeschonnek's vision of air power was its employment in short campaigns of maximum intensity. According to Jeschonnek, the Luftwaffe should maintain no reserves of pilots or materiel. In the case of a war or campaign, everything—including the training units and instructor pilots—would be thrown into the campaign and nothing held back. Such an approach might provide maximum effectiveness and firepower in the short term, but in the long term raiding the training centers for aircraft and personnel mortgaged the Luftwaffe's future. Colonel Plocher, chief of the operations staff, urged Jeschonnek to consider planning for the possibility of a long war but Jeschonnek rejected this sensible suggestion. While Jeschonnek overemphasized the dive bomber he also viewed air warfare almost solely in terms of combat aircraft. Jeschonnek expressed little interest in developing the transport and reconnaissance forces of the Luftwaffe.[20] While the Luftwaffe would go to war with impressive reconnaissance and transport forces—the result of Wilhelm Wimmer's production programs—these forces would also suffer from the neglect of the chief of staff as the war dragged on.

It is ironic to note that numerous historians have commonly described the Luftwaffe's lack of emphasis on heavy bombers or on strategic bombers as the result of what happens when army officers turned airmen, such as Kesselring and Stumpf, took over the leadership of the Luftwaffe. Under their influence, the Luftwaffe supposedly turned from a strategically oriented force into a force that emphasized supporting army operations. Yet, in reality, Kesselring and Stumpf tended to follow the vision of air power set forth by General Wever, which emphasized the bomber and strategic campaigns. It was Jeschonnek—the former fighter pilot and bomber wing commander, the officer who had not served in the ground forces but had always served with the air arm or the air staff—who was the most guilty in turning the Luftwaffe away from the heavy bomber and strategic air warfare. The former army ground officers in the Luftwaffe, notably Wever, Kesselring, and Stumpf, possessed a much broader and more strategically oriented vision of air power than some of the professional airmen.

Although the Luftwaffe experienced upheavals in the organization and leadership at the top levels from 1936 to 1939, the Luftwaffe organization at the tactical and operational level evolved fairly rationally and efficiently. While organizing the Luftwaffe on the basis of territorial commands made good sense in the early stages of rearming, building an infrastructure, and creating the basis of an operational force, it was not an organization that one could efficiently go to war with. By 1938, the territorial commands no longer filled the role as combatant commands. The air districts were primarily logis-

Colonel General Hans Jeschonnek, Luftwaffe chief of staff, 1939–1943. (Photo from USAF HRA.)

tical and administrative in their nature. While the air districts did have control of air defense and civil defense in their regions, their primary mission was in supervising the construction and administration of the Luftwaffe infrastructure such as airfields, depots, and training facilities. For the wartime missions, the Luftwaffe organized air fleet (Luftflotte) headquarters to exercise command of large air units in combat operations. The air fleet headquarters, like the headquarters of a field army, was task-organized for its mission. The air fleet could command significant bomber, fighter, recon, and transport forces. In addition, the air fleet would have its own logistics, engineer, flak, and communications units. The air fleet, like a field army, would be assigned air divisions (Fliegerdivisionen), which would be made up of several groups or wings and might constitute 100 to 300 aircraft. More than one air division might be organized into an air corps (Fliegerkorps). The air divisions and air corps had their own headquarters and supporting troops. Depending on the task, the air division or air corps might be a specialized force—as the VIII Air Corps was for ground support or as other air corps and divisions were organized for the airborne units—or it might be a multipurpose force employing a variety of air units from flak to bombers. This form of organization proved itself to be effective in combat.

MOVING TO A MATURE AIR POWER DOCTRINE

One thing that the Luftwaffe had in its favor in developing practical operational doctrine for the rapidly expanding force in the late 1930s was the general staff tradition that the Luftwaffe had inherited from the army. While the political infighting at the very top of the Luftwaffe was severe, the Luftwaffe was by no means paralyzed. With the exception of a few Göring appointees like Udet and Loerzer, the senior commanders and senior staff officers of the Luftwaffe were experienced professional soldiers and airmen. The release of general staff officers from the army to the Luftwaffe and the recall of airmen with military experience from the old imperial Luftstreitkräfte ensured that the best aspects of the old general staff ethic were employed in developing doctrine and tactics for the new force. The Imperial army and the Reichswehr had emphasized training and maneuvers as a means of testing and modifying operational doctrine. The Luftwaffe set out with an intensive program of war games and exercises with the same philosophy as the army. As new Luftwaffe units were created, the Luftwaffe general staff and the Luftwaffe air district commands directed numerous large-scale exercises so that the new operational doctrine as outlined in Luftwaffe Regulation 16 could be tested under trying field conditions. Each of the major maneuvers was studied intensively and critically by the staffs with the intent of noting deficiencies in training, equipment, tactics, and planning. The lessons learned from these exercises and war games were quickly published and circulated throughout the Luftwaffe commands so that subordinate commands and units could keep abreast of the latest tactical and operational concepts to be employed in their own training plans.

The year 1936 saw three major Luftwaffe regional exercises and large-scale participation of the Luftwaffe in a five-day army/Luftwaffe maneuver in Hessen.[21] An exercise in Dresden tested the civil defense, flak, and air defense systems against a simulated bombing attack.[22] The major army/Luftwaffe maneuvers included coordinating with the army's new panzer units. Both the "red" and "blue" forces had Luftwaffe reconnaissance, fighters, and bombers under their command. Both sides attempted to gain air superiority by bombing the other's airfields. The blue force carried out an interdiction campaign and set its fighter forces to find and attack the red forces' motorized columns on the road. As the exercise progressed, the blue forces successfully "bombed" the bridges across the Main River between Frankfurt and Aschaffenburg, thereby crippling the movement of the red motorized forces.[23]

Under generals Kesselring and Stumpf, the Luftwaffe embarked on a program of the largest peacetime air and joint air/ground exercises seen in the interwar period. The Wehrmacht maneuvers of September 1937 included all services in a six-day exercise across the North German Plain from Hannover north to the coast. The army employed over twenty divisions in the exercise, including two of its new panzer divisions. Most of the Luftwaffe's operational units took part, including seventeen bomber groups, six flak regiments, seven fighter groups, one stuka group, and numerous reconnaissance squadrons and ground support units.[24] Part of the Luftwaffe, especially the reconnaissance, stuka, and fighter units, carried out missions in direct support of the army troops including close air support employed to support attacks and to support defenders. However, most of the Luftwaffe's effort went into strategic campaigns against the enemy cities and transportation net. The ports were a favored target as well as rail yards and industrial facilities. The Luftwaffe bombers practiced flying operational missions at night and in poor weather.[25] The civil defense system of the Reich was strenuously tested with simulated incendiary attacks, gas attacks, and attacks with delayed-fuse bombs.[26] New defense procedures were created. On 22 September, Stettin was covered in artificial fog to protect industrial facilities from attack by bombers.[27] For the first time in maneuvers, the Luftwaffe dropped a paratroop company to seize a vital bridge and hold it until advancing motorized troops relieved them.

Numerous lessons were learned from the exercise. The system for giving orders, particularly for the air defense, was "too slow and bureaucratic."[28] The air reporting system worked too slowly and, in some cases, the tactics of the defending fighter force were criticized. However, for most of the exercise, the Luftwaffe found that the flak and fighter force had done a good job in the defense.[29] The bomber force had performed competently, "sinking" and "damaging" numerous merchant and naval ships in harbor attacks. The new paratroop force had performed especially well and had dropped successfully on the target, had seized and held their bridge in support of the motorized forces. The coordination of air and ground operations needed work but had gone relatively well. The 1937 maneuvers had shown the government and the rest of the Wehrmacht that it could conduct a wide variety of both offensive and defensive operations. Numerous deficiencies at the tactical level were noted, and the Luftwaffe staff went to work to make improvements. Moreover, the 1937 maneuvers confirmed the Luftwaffe in its emphasis of strategic bombing as a primary mission.

In the development of air doctrine, Albert Kesselring proved himself to be a worthy successor to General Wever. As soon as he was appointed chief of staff he set about to rectify some of the weaknesses in air doctrine. At this time, the Luftwaffe had no night fighter forces so in June 1936, Kesselring directed that night fighter exercises be held with the view to develop doctrine and tactics for a specialized night air defense force.[30] The result was the creating of the Luftwaffe's first manual for the conduct of a night fighter defense published in April 1937.[31] Kesselring could lay claim to the title of the founder of German night fighters.

Kesselring strongly supported the program to produce a long-range heavy bomber. General Paul Deichmann, the chief of Kesselring's operations staff, argued strongly for a four-engine bomber program in early 1937, and the Luftwaffe general staff requested that such an aircraft be developed.[32] Erhard Milch was, however, was much less enthusiastic about the program than the Luftwaffe general staff.[33] While the heavy bomber project begun under Wever's tenure was dropped due to the poor performance of the prototypes in April 1937, both Kesselring and Stumpf pushed Milch and the air ministry for a new heavy bomber program. The air ministry gave in and on 2 June 1937, as Stumpf assumed the post of chief of staff, the Heinkel company was told to proceed with the heavy bomber project that was to result in the Heinkel He 177 heavy bomber.[34]

One major change by Kesselring in Luftwaffe doctrine was a greater emphasis put on the development and production of fighter aircraft. In December 1936 Kesselring requested that the air ministry develop and produce two types of fighter aircraft. The first was designated the light fighter plane. It was to have a single engine, high-speed (almost 400 mph at 18,000 feet), instrumentation for night and blind flight, a flight duration of one and a half hours, and moderate armament of two heavy and two light machine guns. The Me 109, just entering production, would meet the standards set by Kesselring. The general staff envisioned the light fighter in the primary role as a bomber and fighter interceptor and a secondary role in conducting low-level ground attacks. Kesselring requested that the light fighter be equipped to carry light bombs.[35] The heavy fighter requested by Kesselring, essentially what was to become the Me 110, was to be long range (three hours flight duration), fast (340–400 mph), with full instrumentation for night flying. It was to be very heavily armed with at least two cannons and two to four machine guns and was to fulfill the primary roles as an interceptor, long-range bomber escort, and long-range reconnaissance aircraft. Its secondary mission was to serve as a light bomber capable of low-level attacks. For this purpose it was to have bomb racks and a simple bombsight.[36]

Kesselring took considerable pride in the role he played in fostering the development of the paratroop and air landing units as an important part of the Luftwaffe.[37] By mid-1937 a full paratroop training program was in place with each paratrooper required to do six jumps at the completion of a three-month training course.[38] By mid-1937, battalion-level training had begun.[39] General Stumpf carried on the initiative that Kesselring had made in building an operational paratroop force with enthusiasm. Stumpf wanted to see the paratroops as an elite force. In addition to being able to jump out of planes, each paratrooper was to be fully trained in a second specialty such as pioneer or machine gunner.[40]

In July 1938 the paratroop forces were put under the command of Major General Kurt Student.[41] In September 1938 the paratroop forces were renamed the 7th *Fliegerdivision* (Air Division) and that same month, took part in Germany's first large-scale airborne exercises.[42] Student, now also given the title of inspector of paratroops, was an imaginative and technically proficient officer who believed that paratroops and air landing forces had the potential to be a major operational weapon. Student had worked extensively with gliders in the early 1920s and in 1938 argued successfully for the production of large numbers of gliders for landing infantrymen and equipment behind enemy lines. A suitable glider that carried ten passengers was already available and it was put into production.[43] Student convinced the Luftwaffe

General der Flieger Kurt Student as chief of the airborne forces. (Photo from USAF HRA.)

staff of the broad possibilities of the use of paratroops for much more than small commando-raids. He saw that paratroops, more than any other force, had the capability of achieving surprise. During the war scare of 1938 Student took an active role in planning to use his full paratroop force to seize vital airfields in Czechoslovakia.[44] In the summer of 1938, as part of his vision for the airborne force to be used in major operations, he directed that airborne artillery units be equipped with light and specially modified field pieces and a full range of support forces such as engineers, signalers, medical units, and antitank units be established to give the airborne forces the same firepower as an infantry division.[45] Six transport groups of Ju 52 aircraft were assigned as part of the 7th Air Division and directed to train as a specialist air-dropping force.

By early 1939, the idea of using airborne forces at the operational level of war had caught on to the point that the army's 22nd Infantry Division was designated as an air landing division and directed to be trained in glider operations to fight alongside the paratroops.[46] Large-scale paratroop exercises with the army in the summer of 1939 convinced the army that this new force could play an important role. The paratroop force made several successful surprise drops and seized objectives in a maneuver directed by Colonel General von Kluge. He and the army were impressed by the fulfillment of Student's prediction that paratroops could indeed achieve surprise and gain strategic objectives.[47]

CONCEPTS OF STRATEGIC BOMBING

The period from the mid-1930s to the start of World War II saw considerable open debate and discussion within the military journals and air power literature concerning the role of a strategic bombing doctrine for Germany. Several Luftwaffe officers wrote about the necessity for the Luftwaffe to be oriented toward a doctrine of strategic bombing.[48] German exponents of a strategic bombing doctrine paralleled much of British and American thought of the time. Major Erwin Gehrts wrote in the Luftwaffe's journal of military theory that the will of an enemy nation is incorporated in its industry as much as in its armed forces and that the destruction of enemy industry by strategic bombing was the fastest and surest way to break the enemy will.[49]

Luftwaffe general staff major Hans-Detlef Herhudt von Rohden was certainly the most prolific and eloquent of Germany's strategic air war theorists.[50] Von Rohden, like so many German military thinkers of the era, was a disciple of the geopolitical theories of Karl Haushofer.[51] Haushofer theorized that Germany needed living space (Lebensraum) to support its security but that it was hemmed in on several sides by hostile nations.[52] Von Rohden, starting with Haushofer, argued that geography worked to Germany's disadvantage making the fatherland vulnerable to air attack from enemies on all sides.[53] This was a common theme in German air power thought of the 1930s and was expressed in numerous books and articles of the period.[54] From this perspective, it was argued that the Luftwaffe was Germany's first line of defense. It was also argued that air power in the form of strategic air attack was the only means by which Germany could strike quickly and put its more populous enemies at a disadvantage.

In a series of articles for the *Militärwissenschaftliche Rundschau* in 1937, von Rohden attempted to outline a comprehensive theory of aerial warfare with strategic bombing at its center, which he called the "operative Luftkrieg" (operational air war).[55] Von Rohden's theory of air war was published in book form the next year with the Clausewitzian title, *On Air War (Vom Luftkriege: Gedanken über Führung und Einsatz moderner Luftwaffen).* Von Rohden's theory started by taking Haushofer's geopolitical theories further. Because modern aircraft were able to span great distances, the air war of the future would not just occur in continental terms—it would become an intercontinental war. The strategic bomber would become the primary weapon of the intercontinental conflict.[56]

Von Rohden started with the concept of "overall conduct of warfare" (Gesamtkriegführung), arguing the air force was an inherently strategic weapon that should be employed primarily as a force directed by the high command. He argued cautiously that air power theory needed to stand between the extremes of Douhet and the army preference for tactical employment. Air power could and should be used in its auxiliary roles of reconnaissance and tactical support for the army. The air force, von Rohden argued, could not win wars alone. At times the air force should be thrown in as a supporting weapon in decisive sea and land engagements but, as a general rule, the air force was best left as a concentrated force that could be employed in striking the enemy heartland directly.

In espousing his theory of strategic employment of air power as the primary role of the air force, von Rohden was arguing from a practical standpoint. Modern ground and sea forces were well equipped with antiaircraft weapons and forces, and attacks directly against the enemy armed forces would result in heavy losses. The enemy, however, could not employ the same level of resources for protecting its industrial base, and attacking enemy industry would be less costly. Von Rohden believed, along with the doctrine expressed in Regulation 16, that the first part of an air campaign should be an attack against the enemy air force, including the airfields and infrastructure of the air force. After this campaign was won and air superiority gained, the air force could then concentrate on the sources of enemy power: "Destruction of enemy production centers and their supply of raw materials is an all-important task of operational air warfare."[57] Destruction of vital factories and the disruption of the enemy transport net would result in a paralysis of the enemy economy and the resultant collapse of morale on the home front. This was not an argument for Douhetian terror bombing. The vital industries and transportation centers that would be targeted for shutdown were valid military targets. Civilians were not to be targeted directly, but the breakdown of production would affect their morale and will to fight. German legal scholars of the 1930s carefully worked out guidelines for what type of bombing was permissible under international law. While direct attacks against civilians were ruled out as "terror bombing," the concept of attacking the vital war industries—and the probable heavy civilian casualties and breakdown of civilian morale—was ruled as acceptable under the Geneva Convention.[58]

Von Rohden's theory of air war was certainly popular within the Luftwaffe and his preference for a strategic air war was probably shared by the majority of Luftwaffe officers on the eve of the war. The problem with von Rohden's theory was that it was simply too general and provided little practical detail about targeting. Questions such as: How many centers should be attacked? How many bombs should be dropped on each type of industry? Which industries should be targeted first? Von Rohden left these essential questions unanswered and so brought the Luftwaffe only partway to a comprehensive strategic air war doctrine. However, von Rohden was important in that he provided the Luftwaffe with strong arguments for keeping strategic bombing at the forefront of German air doctrine.

Technological developments of the mid- and late-1930s were exploited by the Luftwaffe to bring it closer to a vision of strategic bombing. A system was developed in the 1930s that enabled the Luftwaffe bombers to fly a series of narrow radio beams. As the bomber approached the target the plane, flying along the beam, was intersected by three beams. The first alerted the bombardier, the second and third measured ground speed and determined the moment for automatic bomb release. The first of the systems, called Knickebein or "X-Gerät," could bring a bomber and its bombload to within one kilometer of the target at a range of several hundred kilometers. The second apparatus, called the "Y-Gerät," was even more accurate. This would enable the Luftwaffe bomber force to hit enemy industrial centers at night or in bad weather with reasonable accuracy. By the time of the campaign in France in 1940, two X-Gerät stations had been established in Germany and more would soon be ready for deployment.[59] Once the Luftwaffe had tested the prototype radio beam bombing devices in the winter of 1938, a specialized bomber wing was created, KG 100, as a force equipped and trained to use this new bombing method. KG 100 would become the Luftwaffe's pathfinder force for strategic bombing.[60] Use of such new technologies for the bomber force was strongly supported by the Luftwaffe's general staff. As chief of staff, Kesselring stressed the importance of training bomber navigators and bombardiers to operate on long-range missions and at high altitude.[61] Most major Luftwaffe exercises from 1936–1939 included the use of bombers in long-range strategic missions in both day and night operations. For example, the maneuvers of Air Fleet 2 in 1939 were centered on a strategic campaign conducted by the "Blue Force," based in Northwest Germany, against the primary ports (Lübeck and Wismar) of the "Red Force." The "Red Force," based in Northeastern Germany, centered its air campaign on attacking the strategic industries of the Ruhr, Osnabrück, and Münster.[62] Even Jeschonnek's advocacy of joint operations could not shake the senior leaders of the Luftwaffe for practicing for a strategic air campaign.

AIR DEFENSE DOCTRINE

From 1936 on, the Luftwaffe general staff put added emphasis on the development of an air defense doctrine and the fighter force. While the Luftwaffe was still envisioned as a bomber-heavy force, the plans for the production of fighter planes in 1937–1939 were increased—partly due to the experience of the war in Spain and the importance of using fighters for escort of the bombers and for the air superiority battle there. Between April 1937 and September 1938 a total of almost 1,500 fighters were produced, compared to approximately 2,000 bombers.[63] The production plans of 1938 called for the delivery of 335 fighters a month as opposed to 282 bombers.[64]

The concepts of using fighter planes changed between 1934 and 1939. The fighter tactics of the mid-1930s had emphasized combat between single aircraft and small flights. By 1939, the tactics developed by the Luftwaffe's fighter inspectorate emphasized flying in squadron formations and more complex tactics of different flights within a squadron engaging different parts of an enemy squadron or group formation.[65] Fighter tactics also became specialized for the capabilities of the aircraft. The fighter inspectorate also developed special tactics for combating a formation of enemy two-seat fighters.[66] The speed of aircraft had changed tactics since the mid-1930s, when most air powers still relied on biplanes. By 1938, the Luftwaffe was practicing fighter intercepts at 300 mph.[67]

The employment of flak artillery remained central to the Luftwaffe's doctrine of air defense. In a Luftwaffe general staff conference in 1939, it was noted that the effectiveness of the flak had been unappreciated in World War I but that Spain had shown that the modern flak arm could do very well in combat.[68] From the founding of the Luftwaffe, the Luftwaffe's commanders had put enormous resources into flak artillery. By 1939 the flak arm had grown into a force of 100,000 men organized into twenty-seven regiments. Germany in that year had a force of 182 heavy, 23 medium, and 149 light flak batteries, as well as 59 searchlight batteries. At the start of the war, Germany had 5,511 light and medium flak guns and 2,362 heavy guns, for a total of 7,873 air defense guns. Upon mobilization for war, additional reserve units could be added to the total, including flak machine gun units, heavy flak guns mounted on rail cars, and barrage balloon units.[69]

As with the bomber force, technological developments greatly affected the capabilities and doctrine of the air defense force. The development of radar had begun seriously in 1933 and the Gema Company had been formed in 1934 to produce radar for the German navy.[70] Colonel Wolfgang Martini, the Luftwaffe's chief of communications, requested that private industry adapt the radar being used by the navy for the Luftwaffe—especially in regard to developing radar that could measure altitude. By 1936 the prototype "Freya" radar tested by the Luftwaffe could locate an aircraft at an 80-kilometer distance. Martini first ordered twelve of these radar, and soon increased the Luftwaffe order to 200.[71] In the fall 1937 maneuvers, radar was employed by the Luftwaffe for aircraft warning and proved to be a sensation.[72] By 1938 an improved Freya radar was delivered that could spot aircraft at a range of 120 kilometers.[73] In 1936 work began on the Würzburg radar for close-range coordination with the flak. By 1940, when the Würzburg was deployed with the flak, it had a 40-kilometer range *and* the ability to measure altitude accurately.[74]

The Luftwaffe began creating a coastal chain of radar for air defense in 1937–1939—at the same time that the British were developing their coastal chain of radar stations.[75] The effectiveness of the German radar chain was demonstrated on 18 December 1939, when an RAF raid of twenty-four Wellington bombers targeting Wilhelmshafen were picked up 113 kilometers out by the Freya radars. The Luftwaffe managed a fighter intercept of the British raiders, shooting down twelve and badly damaging three for a loss of two Me 109s.[76] German radar progressed so that, by the summer of 1939, aircraft-mounted radar for night interception of bombers was given field tests.[77]

Even in 1939, however, most of the air defense of Germany was a decentralized defense of point targets, and the responsibility for coordinating air defense was given to the air district headquarters. The Luftwaffe general staff directed that point defense of vital industrial and military targets was the primary mission of the home defense forces, and the fighter forces were restricted to small regions for the defense of their assigned sector. Free-ranging fighter sweeps were not approved.[78] Steps were taken, however, to create a central air defense command to coordinate the air defense of the western region of Germany. In 1938 the Western Air Defense Zone (Luftverteidigungszone West) was created, extending 600 kilometers from Münster down to the Swiss border with a depth of 20 to 100 kilometers. Strong flak and fighter defenses were emplaced in this region, primarily for the protection of the industrial heart of Germany, the Ruhr. The commander of the Western Air Defense Zone came under the direct command of the commander in chief of the Luftwaffe.[79]

The core of the Luftwaffe's air defense doctrine, however, remained the offensive air campaign to attack the enemy air force on the ground, crippling its infrastructure and ground installations so that a strategic bombing campaign would not be attempted, and German home defenses not put to the test. A major part of the 1936 and 1937 Wehrmacht and Luftwaffe war games consisted of an air offense against the French air force and its ground bases and infrastructure. The object of the war game was not just to take out the French air force in the border region and gain air superiority along the army's front. The Luftwaffe staff planned to carry the air superiority campaign deep into France and to attack airfields, factories, depots, and facilities in the center of the country.[80] Well into the world war, the Luftwaffe maintained that the best air defense of Germany lay in an aggressive offensive air campaign.[81]

ARMY SUPPORT DOCTRINE

The period 1936 to 1939 saw a noticeable increase in the doctrinal emphasis placed on Luftwaffe operations in coordination with the ground forces. Although army support operations remained a secondary priority for the Luftwaffe, developing the techniques for coordination of air/ground operations and training both services in these tactics took up a great deal of the Luftwaffe's time and resources.

As far as the general staff's fighter inspectorate was concerned, the use of fighter planes in low-level attacks against ground targets was an important secondary mission for the fighter force—after winning the air superiority battle—and the fighter inspectorate worked to create tactics for attacks against ground targets. In a paper presented to the fighter inspectorate in November 1936, Major Raithel described the primary targets for the fighters when supporting the ground battle: enemy reserve forces, artillery positions, and roads and bridges behind the enemy battlefront to tie down enemy forces and prevent their movement or counterattack.[82] Fighter planes were expected to carry light bombs and to be proficient in dropping them. The use of the weather and low-level flying to achieve surprise in the ground attack was stressed.[83] At that time, the use of aircraft to destroy enemy armored vehicles was not really possible with the armament available to the fighter forces—light bombs and machine guns—but Major Raithel assured his fighter inspectorate colleagues that better armament, such as aircraft cannon, would enable the fighter force to assume this important mission. In short, the emphasis for army support missions in Luftwaffe doctrine was on conducting interdiction campaigns rather than on direct close support for troops engaged in combat on the front.

While the fighter forces might be unleashed in an interdiction campaign close behind the enemy lines, the bomber, stuka, and long-range fighter forces would be expected to carry out interdiction campaigns considerably farther behind the fighting front. The Luftwaffe envisioned combining bomber, reconnaissance, heavy fighter, and stuka groups into an aerial task force to carry out specific missions. To effectively destroy a target such as a rail net deep behind the enemy lines, a combination of a reconnaissance squadron, stukas, and horizontal bomber units was envisioned. General Kesselring called this the "combined attack with mixed units."[84] Planning and coordinating such aerial task forces was seen as an important training mission of the Luftwaffe, and the general staff stressed practicing such coordination in its directives for operational war training in 1938.[85]

To further increase the capability of the Luftwaffe in the ground attack role, the Luftwaffe's reconnaissance aircraft were designed to carry light bombloads and were expected to serve as light day bombers as a secondary mission. This concept was tried and endorsed in the Luftwaffe's war games of 1936/1937.[86] The new reconnaissance aircraft ordered by the Luftwaffe after

1936 had light bomber capability. For example, the Focke-Wulf 189, a twin-engine reconnaissance plane especially designed for army cooperation duties and which entered production in 1938, was capable of carrying a 450-pound bombload.[87]

The experience of Spain, however, demonstrated the capability of aircraft to intervene decisively in ground operations. In April 1937, the Luftwaffe requested the development of a heavily armed and armored aircraft specifically designed for ground attack. The Henschel and Focke Wulf companies began the development of what would become the Henschel 129. The Henschel aircraft was designed for survivability against ground fire and thus had two engines. For the attack role, it was envisioned with a variety of weapons including a 30-mm cannon.[88]

The senior Luftwaffe commanders stressed the importance of joint training for Luftwaffe officers. In September 1936, the Luftwaffe general staff directed that the operational commanders assign reconnaissance squadrons to train with specific army divisions and corps.[89] While training in air tactics was given top priority, training in ground tactics was given second priority. Kesselring directed that "Those assigned to support of the ground or sea forces have a duty to understand the operations of those forces."[90] To increase interservice understanding, the army high command agreed that the Luftwaffe could send its junior officers to army maneuvers and exercises to serve as temporary infantry or artillery platoon commanders.[91] After his return from Spain as commander of the Condor Legion, General Sperrle placed great stress on training his 5th Air District Forces (later to become the Third Air Fleet) in joint army/air operations. He directed that Luftwaffe base commanders set up joint war games and exercises with the local army unit commanders. He further insisted that the senior army units in his region include the Luftwaffe in their war games and exercises and mobilization planning. The Luftwaffe officers were not to attend army training and war games as observers but were expected to take a direct part acting as air commanders in training exercises.[92] Under Sperrle, Luftwaffe officers were expected to know army tactics and doctrine, and he expected his officers to educate the army about the roles and capabilities of air power. It was an ethic that was stressed throughout the Luftwaffe.

From the Luftwaffe's and the army's point of view, the most important part of the air/ground partnership was the cooperation of the Luftwaffe with the army's panzer and motorized divisions. Both the army and the Luftwaffe held that air support needed to be concentrated at the decisive point of battle, and that the army's panzer and motorized divisions would be deployed at

Henschel Hs 129 ground attack aircraft. Development of this heavily armed plane began in 1937 after the experience in Spain gave a higher priority to the close air support mission. (Photo from USAF HRA.)

this schwerpunkt (decisive point). The first requirement for the army in conducting a war of maneuver was in obtaining accurate intelligence in a rapidly changing battlefield. For this purpose, the Luftwaffe created a large force of specialized reconnaissance aircraft and divided these aircraft into two different forces. One force consisted of long-range, high-performance aircraft such as the Do 17 bomber and were to be used for "operational air reconnaissance," namely the support of the Luftwaffe's bomber forces engaged in strategic air warfare.[93] The second force was designated as the "tactical air reconnaissance force" and would directly support the army's requirement for intelligence and observation in the battle zone. This second force would be equipped mostly with light aircraft such as the Henschel Hs 126, which were capable of flying in and out of rough forward airfields located in the close proximity of army division and corps headquarters.[94]

The tactical reconnaissance force had to have a thorough understanding of army tactics and operations to spot and identify enemy units, artillery, and armored formations in the battle zone. Reconnaissance pilots had to be able to use their judgment in accurately reporting the significance and threat of enemy movements and formations to the ground commanders. They had to be better at reading a map and understanding terrain than other pilots.[95] Under the operational battle doctrine of the panzer troops, the conduct of extensive reconnaissance was essential in selecting the routes of advance and in selecting the place and time to engage the enemy forces. Heinz Guderian, the noted German armored warfare theorist and panzer force commander, noted the important role that tactical air reconnaissance played in conducting armor operations in his 1937 book *Achtung-Panzer!*[96] From 1936 to 1939, constant exercises with the panzer force were conducted by the tactical reconnaissance units of the Luftwaffe. Many of these exercises were large operations including several army divisions.[97]

To coordinate some aspects of the Luftwaffe's support for the army, each army headquarters and sometimes a corps headquarters would have a senior Luftwaffe officer assigned as the *Koluft* or commander–air force (*Ko*mmandeure der *Luft*waffe). The *Koluft* had command of Luftwaffe flak units attached to the army for air defense on the battlefront and of tactical reconnaissance squadrons assigned to support the field army or corps. He was to advise the army commander on all aviation matters and had responsibility for coordinating Luftwaffe logistical support for the army.[98] The *Koluft* worked under the direction of the army commander and, as the Luftwaffe was not especially happy about subordinating Luftwaffe units to ground commanders, did not have any authority over Luftwaffe combat aircraft.[99] However, the Luftwaffe had a system of air liaison officers in place, by the mid-1930s, who were under Luftwaffe control and had the responsibility for coordinating combat air support. The *Flivos* (air liaison officers) were detached from operational units given the mission of supporting the army and deployed to corps headquarters and down to division level in the case of panzer divisions. The *Flivo* took with him his own communications team and was required to report the ground situation to the supporting air division or air corps commander. This gave the senior Luftwaffe commanders involved in ground operations an accurate and quick picture of the combat situation. With the information of the *Flivo* at hand, the Luftwaffe commander could decide to commit forces to close support operations. The *Flivos* appeared in the 1937 Wehrmacht maneuvers and became a regular part of army/air operations thereafter.[100]

Close air support of army panzer operations were also part of the 1937 maneuvers with a fighter group allocated for direct support on call for a panzer division.[101] With the successful employment of close air support (CAS) on the battlefront in Spain, General Sperrle, commander of the Condor Legion from 1936–1937, became a strong advocate for training the Luftwaffe in CAS operations. The Third Air Fleet, under Sperrle's command, conducted several large exercises with the army in which the Ju 87 stukas and the Hs 123 ground attack planes were employed, flying close air support missions targeting enemy strong points directly in front of the army's armored units.[102] Through 1938 there were numerous army/air force maneuvers in which the stuka and bomber forces practiced close support of armor units in operations such as river-crossing exercises and meeting engagements.[103]

Hans Jeschonnek was especially impressed by the ability of the Luftwaffe to intervene in the ground battle in Spain by destroying strong defensive fortifications. He insisted that airmen had to understand the ground war and put a greater emphasis on close air support as integral to army operational doctrine.[104] While air support for ground operations was still achieved primarily via interdiction campaigns, Jeschonnek diverted significant resources to the CAS mission. Arguing that close air support "is the most difficult mission that can be given to an air force" and that such missions required "the closest liaison between Luftwaffe commanders and the supported army units,"[105] Jeschonnek decided to create a specialized force for CAS. In the summer of 1939 he consolidated more than half of the stuka force into a "close battle division" (Nahkampfdivision), responsible for providing CAS support to the army. In command of the Nahkampfdivision, he placed Wolfram von Richthofen, who had performed so well directing such operations in Spain.[106]

By the eve of the war, with a newly created, specialized CAS force of over 300 combat aircraft as well as extensive training in CAS operations, the Luftwaffe had the largest and most capable force in the world capable of conducting close air support. It has often been remarked that the Luftwaffe emphasized close air support because its higher ranks were filled with ex-army officers, such as Kesselring and Stumpf, who pushed for this mission. In reality the most enthusiastic practitioners and supporters of CAS operations within the Luftwaffe, Hugo Sperrle and Hans Jeschonnek, were long-term professional airmen, involved in the air service since their days as young officers. The Luftwaffe was not somehow pressured into adopting the army support mission by the army—or by army officers-turned-airmen. It was a mission that fit the Luftwaffe's comprehensive approach to warfare, as well as the culture of joint operations that was a central part of the Luftwaffe's mind-set.

Building specialized aircraft and training the airmen in army support operations, however, is only half the formula for developing an effective air war doctrine. The army had a doctrine of conducting a highly mobile war of maneuver, so the Luftwaffe created the organization, logistics, and support units that would enable the air units supporting such a campaign to be as mobile as the army.[107] The fighter, stuka, and reconnaissance squadrons that would support the army's operations were fairly short-range aircraft. To support a mobile army conducting rapid maneuver, the Luftwaffe units needed to operate from bases as close to the front as possible, for the effective range of a fully loaded Hs 123 was about 70 miles, and that of the Ju 87B about 110 miles.[108] To facilitate forward operations, the Luftwaffe had created an impressive logistics force of 117 motorized supply columns that could move with rapidly advancing army units.[109] Mobile airfield companies and Luftwaffe engineer units could set up a rough forward airfield or take over a captured airfield and, supplied by the mobile columns, turn it into a functioning Luftwaffe base in a matter of hours.[110] This mobile logistics force, developed in the 1930s, harked back to the ability of the old imperial Luftstreitkräfte to deploy rapidly during World War I. In any case, the Luftwaffe's decision to employ considerable resources in the creation of a mobile force would pay dividends in battle, as the Luftwaffe logistics system kept Luftwaffe aircraft operating close to the front with a high sortie rate and quick response time.

OFFICER EDUCATION IN THE LUFTWAFFE

Modern aircraft and technology is less important to an air force than the creation and development of its human resources. Immersed in the intellectual tradition of the German military culture, the Luftwaffe leadership knew the importance of establishing a sound educational foundation for its officer corps. With the Luftwaffe growing so rapidly, one of its first major tasks was, accordingly, to create a thorough and comprehensive officer education program for the force.

The Luftwaffe had an advantage in the quality of recruits, both officer and enlisted: It had a special glamour that the army and navy did not possess, and was thus able to set high recruitment standards.[111] When the Luftwaffe was being formally established as an independent branch of the military, the personnel section had recommended that the officer course be three years long. In 1935, however, due to the shortage of officers, the Luftwaffe decided on a two-year training course for commissioning lieutenants.[112] The Luftwaffe officer course started with a four-month basic training course in which the officer cadets learned drill, military discipline, small-unit leadership, infantry tactics, and the basic law and administration of the Luftwaffe. At this point, the officers of the three main branches of the Luftwaffe—the flying troops, the flak artillery, and the signal corps, were sent to their own branch for training for approximately nine or ten months. The flak artillery and signals cadets served in flak and signals units for most of that period, learning the basic duties of the enlisted men they would one day command. A flak branch cadet, for example, was expected to become proficient at every position in a flak gun crew, from the loader to the gunner and aimer. During this period with the troops, the cadet would be promoted to a junior NCO and given the responsibilities of a low-level command.[113] Cadets accepted for the flying troops spent almost a year in pilot training. The German system of pilot training was as thorough as any major air force provided at that time. Officer cadets received their basic flying licenses then moved on through two more stages, including aerobatics, instrument flying, long-distance flying, and navigation, and plenty of instruction on engines, weaponry, radios, and basic tactics. By the time an officer cadet had completed his basic pilot instruction, he had 180 to 200 hours' total flight time.[114]

The officer cadets from all three primary branches of the Luftwaffe spent nine months together at the Luftkriegsschule (Air War School), where all cadets studied a common curriculum. The curriculum of the Luftkriegsschule emphasized the practical subjects that front officers and small-unit leaders needed to know.[115] The emphasis during these nine months was on tactics and operations. Air superiority campaigns, army support operations, and strategic bombing operations were all studied. Students visited active Luftwaffe units and took part in several war games and exercises. A considerable part of the tactical curriculum was devoted to studying army operations, especially the tactics of the panzer and motorized divisions. There was a short course on the basics of naval operations, as well.[116] Because the education was geared to officers who would be serving in air squadrons or flak battalions, relatively little instruction was on strategy or air power theory. There was a short course on air power history of World War I, but far more emphasis was placed on practical subjects. All officer cadets underwent an air observer course, and the flak and signals officers were expected to spend some time in aircraft and develop a basic familiarity with aviation technology.

At the end of the Luftkriegsschule, all officer aspirants were required to take a comprehensive examination and, after passing, would be commissioned lieutenants and sent to active units. The first officers to pass through the Luftwaffe officer schools rather than the army and navy training programs graduated in 1936.[117] Seven more officer schools were soon established and from 1937–1939 approximately 2,500 lieutenants a year were commissioned by the Luftwaffe.[118]

The newly commissioned lieutenants of the Luftwaffe could expect to spend much of their time in special courses and schools once they arrived at their active units. By 1937 the Luftwaffe's training plan listed dozens of one- to three-week schools for junior officers and NCOs, like a squadron weather officer's course, or unit logistics management training.[119] Newly commissioned pilot officers who arrived at their active units with 200-plus hours of flight time in their logbooks were not yet considered to be fully trained pilots or navigators. Each Luftwaffe wing had a squadron or group designated as the training unit, and incoming officers were sent through an intensive course in the unit's aircraft type and in tactics and navigation before they were listed as combat ready.[120] In addition, each Luftwaffe unit commander was enjoined to establish a program of lectures on tactics, aeronautical science, and military history for the continuing education of the officers and NCOs. The Luftwaffe general staff directed that, after every lecture or seminar on military science or history, a discussion period be held to clear up questions and to see that the officers "learn to express themselves freely."[121] To assist this endeavor, the Luftwaffe had hundreds of foreign articles on military aviation and history translated into German and made available for a professional reading and study program.[122]

The next step in the Luftwaffe's formal officer education system came when an officer reached his eighth year of service. At this time, all Luftwaffe officers would attend a four-month course at the Luftkreisschule (Air District School) in Berlin. The Luftkreisschule was created to provide a common curriculum for officers who would go on to the full Luftwaffe general staff course. The Luftwaffe general staff course consisted of two schools: the Luftkriegsakademie (Air War Academy), oriented toward tactics and operations, and the Lufttechnischakademie (Air Technical Academy), which provided a university-level aeronautical engineering program for Luftwaffe officers. After completing either course, the Luftwaffe officer would be assigned to general staff duties. The establishment of the Air Technical Akademy was a continuation of the von Seeckt reforms in which it was acknowledged that the Luftwaffe, being the most technically oriented of the armed forces, would need to have a corps of general staff officers conversant in technology.

All three schools were founded in 1935. The importance placed on them by General Wever was evident in the quality of their faculties. The first commandant of the Luftkreisschule was General Otto von Stülpnagel, one of Germany's first pilots, a general staff officer of long experience.[123] Von Stülpnagel was soon appointed as commander of the Luftkriegsakademie and General Helmuth Wilberg, another experienced general staff officer and commander, was appointed as the commander of the Luftkreisschule. The Air Technical Academy and the Luftkriegsakademie both had superb faculties. The Air Technical Academy faculty was composed primarily of Ph.D.s in engineering and science, and the Luftkriegsakademie faculty consisted of experienced senior general staff officers for the military subjects, and civilian professors for subjects such as geography, economics, and technology. General von Cochenhausen, an army general staff officer and one of Germany's most prolific and highly regarded military writers of the interwar period, was brought out of retirement to serve as the senior tactical instructor for the Luftkriegsakademie.[124] In establishing the Luftwaffe's general staff schools, General Wever had argued his own vision: that general staff education should not be solely tactical/operational, but should also study Gesamtkriegführung (the overall conduct of war), and that the Luftwaffe's general staff should be educated in such subjects as grand strategy, war economics, armament production, and the mentality of potential opponents.[125]

General Wever's vision was not to be realized. The general staff course was planned as a two-and-a-half- to 3-year program, but the shortage of qualified Luftwaffe general staff officers meant cutting both the Luftkriegsakademie and the Air Technical School courses to about eighteen months. The study of grand strategy, economics, and sociology fell mostly to the wayside, because the Luftkriegsakademie curriculum concentrated mainly on the operational/tactical side of warfare. Nearly a third of the curriculum at the Luftkriegsakademie was focused on air operations. The next largest part of the curriculum was devoted to technology—airframe design, aircraft motors, communications equipment, and so on. Army tactics and operations were given a large place in the curriculum, while naval operations were given a much briefer overview. The rest of the curriculum concerned logistics, aerial photography and foreign military forces. Economics was taught, but to a lesser degree than weather and air operations in the curriculum.[126]

The four-month Luftkreisschule course provided a fairly thorough basic staff course, normally to about thirty-five to forty-two officers.[127] The curriculum was built around seminars in military history, air tactics and operations, basic aviation technology, and Luftwaffe staff procedures. There were numerous exercises and war games. As commandant of the school, Wilberg took a broad approach to air power, bringing in outside civilian experts to lecture in economics, aircraft production, and geography. At the end of the course, all officers were required to take a comprehensive examination, and the top examinees were selected for study at the general staff and technical academies.[128]

The main problem with the Luftwaffe's general staff education was the small number of officers that the Luftwaffe could spare to send to higher education. The Luftkriegsakademie admitted only twenty-five to thirty-two officers per year between 1935 and 1939.[129] The Air Technical School had only nine or ten students per year from 1935 to 1938,[130] which meant that it had more faculty than students. The Air Technical School was closed in 1938, and the students and faculty were combined with the Luftkriegsakademie.[131] In many respects, the Luftwaffe's general staff education was admirable. All student officers were required to study a foreign language, and detailed knowledge of the French army and air force in war games and exercises was required. Indeed, the percentage of Luftwaffe general staff officers with real fluency in a foreign language was very high. In 1939, of approximately 220 officers in the Luftwaffe general staff, 98 had passed examinations in French, 77 in English, 28 in Italian, 23 in Spanish, 14 in Russian, and 17 in other languages. Fifty-five general staff officers had diplomas as fully qualified translators and interpreters.[132] Foreign books and articles were available, and openly discussed in the higher Luftwaffe schools. The Luftwaffe general staff officers were, moreover, expected to be conversant with foreign aviation developments and technologies.

The final step in the education process for general staff officers was the Wehrmachtakademie, established in 1935. The Wehrmachtakademie was to provide selected older, experienced general staff officers from all three services with a one-year course that concentrated on higher strategy and war economics. The officers would be prepared for a true joint staff duty to serve as strategists on the staff of the high command of the Wehrmacht. The realization that such a course was needed for modern warfare was already understood in the 1920s and early 1930s, when selected officers spent a year at the University of Berlin studying economics and politics after completing their normal general staff course (the Reinhard course). The initiative for the school came from the army's General von Reichenau. General Wever was an enthusiastic supporter of the concept, which fit in with his idea that officers needed to be educated in political, economic, and social issues as well as in the operational art.[133] The British Imperial Defense College was used as a model for the type of course the Wehrmacht wanted to establish.[134] General Adam, the former chief of the army's Truppenamt and one of the best strategic minds in the German military, was appointed first commander of the Wehrmachtakademie.[135]

The Wehrmachtakademie admitted in only ten students per year: six from the army, and two each from the Luftwaffe and the navy. The professors were mostly civilians, and outside experts such as managers of armament plants were regularly brought in to lecture. That the Luftwaffe had a high regard for the course is shown by the quality of students that it sent. In the three years of the Wehrmachtakademie's existence, future generals Korten, Schwabedissen, Kreipe, and von Rohden attended the Wehrmachtakademie course.[136] As much as such a school was needed by the Wehrmacht, it was nevertheless closed in 1938, primarily due to interservice rivalry and politics. Göring opposed the school when he saw the creation of a true joint staff as a threat to the Luftwaffe, because any such staff would be army-dominated. War Minister von Blomberg had been a supporter of the school, but when Hitler removed him in 1938 there was no one left in the high command willing to speak up for a true joint strategic education for officers.[137]

In comparison with the other major air forces of the time, the Luftwaffe officers and officers selected for the general staff received an education that was equal—and generally better—than the higher officer education offered by the RAF at its staff college in Andover and the U.S. Army Air Corps in the Air Corps Tactical School at Maxwell Field, Alabama. The Air Corps course at Maxwell Field was for officers of the same rank and experience as the Luftwaffe's Luftkriegsakademie and also to prepare them for higher command and staff duties. The American course was only nine months long and was dominated by the theory of precision strategic bombardment as the school doctrine of air warfare. In the American course in the 1930s there was little interest in joint air/ground operations,[138] and air war subjects such as a study of antiaircraft artillery were largely ignored.[139] Essentially, as was common in the U.S. military staff colleges of the 1930s, operations and tactics were studied in regard to the official "school solution" and dissent from the official dogma was not encouraged. At both the Air Corps Tactical School and the RAF Staff College, there was little interest in or study of foreign aviation ideas or recent air operations in foreign lands.

The scope of the Luftwaffe's higher officer education was much larger than that of the Air Corps school. Considerable attention was given to ground and naval operations. There was no official "school solution" taught as dogma. The war games and exercises at the Luftkriegsakademie featured strategic bombing problems just as the Air Corps Tactical School did, but other types of air operations were also thrown into the play, including army support operations and deployment of flak troops. As in the tradition of the army's Kriegsakademie, Luftwaffe officers' solutions to operational problems presented in war game play would be critically examined on their own merits and discussed freely rather than being graded against a set solution.

An attitude of intellectual freedom was also part of the German general staff tradition that was fostered at the Luftkriegsakademie. In strong contrast to the British and American schools, considerable time was given to the study of foreign air forces and operations. By the start of World War II, the Luftwaffe's general staff officers were far more knowledgeable about the British and American air forces and their way of war than the British and Americans were about the Germans. In general, despite deficiencies such as the closure of the Wehrmachtakademie, the Luftwaffe officers who had completed the general staff course in the 1930s had received a broader and more thorough higher military education than their British and American counterparts.

GERMAN STRATEGY AND AIR WAR PLANNING

The grand strategy set by the German government—that is, the political goals of German policy as they were communicated to the military, had a central role in determining the shape of the Luftwaffe's doctrine in the interwar period. German planning and thinking about war were not done in a vacuum. Throughout the entire 1919–1939 period Germany had a clear enemy in France and in France's eastern allies, Czechoslovakia and Poland. These political evaluations by the national government were clearly stated to the Reichswehr, and later to the Wehrmacht in yearly guidance for strategic planning. The Luftwaffe knew who their enemies were and shaped their air doctrine and planning to deal with specific threats.

In May 1935, War Minister von Blomberg issued the Wehrmacht strategic planning guidance from the Nazi government that was essentially a repetition of the strategic advice given by the Weimar Republic's leaders. The Wehrmacht was still a weak organization so Germany would maintain a posture of strategic defense. The greatest threat was an invasion of Germany by France, which would be supported by Poland and Czechoslovakia. Von Blomberg advised the high command that, with their limited resources, the Wehrmacht in case of war would conduct a delaying and defensive operation in the west, while mounting rapid offensives against the weaker partners of the French coalition, Poland and Czechoslovakia.[140] The Luftwaffe prepared specific war plans for this eventuality. In 1937 a revised strategic assessment was issued by von Blomberg, in which the Luftwaffe was told to plan for a war against Czechoslovakia in which the Czechs might be supported by the Russians as well as by the French.[141] Even though the Wehrmacht had grown considerably stronger, it was still not considered strong enough to conduct a two-front offensive war. The basic form of the war plans therefore remained the same: attack quickly in the east and defend in the west.[142] In the variations of the German war plans (Fall Rot-France, Fall Grün-Czechoslovakia, Fall Weiss-Poland), Germany would be fighting continental neighbors with industries and military facilities as fairly close range. Thus, even if a strategic air campaign was decided on, the medium bombers that Germany was rapidly building in the 1930s were sufficient in range and bombload to carry out the mission.

Hitler and the Nazi government frankly admired the British empire and, in the early years of the third Reich, had hoped that Britain might even be a partner in a great, anti-Bolshevik alliance.[143] As late as 1937, the German military was advised that a war with the United Kingdom was "improbable."[144] Not until Britain started to strongly resist the German demands on Czechoslovakia did the Hitler government realize that Britain might be a possible enemy in a future war. The strategic guidance to the Luftwaffe was changed. Finally, in February 1938 Luftwaffe Group Two—soon to be renamed the Second Air Fleet—was told to prepare plans for a possible war with Britain.[145] The Second Air Fleet was stationed in northwest Germany, the closest force to Britain, and as such had the responsibility for conducting an aerial war with Britain.

As tensions were heating up between Germany and Czechoslovakia in the summer of 1938, General Helmuth Felmy, the commander of the Second Air Fleet, sent a long Denkschrift to Göring concerning the plans for an aerial campaign against Britain. First of all, Felmy bluntly pointed out that his air fleet was in no position to wage a major air campaign against Britain at that time. The problem for the Second Air Fleet was basing and logistics. Because the German strategy up to that time had revolved around a war against France, Poland, and Czechoslovakia, virtually all of the class I and II airfields—those with runways, fuel storage, and maintenance facilities to handle a bomber group—had been built close either to the French border, or to the borders of Germany's eastern enemies. Air Fleets One and Four oriented toward Czechoslovakia and Poland had a total of forty-three class I and II airfields at their disposal in case of war. Air Fleet Three, stationed in the southeast and oriented toward France, had forty suitable airfields. Because Britain had not been considered a probable enemy until recently, the Luftwaffe had only built nine class I and II airfields in Air Fleet Two's northwest German region.[146] As things stood in 1938, Felmy's air fleet could only stage a relatively small bomber force of twelve groups out of northern Germany.

Paratroops as another form of air power. Ju 52 transports loaded with paratroops ready to occupy strategic points in Czechoslovakia, 1938. (Photo from USAF HRA.)

As the Luftwaffe's construction plans stood, not until 1941 or 1942 would there be enough airfields in northern Germany to support a major air campaign against Britain.[147]

Felmy identified the British fleet and merchant marine as primary targets for an air campaign, as the Royal Navy was Britain's primary line of defense. He again bluntly told Göring that his bomber force had little training in overwater operations, or in conducting an antishipping campaign. Moreover, long-range operations against Britain called for major improvements in the Luftwaffe's weather reporting service. Felmy closed out his report of 22 September 1938 with the statement, "A war of destruction against England with the resources that we have on hand is ruled out."[148]

Throughout 1938 and 1939, Felmy set out to train his air fleet and to build up his force for an air campaign against Britain. His commanders and staff conducted war games of an air campaign against Britain in the spring of 1939. Felmy wrote a thorough, twenty-eight-page critique of the war games, reporting that the Luftwaffe's capabilities to conduct an air campaign against the British were still insufficient to win a decisive aerial victory. First of all, the German bomber force, then armed with the He 111, would be flying at long range with light bombloads. It would not be until 1942, and the arrival of the planned He 177 heavy bombers, that a successful long-range air campaign against British industry might be effective.[149] British navy and merchant shipping still remained the primary targets of an air campaign, in Felmy's view. He urged that establishment of a naval air division of heavy, long-range bombers, with specialized training in antishipping attacks, be given a high priority.[150] He saw great possibilities in blockading Britain and shutting its ports by an aerial mine-laying campaign. Such minefields might be able to shut down British ports for weeks at a time.[151] After a year of planning, training, and exercises, Felmy was somewhat more optimistic about conducting a future air campaign against Britain, but it was still painfully clear that, with only a year's strategic planning behind it, the Luftwaffe would not be ready for war with the British any time soon.[152]

In the cases of Poland and France, the war planning and strategy process went smoothly. From 1919 to 1939 the German military intelligence had collected a vast amount of information about the French, Polish, and Czech armed forces and their armaments industries. The Luftwaffe's war plans against France and Poland show a sound and realistic assessment of the state of the forces likely to be arrayed against Germany. The war plans against Poland accurately list the airfields where the Polish bomber force was located and include a sound appraisal of Poland's ability to mobilize forces.[153] A campaign to rapidly destroy the Polish air force was developed with the additional Luftwaffe missions of conducting an interdiction campaign against the Polish transport system and close support operations in support of the main army and armored and motorized forces. The initial, main effort of the Luftwaffe was to be the support of the 10th Army.[154]

In the case of France, the Luftwaffe correctly identified the weaknesses of the French air force. Although the French had a large number of aircraft and the French pilots were well trained, the aircraft themselves were mostly obsolete and inferior to their German counterparts. The French flak force was weak, and their air force communications system was poor. The Germans correctly predicted that in case the Wehrmacht invaded Poland, the Luftwaffe could assume a defensive posture in the west with little possibility of a French air attack on German industrial centers.[155] As it turned out, the Luftwaffe's strategic assessment of the French and Poles, and their predictions of enemy capabilities and behavior, were right on the mark. However, in case the French did initiate a strategic campaign against Germany, the Luftwaffe laid out plans for a strategic bombing campaign against France. The German strategy was to first exploit the weaknesses of the French air force—poorly defended airfields and few bunkers for the aircraft—and attack them on the ground, paying special attention to wrecking their weak ground infrastructure. Once the French air force was seriously damaged, the Luftwaffe general staff identified the French oil refineries and storage facilities as the most valuable targets for a strategic campaign.[156] France depended on oil imports for virtually all its needs. A sustained attack on its oil resources would therefore soon cripple the French army and air force. It was a very sound strategy for a strategic air campaign, and the U.S. Army Air Forces would prove the efficacy of such an air strategy when they crippled the German oil refineries in 1944–1945. It was an air strategy that was realistic, and well within the capabilities of the Luftwaffe in 1939.

FOREIGN AIR DOCTRINE, 1936–1939

The way that the major western air forces reacted to the lessons of the war in Spain provides some notable insights into the mind-set of the British, American, and French air staffs in the years preceding the outbreak of World War II. Although the Spanish war was covered extensively by the press and foreign observers and the results of the air campaigns were well known, the attitude of the RAF to the air campaigns of the Spanish Civil War was one of general indifference.

A close look at the *RAF Quarterly,* the official journal of the RAF, during the Spanish Civil War provides some interesting insights about the RAF's view of air power theory and doctrine. The RAF was not completely uninterested in foreign events or ideas. The April 1936 *RAF Quarterly* published a typical article, "General Giulio Douhet—An Italian Apostle of Air Power."[157] However, the prejudice against nonstrategic air power theories is evident. Aside from five paragraphs about the war in Spain in the foreign news section of the July 1937 *RAF Quarterly,* there was no mention of the greatest air war of the time in the RAF journal. The interdiction campaigns, the aerial victory at Guadalajara, and the Condor Legion's air campaign in the north of Spain were all well-known events that had occurred in Spain with the most modern aircraft of the era—and were ignored by the RAF.[158] The RAF Staff College at Andover also took little note of the Spanish War. Although a few lectures were devoted to foreign air thought in the late 1930s, no discussion of the Spanish Civil War air campaigns was included in the curriculum.[159]

In the period leading up to the world war, the RAF rigidly maintained the doctrine of strategic bombardment that had been laid down during the tenure of RAF chief of staff Air Marshal Hugh Trenchard in the 1920s. Voices in the RAF arguing for army/air force cooperation were rare in the RAF.[160] The British air staff insisted on the primacy of bomber procurement and the development of a four-engine bomber during the RAF expansion of the late 1930s. Building up the fighter force was resisted by the RAF staff but Parliament insisted on voting funds for and building up a fighter defense force in the mid-1930s—the force that was to save Britain in 1940.[161]

Ironically, while the RAF staff insisted on the primacy of the strategic bombing campaign virtually to the exclusion of other forms of aerial warfare, the RAF Bomber Command remained a fair-weather air force with little training or emphasis on the skills necessary to fight a strategic bombing war. Training in long-distance navigation and night and bad weather operations was minimal in the RAF in the years leading up to World War II.[162] At the same time, there was little training in army support operations in the RAF in this period and the "army cooperation" squadrons consisted of a few general-purpose light aircraft. The example of the war in Spain did nothing to dispel the RAF's strong prejudice against this form of air force operations.

The U.S. Army Air Corps took slightly more interest in the air war in Spain and drew at least a few lessons from the conflict. In 1938 Major George Kenney, later U.S. Fifth Air Force commander in World War II, wrote an insightful article on the air war in Spain in the *U.S. Air Services,* unofficial journal of the U.S. Army Air Corps.[163] Kenney argued that the small size of the air forces in Spain had not proven or disproven Douhet's theories.[164] He commented on the Battle of Guadalajara, arguing that air power had performed well in the support and interdiction roles.[165] He was also highly impressed by German airlift operations, and predicted that air transport of ground troops would become an important mission of the air force.[166]

For the most part, however, the experience of the Spanish Civil War went against the grain of the strategic bombing dogma of the Air Corps. In May 1938 General Hap Arnold, later chief of the Army Air Forces in World War II, wrote in an editorial in the *U.S. Air Services* that the experience of the Spanish Civil War was essentially irrelevant, because strategic bombing had not been a factor in that war. Because strategic bombing had not been used, he advised against drawing any lessons from that war.[167] At the Air Corps Tactical School (ACTS) at Maxwell Field, Alabama, the center of higher officer education in the Air Corps, the war in Spain was scarcely noticed. Between 1937 and 1938, only one brief lecture on the Spanish air war was given at ACTS.[168] The ACTS was the center of the strategic bombing theorists in the American Air Corps, and the theory of precision strategic bombardment dominated the whole training program.[169]

The driving factor of U.S. Army Air Corps doctrine in the 1930s was the desire to win independence from the army and become a fully separate service. The precision strategic bombing doctrine, in which it was argued that an enemy nation could be paralyzed by bombing a few carefully selected industries, justified an independent air force that could win a war without the efforts of the other services.[170] Although some squadrons of the Air Corps were specialized in the ground attack and army support mission, within the senior leadership of the Air Corps this form of military aviation was downplayed as "support aviation." Within the ground forces of the army, there was considerable interest in the role that air power was playing in Spain. Primarily on the evidence of Spain, the U.S. Army general staff in 1938 requested that the Air Corps develop ground attack aircraft and dive bombers such as the Luftwaffe was employing so effectively in Spain.[171] The Air Corps saw the development of attack aviation as a threat to its strategic bomber programs and resisted strongly. There was such strong feeling in the Air Corps for service independence, to avoid becoming an "army support force," that in discussions with the ground forces in 1938, Air Corps General Frank Andrews objected to the term "air-ground military team" to describe joint operations.[172] The Air Corps would successfully resist developing an effective dive bomber or attack aviation force or in giving any emphasis to the development of joint doctrine up to the outbreak of World War II, although the Air Corps did concede some funds and effort to developing a light bomber force.

The Spanish Civil War era witnessed a renaissance in the thinking of the French air force. Of all the western air forces, the L'Armeé de L'Air followed the air war in Spain most closely in an attempt to learn lessons. French military journals were full of detailed, critical commentary on the conduct of the air war in Spain. The German and Italian use of dive bombers to support ground operations was favorably discussed.[173] The role of air power as a decisive factor in the ground campaign, as exhibited by the Luftwaffe's support in the Nationalist victory at Bilbao, was seen as an important lesson for French airmen.[174] French Air Force General Maginel wrote on the air action at Guadalajara and described it as a model for air operations in support of the ground forces.[175]

The war in Spain coincided with the tenure of a very competent and dynamic French air minister, Pierre Cot (air minister, 1936–1938). Cot was a former world war pilot, well informed on military aviation. During his tenure, Cot attempted to make major changes in the French air force doctrine and organization. Up to this time, the French air force had been viewed primarily as a defensive weapon and an army support force. Until 1936, the French air force was dispersed and organized into small regional commands, which were, in turn, directly under the command of the army regional commander. The official doctrine of the French air force was highly influenced by the defensive orientation of the French army. Cot believed that the role of air power was primarily in the offense and in September 1936 ordered a major reorganization of the L'Armeé de L'Air, with most of the bombers assigned to the First Air Corps, most of the fighters into the Second Air Corps, and the twenty-six remaining groups of aircraft under army command as a support force. The two new air corps, essentially a bomber and a fighter command, were no longer under the control of the army but reported to the air force commander. The previous air rearmament plans, which had given the priority to defensive fighter aircraft, were drastically changed to give bombers the production priority. French Plan II, issued by Cot in 1936, called for the production of 1,339 modern bombers but only 756 fighters and 645 reconnaissance planes.[176]

With the concentration of the bombers and fighters into large functional commands, Cot published a new and offensively oriented doctrine for the L'Armeé de L'Air. Where the French army doctrine had doubted the ability of an air force to gain air superiority for more than a limited period,[177] the new air doctrine stated the need for the air force to attack and gain air superiority over the enemy and maintain that superiority: "The mission of the air force in war is to create conditions so that the sky can be used for all purposes and to see that the enemy's ability to use the air for all purposes is limited."[178]

The bomber force that Cot created had the mission of attacking the enemy centers of industry as well as attacking lines of communication on the battlefield. Regarding the operational air campaign, Cot maintained, "As an offensive battle, the air battle has the goal of destroying the primary power of the enemy by bombing the enemy armed forces as well as attacking the lines of communication, the facilities that ensure the mobility of the enemy forces as well as centers of production which provide the necessary materials to the enemy."[179] Besides moving the French air force toward a doctrine of strategic bombardment, the lessons of Spain had also shown the importance of close air support and interdiction operations. The new air doctrine stated, "Participation in ground operations belongs to the fundamental missions of the air force. All of the operational capabilities can be used for this purpose."[180]

Cot argued for the reform of French air defense. In France, the responsibility for the air defense came under the jurisdiction of three different ministries. Antiaircraft guns were under the control of the army's artillery branch. Civil defense came under the ministry of the interior, and fighter defense was the responsibility of the air force. Cot argued that all aspects of air defense needed to be centralized and under air force command.[181] Cot also instituted some very innovative reforms in the French air force. In 1937 he created a small experimental airborne force, the "Infanterie de L'Air," which took part in the maneuvers that year. The small airborne force showed real promise as an offensive operational arm.[182]

The politics of the Third Republic forced Cot out of office in early 1938. He was replaced by Air Minister Guy LeChambre. LeChambre had no liking for Cot's reforms and the French commander in chief, General Maurice Gamelin, repudiated Cot's attempt to establish an offensive air doctrine. Gamelin believed that the role of air power on the battlefield was exaggerated and that the primary function of the air force was to provide fighter defensive cover for the army.[183] Cot's reforms were quickly undone. The bomber and fighter commands created by Cot were broken up, and the air force was again dispersed to serve under army regional command. The paratroop force, useful in a military with an offensive doctrine, did not fit in with Gamelin's preference for the defense, and they were quickly disbanded. No action was taken to create a unified air defense system. The offensive orientation that Cot had tried to instill in French air doctrine was rejected. In the new production plan, bombers were given a low priority while defensive fighters were given top priority.[184] The attempts of French air force officers to change the doctrine of the air force in light of the Spanish War were stymied and, under the guidance of General Gamelin and Air Minister LeChambre, the French air force returned to the defensive doctrine of the early 1930s.

DEVELOPMENT OF THE NAVAL AIR ARM

The commander in chief of the Reichsmarine, Grossadmiral Erich Raeder, was a firm believer in the primacy of the battleship in war. In 1935 Raeder told Hitler that "the international prestige of a nation is identical with the scale of its naval force."[185] Raeder must have convinced Hitler of his vision because in early 1939 Hitler stood the rearmament strategy of the Third Reich on its head and gave the German navy the top priority for funds and resources to build Raeder's proposed "Z-Fleet." The Z-Fleet would give

Germany an enormous, world-class navy by 1947, with eighteen new battleships and battlecruisers.[186] Aircraft carriers played some role in Raeder's vision, for four new carriers were proposed in the Z-Fleet plan.[187] It would seem, however, that the carriers were more of a prestige item for a major navy rather than an operationally important part of a future fleet. Of the two carriers that the German navy was building, one was envisioned as a training ship and the other, as an experimental model.[188] In any case the construction effort proceeded slowly, since the naval general staff gave the two German carriers a lower construction priority than the light cruisers.[189]

Much of the progress in naval aviation and naval air doctrine was initiated by the Luftwaffe, rather than by the German navy. As commander of Air Fleet 2, General Helmuth Felmy was responsible for conducting the air war against Britain if war broke out. In May 1939 Felmy set up a special air corps within his air fleet, headed by Lieutenant General Hans Geisler,[190] to plan for a naval air campaign against England.[191] With his extensive command and operational experience in naval aviation, both during and after World War I, Geisler was an excellent choice as a senior naval aviation commander. The Luftwaffe high command appointed another experienced naval airmen, Major General Joachim Coeler,[192] as the inspector of naval aviation for the Luftwaffe in 1938. His position was soon upgraded to the title of commander of the naval air forces. Coeler would exercise command of the naval air arm of the Luftwaffe under the operational control of the navy high command.

The naval air arm grew slowly from 1936 to 1939. By the end of 1937 there were four coastal air groups of the naval air service.[193] The naval air squadrons were rearmed with more modern aircraft. The Arado 196 was developed as a short-range reconnaissance and spotter aircraft. The Arado 196 was a two-seat catapult floatplane with a maximum speed of 194 mph and a moderate armament of four machine guns and two 110-pound bombs. It was in production by 1939, and issued to the fleet units before the start of the war.[194] Other improved, long-range patrol craft were developed, such as the Dornier Do 24 flying boat.[195] Until the outbreak of the war, however, no specialized naval strike aircraft had been developed for the naval air arm. In July 1939, the Luftwaffe high command recommended to the navy that the improved model, which was then being developed of the Dornier Do 17—the Do 217—could be adapted to fill the role of a long-range reconnaissance and attack plane. The Do 217 would be fast, and could be equipped to carry torpedoes.[196] In a protocol signed between the navy and the Luftwaffe in January 1939 the navy would have an air arm by 1941, consisting of nine long-distance squad-

Heinkel He 60 seaplane squadron, ca. 1937. (Photo from *Jahrbuch der deutschen Luftwaffe,* 1939.)

rons, eighteen coastal reconnaissance squadrons, twelve carrier squadrons, and two on-board observation squadrons.[197] From the navy's viewpoint, naval aviation was to serve as a patrol and reconnaissance force, and an auxiliary arm of the fleet, rather than a true striking force.

The navy was responsible for developing torpedoes and mines, but by the late 1930s was still unable to produce a reliable, air-dropped torpedo. However, the navy had considerably more success with the development of naval mines that could be air-dropped. A revolutionary magnetic mine was developed in the late 1930s that could be delivered by air, but by the outbreak of the war, only a handful had been produced.[198] General Felmy was a driving force behind the production of the air-dropped mines, for he regarded them as a primary means of attacking Britain by air. Yet despite efforts by Felmy and senior naval airmen Coeler and Geisler to build up a naval air arm capable of making a major contribution to combat operations, by the summer of 1939 the naval air force consisted of a mere 200 operational aircraft, many of them obsolete He 59s. The 200 aircraft were divided into five naval air groups and five separate squadrons, stationed on the north German coast.[199]

TECHNOLOGY AND THE LATER REARMAMENT OF THE LUFTWAFFE

When Ernst Udet was appointed as chief of the Technical Office in the summer of 1936, he brought one simple idea with him: that accurate bombing could only be carried out by dive bombers, so all future bombers of the Luftwaffe should be configured as dive bombers. Udet had visited the United States in 1934 and had the opportunity to fly the Curtis Hawk dive bomber, then in service with the U.S. Navy. Enthralled by the possibilities of the dive bomber, he bought two of the Curtis machines and shipped them back to Germany.[200] Although the Luftwaffe already had some dive bombers in production in 1934–1935 and saw an important role for dive bombers, few officers shared Udet's level of enthusiasm when he demonstrated the capabilities of the Curtis machines.[201] As inspector of fighters and dive bombers in 1935, Udet's enthusiasm had little major effect on the Luftwaffe. His job was to help select the best dive bomber for the next generation of production out of a field of several entries. He helped select the Junkers Ju 87 for serial production, a sound choice.

However, when Udet was named as the chief of the Technical Office with responsibility for developing *all* the Luftwaffe's aircraft, his preference for the dive bomber soon had a major impact on the Luftwaffe. When Udet took over, the third generation of the Luftwaffe's aircraft was in the process of development and selection. The Ju 88 "fast bomber" program had been under way since 1935, and the first flight of the Ju 88 was made in December 1936. The Ju 88 had the qualities that the Luftwaffe staff had wanted. It had a long range, could carry a moderate bombload, and was faster than many of the fighter planes of the time. A later prototype of the Ju 88 reached a speed of slightly over 300 mph in a test run in September 1937.[202] The Ju 88 could have entered production in 1938, but in October 1937 Udet ordered the redesign of the Ju 88 as a heavy dive bomber. This entailed thousands of changes and a virtual redesign of the aircraft to make it capable of carrying the stresses of dive bombing. The production of the Ju 88, later to become one of the great

Colonel General Ernst Udet as chief of aircraft production, 1939. (Photo from USAF HRA.)

medium bombers and night fighters of World War II, would be delayed by approximately two years.[203]

So enthralled was Udet with the dive bomber concept, that he ordered virtually all the bombers under development to be redesigned as dive bombers. For instance, the follow-on aircraft for the Me 110 heavy fighter and the Do 17 bomber, the Me 210 and the Do 217 respectively, were ordered to be redesigned as dive bombers.[204] In a decision that bordered on aeronautical lunacy, Udet ordered the heavy bomber under development, the Heinkel He 177, to be designed as a dive bomber. Udet was a brilliant pilot but had no understanding of aeronautical engineering. It was one thing to build a fairly light aircraft such as the Ju 87 to dive well. On the other hand, it was a virtually impossible task to build a four-engine heavy bomber that could take the stress of diving. Designer Ernst Heinkel tried to talk some sense into Udet and was rebuffed. The He 177 made its first flight in November 1939 and would require over 1,300 structural modifications to even come close to Udet's requirement. As late as 1942, it was discovered that a complete wing design was necessary.[205] In any case, the He 177, which was to be the long-range strategic bomber of the Luftwaffe, was a flawed design from the start. The Heinkel designers attempted to cut the drag of the aircraft by mounting two engines in one wing nacelle, in tandem front to back, which would drive one propeller. There would be one such nacelle on each wing. It was a revolutionary idea that the designers tried mightily to get to work effectively. The primary problem was the difficulty of cooling two engines in one compartment: the heat buildup was so intense that the He 177 engines quite regularly caught fire. Try as they would, the Heinkel Company could never overcome the engine heat problem. Yet Udet's office refused to pull the plug on the program. What was ironic is that, if the He 177 had been designed as a conventional four-engine bomber with a normal engine layout, it would have made a good bomber for its day—fully equal to the British Lancaster or American B-17.[206]

Udet had some justification for his preference for the dive bomber. The early bombsights of the Luftwaffe were not very accurate and the effectiveness of the stuka in getting the bombs on the target as opposed to the inaccuracy of the horizontal bombers such as the He 111 and Do 17 was clearly supported by technical research.[207] Udet was able to convince the Luftwaffe's new chief of the general staff, Hans Jeschonnek, of his theories of the superiority of the dive bomber. Jeschonnek had been a bomber wing commander for two years and was disappointed in the accuracy of his bombers.[208] The factor that Udet—appointed as director of all aircraft production in 1938—and the new chief of staff of the Luftwaffe ignored was the program to develop a precision, high-altitude bombsight. While the bombsights of the mid-1930s had been poor, the Lotfe 7C, available at the start of the war, and Lotfe 7D, which entered service in 1942, were significant improvements. The Lotfe 7D had superb accuracy and, like the famed American Norden bombsight, could be linked to an automatic pilot. When the Lotfe 7D was issued to Luftwaffe bomber units in Russia it proved its worth on the battlefield.[209] Many of the Germans claimed that the Lotfe 7D was superior to the American Norden bombsight for accuracy.

Other aircraft programs were mismanaged under Udet's tenure. Development of the Henschel Hs 129 heavily armed and armored ground attack plane began in 1937. The first Hs 129 flew in the spring of 1939; it was grossly underpowered and overengineered, and difficult to control.[210] More prototypes were produced and the aircraft was tested in combat in 1940—when it predictably proved to be a dud. The whole aircraft had to be redesigned for new engines and hundreds of other modifications made. The redesigned—and much better—aircraft would not enter Luftwaffe service until 1943. It became a useful weapon on the battlefield but, for its whole service life, was plagued by mechanical problems and a low serviceability rate.[211]

Of the whole third generation of Luftwaffe aircraft developed under Udet's tenure, three of the aircraft—the He 177, the Me 210, and the Hs 129—were simply bad designs. The best bomber, the Ju 88, was delayed for years to meet Udet's dive bombing requirements. The only truly successful aircraft program under Udet was the development of the outstanding FW 190 fighter, which entered Luftwaffe service in 1941. Ernst Udet, a man totally unqualified for his position, was simply an unmitigated disaster for the Luftwaffe. Still, the Luftwaffe would enter World War II and fight most of the war with the excellent aircraft that had been developed under Wilhelm Wimmer's tenure—and at the outbreak of the war this generation of aircraft was still superior to most of their enemies'. It would be difficult, however, to judge exactly the degree of damage that Udet inflicted on the Luftwaffe by his poor decisions, how much wasted effort, and how many days of production lost in developing unworkable aircraft.

In many aspects of aviation technology that did not catch the interest of Udet, the Luftwaffe nevertheless made enormous technical strides in the mid- to late-1930s. Development of what would become the V-1 and V-2 rockets of World War II began in the mid-1930s, when Adolf Bauemker and Wolfram von Richthofen selected some promising new technologies and provided subsidies and support.[212] With a Luftwaffe subsidy of less than $20,000, engineer von Ohain and the Heinkel Company developed the world's first jet engine, the He S-3b, in 1937. The world's first jet aircraft, the Heinkel He 176, flew at Peenemünde in August 1939.[213] In the fields of piston engines, Germany was rapidly catching up to Britain and the United States by 1939, and in other fields of technology such as high-altitude flight and development of aircraft cannon and bombs, the Germans led the other air powers. Essentially, despite the foibles of Göring and Udet, and the numerous inefficiencies of the Nazi armament production system,[214] the Luftwaffe had met its goals of developing a first-class air force and the productive and technological infrastructure to support it.

Conclusion

The Luftwaffe was not especially well prepared to go to war with France and Britain as well as Poland on 1 September 1939. Some squadrons still had obsolete equipment, there were severe shortages of bombs and aircraft munitions, and some units needed more training to be fully combat-effective. Right up to the outbreak of the war, Hitler and the top political leadership of the Third Reich seemed confident that the major western powers would not fight for Poland and that Germany had several more years to prepare for a major war for the domination of Europe. Still, the Luftwaffe had grown impressively before 1939. In August 1939 the Luftwaffe had a total force of 373,000 personnel (208,000 in the flying troops, 107,000 in the flak troops, and 58,000 in the signals corps).[1] The Luftwaffe had 4,201 operational aircraft available for combat, including 1,191 bombers, 361 dive bombers, 788 fighters, 431 heavy fighters, and 488 transports.[2] Despite deficiencies, it was by any standards an impressive force.

If the Luftwaffe was not fully ready for war, however, the opposing British and French air forces were in much worse shape as to equipment, logistics, and training. Wars are almost always fought on a "come as you are" basis, and the Luftwaffe would thus enter World War II with several advantages over its opponents. The Luftwaffe was the most capable air force in the world in conducting joint operations with the army. It had an effective system of liaison officers with their own communications *(Flivos)* serving with the leading elements of the ground forces. The Luftwaffe had an extensive doctrine for army support and close support operations and, moreover, had practiced and refined this doctrine since the 1920s. The army and the air force had held numerous joint maneuvers, and 20,000 of the Luftwaffe's personnel had gone through the real school of combat operations in Spain. The Wehrmacht had far more experience in and understanding of joint operations than any other armed forces in the world at the time. While many of the British and French military officers thought a great deal about joint ground/air operations, very few had been out on exercises and maneuvers trying to put their ideas into practice. The Germans had been training under arduous conditions for years to conduct air campaigns such as the campaigns of 1939–1940.

THE AIR CAMPAIGN OVER POLAND

The effectiveness of the Luftwaffe doctrine in supporting a war of maneuver was demonstrated in Poland. In September 1939, the air campaign took place much as General von Seeckt had predicted in the 1920s. The first target for the Luftwaffe was the Polish air force. The Polish air force was a small force armed with 463 mostly obsolete planes.[3] The Poles had transferred most of their operational aircraft from their permanent air bases to camouflaged, emergency fields scattered around the country. When the Luftwaffe attacked the Polish air force in the first three days of the campaign, it did not destroy the Polish operational squadrons on the ground as it had hoped. However, the facilities and infrastructure that make an air force combat-capable—the spare parts, fuel supplies, repair and maintenance facilities, as well as the reserve aircraft and communications facilities were quickly destroyed by the Germans. From then on, scattered in small units around the country, the Poles would fight a losing attrition battle in the air. Damaged aircraft could not be repaired, lost aircraft could not be replaced, and the Polish aircraft that did get into the air were quickly dispatched by the Luftwaffe's fighters.[4]

As the Luftwaffe had planned since the early 1930s, the Polish rail system became a primary target for the bomber force. The rapid destruction of the Polish lines of communication crippled the ability of the Poles to move troops and supplies. In accordance with their battle doctrine, the Luftwaffe massed approximately half its stuka force (160 aircraft) into a "Close Battle Division," which consisted of a further Hs 123 ground attack group (forty aircraft) and a reconnaissance squadron and two fighter groups for escort.[5] This force, under the command of Wolfram von Richthofen, was given the mission of providing close air support to the Tenth Army, which contained the greater part of the army's armored and motorized assets and had been designated as the "schwerpunkt" or "decisive point" of the German invasion. The Close Battle Division of the Luftwaffe provided tremendous firepower to the panzer forces, enabling them to make a rapid advance deep into Poland. As in Spain, strong Polish fortifications such as the Fortress of Modlin were quickly shattered by heavy air attacks by the stukas and conventional bombers.[6]

The Luftwaffe's creation of a large, mobile logistics force enabled the Luftwaffe's units to move into Polish airfields right after the army overran them and to fly army support missions with the fighters, stukas, and reconnaissance aircraft from rough airfields directly behind the German lines. This

Polish air force aircraft hangers at the Warsaw Airfield, September 1939. The Luftwaffe destroyed the main airfields and the infrastructure of the Polish air force in the first days of the 1939 campaign. (Photo from *Jahrbuch der deutschen Luftwaffe*, 1940.)

gave the Luftwaffe a high combat sortie rate of three-plus missions per day and gave the Luftwaffe a fast reaction time when the army and Luftwaffe commanders determined that a Polish target needed to be attacked. The Luftwaffe was used to the full extent of its mobility in Poland, and large air commands could be transferred from one sector of the battlefront to another rapidly and efficiently. For example, von Richthofen's Close Battle Division was transferred from the Second Air Division to Air Fleet 4 after the first week of the campaign without any major problems.[7] The Luftwaffe's large transport force of Ju 52s flew bombs, fuel, parts, and personnel to the forward airfields and ensured a rapid supply to the forward air units. The movement of large air units such as von Richthofen's had been practiced extensively in peacetime maneuvers, and it came off without a hitch. It was a logistics and planning feat that no other air force in the world could have carried out in 1939.

The Poles fought valiantly in 1939, but their forces were decisively defeated in a three-week mobile campaign of unprecedented tempo. The army gave full credit to the Luftwaffe for its interdiction and close support campaign. Army General von Reichenau, commander of the Tenth Army, declared that the Close Battle Division's support had "led to the decision on the battlefield."[8] The tactics of the Spanish War such as attacking in waves and keeping the enemy under constant pressure worked in Poland as well. The effect on the morale of the defending Polish troops was rated as devastating.[9]

The German general staff tradition of critical analysis was still very healthy in the early days of the war and as soon as the air campaign against the Poles was concluded, army and Luftwaffe staffs went to work to determine the lessons learned from the campaign and to modify tactics, equipment, and doctrine for the next campaign.[10] Although the air campaign in Poland had gone very well, there had still been numerous problems of coordinating ground and air operations. There had been numerous instances of Luftwaffe aircraft mistakenly bombing forward German army troops and problems in transmitting reconnaissance reports and air support requests in a timely fashion. The Luftwaffe worked to improve its communications and coordination and issued a series of tactical directives to the air fleets to help them plan for future operations.[11] One of the lessons of Poland was the effectiveness of von Richthofen's air division's close air support attacks. The Close Battle Division was enlarged and renamed the VIII Air Corps for the spring campaign when it would serve as a specialist close air support force.

In contrast, the British and French did little to modify their air doctrine after the Polish campaign. It was not due to a lack of information or analysis. Many Polish officers had gotten out of Poland and were on hand to describe how the Germans had conducted air operations and what the German capabilities were. The RAF, for example, simply had little interest in creating a specialist tactical aviation force for army support. Although the dive bomber had proved to be an effective weapon in Poland, the RAF had already made a decision and rejected the concept and was not about to reconsider its decision.[12] The communications and liaison system of the French army and air force were minimal and little had been done for years to improve the situation. For the French, the Polish campaign held few lessons.[13]

The Luftwaffe's next campaign was the invasion of Norway on 9 April 1940. The German navy took a beating and it was a very close-run operation for the Germans. The Luftwaffe, however, turned the tide for the Wehrmacht. When ships carrying the army landing force were stopped in Oslo Fjord, the city was taken by troops landed by Ju 52 transports at the Oslo airport. As the Royal Navy moved to reinforce Norway, the Luftwaffe seized vital airfields and gained control of the Norwegian skies. For the first time in history, air power proved to be dominant over sea power. Under heavy air attack, the Royal Navy and the British and French divisions that had landed had to evacuate the country.

THE CAMPAIGN IN THE WEST

As the Wehrmacht planned to invade France and the Low Countries, the Luftwaffe could look to a moderate qualitative superiority of aircraft over the British and French air forces. The British Blenheim and Wellington bombers could match their German counterparts, and the RAF's Hurricanes and Spitfires were approximately equal to their Me 109 and Me 110 opponents. The French aircraft inventory consisted mostly of obsolete aircraft, but American equipment had been delivered in quantity, and good, new French aircraft such as the Dewoitane 520 fighter were coming off the production lines. Counting aircraft in reserve and stationed in North Africa and in the south of France, the Allies could even claim a numerical superiority over the Germans in May 1940.[14] In any case, when the attack came, the Germans had a numerical superiority on the front lines with a total of 2,589 bombers, dive bombers, and fighters committed against France and the Low Countries against a total of 1,453 Allied combat aircraft.[15]

In a replay of the Polish campaign the Luftwaffe started with an air superiority campaign designed to destroy the Allied air forces on the ground. On May 10, the start of the German invasion of France and the Low Countries, one-third of the Luftwaffe's bombing missions (fifty of 150) were directed against the French airfields.[16] The Dutch and Belgian air forces were mostly destroyed on the ground. The RAF airfields in France also came under heavy attack. All eighteen of 114 Squadron's Blenheim bombers were destroyed or disabled on the ground by Luftwaffe attacks on 10 May.[17] The French count 757 aircraft lost in the Battle for France. Of those, 229 were destroyed on the ground—many, in the first few days.[18] For the first three days of the campaign, the Luftwaffe made the Allied air forces their priority target. The strategy paid off: the Luftwaffe quickly gained and held air superiority throughout the six-week campaign.

The Luftwaffe demonstrated a major innovation in warfare on 10 May 1940 when the 7th Airborne division was dropped in the west of Holland to seize the Waalhaven airfield and the bridges between Rotterdam and the

The Luftwaffe made the L'Armeé de L'Air and the RAF their primary target in the first days of the May 1940 campaign. General von Richthofen, commander of the Luftwaffe's VIII Air Corps, took this photo of a French fighter destroyed on the ground by the Luftwaffe in May 1940. (Photo from the von Richthofen family.)

Hague. After the initial objective was seized the 7th Airborne was reinforced by the 22nd Air Landing Division that was flown in on the Luftwaffe's air transport force. The seizure of this terrain meant that the Dutch army would be unable to retreat within its defense line of "Fortress Holland" in the west of the country. Between German paratroops and air-landed infantry on one side and the Eighteenth Army advancing from the east, Holland capitulated in only five days—rather than the three weeks that the Dutch general staff had expected to hold the west of the country until Allied reinforcements arrived.[19] In addition to this victory, a detachment of Luftwaffe glider troops had landed on top of Fort Eban Emael at dawn on May 10 and quickly captured the powerful Belgian fortress.[20] This action served to open the Belgian/Dutch border to the rapid advance of German ground troops. The Luftwaffe paratroops had shown how the tempo of a campaign could be speeded up by the employment of a large force deep in the enemy's rear.

One of the lessons of the Polish campaign had been to ensure that the headquarters of the Luftwaffe air divisions and corps were co-located with the headquarters of the armies that they were supporting. The air liaison teams attached to the corps and panzer divisions were directed to simply transmit information on the combat situation at the front to their air corps headquarters and were not to advise the army or request air support. At von Richthofen's VIII Air Corps command post, the commander or his chief of staff were always available to confer with the chief of staff of Panzergruppe von Kleist, which was being supported by von Richthofen's air units. The situation reports of the panzer divisions were transmitted directly to the air corps headquarters, and, with the agreement of the army and Luftwaffe commanders, attack orders for VIII Air Corps units could be issued within minutes. At all times, the VIII Air Corps had one stuka group (forty aircraft) and one fighter group at forward airfields ready for immediate takeoff. With this system, German panzer units could get air support within forty-five to seventy-five minutes of an attack order being issued.[21]

The best-known use of the Luftwaffe in the army support role occurred at the German army breakthrough at Sedan on 13 May. Over 1,000 bomber, stuka, and fighter sorties attacking in waves throughout the day struck the French reserves and artillery positions defending the Meuse River. The constant air attack, a tactic from Spain, demoralized the defending French 55th Division. The Frenchmen were well dug in and actually took few losses, but the French artillery was prevented from firing at the Germans crossing the river. By evening the German troops were across the Meuse and the French troops, who had not seen a friendly aircraft all day, broke and ran.[22]

One of the major innovations in air warfare occurred after the German panzer divisions crossed the Meuse. The rapid advance of the panzer forces had left the supporting infantry divisions far behind, and a large gap had formed between the panzer troops and the unmotorized infantry. This gap caused considerable concern in the German high command so that on 16 May, with the front wide open, the army group commander, von Rundstedt, ordered Panzergruppe von Kleist to slow his advance to allow the infantry divisions to catch up.[23] Von Richthofen requested that his VIII Air Corps be concentrated in the southern area of operations—which von Richthofen saw as the decisive point of the campaign—in support of Panzergruppe von Kleist. Von Richthofen convinced Göring to issue orders directing the VIII Air Corps to "follow Panzer Group Von Kleist to the sea."[24] Von Richthofen urged von Rundstedt to allow von Kleist's panzer army to continue its rapid advance without infantry support on their flanks. Von Richthofen assured a doubtful army staff that his VIIIth Air Corps could protect the flanks of the

French army column caught on the road by Luftwaffe aircraft, May–June, 1940. (Photo from USAF HRA.)

advance. The advance resumed and von Richthofen made good on his promise. The VIII Air Corps' reconnaissance aircraft spotted French divisions moving to counterattack and the air corps' stukas, bombers, and fighters relentlessly bombed the French troop columns, highway traffic, and tank units that appeared on the flanks. The French Ninth Army was effectively routed by air attack.[25] The Luftwaffe played a large role in repelling the attacks of de Gaulle's 4th Armored Division on 17 May at Montcornet and 19 May at Crécy-sur-Serre.[26]

As in Poland, the Luftwaffe's highly mobile logistics and support force enabled the Germans to fly from rough forward areas and achieve a high sortie rate. German fighters flew an average of four sorties per day.[27] The Stuka force flew even more sorties per day.[28] This is a significant contrast to the French air force, which flew remarkably few sorties. The French fighter force flew an average of only 0.9 sorties per day, and the French bombers only 0.25

The victors of the May–June 1940 campaign relaxing. Newly promoted Field Marshal Erhard Milch (left) with General der Flieger Wolfram von Richthofen in France shortly after the French surrender. (Photo from the von Richthofen family.)

sorties per day.[29] This amounts to an astounding misuse of air power. The few air operations that the French and RAF mounted were small, piecemeal attacks. Hampered by poor communications and liaison between air forces and armies, the Allies seem to have taken hours to transmit simple messages or to forward requests for air support. When the decision to attack a vital objective such as the German bridgehead across the Meuse was finally made, it came too little and too late. The Luftwaffe had provided two corps of flak artillery to support the army's advance in France and the Germans had plenty of flak to cover their forward advance and their lines of communications. Allied bombing attacks on the advancing German army were repeatedly torn to shreds by the heavy flak protection that the Luftwaffe provided to the forward areas.[30]

In the May–June 1940 campaign, the Luftwaffe successfully conducted a wide variety of missions successfully: an air superiority campaign, reconnaissance for the ground forces, close air support, flank protection for a panzer army, flak defense against Allied attacks, the world's first major airborne operations, and a conventional interdiction campaign against the French transport system. The Luftwaffe even conducted some strategic bombing raids targeting the French aircraft factories in the Paris area.[31] At several points, such as at Sedan and in von Kleist's advance to the English Channel, the Luftwaffe intervened decisively in the battle and proved that air power had become perhaps the key element in conducting a war of maneuver.

While the Luftwaffe had shown a spirit of innovation in 1940, the French and British air forces seemed bound by doctrinal prisons of their own making. The French had been so defensively oriented that their bomber force of about 800 bombers scarcely made any impact on the campaign.[32] The RAF was just as bad. At the same time that the Germans were forcing the crossing at the Meuse and their support troops and logistics jammed the roads for a hundred miles back into Germany, the RAF Bomber Command sent a force of ninety-nine medium bombers to bomb the Ruhr the night of 15 May.[33] As the German panzer forces began to race across France, the RAF responded to desperate appeals for support from the army and two nights later conducted another large raid against the German homeland, this time against Hamburg and Bremen. The German war effort was untouched by the British strategic air offensive as the major damage to Bremen was the destruction of two warehouses full of furniture confiscated from Jews.[34]

THE BATTLE OF BRITAIN

From July to August 1940, the Luftwaffe conducted an air offensive over England with the objective of defeating the RAF and gaining air superiority over British skies so that the army and navy could carry out a sea invasion of Britain. By the end of September, the Luftwaffe had failed to gain air superiority and the invasion was called off. The Battle of Britain has been extensively studied and there is no need to repeat all of the events of the campaign here. However, the Luftwaffe's attempt to conduct an air war against Britain in 1939–1940 dramatically demonstrates what was the Luftwaffe's single greatest failure in developing an air war doctrine: The Luftwaffe went to war without a coherent naval air war doctrine and without an effective naval air arm.

That the Luftwaffe had failed to create an effective naval air arm became painfully evident on Britain's entry into the war—an event not really expected by the Third Reich's top leadership. General Felmy had already made it clear to Göring and the navy that the most suitable method of conducting a strategic air campaign against Britain would be to strike at the British ports and shipping, because Britain was dependent on imports for much of its food and most of its raw materials. In a letter to Reichsmarschall Göring on 31 October 1939, Grossadmiral Raeder, commander in chief of the navy and bearer of the primary responsibility for carrying out war against Britain, complained that the naval aviation force was incapable for conducting missions against British shipping.[35] The He 115 seaplanes and the Do 18 flying boats were not fast enough nor did they have sufficient range to serve as strike aircraft. The navy required planes such as the Do 217—not yet in serial production—which had the range for overwater operations, the speed for conducting attacks, and the capability to drop bombs and torpedoes. Raeder even complained about the lack of suitable air-droppable torpedoes, although torpedo development had always been the responsibility of the navy ordnance department.[36]

Even though General Felmy had sensibly pointed out in 1938 how an aerial mining campaign could be used to shut British harbors, the Reichsmarine had only a few of the new magnetic mines available at the start of the war. Rather than accumulate a significant stock of mines and then use them against the British, small numbers of mines were sown off the English coast by naval aircraft flying at night. Between 20 November and 7 December 1939 a mere sixty-eight mines were dropped in British waters.[37] Although the magnetic mines would have been very lethal to British shipping had they been dropped in quantity, the British soon dredged one up, examined it, and developed countermeasures.[38] In preparation for the 1940 campaign, the naval air arm operating under the control of the navy dropped a total of 188 mines off the British coast that sank a mere seven ships of 14,564 tons.[39]

Lacking an effective long-range reconnaissance plane/bomber for naval operations, in the fall of 1939 the Luftwaffe began a program to modify the Focke Wulf 200 Condor, a four-engine Lufthansa passenger airliner, as a naval strike aircraft. The FW 200 was never really suitable as a strike aircraft as its structure was too light to carry enough bombs, armor, and armament, but with the aircraft production program in a state of confusion, the FW 200 conversions were the best that the naval air arm could ask for. By August 1940 a few of the modified Condors were ready and began to fly antishipping strikes over the Atlantic.[40] The success that the small force of approximately thirty Condors had was astounding. Between August 1940 and February 1941, the FW 200 force sank eighty-five Allied vessels of a total 363,000 tons.[41]

The success that the Luftwaffe had with a handful of improvised bombers demonstrates what Germany could have done against Britain if it had developed a real naval air striking force in the interwar period. The technology was at hand, the funds and personnel were available. Indeed, the Germans even had a significant advantage in developing the first effective magnetic naval mine. If the fifty-plus German submarines, mostly short-range models, available at the start of the war were enough to seriously threaten the viability of the British nation, one shudders to think what the Germans could have done to Britain with a larger U-boat fleet, a few thousand magnetic mines, and a force of a couple hundred purpose-built, long-range naval attack aircraft. However, Admiral Raeder expressed little interest in such a force before the war, and the mining operations that he supervised in the opening phases of the war show how little understanding of the potential for naval aviation there was in the Reichsmarine. It would not be until 1942 that the Luftwaffe fielded a specially trained and equipped torpedo bomber group, which then did sterling service in conducting antishipping strikes in Norway and the Mediterranean. Ironically, much of the effort to plan for and build an effective naval air strike force came from the Luftwaffe's Helmuth Felmy, who encountered only moderate interest from the Reichsmarine commander and staff when he pushed for a larger naval air arm.

STRATEGIC BOMBING AND THE BATTLE OF BRITAIN

Air power scholars have asserted that one of the primary causes for the German defeat in the Battle of Britain was the lack of four-engine heavy bombers that could have waged a strategic bombing campaign against vital targets.[42] Luftwaffe doctrine is also blamed. John Keegan states that "The Luftwaffe of 1939–1940 did not espouse any strategic bombing theory at all."[43] The Luftwaffe of 1940 is described as a "ground support arm" that had been developed that way because most of its chiefs were "ex-army" officers.[44] In reality, the Luftwaffe of 1940 was quite capable of conducting a strategic air campaign and had the doctrine and equipment to do it. The Luftwaffe had no need of four-engine bombers to reduce Britain; the German bomber force of He 111s, Do 17s, and Ju 88s had enough range and bombload to do the job. The problem for the Luftwaffe—as it would be for the Allied air forces in 1943–1944—was in the lack of a suitable escort fighter that could escort the bombers to the target and get them back without extreme losses. However, the lack of a long-range escort fighter was not a failure of German doctrine. In the interwar period the Luftwaffe, in contrast to the British and Americans, had not believed that the bomber would get through on its own, and Germany was the only nation in the interwar period to develop a true, long-range fighter to escort the bombers—the Me 110 twin-engine fighter. Although the Me 110 was one of the great aircraft of World War II and performed admirably in the fighter-bomber, reconnaissance, and night-fighter roles—it could not win in a dogfight with the lighter single-engine Hurricanes and Spitfires. The other German fighter, the Me 109, was also a great aircraft, but it lacked the range to escort the bombers past London—and then it had only a few minutes of battle time over the target. As for the argument that the Luftwaffe was an "army support arm," it can be noted that the Luftwaffe's bombers and aircrew were far more capable of finding and accurately bombing specific industrial targets in 1940 than was the strategically oriented bomber command of the Royal Air Force.

One major cause for the Luftwaffe's failure in 1940 is its poor intelligence on Britain, its war industries, and the RAF.[45] This is certainly true. The Luftwaffe had a very poor idea of how the RAF defenses worked, what air bases belonged to fighter command, where the most vital aircraft factories were, and so forth. Yet, this failure to collect intelligence was not because the Luftwaffe thought only in terms of army support and not in strategic terms, but because the political leadership of the Third Reich did not advise the Luftwaffe to consider Britain as a possible enemy until a year and a half before the war began. A year and a half is scarcely enough time to collect enough information and develop a true appreciation of how one of the world's largest economies and military establishments worked. In contrast, the Luftwaffe's intelligence on France and Poland, countries that had been seen as enemies for two decades, was thorough. Since it had been given time to prepare, the Luftwaffe had a much better understanding of the Polish and French economies and militaries than it had of the British. The Luftwaffe plans for strategic targeting of French and Polish industries were based on a thorough and accurate assessment of those nations. To illustrate the point, it took the Allies three to four years of war and a massive intelligence effort to get to the point where British and American bombers could start to seriously hurt German industry by strategic attacks.

In any case, the Luftwaffe's chances to win the Battle of Britain were small no matter what doctrine for aerial warfare it used. The Germans had only a few weeks to win the air battle before bad weather closed in and ruled out a naval landing on the English coast. The Germans had just suffered serious losses in a hard battle for France and the Low Countries, and, finally, the RAF always had the option of pulling its fighters out of the south of England and retreating to bases in the north out of the Luftwaffe's way. Such a strategy would have opened up London to bombing but it would have kept the RAF as a "fleet in being"—ready and waiting to redeploy south and intervene if the Germans landed. With such a strategy, Britain would have taken more punishment, but the Luftwaffe could not have assured the army of air superiority in an invasion. With a weak navy and without clear air superiority, it is doubtful that the Wehrmacht would have risked an invasion.

ASSESSMENT OF LUFTWAFFE THEORY AND DOCTRINE

The victors get to write the history and for fifty years the assessment by many military and air power historians has been that the Luftwaffe's theory and doctrine for air war took the wrong approach. The Luftwaffe is characterized as merely a "tactical air force," which was led by "soldiers first and airmen second," men who "lacked a full committment [*sic*] to air power."[46] Such judgments reflect a narrow British/American air forces culture dating from the 1930s in which the true and correct way to conduct air warfare is by strategic bombing, other forms of air power being secondary to winning the air war. The dismissal of Luftwaffe leaders and thinkers such as Walter Wever, Albert Kesselring, and Hans-Jürgen Stumpf as "soldiers first and airmen second" betrays the British/American air force prejudice that only someone who becomes a pilot at a young age and spends his formative years acquiring top-notch flying skills in an air force squadron could possibly be a "true believer" in air power.

Yet the German airmen of the interwar period, such as Helmuth Wilberg, Hugo Sperrle, Helmuth Felmy, Wolfram von Richthofen, Kurt Student, and their colleagues Wever, Kesselring, and Stumpf, cannot be so easily dismissed as second-rate air theorists. German air power theory of the interwar period is remarkable for its broad and comprehensive approach to air power. To the German airmen, air power meant a doctrine of strategic bombing, but it also meant a concept of conducting joint operations with the ground forces, a theory of homeland civil defense and passive defense against a bombing campaign, the creation of a paratroop force capable seizing and holding vital objectives behind the enemy lines, the creation of a large air transport force and a mobile logistics system for keeping one's forces supplied in the field, and the development of a strong antiaircraft artillery arm that could defend the homeland and provide support to the armed forces. In virtually all these aspects of air power, the Luftwaffe was ahead of the British and the Americans in the interwar period.

Rather than being a weakness, the Luftwaffe's doctrine of war developed painstakingly during the interwar period was one of the strengths of the Wehrmacht. It was a concept of air war that showed considerable innovation. The Luftwaffe was able to make a decisive use of airborne force in 1940 in Holland and 1941 in Crete. The Luftwaffe's ability to operate jointly with the army in France in 1940 gave the Wehrmacht its margin of victory in a rapid campaign. Building and hardening vital industrial plants in the 1930s with the possibility of aerial bombing in mind and training the populace in civil defense was one of the reasons why the Allied bombing offensive found it so difficult to take down German armaments production in 1943–1944. The Luftwaffe entered the war with the largest and most effective air transport force in the world. Again, this made a decisive difference in the campaign for Norway. The large flak force of the Luftwaffe remained a potent arm of the Wehrmacht for the entire war and proved its worth time and again. The U.S. Army Air Forces lost 18,418 aircraft in the air campaign against Germany in World War II, and the Luftwaffe's flak arm is credited with 7,821 of those planes.[47] Although one could argue that the creation of such a flak force diverted too many resources from the rest of the war effort, the Wehrmacht certainly never complained about the Luftwaffe flak gunners who used their dual-purpose guns to destroy hundreds of British and American tanks in the Normandy battles of 1944.

The Luftwaffe fought outnumbered on all fronts after the campaign of 1940. Despite this, it was still able to win and hold air superiority in Russia, north Africa, and over northern Europe for a considerable period. It was still able to intervene effectively in ground operations as late as 1943. As Williamson Murray points out in his book, *Strategy for Defeat: The Luftwaffe 1933–1945,* the Luftwaffe lost an attrition war in the air. The Luftwaffe failed to produce enough aircraft and the right aircraft. Even more damaging, the Luftwaffe failed to increase its pilot training programs significantly after the start of the war. Jeschonnek's concept of blitzkrieg operations meant that the Luftwaffe was unready to deal with an aerial attrition war. Mismanagement of the aircraft production programs under Udet also meant that the Luftwaffe went into the campaign in Russia with fewer aircraft than it had in the 1940 campaign. Against vast American, British, and Russian production the Luftwaffe was eventually bled to death. Yet, up to early 1944 the Luftwaffe could still hold its own over the skies of the Reich.

In his book *The German Air War in Russia,*[48] Richard Muller puts to rest the concept that the Luftwaffe as a whole had no concept of strategic bombing. Muller documents that the Luftwaffe came up with a sophisticated plan for strategic attacks against vital Russian industries, and it had a corps of first-rate bomber commanders such as General der Flieger Günther Korten who were ready to conduct such a campaign.[49] However, under Göring's direction, the bomber force was ill-used throughout the war. A large part of the bomber force was destroyed while serving as air transports during the ill-fated attempt to supply Stalingrad by air in the winter of 1942–1943. A pointless attempt to terrorize England by night bomber attacks on London in 1944 resulted in the decimation of Major General Dietrich Peltz's 500-bomber force of the IX Air Corps with few losses on the British side. As with the disastrous Stalingrad airlift, the Luftwaffe bombing campaign was ordered by Hitler and Göring against the objections of the Luftwaffe's senior commanders. Such was the nature of strategic decision-making in the Third Reich.

CONTRAST WITH THE ALLIES

The British and Americans entered the war with a fixation on the strategic bombing concept and only reluctantly adapted to the actual nature of the aerial war. The RAF had to build a doctrine for mobile war operations from scratch in the Western Desert in 1941–1942. Because the RAF had no transport force, a makeshift force of old bombers had to be adapted to the purpose.[50] It would not be until late 1942 that the RAF could effectively fly the kind of close support missions that the Luftwaffe had been doing since 1939. The U.S. Army Air Forces did not work out an effective close support system until 1943–1944. In other aspects of air doctrine, the British and Americans were years behind the Germans. Both allies would copy the German paratroop and glider forces after 1940, but the Allies were never able to use their airborne forces with the same operational effect that the Germans had demonstrated in Holland in 1940 and Crete in 1941. As late as the spring of 1944 many senior British and American air commanders still believed that the war against Germany could be won by strategic bombing alone—that a land invasion of Western Europe was unnecessary.[51] U.S. Air Force General Haywood Hansell persisted arguing long after the end of World War II that strategic bombing alone could have won the war.[52] The dogma of strategic bombing was so pervasive among the interwar British and American air forces that the other important aspects of air power had been ignored. An effective operational theory and doctrine of air power had to be created after the start of the war and lessons learned at great cost in lives and equipment.

SUMMARY

The story of the development of the Luftwaffe in the interwar period is a remarkable one and ought to provide some important lessons to modern military leaders and thinkers. Subject to total aerial disarmament in 1919, only twenty years later a reborn Luftwaffe would emerge as the most combat-effective air force in the world. That this happened was the result of a careful and rational planning process that began under General von Seeckt right after Germany's defeat in World War I. To a greater degree than any other power, the German air and ground forces initiated a program of critical analysis to absorb their experience in the war and to glean useful lessons to guide the formation of a new air force when rearmament came. The Reichswehr of the 1920s and early 1930s maintained a small corps of professional air officers who were able to build on these sound foundations. Even when Germany was disarmed, the Allies could not stop the Germans from thinking and planning. The German army quietly absorbed the experience of other countries by intensive study and, combining this with their own extensive experience, created an original and comprehensive air doctrine. Although they are rarely mentioned in the books about air power today, officers such as Helmuth Wilberg, Hugo Sperrle, Helmuth Felmy, Kurt Student, and Wilhelm Wimmer proved to be outstanding air strategists and thinkers who provided Germany with a practical operational air doctrine and theory when the time came to rearm.

Once rearmament was under way, a new group of air leaders came to the fore. Walter Wever, Albert Kesselring, Hans-Jürgen Stumpf, Robert Knauss, Herhudt von Rohden, Wolfram von Richthofen, and Hans Jeschonnek inherited a sound foundation and built on it. Owing to the German general staff tradition of war games and large-scale maneuvers, the ideas developed in the 1920s matured into an effective air doctrine for battlefield victory. Despite the failure to develop a naval air doctrine and the poor guidance of Hans Jeschonnek, the Germans were able to gain the aerial advantage over the Allied powers in the first years of the World War II not because they had overwhelming numbers of aircraft, but because their conception of a future air war and the training and equipment required for such a war was far more accurate than their opponents' air power vision.

Notes

INTRODUCTION

1. Karl-Heinz Frieser provides some thorough statistical research into the numbers and types of aircraft that were available to the RAF and French air force in May 1940. He argues that if the Allies had brought the full air power available to France and Britain in the European theater to bear against the Luftwaffe in the west in May 1940 the Luftwaffe would have been clearly outnumbered with 4,469 Allied bombers and fighters to 3,578 German combat aircraft. Frieser further points out that the German technological superiority was also very slim. See Frieser, Karl-Heinz, *Blitzkrieg-Legende: Der Westfeldzug 1940* (Munich: Oldenbourg Verlag, 1995), 52–67.

2. Roger Freeman, *The Mighty Eighth* (Garden City, N.Y.: Doubleday, 1970).

3. The only history of the Air Corps Tactical School is a short general official history of less than a hundred pages of text containing only twenty pages on air doctrine. See Robert F. Finney, *History of the Air Corps Tactical School 1920–1940* (Washington, D.C.: Center for Air Force History, 1992).

4. John Keegan, *The Second World War* (New York: Penguin, 1989).

5. Ibid., 91.

6. Telford Taylor, *The March of Conquest* (Annapolis, Md.: Nautical and Aviation Press, 1958, reprinted 1991), 24.

7. Trevor Dupuy, *The Evolution of Weapons and Warfare* (New York: De Capo Press, 1984), 243.

8. Wesley Craven and James Cate, *The Army Air Forces in World War II,* vol. 1 (University of Chicago Press, 1948), 87–88.

9. See Dennis Richards, *The Royal Air Force 1939–1945* (London: Her Majesty's Stationary Office, 1953), 29; and Asher Lee, *The German Air Force* (New York: Harper and Brothers, 1946), 16–17.

10. See Alan Stephens, "The True Believers: Air Power Between the Wars," in *The War in the Air 1914–1994,* ed. Alan Stephens (Fairbairn, Australia: RAAF Air Power Studies Centre, 1994), 70.

11. Robin Cross, *The Bombers* (New York: Macmillan, 1987), 107–9.

12. The best exposition of this view is found in Haywood Hansell, *The Strategic Air War Against Germany and Japan* (Washington, D.C.: Office of Air Force History, 1986), 262–63.

13. The Anglo/American prejudice in favor of strategic bombing as the primary

function of an air force is demonstrated by the large number of scholarly history books written on the strategic bombing campaign in Europe in World War II, as opposed to the very small number of scholarly works on the tactical air forces. On the strategic campaign are excellent works such as Max Hastings's *Bomber Command* (New York: Simon & Schuster, 1989); Martin Middlebrook's *The Nuremberg Raid* (New York: Morrow, 1976), and his *The Schweinfurt-Regensburg Mission* (New York: Penguin, 1985); and Dudley Saward's biography, *Bomber Harris* (Garden City, N.Y.: Doubleday, 1985). One cannot find counterpart books about the Ninth Air Force, Twelfth Air Force, Second Tactical Air Force, or their commanders.

14. See Olaf Groehler, *Geschichte des Luftkriegs: 1910 bis 1980* (Berlin: Militärverlag der DDR, 1981), 196–99.

15. Gerhard Weinberg, *A World at Arms: A Global History of World War II* (New York: Cambridge University Press, 1994), 125.

16. Dominick Pisano, ed., *Legend, Memory and the Great War in the Air* (Washington, D.C.: Smithsonian Institution Press, 1992), 29.

17. Peter Fritzsche, *A Nation of Fliers: German Aviation and the Popular Imagination* (Cambridge, Mass.: Harvard University Press, 1992), esp. 179–219.

18. Edwin Hoyt, *Angels of Death: Goering's Luftwaffe* (New York: Forge, 1994).

19. Samuel Mitcham, *Men of the Luftwaffe* (Novato, Calif.: Presidio Press, 1989).

20. Stephen McFarland and Wesley Newton, *To Command the Sky: The Battle for Air Superiority Over Germany, 1942–1944* (Washington, D.C.: Smithsonian Institution Press, 1991).

21. Ibid., 66.

22. Ibid., 39.

23. Ibid., 68. There are many other examples; these are just a sampling.

24. Ibid., 210–11.

25. David Irving, *Goering: A Biography* (New York: Avon, 1989). In his book, Irving asserts that Göring, one of the Third Reich's inner circle, was unaware of the extermination of Europe's Jews. See also David Irving, *The Rise and Fall of the Luftwaffe: The Life of Luftwaffe Marshal Erhard Milch* (London: Weidenfeld and Nicolson, 1973).

26. Telford Taylor, *The March of Conquest* (Baltimore: Nautical and Aviation Press, reprint 1991), 25–26.

27. Stephen McFarland and Wesley Newton, *To Command the Sky,* 42.

28. Karl-Heinz Völker, *Entwicklung der Militärischen Luftfahrt in Deutschland 1920–1933* (Stuttgart: Deutsche Verlags-Anstalt, 1962).

29. Karl-Heinz Völker, *Die Deutsche Luftwaffe 1933–1939: Aufbau, Führung, Rüstung* (Stuttgart: Deutsche Verlags-Anstalt, 1967).

30. Karl-Heinz Völker, ed., *Dokumente und Dokumentarfotos zur Geschichte der Deutschen Luftwaffe* (Stuttgart: Deutsche Verlags-Anstalt, 1968).

31. Horst Boog, *Die deutsche Luftwaffenführung 1935–1945* (Stuttgart: Deutsche Verlags-Anstalt, 1982).

32. See Horst Boog, "Luftwaffe und unterschiedloser Bombenkrieg bis 1942," in *Luftkriegführung im Zweiten Weltkrieg,* ed. Horst Boog (Herford: E.S. Mittler Verlag, 1993), 435–68.

33. Klaus Maier et al., *Die Errichtung der Hegemonie auf dem Europäischen Kontinent,* vol. II of *Das Deutsche Reich und der Zweite Weltkrieg* (Stuttgart: Deutsche Verlagsanstalt, 1979). See esp. "Totaler Krieg und operativer Luftkrieg," 43–69, and "Die Operative Luftkrieg bis zur Luftschlacht um England," 329–44.

34. Richard Muller, *The German Air War in Russia* (Baltimore: Nautical and Aviation Press, 1992).

35. John Morrow, *German Air Power in World War I* (Lincoln: University of Nebraska Press, 1982).

36. John Morrow, *The Great War in the Air* (Washington, D.C.: Smithsonian Institution Press, 1993).

37. Raymond Proctor, *Hitler's Luftwaffe in the Spanish Civil War* (Westpoint, Conn.: Greenwood Press, 1983).

38. Manfred Zeidler, *Reichswehr und Rote Armee 1920–1933* (Munich: Oldenbourg Verlag, 1993).

39. See Bernd Stegemann, "Der Zweite Anlauf zur Seemacht" and "Die Erste Phase der Seekriegführung bis zum Fruehjahr 1940," in *Das Deutsche Reich und der Zweite Weltkrieg,* vol. II, 70–78 and 159–88.

40. Edward Homze, *Arming the Luftwaffe: The Reich Air Ministry and the German Aircraft Industry, 1919–1939* (Lincoln: University of Nebraska Press, 1976).

41. William Green, *Warplanes of the Third Reich* (New York: Galahad, 1990).

42. Hanfried Schliephake, *The Birth of the Luftwaffe* (Chicago: Henry Regnery, 1971).

43. E. R. Hooton, *Phoenix Triumphant: The Rise and Rise of the Luftwaffe* (London: Arms and Armour Press, 1994).

THE LESSONS OF WORLD WAR I

1. Michael Howard, *The Franco-Prussian War* (London: Methuen, 1979), 167.

2. Ibid.

3. An excellent overview of military aviation of the French and Germans prior to World War I is Militärgeschichtliches Forschungsamt, ed., *Die Militärluftfahrt bis zum Beginn des Weltkrieges 1914* (Frankfurt am Main: Verlag E.S. Mittler und Sohn, 1965). On early balloon use and experiments, see 1–4. Another useful study of German airpower doctrine and organization before World War I is John Morrow, *Building German Airpower, 1909–1914* (Knoxville: University of Tennessee Press, 1976).

4. Ibid., 1.

5. Charles Christienne and Pierre Lissarague, *A History of French Military Aviation* (Washington, D.C.: Smithsonian Institution Press, 1986), 19.

6. Militärgeschichtliches Forschungsamt, *Die Militärluftfahrt,* 35–37.
7. Ibid., 43.
8. Ibid., 44–45.
9. Ibid., 69.
10. Ibid., 78–79.
11. Ibid., 80.
12. Helmut von Moltke, *Letter to War Ministry,* 2 March 1911, in *Urkunden des Obersten Heeresleitung,* Erich von Ludendorff, ed. Berlin: E. S. Mittler, 1920, 24–25.
13. John Morrow, *Building German Airpower, 1909–1914* (Knoxville: University of Tennessee Press, 1976), 15.
14. Ibid.
15. Morrow, *Building German Airpower,* 48.
16. Morrow, *Building German Airpower,* 52.
17. On the Bavarian aircraft industry and air arm, see Peter Pletschacher, *Die königliche bayerische Fliegertruppen, 1912–1919* (Stuttgart: Motorbuch Verlag, 1978). See also John Morrow, *Building German Airpower,* 93–103.
18. Morrow, *Building German Airpower,* 93.
19. Ibid., 21.
20. Militärgeschichtliches Forschungsamt, *Die Militärluftfahrt,* 120–21.
21. Morrow, *Building German Airpower,* 16.
22. Militärgeschichtliches Forschungsamt, *Die Militärluftfahrt bis zum Beginn des Weltkrieges 1914, Technische Band* (Frankfurt am Main: Verlag E. S. Mittler, 2nd edition, 1966), 40.
23. On the relationship between the general staff and war ministry, see Wiegand Schmidt-Richberg, *Die Generalstäbe in Deutschland 1871–1945* (Stuttgart: Deutsche Verlags-Anstalt, 1962), 20–24.
24. There are several useful histories of the pre–World War I general staff, including Walter Goerlitz, *The German General Staff 1657–1945* (New York: Praeger, 1953). See also Wiegand Schmidt-Richberg, *Die Generalstäbe in Deutschland;* and Trevor Dupuy, *A Genius for War: The German Army and General Staff 1807–1945* (McLean, Va.: Dupuy Institute, 1984).
25. Schmidt-Richberg, *Die Generalstäbe in Deutschland,* 18.
26. Chief of the general staff to the war ministry, letter of 2 March 1911, in *Urkunden des Obersten Heeresleitung,* Erich von Ludendorff, ed. (Berlin: E. S. Mittler, 1920), Akt 13.
27. Helmut von Moltke, "Denkschrift," December 1912, in *Urkunden des Obersten Heeresleitung,* Erich von Ludendorff, ed., Akt 19.
28. Helmut von Moltke, letter to inspectorate of military transport, 9 March 1912, in *Urkunden des Obersten Heeresleitung,* Erich von Ludendorff, ed., 25, Akt 14.
29. The Euler machine gun mount was a ring mount that enabled the observer, flying in the rear seat of the aircraft, to shoot above, below, behind, and to the side of the aircraft.

30. Helmut von Moltke, letter to inspectorate of military transport, 23 April 1912, in *Urkunden des Obersten Heeresleitung,* Erich von Ludendorff, ed., 26, Akt 15.

31. Helmut von Moltke, letter to the war ministry, 26 September 1912, in *Urkunden des Obersten Heeresleitung,* Erich von Ludendorff, ed., Akt 17.

32. Ibid.

33. Erich von Ludendorff, "Further Development of Military Aviation to 1 April 1917," letter to Section VII of the war ministry (14 January 1913), in *Urkunden des Obersten Heeresleitung,* Erich von Ludendorff, Akt 20.

34. Peter Supf, *Die Geschichte des deutsche Flugwesens,* vol. I. Berlin: Verlagsanstalt Hermann Klemm, 1935, 377.

35. Supf, *Die Geschichte des deutschen Flugwesens,* 454–55.

36. Peter Kilduff, *Germany's First Air Force 1914–1918* (Osceola: Motorbooks International, 1991), 6–10.

37. Ibid., 377.

38. Helmuth Felmy earned his pilot's license in 1912, and began the Kriegsakademie in 1913. BA/MA *Personnel Records of Helmuth Felmy.*

39. Kilduff, *Germany's First Air Force,* 9–10.

40. Supf, *Die Geschichte des deutschen Flugwesens,* vol. II, 95.

41. *Anhaltspunkte für den Unterricht bei der Truppe über Luftfahrzeuge und deren Bekämpfung,* March 1913.

42. Ibid., paras. 2–16.

43. Ibid., paras. 17–28.

44. Militärgeschichtliches Forschungsamt, *Die Militärluftfahrt bis zum Beginn des Weltkrieges: Technischer Band* (Frankfurt am Main: Verlag E.S. Mittler, 1966), 288–302.

45. Ibid., 81–82.

46. Ibid., 95.

47. Cited in Rudiger Kosin, *The German Fighter Since 1915* (London: Putnam, 1988), 13.

48. See Heinz Nowarra, *50 Jahre Deutsche Luftwaffe,* vol. I (Berlin: Heinz Nowarra, 1961).

49. Dennis Showalter, *Tannenberg: Clash of Empires* (Hamden: Archon, 1991), 152–53, 169–70, 192, and 311–12. See also Peter Supf, *Die Geschichte des deutschen Flugwesens,* vol. II, 257–63.

50. Supf, *Die Geschichte des deutschen Flugwesens,* vol. II, 262.

51. Kilduff, *Germany's First Air Force,* 18–19.

52. In the 1915–1916 airship campaign against England, the Germans sent 220 Zeppelin sorties, dropped 175 tons of bombs, killed 557 civilians, and wounded 1,358. See David Divine, *The Broken Wing: A Study in the British Exercise of Air Power* (London: Hutchinson, 1966), 103.

53. George Questor, *Deterrence Before Hiroshima* (New Brunswick, N.J.: Transaction, 1986), 28.

54. Joachim Kuropka, "Die britische Luftkriegskonzeption gegen Deutschland im Ersten Weltkrieg," in *Militärgeschichtliche Mitteilungen* 27, no. 1 (1980): 8.

55. Von Rieben, ed., *Luftschiffen, Flugwaffe* (August 1940): 1, in BA/MA Potsdam W-10/50825. During World War I, the German navy used seventy-four airships. Of these, fifty-four were lost, with 40 percent of the aircrew becoming casualties. See Heinrich Walle, "Das Zeppelinsche Luftschiff als Schrittmacher technologischer Entwicklung im Krieg und Frieden," in *Militär und Technik: Wechselbeziehung zu Staat, Gesellschaft und Industrie im 19. Und 20. Jahrhunderten,* ed. Roland Foerster (Herford: E. S. Mittler und Sohn, 1992), 196.

56. John Slessor, *Air Power and Armies* (London: Oxford University Press, 1936), 19.

57. Oberstleutnant Hermann von der Lieth-Thomsen, "Denkschrift of 10 March 1916," in *Die Luftstreitkräfte des Deutschen Reiches,* ed. Dr. Klemp (ca. 1936), in BA/MA Potsdam W-10/50845.

58. War Ministry, Abt. 7, *Memo* (March 1916), 25 in BA/MA Potsdam W-10/ 50845.

59. Kontreadmiral Phillips, Marine Luftfahrt Abteilung, letter to naval state secretary (8 June 1916), in BA/MA Potsdam W-10/50845, Appendix 3.

60. A good overview of the dispute over an independent air force is found in Karl Köhler, "Auf dem Wege zur Luftwaffe," in *Wehrwissenschaftliche Rundschau* no. 10 (October 1966): 553–62.

61. A complete table of organization of the Luftstreitkräfte headquarters and an army aviation headquarters is provided in Hermann Cron, ed., *Der Organisation des deutschen Heeres im Weltkriege,* part V (Berlin: E. S. Mittler und Sohn, 1923), 88–95.

62. General der Kavallerie Ernst von Hoeppner was born in Tonnin in 1860, and died in Rügen in 1922. His service record reads: entered army, 1879; second lieutenant, 1879; cavalry officer, 1879–1893; Kriegsakademie, 1889–1892; captain, 1893; squadron commander, 1893–1897; staff positions, 1899–1902; major, 1899; general staff, 1902–1904 and 1905–1906; lieutenant colonel, 1906; section commander, greater general staff, 1906; commander, 13th Hussar Regiment, 1906–1908; colonel, 1909; commander, major general, 1912; 4th Cavalry Brigade, 1912–1914; chief of staff, 3rd Army, 1914–1915; lieutenant general, 1915; commander, 17th Division, 1915; commander, 75th Division, 1916; commanding general of the Luftstreitkräfte, Nov. 1916–Jan. 1919; general der kavallerie, 1919; retired, 1919.

63. General der Flieger Hermann von der Lieth-Thomsen was born in Flensburg in 1867, and died in Berlin in 1942. His military file reads: entered army, 1887; second lieutenant, 1889; engineer officer, 1887–1897; Kriegsakademie, 1897–1900; greater general staff, 1901–1903; captain, 1902; pioneer company commander, 1903–1905; greater general staff, 1905–1914; major, 1911; lieutenant colonel, 1916; airship detachment posen, 1914; chief of field aviation forces, 1915–1916; chief of staff of commander, Luftstreitkräfte, 1916–1919; colonel, 1918; chief, aviation department, Prussian war ministry, 1919; retired, 1919; recalled to duty as officer on special service, 1935–1942; major general, 1935; lieutenant general, 1937; General der Flieger, 1939.

64. Kommandierende General der Luftstreitkräfte, *Weisungen für den Einsatz und die Verwendung von Fliegerverbänden innerhalb einer Armee,* May 1917.

65. Ibid., paras. 34–40.

66. Ibid., para. 43.

67. Ibid., para. 45.

68. Von Richthofen's detailed fighter tactics manual of 1918 is translated and reproduced in Peter Kilduff, *Richthofen: Beyond the Legend of the Red Baron* (New York: Wiley, 1993), 231–40.

69. Georg Neumann, *Die deutschen Luftstreitkräfte im Weltkrieg* (Berlin: E. S. Mittler und Sohn, 1921), 268–69.

70. Richard Hallion, *Rise of the Fighter Aircraft, 1914–1918* (Baltimore: Nautical and Aviation Press, 1984), 72–73 and 160–61.

71. British Royal Flying Corps losses in April 1917 were: 222 aircraft lost, and 316 RFC pilots and observers KIA/MIA. See Peter Liddle, *The Airman's War 1914–1918* (New York: Blandford Press, 1987), 55.

72. See General Max Schwarte, *Der Grosse Krieg 1914–1918,* vol. IV (Leipzig: Barth Verlag, 1922), 603.

73. H. A. Jones, *The War in the Air,* vol. IV (Oxford: Clarendon, 1934), 112–13.

74. Reichsarchiv Air History Branch, Account of 1917 Air Campaigns (Nov. 1923), in BA/MA Potsdam W-10/50097, 332.

75. Ibid., 331.

76. See Hermann Cron, ed., *Die Organisation des deutschen Heeres im Weltkriege* (Berlin: E. S. Mittler, 1923), 99–101. For accounts of the German ground attack units in 1917, see Hauptmann Friedrich Ritter von Krauser, "Schlacht und Nachtflüge in Flandern 1917," in *In der Luft Unbesiegt,* ed. Georg Neumann (Munich: J. F. Lehmanns Verlag, 1923), 79–91. See also, Major Freiharr von Bülow, *Geschichte der Luftwaffe* (Frankfurt am Main: Verlag Moritz Diesterweg, 1934), 91–100.

77. A translation of this manual is found in H. A. Jones, *The War in the Air,* vol. IV, Appendix: Chief of Staff, German Field Army, "Employment of Battle Flights" (20 February 1917).

78. Ibid., para. 7.

79. Ibid., para. 12.

80. Ibid.

81. Ibid., para. 2.

82. Richard Hallion, *Strike from the Sky* (Washington, D.C.: Smithsonian Institution Press, 1989), 20.

83. Chief of staff, German field army, "Employment of Battle Flights," para. 27.

84. Jones, *The War in the Air,* vol. IV, 149.

85. Ibid., vol. VI, 161.

86. Ibid., vol. IV, 99–100.

87. Ibid., vol. VI, 161.

88. Kriegsgeschichtliches Forschungsanstalt, *Die Angriffe auf französiche Kanalhäfen,* in BA/MA Potsdam W-10/50824, 5–10.

89. Ibid., 7–9.

90. Rolf Roenigh, *Webereiter der Luftfahrt* (Berlin: Deutscher Archiv-Verlag, ca. 1939), 96.

91. W. M. Lamberton, *Reconnaissance and Bomber Aircraft of the 1914–1918 War* (Letchworth, U.K.: Harleyford, 1962), 193.

92. Kommandierende General der Luftstreitkräfte, *Utilization and the Role of Artillery Aviators in Trench Warfare,* German manual of early 1917, translated by the U.S. Army War College (July 1917).

93. John Morrow, *The Great War in the Air* (Washington, D.C.: Smithsonian Institution Press, 1993).

94. Roenigh, *Wegbereiter der Luftfahrt,* 136.

95. Peter Supf, *Das Buch der deutschen Fluggeschichte,* vol. II (Berlin: Verlags-Anstalt Hermann Klemm, 1935), 294–95.

96. Kommandierende General der Luftstreitkräfte, "Der Infanterieflieger und der Infanterieballon" (1 September 1917), in *Urkunden der Obersten Heeresleitung,* Erich Ludendorff, ed. (Berlin: E. S. Mittler, 1920).

97. David Divine, *The Broken Wing: A Study in the British Exercise of Air Power* (London: Hutchinson, 1966), 103.

98. Joachim Kuropka, "Die Britische Luftkriegskonzeption gegen Deutschland im Ersten Weltkrieg," in *Militärgeschichtliche Mitteilungen* no. 1 (1980): 8.

99. David Divine, *The Broken Wing,* 103–10.

100. Raymond Fredette, *The Sky on Fire* (New York: Holt, Reinhart and Winston (1966), 262. The total losses from all airship and airplane raids on Britain from 1915–1918 were 1,414 dead and 3,416 wounded.

101. Reichsarchiv, Abt. B., Ref., *Luftstreitkräfte Study of 1918 Air War* (2 April 1926), in BA/MA 2/2195, 5.

102. Morrow, *The Great War in the Air,* 218–19.

103. Ibid.

104. Oberste Heeresleitung, "Der Angriff im Stellungskriege" (1 January 1918), in *Urkunden des Obersten Heeresleitung,* Erich Ludendorff, ed. (Berlin: E. S. Mittler und Sohn, 1920), 641–85.

105. Ibid., chapter 6, paras. 82–84.

106. Ibid., para. 95.

107. Ibid., para. 98.

108. *Ausbildungsplan der Infanteriekommandos* (January 1918), in BA/MA PH 17/98.

109. See Kommandierende general der Luftstreitkräfte, "Hinweise für die Führung einer Fliegerabteilung in der Angriffschlacht und im Bewegungkrieg" (10 February 1918). This pamphlet gives advice on how to organize the fighter and ground attack groups for close air support during different phases of the ground battle.

110. Morrow, *The Great War in the Air,* 296–97.

111. Reichsarchiv, *Study of 1918 Campaign* (April 1926), in BA/MA RH 2/2195.

112. Brereton Greenhous, "Evolution of a Close-Ground Support Role for Aircraft in World War I," in *Military Affairs* (February 1975): 26–27.

113. Reichsarchiv Study of April 1926, in BA/MA RH 2/2195, 12–14.

114. Jones, *The War in the Air,* vol. V (Oxford: Clarendon Press, 1935), 424–27.

115. On the bombing of Paris in 1918, see Jean Hallade, "Big Bertha Bombs Paris," in *Tanks and Weapons of World War I,* Bernard Fitzsimons, ed. (London: Phoebus, 1973).

116. Morrow, *The Great War in the Air,* 302.

117. Ibid., 303.

118. Maj. Arnd, Reichsarchiv Study, *Tätigkeit der amerikanischen Fliegerverbände in Zusammenhang mit den Operationen bei St. Mihiel, September 1918* (1925), in BA/MA PH 17/55.

119. Morrow, *The Great War in the Air,* 316–17.

120. Ibid., 310.

121. See *Revue De L'Aeronautique Militaire* (July/August 1925).

122. Morrow, *The Great War in the Air,* 125–28.

123. See Truppenamt T-Luft, letter of 4 February 1927, in BA/MA RH 12-1/53, fol. 5.

124. Divine, *The Broken Wing,* 141–43.

125. Ibid.

126. Capt. Hoth, Report to Commanding General of the Luftstreitkräfte (7 August 1918), in BA/MA PH 17/96.

127. Neumann, *Die deutschen Luftstreitkräfte,* 275–86.

128. See Olaf Groehler, *Geschichte des Luftkriegs: 1910 bis 1980* (Berlin: Militärverlag der DDR, 1981), 81–85, for a good summary of World War I German air defense.

129. Kriegsgeschichtlichen Abteilung der Luftwaffe, *Entwicklung und Einsatz der deutschen Flakwaffe und des Luftschutzes im Weltkrieg* (Berlin: E. S. Mittler und Sohn, 1938), 93 and 97–98.

130. Jones, *The War in the Air,* vol. IV, 94.

131. Kriegswissenschaftliche Abteilung der Luftwaffe, *Entwicklung und Einsatz der deutschen Flakwaffe,* 115.

132. Neumann, *Die deutschen Luftstreitkräfte,* 590.

133. A good account of the army/navy rivalry over aircraft is found in John Morrow, *German Air Power in World War I* (Lincoln: University of Nebraska Press, 1982), 117–18.

134. Ibid., 209.

135. Neumann, *Die deutschen Luftstreitkräfte,* 589.

136. Ibid.

137. The British official history acknowledges the inferiority of Allied naval aircraft. See H. A. Jones, *The War in the Air,* vol. VI, 380. See also John Morrow, *German Air Power in World War I,* 135–36.

138. Neumann, *Die deutschen Luftstreitkräfte,* 589.

139. Erich Groener, *Die deutschen Kriegsschiffe 1815–1945,* vol. 1 (Koblenz: Bernard und Graefe Verlag, 1989), 98.

140. Morrow, *The Great War in the Air,* 371.

141. Ibid., 223.

142. See Brian Philpott, *The Encyclopedia of German Military Aircraft* (London: Bison, 1981), 53–54.

143. Morrow, *The Great War in the Air,* 316–17.

144. Kenneth Munson, *Aircraft of World War I* (Garden City, N.Y.: Arco, 1977), 93–94; and Richard Hallion, *Rise of the Fighter Aircraft 1914–1918* (Annapolis, Md.: Nautical and Aviation Press, 1984), 117.

145. Brigadier General William Mitchell, *Memoirs of World War I* (New York: Random House, 1960 reprint of 1926 edition), 306.

146. Morrow, *The Great War in the Air,* 369, 371.

147. Ibid., 278.

148. W. M. Lamberton, *Reconnaissance and Bomber Aircraft of the 1914–1918 War,* 197. A good overview of German radio technology of World War I is found in Georg Neumann, *Die deutschen Luftstreitkräfte,* 190–211.

149. Morrow, *The Great War in the Air,* 298–99.

150. Neumann, *Die deutschen Luftstreitkräfte,* 218–27.

151. Brigadier General William Mitchell, *Memoirs of World War I,* 268.

152. See Morrow, *The Great War in the Air,* 309. The Luftstreitkräfte had 16,054 casualties from all causes—combat and operational accidents—with 5,953 dead and 2,751 missing or captured. The British flying forces lost 16,623. The French air service lost 7,255 men in combat but their accident losses are unknown. A sound estimate would be to double the number, figuring one accident loss for every combat loss. Add in the American, Belgian, Russian, and Italian losses, and a 3:1 German kill ratio is probable.

153. General Hoeppner's account of World War I shows a very broad definition of airpower, which included flak artillery, home air defense, and naval air operations, as well as bomber, fighter, and ground support operations. See General der Kavallerie Ernst von Hoeppner, *Deutschland's Krieg in der Luft* (Leipzig: Koehler und Amelang, 1921).

RESPONSE TO DISARMAMENT

1. John Morrow, *The Great War in the Air* (Washington, D.C.: Smithsonian Institution Press, 1993).

2. Ibid., 354–55.

3. Ibid., 353.

4. Ibid., 354.

5. The primary biography of Hans von Seeckt is Hans Meier-Welcker's *Seeckt.* There is also his autobiography, *Aus Meinem Leben,* edited by Friedrich von Rabenau (1866–1918) (Leipzig: Haase-Koehler Verlag, 1938). Both are highly detailed accounts.

6. Hans von Seeckt, *Report to the Army High Command* (18 February 1919), NARA. File M-132, Roll 21, Item 110, von Seeckt Papers.

7. Karl-Heinz Völker, *Die Entwicklung der militärischen Luftfahrt in Deutschland 1920–1933* (Stuttgart: Deutsche Verlags-Anstalt, 1962), 136–37. Wilberg had served under von Seeckt in Macedonia as air staff officer for the Southern Army Group. See Maj. Gen. Hermann Franke, *Handbuch der neuzeitlichen Wehrwissenschaften,* vol. II: *Die Luftwaffe* (Berlin: Verlag von Walter de Gruyter, 1939), 443.

8. Cooper, *The German Air Force 1922–1945* (London: James, 1981), 379.

9. Völker, *Die Entwicklung der militärischen Luftfahrt,* 136–37.

10. Cited in Richard Suchenwirth, *The Development of the German Air Force, 1919–1939.* U.S. Air Force Historical Study No. 160 (Maxwell AFB: Air University, 1968), 5.

11. Hans von Seeckt, *Gedanken eines Soldaten* (Berlin: Verlag für Kulturpolitik, 1929), 93–95.

12. Ibid., 91–93.

13. Mathew Cooper, *The German Air Force 1922–1945* (London: Janes', 1981), 383.

14. Von Seeckt, *Gedanken,* 91–93.

15. James Corum, *Roots of Blitzkrieg* (Lawrence: University Press of Kansas, 1992), 100–102.

16. Wiegand Schmidt-Richberg, *Die Generalstäbe in Deutschland 1871–1945* (Stuttgart: Deutsche Verlags-Anstalt, 1962), esp. 49–69.

17. General der Flieger Helmuth Wilberg was born to a portrait painter and his wife in 1880, and died in 1941 in an air accident. His service record: entered army, 1899; lieutenant, 1900; Infantry Regiment 80, 1899–1906; first lieutenant, 1909; Kriegsakademie, 1910–1913; pilot training, 1910; captain, 1913; adjutant for inspectorate of air units, 1913–1914; commander, Air Detachment 11, 1914–1915; air commander, several armies—primarily Fourth Army, 1915–1918; Reichswehr ministry air staff, 1918–1927; major, 1926; infantry battalion commander, 1928–1929; colonel, 1929; commander Breslau garrison, 1929–1932; major general, 1932; department chief, air ministry, 1934–1935; lieutenant general, 1935; commander, Luftkreis School, 1935–1937; commander, Special Staff W (Condor Legion Staff), 1936–1938; General der Flieger, 1938; retired, 1938; recalled to service, 1939; senior training commander, 1939–1941.

18. Wilberg flew in the 1912 Suddeutsche Rundflug in which two of the sixteen military pilots were killed in air crashes. See Willi Hackenberger, *Die Alten Adler: Pioniere der deutschen Luftfahrt.* (Munich: J. F. Lehmanns Verlag, 1960), 111.

19. Suchenwirth, *The Development of the German Air Force,* 7.

20. Hans von Seeckt, letter to the Truppenamt et al., 1 December 1919, BA/MA 2/2275.

21. Ibid.
22. Ibid.
23. Flugmeisterei, letter of 13 November 1919, BA/MA RH 2/2275, folios 21–26.
24. See Flugmeisterei, Abteilung 2, letter of 4 December 1919, BA/MA RH 2/2275, folios 38–40.
25. See Waffenamt, letter of 24 December 1919, BA/MA RH 2/2275, folios 85–87.
26. Ibid.
27. Ibid.
28. Ibid.
29. BA/MA RH 2/2275 contains about twenty such reports.
30. Kriegsgliederung der Divisions VI, 1920, in BA/MA RH 2/2275, folios 156–59.
31. Kriegserfahrung der Flieger, 30 July 1920, in BA/MA RH 2/2275.
32. Ergebniss des Diskussions—Vortrages über Luftkampfführung, 13 October 1920, in BA/MA RH 2/2275, folios 162–63.
33. Ibid.
34. Hoth, *Kriegserfahrungen,* 3 May 1921, BA/MA RH 2/2275, folios 251–59.
35. Ibid.
36. Major Wilberg, letter to Colonel Thomsen, 8 February 1922, in BA/MA RH 2/2275, folios 384–85.
37. Seydel was wartime commander of Flakgruppe XX. See Cpt. Seydel, "Flak," *Militärwochenblatt* no. 33 (1921).
38. *Heeresdienstvorschrift 487: Führung und Gefecht der Verbundenen Waffen.*
39. *Heeresdienstvorschrift 487,* part I, para. 71.
40. Ibid., paras. 72–74.
41. Ibid., para. 75.
42. Ibid., para. 76.
43. Ibid., para. 77.
44. *Heeresdienstvorschrift 487,* part II (20 June 1923), para. 472.
45. Ibid.
46. Hans von Seeckt, letter to all branch schools, 8 November 1924, in BA/MA RH 12-12/22.
47. T-4 Truppenamt, directive to the Waffenschulen (late 1920), in BA/MA RH 12-2/54, 9.
48. Ibid.
49. Ibid., 4–5.
50. Truppenamt T-4, *Ausbildung der aus Führergehilfen im Aussicht genommenen Offiziere* (31 July 1922), in BA/MA 12-21/94, 4.
51. Ibid., 8.
52. Ibid., 14–15, 17.
53. Hans von Seeckt, letter to the Waffenamt and branch inspectorates (24 January 1924), in BA/MA RH 12-2/21.
54. Among the generals who had received engineering degrees in the 1920s were:

Lieutenant General Wilhelm Becker, who studied at the Technische Hochschule in Charlottenburg, Berlin, 1929-1933; General Kurt August, who studied at the Technische Hochschule in Danzig from 1919–1922, after which he was employed by the army as a civilian; Major General Robert Fuchs, who received his degree in Engineering at Charlottenburg Technische Hochschule in the 1920s; and Major General Gerhard Bassenge, who studied at the Technische Hochschule in Hannover from 1922–1927.

55. Interview by the author with Freiherr Götz von Richthofen, son of Field Marshal Wolfram von Richthofen, 4 September 1993.

56. Konstantin von Altrock, born in 1861 in Breslau, was commissioned in 1881. His service record: appointed to general staff, 1901; promoted to major general, 1914; commanded 60th Infantry Brigade, 1914–1915; promoted to lieutenant general, 1917; commanded 28th Reserve Division, 1918; retired, 1919. Konstantin von Altrock edited *Taktik und Truppenführung* (Berlin: E. S. Mittler und Sohn, 1929), one of the best-known Reichswehr tactical handbooks of his era.

57. In the early 1920s almost every issue of the *Militärwochenblatt* featured a section entitled "Luftfahrwesen" ("Aviation News"), which contained abstracts of foreign articles, books, and speeches on air power. British air thought was carefully followed. See the summary of a lecture on "Future Air War" by RAF Captain Green in *Militärwochenblatt* no. 27 (1921).

58. For translations of Gen. Mitchell's articles, see "How We Should Organize an Air Force," in *Militärwochenblatt* no. 47 (18 June 1925); and "The Era of Aviation," in *Militärwochenblatt* no. 32 (25 Feb. 1925).

59. General Mitchell's famous experiments re sinking the USS *Alabama* and the SMS *Ostfriesland* were covered in detail in *Militärwochenblatt* nos. 8, 19 (1921).

60. *Luftfahrt Nachrichten* no. 1 (August 1919), BA/MA RH 2/2277.

61. See Gen. William Mitchell, Lecture on Aerial Technology (translation), 1 July 1920, in BA/MA RH 2/2277, 471–80.

62. Waffenamt, letter of 12 May 1920, in BA/MA RH 2/2277. See also Waffenamt, letter of 22 October 1919, ibid., 23, which asks T-3 to subscribe to seventeen additional foreign journals. See ibid., 230–40 for a list of the German journals on file.

63. Cpt. Hans Ritter, *Der Luftkrieg* (Berlin: F. Köhler Verlag, 1926), 189–90.

64. Hans Ritter, *Der Zukunftskrieg und seine Waffen* (Leipzig: Verlag von K.F. Koehler, 1924), 85–88.

65. TA-L, Referat VI, *Militärische Faktoren für die Bewertung der Modernen Luftmächte,* 9 April 1926, in BA/MA RH 2279.

66. Maj. Helmuth Wilberg, *Reisebericht,* 1925–1926, in BA/MA RH 2/1820, 199.

67. T-3, *Die französischen Herbstmanöver 1923,* 10 July 1924, in BA/MA RH 2/1547.

68. Truppenamt, report of 25 April 1925, *Nachschubstab,* in NARA T-78, roll 178.

69. *Studie eines Offizieres über die Fliegerwaffe und ihre Verwendung,* a manual published by the army ca. 1925, is in the author's collection.

70. Ibid.

71. Ibid.

72. Ibid.

73. General Giulio Douhet was born in 1869 and died in 1930. An artillery officer, he first wrote on air power in 1909. At the outbreak of World War I, he was commander of an aviation battalion. Court-martialed and imprisoned for a time for his open and extreme criticism of the Italian High Command's direction of the war, he was later pardoned and, in February 1918, made chief of the Central Aeronautical Bureau. He made general in 1921. Having joined the Fascist party, he was appointed air minister by Mussolini in 1922. After his retirement in 1923, he continued to write exclusively on air power subjects for the *Rivista Aeronautica.*

74. Luftschutzübungsreise 1924, in BA/MA RH 2/2244, microfiche 1.

75. Manfred Zeidler, *Reichswehr und Rote Armee 1920–1933* (Munich: R. Oldenbourg Verlag, 1993), 109.

76. Manfred Zeidler, "Luftkriegsdenken und Offizierausbildung an der Moskauer Zukovskij Akademie im Jahre 1926," in *Miliärgeschichtliche Mitteilungen* 27 (1980): 127–74, esp. 146–52.

77. Ibid., 153–56.

78. Ibid., 156.

79. See Herbert Molloy Mason, *Rise of the Luftwaffe* (New York: Ballantine, 1973), 140–56.

80. Völker, *Die Entwicklung der militärischen Luftfahrt,* 140.

81. According to the Lipetsk Observer Training Curriculum for 1926/27, found in BA/MA RH 2/2299.

82. Zeidler, *Reichswehr und Rote Armee,* 123–27.

83. Karl Ries, *The Luftwaffe: A Photographic Record 1919–1945* (London: B. T. Batsford, 1987), 9.

84. David Irving, *The Rise and Fall of the Luftwaffe: The Life of Luftwaffe General Erhard Milch* (London: Weidenfeld and Nicolson, 1973), 12–16.

85. Extensive correspondence files from the 1920s between the Reichswehr air staff and Erhard Milch remain extant. See Erhard Milch, letter to Helmuth Wilberg (4 April 1927), in BA/MA RH 2/2187. See also BA/MA RH 2/2191, on aircraft development in the 1920s.

86. Suchenwirth, *The Development of the German Air Force,* 12–13.

87. Mason, *Rise of the Luftwaffe,* 100.

88. Service record of General Wilhelm Haehnelt.

89. Völker, *Die Entwicklung der Militärische Luftfahrt,* 137–38.

90. Army commander to Reichswehr air ministry, letter of 4 June 1920, in BA/MA RH 2/2198. An extensive list of machine shops, airfields, and industrial facilities available to the Reichswehr by the mid-1920s, in case of war, may be found in Truppenamt Air Staff Records in BA/MA RH 2/2191.

91. See Georg Thomas, *Geschichte der deutschen Wehr und Rüstungswirtschaft, 1918 to 1945* (Boppard am Rhein: Harold Boldt Verlag, 1966), 53–57.

92. See Ernst Hansen, *Reichswehr und Industrie* (Boppard am Rhein: Harald Boldt Verlag, 1978), 82–85.

93. E. R. Hooton, *Phoenix Triumphant* . . . , 24–29.

94. Völker, *Entwicklung der Militärischen Luftfahrt,* 134–37.

95. Werner Rahn, *Reichsmarine und Landesverteidigung 1919–1928* (Munich: Bernard und Graefe Verlag, 1976). On joint army/navy war games conducted in 1924–1925, see 150–51. On joint army/navy staff exercises conducted in May 1928, see 153.

96. Rahn, *Reichsmarine und Landesverteidigung,* 96–100.

97. Homze, *Arming the Luftwaffe,* 38.

98. Ernst Heinkel, *He 1000* (London: Hutchinson, 1956), 78–79. See also Heinkel's *Stürmisches Leben* (Stuttgart: Landesverlag, 1953), 116–26.

99. Hooton, 29.

100. Ronald Miller, *The Technical Development of Modern Aviation* (London: Routledge and Kegan Paul, 1968), 56.

101. Truppenamt T-Luft, *Richtlinien für die Führung des operativen Luftkrieges.*

102. Ibid., para. 5.

103. Ibid., para. 4.

104. Ibid., para. 66.

105. Ibid., paras. 68 and 70.

106. Ibid., para. 69.

107. Ibid., para. 11.

108. Ibid., paras. 106–27.

109. Ibid., paras. 91–92.

110. Ibid., para. 95.

PREPARATION FOR AERIAL REARMAMENT

1. Hans von Seeckt was ordered to resign by the government because he had invited the Kaiser's grandson to take part in the army fall maneuvers of 1926 as an observer. In the oftentimes bizarre politics of the Weimar Republic, such a minor action constituted a major political scandal.

2. Wulf Bremer and Hans Dollinger, *Die deutsche Reichswehr* (Frankfurt am Main: Bernard und Graefe Verlag, 1972), 127.

3. Waffenamt, Organization and Personnel Roster 1928/1929, in BA/MA RH 8/v. 3667.

4. Born the son of a brewery owner in Ludwigsburg in 1885, Hugo Sperrle died in 1953 in Munich. His military service record is taken from BA/MA MSG 1/124 G: entered army, 1903; lieutenant, 1904; infantry regiment 126, 1903–1914; Kriegsakademie, 1914; captain, 1914; Field Air Detachment 4, 1914–1915; commander, Field Air Detachment 42, 1915–1916; commander, Observer School, Cologne, 1916–1917; commander, 7th Army Aviation, 1917–1918; Fifth Division staff, 1920–1924; Reichs-

wehr air ministry, 1924–1929; major, 1926; battalion commander, 14th Infantry Regiment, 1929–1931; lieutenant colonel, 1931; colonel, 1933; commander, First Luftwaffe Division, 1934–1935; major general, 1935; commander, Air District Five, 1935–1936; commander, Condor Legion, 1936–1937; lieutenant general, 1937; General der Flieger, 1937; commander, Third Air Command/Third Air Fleet, 1938–1944; field marshal, 1940; Führerreserve, September 1944–May 1945.

5. General der Flieger Hellmuth Felmy was born in Berlin in 1885, and died in Darmstadt in 1965. His military service record reads: entered army, 1904; lieutenant, 1905; infantry service, 1905–1912; pilot training, 1912; Kriegsakademie, 1913–1914; pilot, 1914–1915; commander, Air Detachments 51, 300, A256, 1915–1918; captain, 1914; commander, Lübeck Flying School, 1918–1919; Reichswehr air staff, 1924–1926 and 1929–1931; lieutenant colonel, 1931; chief of staff, branch schools, 1931–1933; transferred to air ministry, 1933; colonel, 1933; major general, 1936; chief of staff of Luftwaffe schools, 1933–1935; commander, District V, 1935–1936; commander, Air District VII, 1936–1938; lieutenant general, 1937; General der Flieger, 1938; commander, Luftwafe Gruppenkommando 2, 1938–1939; commander, Second Air Fleet, 1939–12 January 1940; chief, Wehrmacht Mission Iraq, 1941; commander, southern Greece, 1941–1942; commander, army corps, 1943–1945.

6. General der Flieger Wilhelm Wimmer was born in Bavaria in 1889, and died in Garmisch in 1973. His service record: entered army, 1909; lieutenant, 1911; 16th Bavarian Infantry Regiment, 1909–1914; pilot training, 1914; pilot at front, 1914–1916; Bavarian air inspectorate, 1916–1918; commander, Bavarian Air Detachment 294; infantry officer and company commander, 1919–1926; captain, 1918; major, 1928; Reichswehr air staff, 1926–1930; Waffenamt, 1930–1933; lieutenant colonel, 1933; department chief, air ministry, 1933–1935; colonel, 1934; major general, 1936; chief, Luftwaffe Technical Office, October 1935–June 1936; air commander, Air District III, 1936–1938; lieutenant general, 1938; General der Flieger, 1939; commander, Luftwaffe Command East Prussia, 1939–1940; commander, Field Air District Belgium-Northern France 1940–1944.

7. Lieutenant General Walter Schwabedissen was born in Pommerania in 1896, and died in Munich in 1989. His service record reads: entered army, 1914; lieutenant, 1915; field artillery officer, 1914–1915; observer training, 1915; observer, various squadrons, 1915–1918; first lieutenant, 1918; artillery postings, 1919–1923; General Staff Course, 1923–1928; captain, 1928; Reichswehr air staff, 1928–1931; "Reinhard Courses," University of Berlin, 1931–1932; battery commander, Artillery Regiment 6, 1932–1933; air ministry training section, 1933–1934; major, 1934; bomber group commander, 1935–1936; lieutenant colonel, 1936; Wehrmachtakademie, 1936–1937; chief of staff, Air District II, 1937–1939; colonel, 1938; chief of staff, First Flak Corps, 1939–1940; major general, 1940; commander, Night Fighter Division 2, Fighter Division 2, and Fighter Division 5, 1942–1943; lieutenant general, 1942; commander, Luftwaffe Forces Denmark, 1944.

8. Albert Kesselring, *Memoirs of Field Marshal Kesselring* (Novato, Calif.: Presidio Press, 1989), 22–23.

9. Homze, *Arming the Luftwaffe*, 24.

10. Richard Suchenwirth, *The Development of the German Air Force, 1919–1939.* U.S. Air Force Historical Study No. 160 (Maxwell AFB: Air University, 1968), 19–21. See also Bruno Maass, "Vorgeschichte der Spitzengliederung der früheren deutschen Luftwaffe 1920–1933," in *Wehrwissenschaftliche Rundschau* 7 (1957): 505–23.

11. Völker, *Die Entwicklung der Militärischen Luftfahrt in Deutschland 1920–1923: . . . Planung und Massnahmen,* vol. III (Stuttgart: Deutsche Verlag-Anstalt, 1962), 175–77.

12. Karl-Heinz Völker, *Die Deutsche Luftwaffe 1933–1939. . . . Aufbau, Führung und Rustung der Luftwaffe* (Stuttgart: Deutsche Verlags-Anstalt), 17.

13. Chef der Heeresleitung, letter to the Sixth Division on the activities of the Sixth Signal Battalion, Hannover, 29 August 1932, reproduced in *Dokumente und Dokumentarfotos: Zur Geschichte der deutschen Luftwaffe,* Karl-Heinz Völker, ed., vol. 9 (Stuttgart: Deutsche Verlags-Anstalt, 1968), 101–2.

14. Ibid. The document is reproduced on pages 109–10.

15. Chief of the Heeresleitung, letter to the Waffenamt, July 1931, in BA/MA RH 8/v.993.

16. H. G. Wells, *The War in the Air* (London: George Bell and Sons, 1908).

17. R. P. Hearne, *Aerial Warfare* (London: John Lane, 1909).

18. Olaf Groehler, *Geschichte des Luftkrieges, 1910 bis 1980* (Berlin: Militärverlag der Deutschen Demokratischen Republik, 1981), 112–13.

19. See Conrad C. Crane, *Bombs, Cities, and Civilians: Airpower Strategy in World War II* (Lawrence: University Press of Kansas, 1993), 12–15.

20. Edward Warner, "Douhet, Mitchell, Seversky: Theories of Air Warfare," in *Makers of Modern Strategy,* ed. Ed Wood Meade Earle (Princeton, N.J.: Princeton University Press, 1943), 485–503, esp. 489–490.

21. Giulio Douhet, *The Command of the Air* (New York: Coward McCann, 1942), 188.

22. Ibid., 20–21. See also 57–58.

23. Ibid., 58.

24. Neville Jones, *The Beginnings of Strategic Airpower: History of the British Bomber Force 1923–1939* (London: Frank Cass, 1987), 29.

25. Ibid., 30.

26. Ibid., 42.

27. Basil Liddell Hart, *Paris, The Future of War* (London: K. Paul, Trench, Trubnee and Co., 1925).

28. Ibid., 46–48.

29. B. H. Liddell Hart, *The Remaking of Modern Armies* (London: John Murray, 1927), 83–87.

30. J. C. Slessor, *Airpower and Armies* (London: Oxford University Press, 1936).

31. Jones, 69–70.

32. *Revue du Aéronautique Militaire* covered air support for the Morroccan campaign in great detail in 1922–1923. In this period, there was, for instance, "The Devel-

opment of Air Doctrine in the Army Air Arm, 1917–1921," 66–67, but no articles appeared on independent air operations.

33. The first significant expression of Douhet's theories in France was written by Lieutenant Colonel P. Vauthier, *La Danger Aérienne de Pais* (Paris: Bergère-Levreault, 1930). France's premier commentators on Douhet were Lieutenant Colonel P. Vauthier, *La Doctrine de Guerre de Général Douhet* (Paris: Bergère-Levreault, 1934); and Navy Engineer Camille Brougeron, who wrote numerous articles on Douhet for *Revue de l'Armée de l'Air* during the 1930s.

34. Charles Christienne and Pierre Lissarague, *A History of French Military Aviation* (Washington, D.C.: Smithsonian Institution Press, 1986), 259.

35. Ibid., 259–60. On the role of air doctrine and the BCR aircraft, see J. Hebrand, *Vingt-cinq Armées de l'Aviation Militaire,* vol. I (Paris: Alvin Michel, 1946), 135–48.

36. Patrick Façon, "Douhet et sa Doctrine à Travers la Littérature Militaire et Aéronautique Française de l'Entre Deux Guerres: Étude de Perception," in *La Figure et l'Opéra de Guilio Douhet,* eds. Caserte-Pozzuoli (Rome: Società di Historia Patria, 1988).

37. J. Mencarelli, *Amadeo Mecozzi* (Rome: Offizio Historico Aeronautica Militare, 1979).

38. Captain Amadeo Mecozzi, "Il Volo Rasente e le sue Possibilita Tattiche," in *Rivista Aeronautica* (June 1926): 53–69.

39. Captain Amadeo Mecozzi, "Il Conqueto di Contra-Aviazione," in *Rivista Aeronautica* (March 1926): 58–62.

40. Major Amadeo Mecozzi, "Les Grandi Unità Aviatori," in *Rivista Aeronautica* (March 1929): 533–76.

41. Claudio Segre, "Balbo and Douhet: Master and Disciple," in *La Figura e l'Opera di Giulio Douhet,* ed. Casserte Pozzuoli (Rome: Societa di Historia Patria, 1988), 58.

42. Lee Kennett, "Developments to 1939," in *Case Studies in the Development of Close Air Support,* ed. B. J. Cooling (Washington, D.C.: Office of Air Force History, 1990), 30.

43. Neal Hyman, "NEP and Industrialization to 1928," in *Soviet Aviation and Airpower,* eds. Robin Higham and Jacob Kipp (Boulder, Colo.: Westview Press, 1977), 35–46, esp. 39.

44. Richard Simpkin, *Deep Battle: The Brainchild of Marshall Tukhachevskii* (London: Brassey's, 1987), 43.

45. Ibid., 139.

46. Neal Hyman, "NEP and Industrialization," 41.

47. Groehler, *Geschichte des Luftkrieges,* 130.

48. Ibid., 130.

49. Ibid.

50. V. K. Triandafrillov, *The Nature of the Operations of Modern Armies,* trans. William Buhrans (London: Frank Cass, 1994).

51. Ibid., 43-45 and 61-63.

52. John Erickson, *Soviet High Command; A Military Political History 1918-1941* (Boulder, Colo.: Westview Press, 1962), 382-83.

53. I. B. Holley, Jr., *Ideas and Weapons* (Washington, D.C.: Office of Air Force History, 1983), 58-62.

54. Ibid., 170-71.

55. Ibid., 160-73.

56. For a detailed exposition of the early development of U.S. air doctrine, see Thomas H. Greer, *The Development of Air Doctrine in the Army Air Arm, 1917-1941* (Washington, D.C.: Office of Air Force History, 1985), esp. chapter 2.

57. Robert F. Futrell, *Ideas, Concepts, Doctrine; Basic Thinking in the United States Air Force, 1907-1960,* vol. I (Maxwell AFB: Air University Press, December 1989), 39.

58. Haywood Hansel, *The Strategic Air War Against Germany and Japan* (Washington, D.C.: Office of Air Force History, 1986), 10-17.

59. Crane, *Bombs, Cities and Civilians,* 18-22.

60. David R. Mets, *Master of Air Power: General Carl A. Spaatz* (Novato, Calif.: Presidio Press, 1988), 54. See also Thomas Grier, *The Development of Air Doctrine in the Army Air Arm, 1917-1941.* (Washington, D.C.: Office of Air Force History, 1985), 66-67.

61. Grier, *The Development of Air Doctrine in the Army Air Arm, 1917-1941,* 62-65.

62. Major Welsch, a.D., in *Militärwochenblatt* no. 37 (4 April 1928).

63. "Oberst J. F. C. Fuller: Probleme der Luftkriegführung," in *Militärwochenblatt* no. 26 (1928).

64. "Das Werden einer französischen Luftmacht," in *Militärwochenblatt* no. 12 (25 September 1929).

65. "Das Hauptquartier der Luftverteidigung Englands und der Nächste Luftangriff auf London," in *Militärwochenblatt* no. 12 (1927).

66. Lt. Col. Freiherr von Lutzoff, "Die italienischen Luftmanöver 1927," in *Militärwochenblatt* no. 21 (1927).

67. See the Review of E. Gemio's *Rivista di Artilleria, Militärwochenblatt* no. 2 (29 May 1929), for a discussion of articles by Douhet.

68. Major von dem Hagen, *Reisebericht* (November 1928), BA/MA RH 2/1822.

69. Kurt Hesse, *Reisebericht* (9 February 1925), BA/MA RH 2/1820.

70. See Lt. Col. Becker and Lt. Col. Zimmerle, *Reisebericht* (1928), BA/MA RH 2/1823, and Maj. Radelmeier, *Reisebericht* (31 January 1929), BA/MA RH 2/1822.

71. Oberst von Boetticher, *Das Heerwesen der vereinigten Staaten vom America* (*Reiseberichte* 1923-1927), BA/MA RH 2/1820.

72. Captain Speidel, *Berichte,* in MA/DBR, R 06 10/4, 138-41.

73. Ibid., 145-58.

74. MA/DDR, R 06 10/4.

75. Field Marshal Dr. Wolfram von Richthofen was born in Silesia in 1895, and died in Bad Ischl in 1945. His personnel record reads: entered army, 1913; lieutenant,

1914; cavalry officer, 1913–1917; pilot training, 1917; pilot, JG 1, 1918; first lieutenant, 1920; left army in 1920 to study for engineering degree at the Technische Hochschule in Hannover, 1920–1923; return to army, 1923; Berlin Garrison, 1923–1928; captain, 1929; company commander, motor troops, 1928–1929; Truppenamt Intelligence Section, 1929; air attaché, Italy, 1929–1932; company commander, motor troops, 1932–1933; to air ministry, 1933; major, 1934; section chief, Technical Office, 1934–1936; lieutenant colonel, 1936; chief of staff, Condor Legion, 1936–1937; commander, KG 257, 1938; colonel, 1938; major general, 1938; commander, Condor Legion, 1938–1939; commander, Special Air Division, 1939; commander, VIII Air Corps, 1939–1942; General der Flieger, 1940; commander, Air Fleet 4, 1942–1943; field marshal, 1943; commander, Air Fleet 2, 1943–1944; sick leave, 1944–1945; died of brain tumor, July 1945.

76. MA/DDR, R 06 10/4, 305.

77. A good study of the German/Russian military relationship in the 1920s is found in the memoirs of one of the senior officers who coordinated the German programs in Russia. See Hermann Teske, ed., *General Ernst Köstring: Der militärische Mittler zwischen dem Deutschen Reich und der Sowjetunion* (Frankfurt a.M.: E. S. Mittler und Sohn, 1966).

78. See Manfred Zeidler, *Reichswehr und Rote Arme,* 263–67.

79. General von Blomberg said, in 1928, there was much to learn from the Russians. See General von Blomberg, *Lebenserinnerungen,* in BA/MA N/52/2, 137 and 154.

80. See James McCudden, *Flying Fury* (London: Aviation Book Club, 1930).

81. Charles Nordhoff and James Norman Hall, *Falcons of France* (New York: Little Brown, 1929).

82. Dominick Pisano, ed., *Legend, Memory and the Great War in the Air* (Washington, D.C.: Smithsonian Institution Press, 1992), 29.

83. For a translation see Giulio Douhet, *Command of the Air* (New York: Arno, 1972), 295–394.

84. *Luftkrieg 1936: Die Zertrümmerung von Paris* (Berlin: Verlag Tradition Wilhelm Kolk, 1932).

85. Ibid., 25.

86. Ibid., 40–43.

87. Ibid., 52–57.

88. Axel Alexander, *Die Schlacht über Berlin* (Berlin: Verlag Offener Worte, 1933).

89. Ibid., 48–49, 67–71, and 88–89.

90. Ibid., 67–71.

91. Ibid., 93–96.

92. Captain a.D. Hans Ritter, *Der Zukünftskrieg und seine Waffen* (1924), 6.

93. Ibid.

94. For a representative article of this type, see "Land Ohne Grenzen," in *Militärwochenblatt* no. 31 (18 February 1930).

95. General a.D. Schwarte, *Vortrag* (1928), BA/MA RH 12-1/53, folios 51–58.

96. T-2 Luft, letter of 26 September 1928, BA/MA RH 12-1/53, folio 59.

97. R. Spies, *Report on Bombing Accuracy and Patterns* (ca. 1927), BA/MA RH 2/2187.

98. TA Luft Correspondence File, letter of 10 December 1927 from Technische Hochschule Berlin to TAL, in BA/MA RH 2/2187. See also Translation of a Technical Article on French Bombs (11 December 1925), in BA MA RH 2/2206.

99. Luftschutz Liga and Ring Deutscher Flieger, *Correspondence with Defense Ministry* (1931-1933), in BA/MA RL 4/313.

100. Air Ministry Correspondence File, in BA/MA RL 4/313.

101. Generaloberst Hans von Seeckt, "Über Heere und Kriege der Zukunft," in *Militärwochenblatt* no. 38 (11 April 1928).

102. Peter Fritzsche, *A Nation of Fliers* (Cambridge, Mass.: Harvard University Press, 1992), 203-15.

103. "Luftschutz Probleme in französischen Beleuchtung," in *Militärwochenblatt* no. 16 (1929).

104. Heinz Sperrling, *Die Tätigkeit und Werksamkeit des Heereswaffenamtes der Reichswehr für die materiel-technische Ausstattung eines 21-divisions Heeres als Übergangsstufe zu einem kriegsstarken Aggressionsinstrument des deutschen Imperialismus* Diss., Militärgeschichtlichen Institut der DDR (1924-1934), 68.

105. See "Fliegerabwehrartillerie eines Armeekorps in den U.S.A," in *Militärwochenblatt* no. 24 (1929). Also see "Luftschutz in America," in *Militärwochenblatt* no. 6 (1929); and "Schutz friedlichen Hinterlandes gegen Luftangriffe," in *Militärwochenblatt* no. 40 (25 April 1928).

106. Oberstleutnant a.D. von Keller, *Die heutige Wehrlosigkeit Deutschlands im Leuchte seiner Verteidigung gegen die Fliegerangriffe in Kriege 1914/18* (Berlin: Verlag Offene Worte, 1929).

107. "Luftangriffe und Paniken" in *Militärwochenblatt* no. 24 (1928).

108. Manfred Zeidler, *Reichswehr und Rote Armee 1920-1933* (Munich: Oldenbourg Verlag, 1993), 124-25.

109. Helmuth Wilberg, letter to Heeresleitung, 2 April 1924; and Joachim von Stulpnagel, letter to Wilberg, 24 March 1924, in BA/MA RH 2/2207.

110. Manfred Zeidler, *Reichswehr und Rote Armee 1920-1933,* 123-27.

111. Rolf-Dieter Müller, "World Power Status Through the Use of Poison Gas? German Preparations for Chemical Warfare, 1919-1945," in *The German Military in the Age of Total War,* ed. Wilhelm Deist (Leamington Spa: Berg, 1985), 171-209.

112. Von Seeckt, *Bemerkungen des Chefs der Heeresleitung* (1923), in NARA, File T-177, Roll 25, Stück 133, para. 15.

113. American Military Attaché to Germany, *Report on Fall Maneuvers of the German Army,* 13-21 September 1926.

114. Richard Chalmer, ed., "Report of 1 November 1924 by U.S. Attaché," in *Weekly Summaries 1924* (*United States Military Intelligence,* vol. XXIII) (New York: Garland, 1978).

115. Robert Citino, *The Evolution of Blitzkrieg Tactics: Germany Defends Itself Against Poland, 1918–1933* (Westport, Conn.: Greenwood Press, 1987), 90, 183–84.

116. For an example, see Major Siebert, *Atlas zu F.u.G. I. Führung und Gefecht der Verbundenen Waffen: Ein Anschauungs-Lehrbuch* (Berlin: Verlag Offene Worte, 1929). This is one of the more elaborate, well-illustrated manuals of the Reichswehr era. A whole array of military air power doctrine is depicted, including the use of close air support (41); deep interdiction (42); and aircraft in close support to mass tank attacks (52).

117. David Speiers, *Image and Reality: The Making of a German Officer, 1921–1933* (Westport, Conn.: Greenwood Press, 1984), 107.

118. Ibid., 256.

119. In 1925–1926, thirty-four artillery officers underwent a two-week course on flak in Königsberg. In 1928–1929, three officers from each Reichswehr division attended a four-week flak artillery course in Königsberg. See David Speiers, *Image and Reality,* 251–56.

120. T-1, letter of November 1926, in BA/MA RH 12-1/15, 112–13.

121. Ibid.

122. Robert Citino, *The Evolution of Blitzkrieg Tactics,* 147–50.

123. Ibid.

124. Werner Rahn, *Reichsmarine und Landesverteidigung, 1919–1928* (Munich: Bernard und Graefe Verlag, 1976), 274–76.

125. Naval Staff, "Braucht Deutschland grosse Kriegsschiffe?" (*Denkschrift* of May 1929), in Werner Rahn, *Reichsmarine,* 281–86, esp. 282.

126. Ibid.

127. Suchenwirth, *Development of the German Air Force, 1919–1939,* 41–44.

128. William Green, *Warplanes of the Third Reich* (New York: Galahad, 1990), 273–77.

129. Green, *Warplanes of the Third Reich,* 112–13.

130. Suchenwirth, *Development of the German Air Force,* 44.

131. Reichswehr ministry to Marineamt, *Vorschläge für die Entwicklung der Luftfahrtindustrie,* letter of 11 January 1927, in BA/MA RH2/2187. See also Marineamt to TA-1, January 1927, ibid.

132. Citino, *The Evolution of Blitzkrieg Tactics,* 156–58.

133. Ibid., 161–63.

134. Green, *Warplanes of the Third Reich,* 267.

135. Ibid., 264–66.

136. Rahn, *Reichsmarine,* 193.

137. Ibid.

138. *La Armée aeronautique 1928–1929,* eds. L. Hirschauer and C. H. Dolphus (Paris: Dunoud, 1929), 386 and 392.

139. Ronald Miller and David Sawers, *The Technical Development of Modern Aviation* (London: Routledge and Kegan Paul, 1968), 15.

140. Ibid., 166–69.

141. Peter W. Brooks, *The Modern Airliner: Its Origins and Development* (London: Putnam Press, 1961), 52–53.

142. Brooks, ibid., 71–73. See also Peter Supf, *Das Buch der deutschen Fluggeschichte,* vol. II, 485–86, 613.

143. Brooks, ibid., 53.

144. Brooks, ibid., 613.

145. Green, *Warplanes of the Third Reich,* 109.

146. Tony Devereaux, *Messenger Gods of Battle* (London: Brassey's, 1991), 79.

147. Ibid., 84.

148. Helmut Schmidt-Rops, "Das Funkwesen in der Luftfahrt," in *Luftfahrt is Not!,* Ernst Junger, ed. (Leipzig: Deutschen Luftfahrtverbandes, 1930), 278–89.

149. Ernst Kredel, "Der deutscher Luftverkehr," in *Luftfahrt is Not!,* 264–77.

150. Martin Mäder, "Technische Hilfsmittel für die Navigation und Steuerung am Bord neuzeitlicher Verkehrsflugzeuge," in *Luftfahrt is Not!,* 305–22.

151. On engine development in the interwar period, see Bill Gunston, *The Development of Piston Aero-Engines* (Somerset, England: Patrick Stevens Ltd., 1993), 123–58.

152. Ibid., 159.

153. For a good account of the Reichswehr's Lipetsk operation, see Hanfried Schliephake, *The Birth of the Luftwaffe* (Chicago: Henry Regnery, 1971), 16–22.

154. Michael Taylor, *Warplanes of the World: 1918–1939* (New York: Charles Scribner's Sons, 1981), 171.

155. BA/MA RH 2/2299, T-A Luft, *Ausbildung Lehrgang L 1927* (30 November 1926).

156. Schliephake, *The Birth of the Luftwaffe,* 18.

157. Karl-Heinz Völker, *Die deutsche Luftwaffe, 1933–1939* (Stuttgart: Deutsche Verlagsanstalt, 1967), 16.

158. See Manfred Zeidler, *Reichswehr und Rote Armee,* 303.

159. Schliephake, *The Birth of the Luftwaffe,* 20–21.

160. Edward Homze, *Arming the Luftwaffe: The Reich Air Ministry and the German Aircraft Industry, 1919–1939* (Lincoln: University of Nebraska Press, 1976), 21.

161. Herbert Mason, *The Rise of the Luftwaffe* (New York: Ballantine, 1973), 148.

162. Schliephake, *The Birth of the Luftwaffe,* 17.

163. Suchenwirth, *The Development of the German Air Force, 1919–1939,* 27–28.

164. Ibid.

165. Ibid.

166. Hans von Fichte, "Erfahrungsberichte Nachtjäger" (22 May 1928), in BA/MA RH 2273.

167. BA/MA RL 4/80, *Abschrift vom Thomsen, 5 Oktober 1931.*

168. Ibid., 18.

169. Ibid., 10.

170. Ibid., 4–9.

171. BA/MA RL 2/II 364 Entwurf, *Grundsätze für den Einsatz der Luftstreitkräfte* (ca. 1930).

172. BA/MA RL 2/IV, 12–14.

173. See "Tiefflieger und ihre Bekämpfung durch die Truppe," in *Militärwochenblatt* (1928), no. 11. See also "Die Sturzbombe," in *Militärwochenblatt* no. 13 (1931), as well as "Die Opfer des Sturzbombes" and "Einsatz von Luftstreitkräften im Bewegungskriege," both in *Militärwochenblatt* (1930), no. 30.

174. "Operative Luftaufklärung und Erkundigungsflugzeuge," in *Militärwochenblatt* (1931), issues 6–8.

175. BA/MA RH 8/b 923, Heeresausbildungsabteilung to Waffenamt, memo of 29 November 1926, *Heeresmotorisierung und Kreigsgliederung einer motorisierte Division.*

176. See *Wissen und Wehr* (10 December 1929), also "Vertikale strategische Umfassung?" in *Militärwochenblatt* (1930), no. 28.

177. Waffenamt Correspondence, *Conference Memo* (18 February 1932), BA/MA RH 8/v 9916.

178. *Grundsätze für die Einsatz der Luftstreitkräfte,* in BA/MA RL 2/II 364, 2.

179. Ibid.

180. Ibid., 2.

181. Ibid.

182. Ibid.

183. Ibid.

184. Truppenamt, *Zusammenstellung der Gesamtstärken und Ausrüstung der Kommandobehörden und Truppeneinheiten des Feldheers,* National Archives, von Seeckt Papers File M-132, Roll 430.

185. Ibid., F. 2, Luftstreitkräfte.

186. On German rearmament planning during this period, see Richard Suchenwirth, *Development of the German Air Force, 1919–1939,* 34–48.

187. Ibid., 37. See also Waffenamt, *Rüstungsgrundlagen, Heer, Marine und Luftstreitkräfte Übersicht* (June 1930), in BA/ MA RH 8/b997.

188. Burkhart Müller-Hillebrand, *Das Heer bis zum Kriegsbeginn* (Darmstadt: E. S. Mittler und Sohn, 1954), 19–20.

189. Ibid., 20.

190. Matthew Cooper, *The German Air Force 1933–1945* (London: Janes, 1981), 2.

191. Homze, *Arming the Luftwaffe,* 34–35.

192. Karl-Heinz Völker, "Die geheime Luftrüstung der Reichswehr und ihre Auswirkung auf dem Flugzeugbestand der Luftwaffe bis zum Beginn des Zweiten Weltkrieges," in *Wehrwissenschaftliche Rundschau* 12, no. 9 (1962): 544–45.

193. Ibid.

194. Green, *Warplanes of the Third Reich,* 259–60.

195. Ibid., 261–64.

196. Ibid., 267–73.
197. Ibid., 110.
198. Enzo Angelucci, *Rand-McNally Encyclopedia of Military Aircraft* (New York: Gallery, 1990), 145 and 155.
199. Green, *Warplanes of the Third Reich,* 264–66.
200. Ibid., 273 and 277. Also see Karl-Heinz Völker, *Die geheime Luftrüstung,* 245.
201. Green, *Warplanes of the Third Reich,* 405–13.

THEORY AND AIR DOCTRINE IN THE WEVER ERA

1. David Irving, *Göring: A Biography* (New York: Avon, 1989), 130–31.
2. Interview with Götz, Freiherr von Richthofen, son of Field Marshal von Richthofen, Aumühle, Germany, 21 June 1992.
3. Field Marshal Erhard Milch was born in Wilhelmshaven in 1892, and died in 1972 in Wuppertal. His military personnel file reads: entered army, 1910; lieutenant, 1911; artillery officer, 1911–1915; first lieutenant, 1915; aircraft observer training, 1915; observer, Artillery Air Detachments 205 and A204, 1915–1916; adjutant, Artillery Aircraft School East, 1916–1917; General Staff Course, 1918; commander, Fighter Group 6, 1918; commander, Air Police Squadron Königsberg, 1919; captain, 1918; left army, 1920. Joined Junkers and Lufthansa airlines, 1920–1933; director, Lufthansa, 1926–1933; rejoined in Luftwaffe, 1933; colonel, 1933; state secretary for aviation, 1933–1934; major general, 1934; lieutenant general, 1935; General der Flieger, 1940; chief of aircraft production, 1941–1944.
4. Irving, *Göring: A Biography,* 98.
5. Interview with Hans-Joachim Wilberg, son of General der Flieger Helmuth Wilberg, 19 June 1992.
6. Homze, *Arming the Luftwaffe,* 119 and 121.
7. Ibid., 121.
8. Interview with Freiherr Götz von Richthofen, son of Field Marshal Wolfram von Richthofen, 4 September 1993.
9. A memo written by the army commander in chief, 10 April 1933, proposed a plan for the development of an air service within the army. From 1933 to 1936, Freiherr von Hammerstein-Equord's concept of an air force argued for the development of sixteen reconnaissance squadrons for army support, but only nine bomber squadrons. See Karl-Heinz Völker, *Dokumente und Dokumentarphotos zur Geschichte der deutschen Luftwaffe* (Stuttgart: Deutsche Verlags-Anstalt, 1968). Document reproduced on 119–21.
10. For a good commentary on the content and impact of *Truppenführung,* see Martin van Creveld, *Fighting Power* (Westport, Conn.: Greenwood Press, 1982), 28–41.
11. *Heeresdienstvorschrift 300* (1933), para. 759.

12. Ibid.
13. Ibid.
14. Ibid., para. 761.
15. Ibid., para. 765.
16. Ibid., para. 764.
17. Ibid., para. 771.
18. Ibid., para. 779.
19. The *Militärwochenblatt* of 1934 contains numerous articles on foreign air powers. See "Die Vorführung der englische Luftstreitkräfte in Hendon," in issue no. 3; "Luftschutzübungen bei London," in no. 5 and no. 11; "Zivilluftfahrt und passive Luftschutz in Frankreich," in no. 8; "Die Luftschutzübungen bei London," in no. 12; "Luftschutzübungen bei Paris," in no. 15; "Neues von der italienischen Luftarmee," in no. 29; and "Französische und englische Gedanken über den Luftkrieg," in nos. 42–43.
20. "Autogyro in Kleinkrieg," in *Militärwochenblatt* no. 4 (1934) and "Die Verstärkung der englische und amerikanische Luftmacht," in *Militärwochenblatt* no. 9; "Taktik und Bewaffnung französicher Jagdflugzeuge," in *Militärwochenblatt* no. 17; "Flugzeugschiffe," in *Militärwochenblatt* no. 34; "Kanonenjagdflugzeuge und Taktik des Luftkampfes," in *Militärwochenblatt* no. 47.
21. See Rittmeister Cristolki's "Die Luftwaffe im Angriff," in *Militärwochenblatt* no. 34.
22. Luftwaffedienstvorschrift 10: *Der Kampfflugzeug* (1934), para. 10.
23. Ibid., paras. 12–19.
24. See *Der Jagdflieger: Entwurf für Vorschrift,* in BA/MA RL 2/283 (1934).
25. Ibid., 4.
26. Ibid., 7–8.
27. Ibid., 27.
28. Ibid., 55–56.
29. Ibid., 53–54. On fighter tactics of the era, see also Abteilung LLA III/3, *Ungültiger Entwurf für Vorschrift* (1934), in BA/MA RL II/14. This proposed manual contains numerous charts showing dogfight tactics of the era.
30. Oberleutnant a.D. Feuchter, "Flugzeuge als Truppentransportmittel," in *Militärwochenblatt* no. 22 (1933).
31. Dr. Robert Knauss was born in Stuttgart in 1892, and died in 1955. His military personnel record reads: entered army, 1910; lieutenant, 1911; Infantry Regiment 125, 1910–1915; Observer Air Detachments 59 and A269, 1915–1918; first lieutenant, 1915; captain, 1918; general staff officer, 52nd Division, 1918–1919; general staff, Reichswehr, 1919–1920; left army in 1920. With Aero-Lloyd and Lufthansa airlines, 1924–1935; rejoined Luftwaffe with rank of major, 1935; commander, Bomber Group I in KG Boelcke, 1936–1937; commander, Lehrgeschwader Greifswald, 1937–1940; lieutenant colonel, 1935; colonel, 1938; chief of staff, Luftwaffe Norway, major general, 1940; commandant, Luftkriegsakademie, 1940–1944; lieutenant general, 1942; General der Flieger, 1944.

32. Service record of General der Flieger Robert Knauss and interview with Dr. Professor von Sietencron, stepson of Robert Knauss, 11 September 1993. Also interview with Frau Siess, daughter of Robert Knauss, 11 September 1993.

33. The full text of the Knauss Denkschrift is provided in "Eine geheime Denkschrift zur Luftkriegskonzeption Hitler-Deutschlands von Mai 1933," in *Zeitschrift für Militärgeschichte,* eds. Major Bernhard Heinmann and Major Joachim Schunke, no. 1 (1964), 72–86.

34. Interview with Hans-Joachim Wilberg, Diplomingenieur, son of General der Flieger Helmuth Wilberg, 19 June 1992.

35. The bomber "must be capable of carrying at least 2,000 kilograms of bombs, and of reaching targets 800 kilometers away." Robert Knauss's Denkschrift (1933), 81.

36. Ibid., 77–78.

37. Ibid., 78.

38. Ibid.

39. Ibid., 79.

40. Ibid.

41. Ibid., 80.

42. Ibid.

43. Ibid., 79.

44. Klaus Maier, "Totaler Krieg und operative Luftkrieg," in *Die Errichtung der Hegemonie auf dem europäischen Kontinent,* ed. Klaus Maier, Horst Rohde, et al. (Stuttgart: Deutsche Verlagsanstalt, 1979), 44.

45. German air officers at this time were well familiar with Douhet's theory. For example, Helmuth Wilberg had collected Douhet's writings. From an interview with Hans-Joachim Wilberg, son of General der Flieger Helmuth Wilberg, 19 June 1992.

46. Suchenwirth, *Command and Leadership in the German Air Force* (USAF Historical Study No. 174) (Maxwell AFB: USAF Historical Division, 1969), 2.

47. Lieutenant General Walther Wever was born in 1887 in Wilhelmsort, West Prussia, and died 3 June 1936 in Dresden. His military service record reads: entered army, 1905; lieutenant, 1906; infantry officer, 10th Grenadier Regiment, 1905–1914; captain, 1915; adjutant, 21st Infantry Brigade, 1915–1916; battalion commander, 1915; general staff, VIII Reserve Corps, 1916; general staff, Fourth Army, 1917; general staff, high command, 1917–1918; battalion commander, 10th Grenadier Regiment, 1918–1919; general staff, 7th Division, 1921–1924; major, 1926; Reichswehr air ministry, 1927–1929; battalion commander, 12th Infantry Regiment, 1929–1931; lieutenant colonel, 1930; colonel, 1933; section chief, Reichswehr air ministry, 1932–1933; major general, 1934; chief, Luftwaffe Command Staff, 1933–1935; lieutenant general, 1936; chief, Luftwaffe general staff, 1935–1936. See Personnel Record of Walter Wever in BA/MA Personnel 6/993.

48. Hooton, 98–99.

49. Suchenwirth, *Command,* 2–3.

50. Ibid., 2.

51. Ibid.

52. Hooten, 98.

53. See Andreas Nielsen, *The German Air Force General Staff* (USAF Historical Study No. 173) (Maxwell AFB, Ala., 1959). See also Suchenwirth, *Command,* 1–16.

54. Suchenwirth argues that Göring was enthusiastic about the ideas of Giulio Douhet, and that "Göring felt in Wever a colleague who was equally imbued with these ideas and was capable of translating them into exact General Staff planning." See Suchenwirth, *Command,* 4.

55. Cited in Suchenwirth, *Command,* 4.

56. Suchenwirth, *Command,* 4.

57. Wever lectured at the Air Technical Academy on 1 November 1935. A transcript is preserved as a USAF HRA Karlsruhe collection document, K 239.716251–31.

58. Ibid.

59. Ibid., 3–4.

60. Ibid.

61. Ibid., 6.

62. Ibid., 7.

63. Ibid.

64. Ibid.

65. Ibid., 7.

66. Ibid., 8.

67. Ibid.

68. Ibid., 5.

69. Ibid.

70. Ibid., 6.

71. Ibid.

72. Ibid., 8–9.

73. Luftwaffe Dienstvorschrift 16, *Luftkriegführung* (1935), para. 2.

74. Ibid.

75. Ibid., para. 9.

76. Ibid., para. 6.

77. Ibid., para. 10.

78. Ibid., para. 11.

79. Ibid., paras. 20–21.

80. Ibid., para. 8.

81. Ibid., paras. 103–6.

82. Ibid., para. 17.

83. Ibid., para. 18.

84. Ibid., para. 143.

85. Ibid., para. 157.

86. Ibid., para. 166.

87. Ibid., para. 11.

88. Ibid., paras. 59–67.
89. Ibid., paras. 79–82.
90. Ibid., paras. 137–42.
91. Ibid., paras. 258–80.
92. Ibid., para. 186.
93. Ibid., para. 186.
94. Ibid., para. 87.
95. Ibid., para. 184.
96. Ibid., paras. 183–85.
97. Ibid., para. 185.
98. Ibid., para. 185.
99. Edward Homze, *Arming the Luftwaffe: The Reich Air Ministry and the German Aircraft Industry, 1919–1939* (Lincoln: University of Nebraska Press, 1976), 132.
100. Ibid.
101. Adolf Hitler, *Mein Kampf*, John Chamberlain, trans. (New York: Reymal & Hitchcock, 1940), 978–79.
102. Erich von Ludendorff, *The Coming War* (London: Faber & Faber, 1931), 100–101 and 110–11.
103. Erich von Ludendorff, *Der Totaler Krieg* (Munich: Ludendorff's Verlag, 1935), 3–10.
104. Luftwaffe Dienstvorschrift 16 (1935), para. 187.
105. Samuel Mitcham, *Men of the Luftwaffe* (Novato, Calif.: Presidio Press, 1988), 16.
106. General von Fritsch issued a directive on 13 May 1935 stressing the importance for the army to deepen its relationship with the Nazi party, and to understand the mission of the party. The document is reproduced in Klaus Morgen and Jürgen Müller, *Das Heer und Hitler* (Stuttgart: Deutsche Verlags-Anstalt, 1969), 613–14.
107. Luftwaffe Dienstvorschrift 7: *Richtlinien für die Ausbildung der Luftwaffe* (Berlin, 1937), 38.
108. Ibid.
109. Manfred Messerschmidt, *Die Wehrmacht im N. S. Stadt* (Hamburg: R. E. Dekkers Verlag, 1969), 240–41.
110. Generalstab der Luftwaffe, III Abteilung: Ausbilding, *Generalstabsoffiziere: Erziehung und Ausbildung auf der Luftkriegsakademie, Richtlinien* (5 July 1937), in BA/MA RL 2 II/164, 2.
111. Horst Boog, *Die deutsche Luftwaffenführung 1935–1945* (Stuttgart: Deutsche Verlagsanstalt, 1982), 450.
112. On the use of a civil defense program to educate the public on air power, see Peter Fritzsche, "Machine Dreams: Airmindedness and the Reinvention of Germany," *American Historical Review* (June 1993), 685–709.
113. Hans Schoszberger, *Bautechnischer Luftschutz* (Berlin: Bauwelt Verlag, 1934), 230–40.
114. See Homze, *Arming the Luftwaffe*, 91–92.

115. Heereswaffenamt Memo, *Vortragsbemerkungen über Aufbau und Stand der kriegswirtschaftlichen Vorarbeiten* (16 April 1934), in BA/MA RH 8/v.1369.

116. Reichsminister der Luftfahrt, *Bemerkungen zu den Übungen des Zivilluftschutzes im Jahre 1934* Berlin (1935), in NARA File T-321, Roll 68, 5.

117. Reichsminister der Luftfahrt, *Vorläufige Ortsanweisung für den Luftschutz der Zivilbevölkerung,* Abschnitt VIII (1936), in NARA File T-321, Roll 68.

118. Reichsminister der Luftfahrt, "Luftschutzveterinärdienst," in *Vorläufige Ortsanweisung für dem Luftschutz der Zivilbevölkerung,* Abschnitt XII (1935), in NARA File T-321, Roll 68.

119. Oberbefehlshaber der Luftwaffe, *Erfahrungsbericht: Über die Übungen des zivilen Luftschutzes im Rechnungsjahr 1936* (Berlin 1937), in NARA File T-321, Roll 68.

120. Reichsanstalt für Luftschutz, "Wesen und Organization des Zivilluftschutzes," in BA/MA RL 4/317, 4.

121. Charles Burdick, "Die deutschen militärischen Planungen gegenüber Frankreich 1933–1938," in *Wehrwissenschaftliche Rundschau* no. 12 (1956): 678–79.

122. Klaus Meier, "Totaler Krieg und operativer Luftkrieg," in *Das deutsche Reich und der Zweite Weltkrieg,* vol. II, 50–51.

123. Luftwaffe Air Staff Denkschrift, *Die zukünftige Kriegführung in der Luft und ihre Auswirkung auf die Bewegungen des Heeres* (26 April 1934), para. 6, in NARA German Records File T 78, Roll 128.

124. Ibid., section 2.

125. Ibid., section 3, para. 2.

126. Ibid., section 2.

127. Ibid.

128. Homze, *Arming the Luftwaffe,* 127–28.

129. Ibid.

130. Reichsminister der Luftfahrt, *Winter Kriegsspiel 1934–1935* (27 September 1934), in BA/MA RL 2II/76.

131. Ibid., folios 7–9.

132. Ibid., folio 9.

133. Ibid., folios 9–10.

134. Ibid.

135. Ibid., folio 10.

136. Ibid.

137. Walter Wever, *Letter to Commander in Chief Army* (29 September 1934), in Völker, *Dokumente und Dokumentarfotos, Akt 184.*

138. *Anlagen zum Winter Kriegsspiel 1934–1935,* in BA/MA RL2II/77.

139. Richard Suchenwirth, *The Development of the German Air Force 1919–1939,* (U.S. Air Force Historical Study No. 160) (Air University, 1968), 172–73.

140. Suchenwirth, *Command,* 12.

141. Ibid.

142. Richard Suchenwirth, *The Development of the German Air Force 1919-1939,* 174.

AIR ORGANIZATION AND TECHNOLOGY IN THE WEVER ERA

1. Karl-Heinz Völker, "Daten zur Gliederung und Organization der Luftwaffe 1933-1939," in *Wehrwissenschaftliche Rundschau* no. 4 (April 1967): 113-17.

2. Richard Suchenwirth, *The Development of the German Air Force, 1919-1939* (U.S. Air Force Historical Study No. 160) (Air University, 1968), 46-48.

3. Karl-Heinz Völker, "Die geheimen deutschen Luftstreitkräfte und Luftschutzprogramm von der Befehlsübernahme des Reichsminister der Luftfahrt am 15. Mai bis zum Endes des Jahres 1933," in *Wehrwissenschaftliche Rundschau* no. 4 (April 1967), 199-213.

4. Karl-Heinz Völker, "Daten zur Gliederung und Organization der Luftwaffe," 113. See also Suchenwirth, *Development,* 58.

5. Karl-Heinz Völker, "Die geheimen deutschen Luftstreitkräfte," 203-4.

6. Ibid., 202-3. See also Suchenwirth, *Development,* 88-89.

7. Suchenwirth, *Development,* 89.

8. Karl-Heinz Völker, "Daten zur Gliederung und Organization der Luftwaffe," 113.

9. Ibid.

10. Suchenwirth, *Development,* 66-67.

11. Karl-Heinz Völker, "Daten zur Gliederung und Organization der Luftwaffe," 113.

12. Ibid., 113.

13. Ibid., 114.

14. See Manfred Kehrig, *Die Wiedereinrichtung des deutschen militärischen Attachédienstes nach dem ersten Weltkrieg (1919-1933)* (Boppard am Rhein: Harald Boldt Verlag, 1966).

15. Karl-Heinz Völker, "Daten zur Gliederung und Organization der Luftwaffe," 114.

16. By 1933 about 120 pilots and 100 observers had been trained at Lipetsk. Two hundred pilots had been trained in civilian schools, and 100 observers trained in the school at Brunswick. The navy had also sent a few officers to flight training each year. See Karl-Heinz Völker, *Die deutsche Luftwaffe 1933-1939* (Stuttgart: Deutsche Verlags-Anstalt, 1967), 16.

17. James Corum, *The Roots of Blitzkrieg* (Lawrence: University Press of Kansas, 1992), 179-80.

18. General der Flieger Karl Koller served as Luftwaffe chief of staff from August 1943 to July 1944.

19. Personnel information from Karl-Friedrich Hildebrand, *Die Generale der*

deutschen Luftwaffe 1935–1945, vols. I–III (Osnabrück: Biblioverlag, 1990). Hildebrand has published the official service records of all 688 men who reached the rank of general in the Luftwaffe.

20. Of the 318 navy officers commissioned in 1934, thirty-six left the navy in 1936 and transferred to the Luftwaffe. See Eric Rust, *Naval Officers Under Hitler* (Westport, Conn.: Praeger Press, 1991), 83.

21. Overy asserts that the inclusion of so many reactivated officers and officers from the army "had the unfortunate consequence of dividing the air officer corps into those who regarded themselves as heirs of the Prussian tradition, and those who came from an unorthodox, particularly technical background. Part of the hostility felt between regular soldiers and the parvenues rose from the fact that the newcomers were given high military office without having followed the normal army channels." See Richard J. Overy, *The Air War 1939–1945* (Chelsea, Mich.: Scarborough House, 1980), 137.

22. "The result of all this was that the Luftwaffe was shaped by aviators who were immature soldiers, and soldiers who were immature aviators." From Telford Taylor's *The March of Conquest* (Baltimore: Nautical and Aviation Press, 1991 reprint), 25–26.

23. Overy, *The Air War,* 136.

24. Edward Homze, *Arming the Luftwaffe: The Reich Air Ministry and the German Aircraft Industry, 1919–1939* (Lincoln: University of Nebraska Press, 1976), 73.

25. Homze, *Arming the Luftwaffe,* 74.

26. William Green, *Warplanes of the Third Reich* (New York: Galahad, 1990), 259–61.

27. Ibid., 261–64.

28. Ibid., 259–61 and 264.

29. Karl-Heinz Kens and Heinz Nowarra, *Die deutsche Flugzeuge 1933–1945* (Munich: J. F. Lehmann Verlag, 1961), 257–58.

30. Green, *Warplanes of the Third Reich,* 26–27, 267–73.

31. Ibid., 405–13.

32. Ibid., 110–12.

33. Ibid., 111, 130.

34. Ibid., 267–73.

35. Enzo Angelucci, *Rand-McNally Encyclopedia of Military Aircraft* (New York: Gallery, 1990), 119–22, 130.

36. Homze, *Arming the Luftwaffe,* 79.

37. Green, *Warplanes of the Third Reich,* 112.

38. Ibid., 266.

39. Homze, *Arming the Luftwaffe,* 79–80.

40. Overy, *The Air War,* 21.

41. Homze, *Arming the Luftwaffe,* 98.

42. Ibid., 104–5.

43. Ibid.

44. For a thorough analysis of German aircraft industry production and efficiency, see Willi Boelcke, "Stimulation and Attitude of the German Aircraft Industry During Rearmament and War," in *The Conduct of the Air War in the Second World War,* Horst Boog, ed. (New York: Berg, 1992), 55–84.

45. Homze, *Arming the Luftwaffe,* 109.

46. *Ergebniss der Ersprechung zwischen A-Amt und C-Amt am 11. Mai 1934, betretend taktische Förderungen und Dringlichkeit der Flugzeugentwicklungs-Aufgaben,* in NARA File T-177, Roll 9.

47. Hans Redemann, *Innovations in Aircraft Construction* (West Chester, Pa.: Schiffer Military History, 1991), 28–31.

48. Green, *Warplanes of the Third Reich,* 428–31.

49. Ibid., 287–90.

50. Ibid., 165–68 and 385–89.

51. Hans Redemann, *Innovations in Aircraft Construction,* 58–61.

52. Green, *Warplanes of the Third Reich,* 573–77.

53. Brown, *Wings of the Luftwaffe,* 166.

54. See Georg Tessin, *Formationsgeschichte der Wehrmacht 1933–1939* (Koblenz: Harald Boldt Verlag, 1959).

55. Reichsminister der Luftfahrt und Oberbefehlshaber der Luftwaffe, *Bemerkungen des Oberbefehlshabers der Luftwaffe zur Ausbildung und zu den Übungen im Jahre 1935,* NARA File T-177, Roll 1 (4 January 1936), 6.

56. Oberbefehlshaber der Luftwaffe, *Bemerkungen . . .* (1935), paras. 8–9.

57. Kommandeur der Panzertruppen, *Zusammenarbeit zwischen Panzereinheiten und die Luftwaffe* (9 December 1936). NARA File T 405, Roll 6.

58. See Georg Tessin, *Formationsgeschichte,* 65–67.

59. Horst-Adalbert Koch, *Flak: Die Geschichte der deutschen Flakartillerie 1935–1945* (Bad Neuheim: Verlag Hans Heming, 1954), 19.

60. See Georg Tessin, *Formationsgeschichte,* 92.

61. Ibid.

62. Horst-Adalbert Koch, *Flak,* 19.

63. See Luftwaffedienstvorschrift 16, paras. 258–80.

64. On artillery late in World War I, see Reichsluftministerium, *Die technische Entwicklung der Flakwaffe bis zum Ende des Weltkrieges,* Kriegswissenschaftliche Abteilung der Luftwaffe, vol. V (Berlin: E. S. Mittler und Sohn, 1942).

65. See Reichsminister der Luftfahrt, *Merkblätter über Flakartillerie, A: Kampfmittel der Flakartillerie* and *B: Richtlinien für Aufstellung vom Flakabwehrwaffen zum Schutz eines Objektes* (Berlin, 1935). This document contains well-developed tactical doctrine for the emplacement of flak batteries and battalions in the establishment of inner and outer rings of flak protection for the defense of vital targets.

66. For a good outline of interwar air defense doctrine in Germany, see Horst Boog, "Die Luftverteidigung in der deutschen Luftkriegsdoktrine und der Aufbau der deutschen Luftverteidigung in Frieden," in *Das deutsche Reich und der Zweite*

Weltkrieg, vol. VI, Militärgeschichtliche Vorschungsamt, ed. (Stuttgart: Deutsche Verlags-Anstalt, 1990), 437–48.

67. Ibid., 438.

68. Ibid. One study of 1936/1937 argued that only forty-seven rounds of heavy flak gun ammunition would be necessary to shoot down one high-flying aircraft.

69. Ibid., 437–38.

70. Army general staff letter of 16 June 1936, cited in Völker, *Akt,* 185.

71. On Russian airborne maneuvers, see "Überblick über Manöver von der Heere im Jahre 1935," in *Militärwissenschaftliche Rundschau* no. 2, ed. Reichskriegsministerium (1936), 262–63.

72. David Glantz, *A History of Soviet Airborne Forces* (London: Frank Cass, 1994), 13–14.

73. Ibid., 14–20.

74. Sturmabteilung Koch, Fliegerdivision VII, *Entstehung der Sturmabteilung und Auszug aus dem Kriegstagebuch,* Hildesheim (summer 1940), 2 in BA/MA RL 33/97.

75. Volkmar Kühn, *Deutsche Fallschirmjäger im Zweiten Weltkrieg* (Stuttgart: Motorbuchverlag, 1993), 14–16.

76. Ibid., 16.

77. Ibid., 17.

78. Luftwaffe staff, *Ergebniss der Besprechung zwischen A-Amt und C-Amt am 11. Mai 1934,* in NARA German Records T-177, Roll 9.

79. Samuel Mitchem, *Men of the Luftwaffe* (Novato, Calif.: Presidio Press, 1988), 16.

80. Interview with Götz Freiherr von Richthofen, son of Field Marshal Wolfram von Richthofen, 21 June 1992: "When Germany went to war in 1939, General von Richthofen expressed the view that the Luftwaffe was likely to suffer for not having developed a heavy strategic bomber force." Wolfram von Richtofen wrote an article in 1931 extolling the Douhetian doctrine of the Italian Air Force: "Die italienischen Luftmanöver im Zeichen des Douhetismus." See Reichsluftministerium, *Sammlung ausländischen Aufsätze über Luftkriegsfragen* (1 March 1937), in NARA File T-177, Roll 1, 32.

81. Robin Cross, *The Bombers* (New York: Macmillan, 1987), 74–75.

82. Angelucci, *Encyclopedia of Military Aircraft,* 293.

83. Redemann, *Innovations in Aircraft Construction,* 42.

84. On the initiation of the British four-engine bomber project in 1936, see Neville Jones, *The Beginnings of Strategic Airpower,* 106–7. On the development of the Italian Piaggio P-108 B four-engine bomber, which first flew in 1939, see Enzo Angelucci, *Encyclopedia of Military Aircraft,* 284.

85. Rudolph Lusar, *Die deutschen Waffen und Geheimwaffen des 2. Weltkrieges und ihre Weiterentwicklung* (Munich: J. Lehmanns Verlag, 1962), 126–27.

86. Bill Gunston, *The Development of Piston Aero Engines* (Sparkford, Somerset: Patrick Stephens, 1993), 157–59.

87. Ibid., 159–63.

88. Green, *Warplanes of the Third Reich,* 127–29.

89. Ibid., 483–84.

90. Edward Homze, *Arming the Luftwaffe,* 122–23.

91. See Werner Niehaus, *Die Rädarschlacht 1939–1945* (Stuttgart: Motorbuch Verlag, 1977), 35–37. See also Horst Boog, "The Luftwaffe and Indiscriminate Bombing up to 1942," in *The Conduct of the Air War in the Second World War,* ed. Horst Boog (New York: Berg, 1992), 381–83.

92. Rudolf Lussar, *Deutsche Geheimwaffen des 2. Weltkrieges und ihre weitere Entwicklung* (Munich: J. F. Lehmanns Verlag, 1962), 176–77.

93. On the Kommando Gerät 36, see Rudolf Lussar, *Deutsche Geheimwaffen des 2. Weltkrieges,* 162.

94. Michael Neufeld, *The Rocket and the Reich* (New York: Free Press, 1995), 44–45.

95. Ibid., 43–49.

96. Rudolf Lussar, *German Secret Weapons of the Second World War* (New York: Philosophical Library, 1959), 163–64.

97. Ministerial-dirigent Adolf Baeumker was born in Breslau in 1891, and died in 1976. His service record reads: entered army, 1908; lieutenant, 1910; first lieutenant, 1915; infantry officer, 1910–1919; captain, 1921; served in defense ministry, 1920–1927; retired, 1927; civilian official with defense ministry, 1927–1933; department chief, air ministry, 1933–1944.

98. Letter of Admiral Raeder to army commander in chief on Luftwaffe issues (18 November 1932), in Ernst Völker, *Dokumente und Dokumentarfotos,* Akt. 33. See also Grand Admiral Erich Raeder, *My Life* (Annapolis, Md.: U.S. Naval Institute, 1960), 232–35.

99. For an overview of naval aviation activities in the period of the Versailles Treaty: 1919–1934, see Denkschrift by Naval Captain Schüssler, "On Naval Aviation Against Versailles," Akt. 39, in Karl-Heinz Völker, *Dokumente und Dokumentarphotos,* 121–30. The degree of importance placed by the navy on aviation is apparent in the naval officer school class of 1934. Of this class of 318 officer cadets, only sixteen were designated for the naval air arm and sent to flight training in 1933. See Eric Rust, *Naval Officers Under Hitler* (Westport, Conn.: Praeger Press, 1991), 16–17.

100. Raeder, *My Life,* 233.

101. Walter Wever, directive, *Abstellung des Stabes des Führers der Marineluftstreitkräfte* (4 June 1934), in NARA File T-177, Roll 18.

102. *Bestimmungen für den F. D. Luft und die Marine* Luftstreitkräfte, Anlage to directive of 4 June 1934, in NARA File T-177, Roll 18.

103. Admiral Raeder, letter to Reichs Air Ministry (3 December 1934), cited in Ernst Völker, *Dokumente und Dokumentarfotos,* Akt. 85.

104. Ibid.

105. Ibid.

106. For the plans and description of the Graf Zeppelin, see Erich Gröner, *Die deutsche Kriegsschiffe,* vol. I (Koblenz: Bernard und Graefe Verlag, 1989), 98–101.

107. Ibid.

108. Captain Lieutenant Metzner, "Die Luftwaffe im Seekrieg," in *Militärwissenschaftliche Rundschau* Heft 4 (1936), 477.

109. Ibid., 481.

110. Ibid., 481-82.

111. Ibid., 485-87.

112. Ibid., 481-82.

113. Ibid., 483.

114. Green, *Warplanes of the Third Reich,* 273-77.

115. Ibid., 124-27.

116. Morris Allward, *An Illustrated History of Seaplanes and Flying Boats* (New York: Dorset Press, 1981), 64.

117. Olaf Groehler, *Geschichte des Luftkrieges* (Berlin: Militärverlag der DDR, 1981), 220.

118. Ibid., 220. For information on numbers and personnel in the Luftwaffe during this era, see Karl-Heinz Völker, *Die deutsche Luftwaffe 1933-1939: Aufbau, Führung, und Rüstung der Luftwaffe* (Stuttgart: Deutsche Verlagsanstalt, 1967), 54-60.

THE LUFTWAFFE IN THE SPANISH CIVIL WAR

1. The best general work on the Spanish Civil War is Hugh Thomas's *The Spanish Civil War* (New York: Harper and Row, 1961).

2. The best account of the Luftwaffe's operations in Spain is Raymond Proctor's *Hitler's Luftwaffe in the Spanish Civil War* (Westport, Conn.: Greenwood Press, 1983). On the origin of the German involvement in Spain, see 1-23.

3. Proctor, *Hitler's Luftwaffe in the Spanish Civil War,* 20-21.

4. Ibid.

5. Proctor, 21-22.

6. Ibid.

7. Ibid., 26.

8. Hugh Thomas, *The Spanish Civil War* (New York: Harper and Row, 1961). Thomas gives the figures of 10,500 Nationalist soldiers airlifted in August and 9,700 soldiers airlifted in September, 244.

9. Proctor, 31.

10. Foot Brigadier General Hap Arnold, "Air Lessons from Current Wars," *U.S. Air Services.* May 1938, 17.

11. Karl Ries and Hans Ring *The Legion Condor: A History of the Luftwaffe in the Spanish Civil War, 1936-1939* (West Chester, Pa.: Schiffer Military History, 1992), 18-23.

12. Howson, Gerald, *Aircraft of the Spanish Civil War* (Washington, D.C., Smithsonian Institution Press, 1990), 26.

13. Proctor, 44-45.

14. Ries and Ring, 28.
15. Ibid.
16. Hugh Thomas, 295-96.
17. Ibid., 292-94.
18. Ibid., 304-6.
19. Ibid., 315-16.
20. Jesús Salas Larrazabal, *Air War Over Spain* (London, Ian Allen, 1969), 95.
21. Proctor, 55.
22. Ries and Ring, 32-35. See also Larrazabal, 103-8. See also Proctor, 64.
23. Howson, 21. Before the end of 1936 the Russians had eight air squadrons in Spain, which included two squadrons of I-15 fighters, two squadrons of I-16 fighters, two squadrons of SB-2 bombers, and two squadrons of R-5 Rasante observation/reconnaissance planes.
24. Proctor, 66.
25. Proctor, 66-67.
26. Larrazabal, *Air War Over Spain*, 108-9.
27. Reich foreign minister to Ambassador von Hassell. Message of 30 October 1936 in Akten zur Deutschen Auswärtigen Politik 1918-1945, Serie D (1937-1945) Band III, *Deutschland und der Spanischen Bürgerkrieg 1936-1939.* Henceforth referred to as "Akt." See also Ries and Ring for a table of organization for the Condor Legion, 38-40.
28. Proctor, 59-60.
29. General der Flieger Karl Drum, "Die deutsche Luftwaffe im spanischen Bürgerkrieg," USAF HRA Karlsruhe Collection, DOC K113.106-50, 6-16.
30. Manfred Merkes, *Die deutsche Politik gegenuber dem spanischen Bürgerkrieg: 1936-1939* (Bonn: Ludwig Rohrscheid Verlag, 1961), 25-26.
31. Ibid. On the economic advantages of German intervention, see also Robert Whealey, *Hitler and Spain: The Nazi Role in the Spanish Civil War: 1936-1939* (Lexington: University Press of Kentucky, 1989), 74-87.
32. Proctor, 40-42.
33. Whealey (note 4), 54.
34. Proctor, 74-75.
35. Proctor, 76-77.
36. See Chief of the Wehrmacht High Command, General Keitel's message to the foreign minister of 22 March 1938, in Akt. 549.
37. Ibid.
38. Akt. 549. On Franco's wish to prevent combat see Akt. 552.
39. Akt. 113, memo from foreign minister. "General Faupel should not concern himself with military matters . . ."
40. Akt. 148. *Message by Faupel to Foreign Minister,* 10 Dec. 1936. Faupel reports how he advised Franco to deal with the Madrid battle, troop training, etc.
41. Akt. 248, Faupel message of 1 May 1937.

42. Whealey (note 4), 65.
43. Akt. 386, Faupel message of 7 July 1937.
44. Interview with Freiherr Götz von Richthofen by J. S. Corum, 21 June 1992.
45. See von Richthofen report of 4 Dec 1936, in BA/MA N/671/1.
46. One example of German Spanish disagreement was in 1937 when Franco decided to defend the strategically unimportant town of Teruel. However, after expressing their disagreement the Condor Legion carried out Franco orders with the will. See Proctor, 175–76.
47. Proctor, 85.
48. Proctor, 91.
49. Proctor, 90.
50. Richard Hallion, *Strike From the Sky: The History of Battlefield Air Attack, 1911–1945* (Washington, D.C., Smithsonian Institution Press, 1989), 97–102.
51. Proctor, 119.
52. Hugh Thomas, 437.
53. Report of von Richthofen 1 April 1937, in BA/MA N/671/2.
54. General der Flieger Karl Drum, "Die deutsche Luftwaffe im spanischen Bürgerkrieg," USAF HRA Karlsruhe Collection, Doc K113.106–150, 199.
55. Proctor, 122–23.
56. Proctor, 126.
57. Proctor, 136.
58. Von Richthofen report of 3 April 1937, in BA/MA N/671/2.
59. Von Richthofen report of 30 April 1937, in BA/MA N/671/2.
60. Von Richthofen report of 4 April 1937, in BA/MA N/671/2
61. Proctor, 119. Personally observing and coordinating major close air support operations soon became a tradition for senior Luftwaffe commanders that extended into World War II.
62. Drum, 186.
63. For description of the Iron Belt see Proctor, 138–39.
64. Drum, 182–84. See also Proctor, 138–41.
65. Drum, 182–84, and Proctor, 104.
66. For detailed information on the Guernica attack, see Gordon Thomas and Max Witts, *Guernica: The Crucible of World War II* (New York: Stein & Day, 1975); and Hans-Henning Abendroth, "Guernica: Ein fragwürdiges Symbol," in Militärgeschichtliche Mitteilungen 1/87, 111–26.
67. Account of George Steer of the *London Times* cited in Peter Wyden's *The Passionate War: The Narrative History of the Spanish Civil War* (New York: Simon & Schuster, 1983), 357–58
68. Cited in Allen Guttmann *The Wound in the Heart: America and the Spanish Civil War* (New York: Free Press, 1962), 106.
69. Ibid., 108.
70. Ibid., 107.

71. See Hugh Thomas, 419.

72. For examples of what has become the conventional description of Guernica, see James Stokesbury, *A Short History of Air Power* (New York: William Morrow, 1986), 146. Also see Alan Stephens, "The True Believers: Air Power Between the War," in *The War in the Air, 1914–1994,* ed. Alan Stephens (Fairbairn, Australia: RAAF Air Power Studies Centre, 1994), 60–61. Also Robin Cross, *The Bombers* (New York: Macmillan, 1987), 85. "There is also little doubt that Oberstleutnant von Richthofen had a wider purpose in mind—the deliberate terror bombing of the town in an attempt to destroy the morale of the government's troops and its supporters," 196. William Shirer, *The Rise and Fall of the Third Reich* (New York: Simon & Schuster, 1960), 297 refers to "the obliteration of the Spanish town of Guernica and its civilian inhabitants."

73. Von Richthofen report of 30 April 1937 in BA/MA N/671/2.

74. The reports by Lt. Col. Von Richthofen as Condor Legion chief of staff, later commander of the Condor Legion, are found in BA/MA N/671/1, N/671/2 and N/671/3. Files contain numerous reports and extensive daily entries for the air campaign in 1937.

75. See Thomas and Witts, *Guernica,* 254.

76. See Richthofen report of 30 April 1937, in BA/MA N/671/2.

77. Ibid.

78. Ries and Ring, 63–64.

79. Daily report of the Condor Legion, 11 February 1938 in BA/MA RL 35/4.

80. Manuel Azner, *Historia Militar de la Guerra de España,* vol. I (Madrid: Editoria Nacional, 1958), 302 (Bombing of Brunete) and 304 (Bombing of Azuara). See also Estado Mayor del Ejercito, *Historia Militar de la Guerra de España,* vol. III (Madrid: Altimira S. A., 1963), 82 (photo of Alcubierre).

81. George Quester, *Deterrence before Hiroshima* (Oxford: Transaction, 1986), 93.

82. Richard Overy and Andrew Wheatcroft, *The Road to War: The Origins of World War II* (London: Macmillan, 1989), 304.

83. Proctor, 145.

84. Ries and Ring, 68.

85. Proctor, 146–47.

86. Ries and Ring, 68.

87. Ibid., 70–72.

88. Howson, 22.

89. Ibid., 19.

90. Von Richthofen Report of 18 July 1937. In BA/MA N/671/2.

91. Report of von Richthofen, 24–26 July 1937 in BA/MA N/671/2.

92. Von Richthofen Report, 24 July 1937 in BA/MA N/ 671/2.

93. Proctor, 174–75.

94. Proctor, 177.

95. Ibid., 176–77.

96. Ibid., 177.
97. Ries and Ring, 123–24.
98. Larrazabal, *La Guerra de España desde el aire,* 312–28.
99. Ibid., 318.
100. Proctor, 191–92.
101. Ries and Ring, 135–36.
102. Proctor, 191.
103. Ibid., 191–92.
104. Proctor, 193–95.
105. Drum, 120–23.
106. Proctor, 195.
107. Report by General Volkmann, 28 July 1938, Condor Legion Lageberichte BA/MA RL 35/4. See also Condor Legion report, letter from Captain Christ, 11 December 1938, in BA/MA RL 35/3, 3.
108. Letter from Captain Christ, 9 August 1938, in BA/MA RL 35/3. This report contains a description of Nationalist operations to date.
109. Ries and Ring, 178.
110. Condor Legion Reports, Captain Christ, letter of 9 August 1938, in BA/MA RL 35/3.
111. Norman Franks, *Aircraft Versus Aircraft* (New York: Crescent, 1986), 68.
112. Ries and Ring, 271–72.
113. Howson, 186–87, 211.
114. Condor Legion, *Reports of 26 July 1938 and 28 July 1938,* in BA/MA RL 35/4.
115. Drum, 193.
116. The Condor Legion reported on 28 July 1938, "Due to heavy air attacks by our whole force the temporary defensive positions on the Ebro can be held against strong Red attacks." See *Condor Legion Report of 28 July 1938,* in BA/MA RL 35/4.
117. *Condor Legion Reports from July–Sept. 1938,* in BA/MA RL 35/4.
118. Larrazabal, *La Guerra de España desde el Aire,* 499.
119. Herbert Mathews, *Half of Spain Died* (New York: Charles Scribners Sons, 1973), 152.
120. Proctor, 66–67. See also Stanley Payne, *Politics and the Military in Modern Spain* (Stanford University Press, 1967), 384.
121. Oberst Jaenecke, "Lehren des spanischen Bürgerkrieges," *in Jahrbuch des deutschen Heeren 1940* (Leipzig: Verlag von Breitkopf und Hörtl, 1940), 143.
122. Ries and Ring, 118–99.
123. Ibid., 128.
124. According to von Richthofen's report of 9 April 1937, German bombers accompanied by Italian bombers attacked a Republican munitions factory in Northern Spain. See BA/MA N 671/2.
125. Thomas, *The Spanish Civil War,* 523.
126. Ibid.

127. John Coverdale, *Italian Intervention in the Spanish Civil War* (Princeton, N.J.: Princeton University Press, 1975), 337–49.

128. Thomas, *The Spanish Civil War,* 524.

129. Ambassador Stohrer, report to the foreign ministry (23 March 1938), from Akt. 550.

130. Ibid.

131. Colonel Conrad Lanza, U.S. Army, "Open Warfare," in *Field Artillery Journal* (November–December 1939): 538–40. See also Major Robert Mackin, U.S. Army, "Airplanes Can Be Stopped," *Coast Artillery Journal* (September–October 1937), 398.

132. Ries and Ring, 83.

133. Ibid., 83–84 and 256.

134. Ibid., 257.

135. Ibid., 256–57.

136. R. Richardson, "The Development of Air Power Concepts and Air Combat Techniques in the Spanish Civil War," in *Air Power History* (spring 1993): 13–21, esp. 18–19.

137. Stanley Payne, *The Franco Regime: 1936–1975* (Madison: University of Wisconsin Press, 1987), 154.

138. Drum, 218–26.

139. BA/MA RM 7/168 and RM 7/69 contain reports on the early naval air operations of the Condor Legion.

140. Ries and Ring, 207. See also *Deutsche Kämpfen in Spanien* (Berlin: Wilhelm Limpert Verlag, 1939), 86–88.

141. *Deutsche Kämpfen in Spanien,* 83–85.

142. Larios, *Combat Over Spain,* 183 and 258. The Nationalists commented that German seaplanes had done an excellent job of attacking the Republican logistics in their attacks on the ports of Valencia, Tarragona, Barcelona, and Almeira. In the latter part of the war, a total of 100 ships had been sunk directly in the Republican ports.

143. On the strategy behind Italy's intervention in Spain, see John Coverdale, *Italian Intervention in the Spanish Civil War;* and Glen Barclay, *The Rise and Fall of the New Roman Empire* (London: Sidgwick and Jackson, 1973).

144. John Coverdale, *Italian Intervention in the Spanish Civil War,* 396; and Glen Barclay, *The Rise and Fall of the New Roman Empire,* 163.

145. Proctor, 79–80.

146. Von Richthofen complained in his report of 3 February 1937, "No one knows what the Italian plans are. Even Franco doesn't know." See von Richthofen report of 3 February 1937 in BA/MA N/671/1.

147. Von Richthofen reported on 13 March 1937, "Abyssnia was a bluff . . . No fighting spirit . . . Sensitive to panic." About the performance of an Italian division at Guadalajara, he commented "Schweinerei." See von Richtofen reports of 13 and 14 March 1937 in BA/MA N/671/1.

148. Proctor, 58–59, provides a good picture of Sperrle and his personality.

149. Von Richthofen's report of 20 January 1937. In BA/MA N/671/1.

150. Von Richthofen's diary, 5 February 1937 in BA/MA N 671/1. Von Richthofen said of Colonel Barosso, chief of Franco's operations section, "I trust him with my operational plans." Ibid., von Richthofen report of 22 January.

151. On Vigón see James Cortada, ed., *Historical Dictionary of the Spanish Civil War* (Westport, Conn.: Greenwood Press, 1982), 473–74.

152. Ernst Obermaier and Werner Held, *Jagdflieger Oberst Werner Mölders* (Stuttgart: Motorbuch Verlag, 1986), 79.

153. José Larios, *Combat Over Spain* (London: Neville Spearman, 1965), 141, 238.

154. Von Richthofen report of 25 July 1937. In BA/MA N/671/1. Von Richthofen referred to the "excellent" attack of the Spanish fighters and bombers north of Brunete.

155. Ries and Ring, 210.

156. Coverdale, 334–35.

157. See General Volkmann report of 14 September 1938 and the daily reports of the Condor Legion BA/MA RL 35/6.

158. Coverdale, 336.

159. Horst Boog, "Higher Command in Leadership in the German Luftwaffe, 1935–1945," in *Airpower and Warfare,* ed. Alfred Hurley (USAF Office of History, 1979), 129–30.

160. Michael Geyer, *Germany Strategy in the Age of Machine Warfare, 1914–1945, Makers of Modern Strategy* (Princeton, N.J.: Princeton University Press, 1986), 572.

161. In 1936–1938 the Nationalist sector of Spain alone provided 2.45 million tons of iron ore and 2.13 million tons of pyrites to Germany. By 1939, Spain was exporting 95.65 million reichsmarks worth of goods to Germany annually. Robert Whealey, 86–94.

162. See Gerald Kleinfeld and Louis A. Tambs, *Hitler's Spanish Legion: The Blue Division in Russia* (Carbondale: Southern Illinois University Press, 1979), 346.

163. Stanley Payne, *The Franco Regime, 1936–1975* (Madison: University of Wisconsin Press, 1978), 158.

164. On the Italian cost of the war, see John Coverdale, *Italian Intervention in the Spanish Civil War,* 392.

165. Proctor, 253.

166. Ibid.

167. Ibid.

168. Ibid.

169. Ibid.

170. Ibid., 254.

171. Samuel W. Mitcham, Jr., *Men of the Luftwaffe* (Novato, Presidio Press, 1988), 51.

172. Proctor, 259.

173. Luftwaffe Chef des Ausbildungswesen, "Folgerungen aus dem rotspanischen Luftschutz" (September 1939), in NARA file T-321, Roll 90.

174. Proctor, 263.

175. Headquarters Luftwaffekommando 5. Directive 8 October 1937 in BA/MA RL 4/15.

176. Neville Jones, *The Beginning of Strategic Air Power* (London: Frank Cass, 1987), 112–13.

177. Luftflotte III, Verlauf der Generalstabsreise, June 1939, 15, 17 in BA/MA RL 7/159

THE LUFTWAFFE PREPARES FOR WAR

1. Field Marshal Albert Kesselring was born in Bavaria in 1885, and died in Bad Neuheim in 1960. His military record reads: joined army, 1904; lieutenant, 1906; service in 2nd Bavarian Foot Artillery Regiment, 1904–1914; service with artillery units, 1915–1917; General Staff Course, 1917; general staff, III Bavarian Corps and Sixth Army, 1918; captain, 1916; battery commander, Artillery Regiments 7 and 24; Reichswehr headquarters, 1922–1925; major, 1925; army commander's staff, 1925–1926; Reichswehr air ministry staff, 1926–1929; lieutenant colonel, 1930; colonel, 1932; battalion commander, artillery, 1932–1933; transferred to Luftwaffe, 1933; major general, 1934; chief of Luftwaffe administration, 1933–1936; Luftwaffe chief of staff, June 1936–31 May 1937; lieutenant general, 1936; General der Flieger, 1937; commander, 3rd Air District, 1937–1938; commander, Air Fleet I, 1938–January 1940; commander, Air Fleet II, 1940–1943; field marshal, 1940; commander in chief, south, 1942–1945.

2. Kesselring is generally kind about Göring in his memoirs but alludes to bad blood between himself and Milch when he was Luftwaffe chief of staff. See Albert Kesselring, *Memoirs of Field Marshal Kesselring* (Novato, Calif.: Presidio Press, 1989).

3. Edward Homze, *Arming the Luftwaffe: The Reich Air Ministry and the German Aircraft Industry, 1919–1939* (Lincoln: University of Nebraska Press, 1976), 61.

4. Colonel General Ernst Udet was born in 1896, and died in 1941 by his own hand. His service record reads: entered army, 1914; pilot training, 1915; lieutenant, Fighter Squadron 5, 1916; commander, Fighter Squadrons 11 and 37, 1917; commander, Fighter Squadron 4 in JG 1, 1918; received Pour le Mérite for sixty-two aerial victories—second highest victory count in Luftstreitkräfte, 1918; first lieutenant, 1918; discharged from army, 1920; owner/operator of an aviation company, worked as a stunt pilot, 1920–1935; reentered Luftwaffe as colonel, 1935; inspector of fighters and stukas, 1935–1936; chief, Technical Office, 1936–1939; major general, 1937; lieutenant general, 1938; chief of aircraft production, 1939–1941; General der Flieger, 1940; colonel general, 1940.

5. Interview with von Richthofen, June 1993.

6. Colonel General Hans-Jürgen Stumpf was born in Kolberg in 1889, and died in Frankfurt am Main in 1968. His service record reads: entered army, 1907; lieutenant, 1908; infantry and engineer units, 1907–1916; general staff, Ninth Army, 1916–1917; captain, 1916; General Staff Course, 1917; general staff of high command, 1918–1919; Truppenamt, 1919–1922; infantry company commander, 1922–1924; general staff,

First Division, 1924–1927; major, 1927; adjutant to army chief, 1927–1929; Reichswehr air ministry, 1929–1933; lieutenant colonel, 1931; colonel, 1934; chief of Luftwaffe personnel office, 1933–1937; major general, 1936; Luftwaffe chief of staff, June 1937 to January 1939; lieutenant general, 1937; General der Flieger, 1938; colonel general, 1940; commander, Air Fleet I, 1940; commander, Air Fleet 5, 1940–1943; commander, Luftflotte Reich, 1944–1945.

7. Horst Boog, *Die deutsche Luftwaffenführung 1935–1945* (Stuttgart: Deutsche Verlags-Anstalt, 1982), 223.

8. Ibid.

9. The chief of the Luftwehr had a wide range of responsibilities, including oversight of civil defense, coordination with the aircraft industry, and planning for the mobilization of raw materials. See Luftwaffe, *Anlage I zum Mobilization—Plan Luftwaffe: Kriegsspitzeingliederung der Luftwaffe* (28 January 1937), in NARA File T-321, Roll 245.

10. Boog, *Die deutsche Luftwaffenführung 1935–1945,* 222.

11. Ibid., 224.

12. Ibid.

13. Ibid., 225.

14. Ibid., 367.

15. Ibid.

16. Hans Jeschonnek was born in 1899 in Hohensulza, the son of a schoolmaster, and he committed suicide in August 1943. His service record reads: entered army, 1914; served with 50th Infantry Regiment, 1914–1917; commissioned, 1915; entered Air Service and took pilot training, 1917; served with Jagdstaffel 40, 1918; served with Reiter Regiment 11, 1919; service with Reichswehr staff and attendance at general staff course, 1928–1931; captain, 1931; Reichswehr staff, 1932–1934; transferred to Reichs Air Ministry, 1934; adjutant to State Secretary Milch, 1934–1935; major, 1935; group commander in KG 35 and commander, Lehrgeschwader, 1935–1937; lieutenant colonel, 1937; chief of Section 1, Luftwaffe general staff, 1937; colonel, 1938; chief of the Luftwaffe operations staff, 1938; chief of the Luftwaffe general staff, 1 February 1939; General der Flieger, July 1940; colonel general, March 1942.

17. Horst Boog, *Die deutsche Luftwaffenführung 1935–1945,* 228–29. For a thorough overview of Jeschonnek's life and career, see Richard Suchenwirth, *Command and Leadership in the German Air Force* (USAF Historical Study No. 174) (Maxwell AFB: USAF Historical Division, 1969), 213–92.

18. Boog, *Die deutsche Luftwaffenführung 1935–1945,* 231.

19. Richard Suchenwirth, *Historical Turning Points in the German Air Force War Effort* (USAF Historical Study No. 189) (Maxwell AFB: USAF Historical Division, 1959), 7.

20. Boog, *Die deutsche Luftwaffenführung 1935–1945,* 229–30.

21. Heinz Orlovius, ed., *Die Deutsche Luftfahrt Jahrbuch 1937* (Frankfurt a.M.: Verlag Fritz Knapp, 1938), 7.

22. Ibid.
23. Ibid., 19–22.
24. Luftwaffe Generalstab, 3 Abt., *Bericht: Wehrmachtmanöver* (Luftwaffe) (1937), in BA/MA RL 2 II/835.
25. Ibid., 44–54.
26. Ibid.
27. Ibid.
28. Ibid., 46–47.
29. Ibid., 55.
30. Karl-Heinz Völker, ed., *Dokumente und Dokumentarfotos zur Geschichte der Deutschen Luftwaffe* (Stuttgart: Deutsche Verlags-Anstalt, 1968), 450–53.
31. Horst Boog, "Die Luftverteidigung in der deutschen Luftkriegsdoktrin und der Aufbau der deutschen Luftverteidigung im Frieden," in *Das Deutsche Reich und der zweite Weltkrieg,* vol. 6, ed. Militärgeschichtliches Forschungsamt (Stuttgart: Deutsche Verlags-Anstalt, 1990), 443–44.
32. General der Flieger Paul Deichmann was born in 1898 in Fulda, and died in 1981 in Hamburg. His military record reads: entered army, 1916; lieutenant, 1916; infantry platoon leader, 1916–1917; observer training, 1917; observer with Flieger Abteilung 8, 1918; infantry officer, 1920–1925; air photography officer, 1st Division, 1925–1928; pilot training at Lipetsk and service with air staff, 1928–1931; captain, 1933; General Staff Course, 1931–1934; Luftwaffe general staff, 1934–1937; major, 1935; commander, II/KG 253, 1937–1939; lieutenant colonel, 1938; colonel, 1940; chief of staff of Luftwaffe training; chief of staff, II Air Corps, June 1940–August 1942; major general, 1942; chief of staff, Second Air Fleet, 1942–1943; commander, I Fliegerkorps; lieutenant general, 1944; General der Flieger, 1945.
33. Homze, *Arming the Luftwaffe,* 166.
34. William Green, *Warplanes of the Third Reich* (New York: Galahad, 1990), 336.
35. Albert Kesselring, letter of 19 December 1939, in BA/MA RL 2 II/73.
36. Ibid.
37. Kesselring, *Memoirs of Field Marshal Kesselring,* 36.
38. Chief of the Luftwaffe general staff, *Directive on Paratroops* (28 June 1937), in BA/MA RL 2 II/163.
39. Volkmar Kuehn, *Deutsche Fallschirmjäger im Zweiten Weltkrieg* (Stuttgart: Motorbuch Verlag, 1993), 16–17.
40. Chief of the Luftwaffe general staff, *Directive on Paratroops.*
41. Colonel General Kurt Student was born in May 1890 in Birkholz, and died in 1978. His service record reads: entered army, 1910; lieutenant, 1911; infantry officer service, 1910–1913; pilot training, 1913; pilot, Flight Detachment 17, 1914–1916; pilot, KG 4, 1916; commander, Fighter Squadron 9, 1916–1917; fighter group commander, Third Army, 1917–1918; Aircraft Testing Department, aviation inspectorate, 1919–1920; section leader, Waffenamt, 1922–1928; infantry service, 1928–1931; major, 1930; commander, 1st Battalion, 3rd Infantry Regiment, 1931–1933; lieutenant colonel,

1934; commander, Luftwaffe technical schools, 1933–1935; colonel, 1935; commander, Aviation Testing Station, Rechlin, 1935–1936; commander, aviation weapons schools, 1936–1937; inspector of aviation schools, 1937; major general, 1938; commander, 3rd Air Division, 1938; commander of paratroops, 1938–1941; lieutenant general, 1940; General der Flieger, 1940; commander, XI Air Corps, 1941; commanding general of paratroops, 1941–1944; colonel general, 1944; commander, First Airborne Army, 1944; commander, Army Group H, 1944–1945.

42. Kuehn, *Deutsche Fallschirmjäger,* 17-20.

43. Ibid., 20.

44. Ibid., 19.

45. Ibid., 23.

46. Ibid., 21.

47. Ibid., 23.

48. See Major Erwin Gehrts, "Gedanken zum operativen Luftkrieg," in *Die Luftwaffe* 2 (1937): 16-39. *The Luftwaffe* was a journal of military thought published by the Luftwaffe for use within the Luftwaffe. Col. Hans von Bülow propounded a similiar view in "Die Grundlagen neuzeitlichen Luftstreitkräfte," in the prestigious *Militärwissenschaftliche Rundschau* no. 1 (1936): 78–107.

49. Klaus Maier, "Totaler Krieg und Operativer Luftkrieg," in *Das Deutsche Reich und der Zweite Weltkrieg* (Stuttgart: Deutsche Verlags-Anstalt, 1979), 47.

50. Major General Hans-Detlef Herhudt von Rohden was born in Liegnitz in 1899, and died in Wiesbaden in 1951. His military personnel file reads: entered army, 1917; lieutenant, 1918; foot artillery, 1917–1918; service with artillery regiments, 1919–1929; first lieutenant, 1925; pilot training in Germany and Russia, 1929–1931; general staff training, 1931–1934; captain, 1933; major, 1935; air ministry staff, 1935–1937; group commander, JG 334; Wehrmachtakademie, July 1937–March 1938; lieutenant colonel, 1938; bomber group commander, KG 152 and Lehr-Geschwader I, 1938–1939; staff, Air Fleet 2, 1939; faculty, Luftkriegsakademie, 1940–1941; chief of staff, IV Air Corps, 1941; chief of staff, Air Fleet 4, 1942–1943; major general, 1943; chief, military history section of Luftwaffe general staff, 1943–1945.

51. For a useful overview of Haushofer's theories, see Derwnet Whittlesey, "Haushofer: The Geopoliticians," in *Makers of Modern Strategy,* ed. Edward Meade Earle (Princeton, N.J.: Princeton University Press, 1943), 388–411.

52. Ibid., 405–10.

53. Hans-Detlef von Rohden, *Vom Luftkriege: Gedanken über Führung und Einsatz moderner Luftwaffen* (Berlin: E. S. Mittler und Sohn, 1938), 10.

54. A fairly typical book of the era is Wulf Bley and Richard Schulz, *Luftarmeen Ringsum* (Berlin: Verlag Kultur-Wacht, 1935). This book stresses the air power of Germany's possible enemies and the ease with which their aircraft could reach Germany.

55. Hans-Detlef von Rohden, "Betrachtungen über den Luftkrieg," parts 1–4, in *Militärwissenschaftliche Rundschau* no. 2 (1937).

56. Von Rohden, *Vom Luftkrieg,* 4.

57. Ibid., 10.

58. See Georg Röhrig, *Die Ziele selbständiger Luftangriffe* (Königsberg: Ost-Europa Verlag, 1938). For a useful overview on the issues of morality and bombing as seen from the German viewpoint, see Horst Boog, "The Luftwaffe and Indiscriminate Bombing up to 1942," in *The Conduct of the Air War in the Second World War,* ed. Horst Boog (New York: Berg, 1992), 373–404.

59. Tony Devereux, *Messenger Gods of Battle* (London: Brassey's, 1991), 139–47.

60. Werner Niehaus, *Die Rädarschlacht* (Stuttgart: Motorbuch Verlag, 1977), 39–40.

61. OB Luftwaffe, *Ausbildungsverfügung für das Winterhalbjahr 1936-1937,* in NARA File T-321, Roll 90 RLM.

62. Luftflotte 2, *Beiheft für die Blaue Partei: Manöver der Luftflotte 2* (1939), in BA/MA RL/41.

63. Homze, *Arming the Luftwaffe,* 152.

64. Ibid., 190.

65. *Jagdflieger-Anleitung 1939,* in BB/MA RL 2 II/283, 47–59.

66. Ibid., 41.

67. Luftkreiskommando 5, *Ausbildung im Sommerhalbjahr 1938* (10 March 1938), in BA/MA RL 4/16.

68. Luftwaffe Generalstab, Abt. 1, *Generalstabsreise der Luftwaffe* (29 June 1939), in BA/MA RL 7/160.

69. Boog, "Die Luftverteidigung," 45.

70. Devereux, *Messenger Gods of Battle,* 104.

71. Niehaus, *Die Rädarschlacht,* 32.

72. Ibid., 32–33.

73. Ibid.

74. Ibid., 33.

75. Ibid., 77.

76. Ibid., 33.

77. Ibid., 34.

78. Generalstab, Abt. 1, *Planstudie 1939* (7 February 1939), in BA/MA RL 2 II/1.

79. Horst Boog, "Die Luftverteidigung," 43–49.

80. Generalstabsausbildung, *Planübung I 1936/1937 for 16–17 Oct 1936,* in NARA File T-321, Roll 2.

81. Boog, "Die Luftverteidigung," 443.

82. Fliegerinspektion 3. Vortrag by Major Raithel, *Technik, Organisation und Einsatz der Jagdkräfte* (11 November 1936), in BA/MA RL 4/237, 21.

83. Ibid.

84. General Kesselring, chief of staff of Air Fleet I, *Vortrag* (21 April 1939), in BA/MA RL 2 II/101.

85. Luftwaffe Generalstab, Abt. 3, *Ausbildungsrichtlinien für das Sommerhalbjahr 1938* (15 February 1938), in BA/MA RL4/16.

86. Oberbefehlshaber der Luftwaffe, *Generalstabsausbildung 1936/1937. Planuebung 1* (17 October 1936).

87. Deutsches Museum, *Heft Focke Wulf,* no. 740.10.

88. Ibid.

89. Oberbefehlshaber Luftwaffe, *Ausbildungsverfügung für das Winterhalbjahr 1936/1937* (17 September 1936).

90. Ibid.

91. Ibid., 5.

92. Luftkreiskommando 5, *Zusammenarbeit der Luftwaffe mit dem Heer* (15 November 1937), in BA/MA RL 4/15.

93. Luftwaffe Dienstvorschrift 2/2, *Der Aufklärungsflieger (Land): Luftaufklärung für die Kriegführung des Heeres* (1938), para. 1.

94. Ibid.

95. The Luftwaffe doctrine for tactical reconnaissance is set out in Luftwaffedienstvorschrift 2/3, *Der Aufklärungsflieger (Land)* (1938).

96. Heinz Guderian, *Achtung-Panzer* (Stuttgart: Union Deutscher Verlagsgesellschaft, 1937), 189–90.

97. See Luftwaffe Gruppenkommando 3, *Bericht über die Reise für Führer obere Dienststellen 15–22 May 1938,* in BA/MA RL 7, for an analysis of Luftwaffe operations with the army's panzer divisions in an exercise in Thuringia.

98. Luftwaffedienstvorschrift 90, *Die Versorgung der Luftwaffe im Kriege* (1938), paras. 13–16.

99. Ibid., para. 13.

100. Oberbefehlshaber Heer, *Anlagen zum Bericht über die Wehrmachtmanöver (Heer) 1937,* Berlin (1938), Anlage 79.

101. Ibid., Anlage 64.

102. Luftflotte 3 Staff, *Aktennotiz Besprechung beim Lehrstab für Heerestaktik: Manöver der Schnellen Truppen* (23 June 1939), in BA/MA RL 7/169.

103. Oberbefehlshaber der Luftwaffe, *Ausbildungsrichtlinien für das Sommerhalbjahr 1938,* Berlin (1938).

104. Luftwaffe Generalstab, Abt. 1, *Generalstabreise der Luftwaffe 1939, Anlage 2* (29 June 1939), in BA/MA RL 7/160.

105. *Verlauf der Generalstabreise* (June 1939), in BA/MA RL 7/159, 15 and 17.

106. Wilhelm Speidel, *Die Luftwaffe im Polenfeldzug 1939,* USAF HRA, Karlsruhe Collection, K113.106–151, 18.

107. The Luftwaffe made extensive preparations for ensuring the mobility of its units in the mid-1930s. See Fliegerinspektorat 3, *Merkblatt über die Verlegung von Jagdverbänden auf Feldflugplätze* (10 Sept. 1936), in BA/MA RL 4/237. This is full of detail, TOEs, etc., on how to quickly move and set up a Luftwaffe airfield and transfer air units.

108. Wilhelm Speidel, *The Campaign for Western Europe, Part 1,* HRA Karlsruhe Collection, K113.107–152, Appendix B.

109. Ibid.

110. See Richard Suchenwirth, *The Development of the German Air Force, 1919-1939* (Maxwell AFB: USAF Historical Division, 1968), 140; and H. von Rohden, *Die Planung und Vorbereitung des Luftkrieges gegen Polen 1939,* Luftkrieg Heft 5, Anlage 6, unpublished ms. (Maxwell AFB: Air University Library, 1946).

111. See Karl-Heinz Völker, *Die deutsche Luftwaffe 1933-1939,* 119-21.

112. Ibid., 121.

113. See *Vorläufige Richlinien für die Ausbildung der Offizieranwärter der Luftwaffe, Teil III* (1936), in NARA File T-321, Roll 68.

114. Luftwaffe Dienstvorschrift 21, *Die Flugzeugführerausbildung* (1937).

115. *Vorläufige Richtlinien für die Ausbildung der Offizieranwärter der Luftwaffe, Teil IV* (1936), in NARA File T-321, Roll 68.

116. Ibid., 17-19.

117. Karl-Heinz Völker, *Die deutsche Luftwaffe,* 121.

118. Ibid., 122-23.

119. Luftwaffe General Staff, *Ausbildungsrichtlinien für das Winterhalbjahr 1937/38* (15 August 1937), in BA/MA RL 4/16.

120. Alfred Price, *Luftwaffe Handbook* (New York: Charles Scribner's Sons, 1977), 60-61.

121. Luftwaffe general staff, *Ausbildungsverfügung für das Winterhalbjahr 1936-37* (17 September 1936).

122. See Reichsluftministerium, *Sammlung ausländischer Aufsätze über Luftkriegsfragen* (1 March 1937), for a listed collection of several hundred foreign articles on all aspects of aviation.

123. General der Flieger Otto von Stülpnagel was born in Berlin in 1878, and died in France in 1948. His military record reads: entered army, 1897; lieutenant, 1898; infantry officer, 1898-1905; Kriegsakademie, 1905-1908; operations section, general staff, 1909-1912; captain, 1911; pilot training, 1911; air section of the transport inspectorate, 1912-1914; infantry company commander, 1914; general staff duties, 1914-1918; major, 1916; faculty, general staff course, 1918; battalion commander, 1919; Reichswehr air ministry, 1919-1925; lieutenant colonel, 1921; colonel, 1925; department chief, Reichswehr air ministry, 1926-27; commander, 7th Infantry Regiment, 1927-28; major general, 1929; inspector of transport troops, 1929-1933; lieutenant general, 1931; commander, Air District School II, 1934-1935; General der Flieger, 1935; commander, Luftkriegsakademie, 1935-1939, also commander of the Air Technical Academy, 1938-1939; commander, XVII Military District, 1939-1940; military commander, France, 1940-1942.

124. General der Flieger, Dr. Phil. Friedrich von Cochenhausen, was born in Marburg in 1879, and died in Hochstadt, Bavaria, in 1946. His military file reads: entered army, 1897; lieutenant, 1898; field artillery service; Kriegsakademie, 1907-1910; captain, 1913; major, 1917; lieutenant colonel, 1922; general staff duties, 1911-1919; Truppenamt training section, 1919-1920; artillery battalion commander, 1923-1925; chief

of staff of training inspectorate, 1925–1928; colonel, 1927; commander, 4th Artillery Regiment 1929–1931; major general, 1930; artillery commander, 4th Division, 1931–1932; tactical instructor, Luftkriegsakademie, 1935–1938; lieutenant general, 1935; General der Flieger, 1938; commanding general, XIII Army Corps, 1939–1942.

125. Boog, *Die deutsche Luftwaffenführung,* 415–16.

126. Generalstab, Abt. 3, *Richlinien für die Ausbildung auf der Höheren Luftwaffenschule und auf der Luftkriegsakademie* (5 July 1937), in RL 2II/164.

127. Boog, *Die deutsche Luftwaffenführung,* 369–70.

128. Ibid.

129. Boog, *Die deutsche Luftwaffenführung,* 375–77.

130. Ibid., 391–92.

131. Ibid., 396–97.

132. Boog, *Die deutsche Luftwaffenführung,* 493.

133. Ibid., 406–7.

134. Ibid., 448–49.

135. A good overview of the Wehrmachtakademie is found in Hans-Georg Model, *Der deutsche Generalstabsoffizier* (Frankfurt a.M.: Bernard und Graefe Verlag, 1968), 105–7.

136. Boog, *Die deutsche Luftwaffenführung,* 405–6.

137. Model, *Der deutsche Generalstabsoffizier,* 106–7.

138. Robert Finney, *History of the Air Corps Tactical School 1920–1940* (Washington, D.C.: Center for Air Force History, 1992), 64 and 72–73.

139. Ibid., 62.

140. Charles Burdick, "Die deutschen militärischen Planungen gegenüber Frankreich 1933–1938," in *Wehrwissenschaftliche Rundschau* 6, no. 12 (1956): 678.

141. Ibid., 680–81.

142. Ibid.

143. Manfred Messerschmidt, "Foreign Policy and Preparation for War," in *Germany and the Second World War,* ed. Militärgeschichtliches Forschungsamt (Oxford: Clarendon Press, 1990), 541–694, esp. 626–32.

144. Klaus Maier, "Totaler Krieg und Operativer Luftkrieg," 51–52.

145. Ibid., 54.

146. Karl Gundelach, "Gedanken über die Führung eines Luftkrieges gegen England bei der Luftflotte 2 in den Jahren 1938/39," in *Wehrwissenschaftliche Rundschau* 10, no. 1 (January 1960): 33–46, esp. 39.

147. Ibid., 35.

148. Ibid., 35–37.

149. General Felmy, commander, Air Fleet Two, *Schlussbesprechung des Planspiels 1939* (13 May 1939), in BA/MA RL 7/43, 13–14.

150. Ibid., 16–17.

151. Ibid., 16–18.

152. Ibid., 27–28.

153. Luftwaffe General Staff, *Planstudie 1939, Heft II* (1 May 1939), in BA/MA RL 2 II/2–3.

154. Ibid., 7–9.

155. Ibid., 2–9.

156. Ibid., 9.

157. "General Giulio Douhet—An Italian Apostle of Air Power," *RAF Quarterly* (April 1936): 148–51.

158. "Foreign News," *RAF Quarterly* (July 1937): 322–23.

159. See RAF Staff College Records, 15th Course File. While Spain was ignored, on 1 October 1937 a lecture was presented at the Staff College on "Air Operations: Italo-Ethiopian Campaign, 1935–36," by Wing Commander L. N. Hollinghurst.

160. Group Captain (later air marshal) Arthur Tedder had argued for greater army/air cooperation when he lectured at the RAF Staff College in the early 1930s. See A. W. Tedder, "Air Aspects of Combined Operations," lecture presented to the RAF Staff College, Andover, preserved in the Tedder Papers, RAF Museum, Hendon.

161. Max Hastings, *Bomber Command* (New York: Simon & Schuster, 1989), 49–50.

162. Neville Jones, *The Beginnings of Strategic Air Power* (London: Frank Cass, 1987), 111–17 and 146–48.

163. Major George Kenney, "The Airplane in Modern Warfare," in *U.S. Air Services* (July 1938), 17–21.

164. Ibid., 18–19.

165. Ibid., 21.

166. Ibid.

167. Brigadier General Hap Arnold, "Air Lessons from Current Wars," in *U.S. Air Services* (May 1938), 17.

168. Maj. G. Crocker, "The Use of Aviation in the Spanish War, 1937–1938," Maxwell AFB: USAF Historical Research Agency, Air Corps Tactical School Records, File No. 168.7045–34.

169. A detailed description of the Air Corps' concepts of strategic bombardment in this period is found in the memoirs of General Haywood Hansell, a faculty member of ACTS in the late 1930s. See Haywood Hansell, *The Strategic Air War Against Germany and Japan* (Washington, D.C.: Office of Air Force History, 1986), 7–19. On the predominance of the strategic bombing concept at the Air Corps Tactical School, see Robert Finney, *History of the Air Corps Tactical School 1920–1940* (Washington, D.C.: Center for Air Force History, 1992), 64–68 and 73–75.

170. On the dominance of strategic bombing doctrine in the air corps of the 1930s, see Frank Futrell, *Ideas, Concepts, Doctrine: Basic Thinking in the United States Air Force 1907–1960* (Maxwell AFB: Air University Press, 1971), 78–82.

171. Ibid., 85–86.

172. Ibid., 84.

173. See General Armengaud, "La Guerre d'Espagne: La Combinaison des forces

de l'air avec les forces navales et avec l'armée de terre," in *Revue Militaire Générale* (March 1938), 259–82, and "La Guerre d'Espagne: Technique et Tactique des forces de l'air," in *Revue Militaire Générale* (April 1938): 413–19.

174. Ibid.

175. General Maginel, "L'Intervention de l'aviation dans la lutte terrestre," in *Revue Militaire Générale* (October 1938): 505–29.

176. Groehler, *Geschichte des Luftkrieges,* 211.

177. "Air superiority can be achieved on the front lines and then for only limited periods." From Ministère de la Defense, *Instruction sur l'Emploi Tactique des Grandes Unites* (1936), para. 10.

178. Ministère de L'Air, *Instruction sur L'Emploi Tactique des Grandes Unités Aériennes* (31 March 1937), para. 169.

179. Ibid., para. 127.

180. Ibid., para. 169.

181. Pierre Cot, *L'Armée de L'Air* (Paris: Éditions Bernard Grasset, 1938).

182. P. Buffotot, "La Perception du Réarmament Allemand par les organismes de renseignements françaises de 1936 à 1939," *Revue Historique des Armées* no. 3 (1979): 173–84.

183. Adam Adamthwaithe, *France and the Coming of the Second World War* (London: Frank Cass, 1977), 62.

184. The air rearmament plan of 1938, Plan V, specified production of 1,490 bombers, 2,127 fighters, and 1,081 reconnaissance planes. See Groehler, 211.

185. Jost Duelffer, "Aufrüstung zur Weltmacht: Die deutsche Marinepolitik 1919/30–1941," in *Revue Internationale d'Histoire Militaire* no. 73 (1991): 101.

186. Ibid., 111.

187. Ibid.

188. Stegemann, "Der Zweite Anlauf zur Seemacht," 73.

189. Ibid.

190. General der Flieger Hans Geisler was born in Hannover in 1891, and died in 1966. His service record reads: entered navy, 1909; commissioned an ensign, 1910; sea duty, 1911–1915; lieutenant JG, 1912; lieutenant, 1915; observer, naval air detachments, 1915–1917; naval aviation staff duties, 1917; observer, Seaplane Detachment Holtenau, 1919–1920; lieutenant commander, 1920; unit and ship command, 1920–1925; General Staff Course, 1925–1926; naval staff duties, 1926–1928; commander, 1928; sea duty, 1932–1933; promoted to naval captain, 1933; transferred to Luftwaffe, 1933; chief of training section, air ministry, 1933–1935; major general, 1937; commander, naval air forces, 1935–1939; lieutenant general, 1939; commander, 10th Air Division, 1939; commander, X Air Corps, 1939–1942; General der Flieger, 1940.

191. Klaus Maier, "Totaler Krieg und operativer Luftkrieg," 65.

192. General der Flieger Joachim Coeler was born in Posen in 1891. His naval service record reads: entered navy, 1912; ensign, 1913; lieutenant, 1915; sea duty, 1914–1915; pilot training, 1915; seaplane pilot, First Seaplane Detachment, 1915–1919; sea

duty, 1920–1923; Naval Flak School, 1923; lieutenant commander, 1924; naval air staff, 1928–1930; commander, Naval Air Testing Office, Warnemünde, 1932–1933; lieutenant colonel, Luftwaffe, 1934; inspector of seaplanes, Air District 6, 1936–1939; commander, naval air forces (west), 1939–1940; major general, 1939; lieutenant general, 1940; commander, 9th Air Division, 1940; commander, IX Air Corps, 1940–1942; lieutenant general, 1940; General der Flieger, 1942; General der Transportflieger, 1944–1945.

193. Michael Salewski, *Die bewaffnete Macht im Dritten Reich 1933–1939* (Munich: Bernard und Graefe Verlag, 1978), 470.

194. Green, *Warplanes of the Third Reich,* 38–42.

195. Ibid., 133–37.

196. Salewski, *Die bewaffnete Macht,* 470–71.

197. Ibid.

198. Bernd Stegemann, "Der Minenkrieg," in *Der Errichtung der Hegemonie auf dem europäischen Kontinent* (Stuttgart: Deutsche Verlags-Anstalt, 1979), 180–81.

199. Salewski, *Die bewaffnete Macht,* 487–88.

200. Ernst Udet, *Ein Fliegerleben* (Berlin: Verlag Ullstein, 1954), 144–46.

201. Ibid., 145–53.

202. Joachim Dressel and Manfred Griehl, *Bombers of the Luftwaffe* (London: Arms and Armour, 1994), 71–73.

203. Ibid.

204. Boog, *Die deutsche Luftwaffenführung,* 187.

205. Dressel and Griehl, *Bombers of the Luftwaffe,* 101–5.

206. The He 277 was designed with a conventional four-engine layout, and a few prototypes were built. The He 277 used many of the components of the He 177, and had impressive performance, with none of the He 177's vices. See Green, *Warplanes of the Third Reich,* 359–61.

207. Boog, *Die deutsche Luftwaffenführung,* 185.

208. Richard Suchenwirth, *Command and Leadership in the German Air Force* (Maxwell AFB: USAF Historical Division, 1969), 151.

209. Boog, *Die deutsche Luftwaffenführung,* 100 and 184. See also Wolfgang Dierich, *Kampfgeschwader 55 "Greif"* (Stuttgart: Motorbuch Verlag, 1994), 487–97.

210. Green, *Warplanes of the Third Reich,* 390–97.

211. According to Heft Henschel, Deutsches Museum, Munich.

212. Papers of D. A. Dickey, USAF civilian engineer, Wright Patterson Field, report on Luftwaffe technology (June 1945), USAF Historical Research Agency.

213. Walter Boyne, *Messerschmitt Me 262: Arrow to the Future* (Washington, D.C.: Smithsonian Institution Press, 1980), 18–20.

214. On the inefficiencies of the Nazi aircraft production system, see Willi Boelcke, "Stimulation und Verhalten von Unternehmen der deutschen Luftrüstungsindustrie während der Aufrüstungs-und Kriegsphase," in *Luftkriegführung im Zweiten Weltkreig,* ed. Horst Boog (Herford: E. S. Mittler Verlag, 1993), 81–112.

CONCLUSION

1. Olaf Groehler, *Geshichte des Luftkrieges* (Berlin: Militärverlag der DDR, 1980), 220.

2. Michael Salewski, *Handbuch zur deutschen Militärgeschichte 1648–1939* (Munich: Bernard und Graefe Verlag, 1978), 570.

3. Groehler, *Geshichte des Luftkrieges,* 219.

4. For an exellent overview of the Polish air force and its strategy in September 1939, see Michael Alfred Peszke, "The Forgotten Campaign: Poland's Military Aviation in September 1939," in *The Polish Review* no. 1 (1994): 51–72, esp. 65–72.

5. Herhudt Von Rohden, ed. *Luftkrieg, vol. V: Die Planungen und Vorbereitung des Luftkrieges gegen Polen 1939* (Maxwell AFB, unpublished ms. in the Air University Library, November 1946), Appendix 3.

6. Ibid., 62, 66–67.

7. Wilhelm Speidel, *Die Luftwaffe im Polenfeldzug 1939,* USAF HRA, Karlsruhe Collection, Doc. K 113.106-151, 9–10.

8. Ibid., part II, 26–27.

9. Ibid., 157.

10. An example of the "lessons learned" from the Polish campaign is : Oberkommando des Heeres, *Richtlinien für die Zusammenarbeit Heer-Luftwaffe auf Grund der Erfahrungen im polnischen Feldzüge (Guidelines for Army/Air Force Cooperation in Light of the Experience of the Polish Campaign)* (25 November 1939). In BA/MA H35/88. See also Luftwaffe Staff, "Taktische Erfahrungen Nr. 2: Ausfertigung für Führerstellen" (1939), in RL 2 II/ 280. This document was part of a regular series of lessons-learned pamphlets sent to operational commanders.

11. An example of this is found in Luftwaffe general staff, operations branch, *Richtlinien (Directives) to Luftflotte 2* (October 1939–January 1940), in NARA file T-321, Roll 172.

12. R. J. Overy, "Air Power, Armies and the War in the West, 1940," in *The Harmon Memorial Lectures in Military History* (U.S. Air Force Academy, 1989), 1–24. See esp. 8–10.

13. See Michel Forget, "Die Zusammenarbeit zwischen Luftwaffe und Heer bei den französischen und deutschen Luftstreitkräften im Zweiten Weltkrieg," in *Luftkriegführung im Zweiten Weltkrieg,* ed. Horst Boog (Herford: E. S. Mittler und Sohn, 1993).

14. For a very thorough discussion of this issue, see Karl-Heinz Frieser, *Blitzkrieg-Legende: Der Westfeldzug 1940* (Munich: Oldenbourg Verlag, 1995), 52–65.

15. Ibid., 57.

16. David Griffin, "The Battle of France 1940," *Aerospace Historian* (fall 1974): 144–53. See esp. 147.

17. Alistair Horne, *To Lose a Battle: France 1940* (London: Penguin, 1969), 247.

18. Griffin, "The Battle of France 1940," 147.

19. Volkmar Kühn, *Deutsche Fallschirmjäger im Zweiten Weltkrieg* (Stuttgart: Motorbuch Verlag, 1993), 49–65.

20. Ibid., 38–49.

21. Wilhelm Speidel, *The Campaign for Western Europe, Part 1,* USAF HRA, Karlsruhe Collection, Doc. K113.107-152, 181.

22. The most detailed account of the Sedan Battle of 1940 is found in Robert Doughty, *The Breaking Point* (Hamden, Conn.: Archon, 1990).

23. Alistair Horne, *To Lose a Battle,* 474–75.

24. Wilhelm Speidel, *The Campaign for Western Europe, Part 1,* 171.

25. Alistair Horne, *To Lose a Battle,* 506–7.

26. Ibid., 481–82, 527–28.

27. R. J. Overy, "Air Power, Armies and the War in the West," 13.

28. Wilhelm Speidel, *The Campaign for Western Europe, Part 1,* 156.

29. R. J. Overy, "Air Power, Armies and the War in the West," 13.

30. Alistair Horne, *To Lose a Battle,* 276–77, 285–86.

31. Janusz Piekalkiewicz, *The Air War: 1939–1945* (Poole, Dorset: Blandford Press, 1985), 78.

32. David Griffin, "The Battle of France 1940," 147.

33. Martin Middlebrook and Chris Everitt, *The Bomber Command War Diaries* (London: Penguin, 1985), 43.

34. Ibid.

35. Admiral Raeder, letter to Göring (31 October 1939), in BA/MA RM 7/168.

36. Ibid., 6–7.

37. Bernd Stegemann, "Der Minenkrieg," in *Das Deutsche Reich und der Zweite Weltkrieg, Band 2,* ed. Klaus Maier, et al. (Stuttgart: Deutsche Verlags-Anstalt, 1979), 180–81.

38. Ibid.

39. Ibid.

40. Green, *Warplanes of the Third Reich,* 225-26.

41. Ibid., 226.

42. Derek Wood and Derek Dempster, *The Narrow Margin* (Washington, D.C.: Smithsonian Institution Press, 1990), 29.

43. John Keegan, *The Second World War* (New York: Penguin, 1989), 91.

44. Ibid.

45. See Wood and Dempster, *The Narrow Margin,* 64–71.

46. Alan Stephens, "The True Believers: Air Power Between the Wars," in *The War in the Air,* ed. Alan Stephens (Fairbairn, Australia: Air Power Studies Centre, 1994), 70.

47. Kenneth Werrell, *Archie, Flak, AAA and SAM* (Maxwell AFB: Air University Press, 1988), 42.

48. Richard Muller, *The German Air War in Russia* (Annapolis, Md.: Nautical and Aviation Press, 1992).

49. Ibid., 151–52. Korten was another ex-ground officer with a general staff background who transferred to the Luftwaffe in 1934. He is yet another former army officer-turned-airman who became a believer in strategic bombing.

50. For a good overview to the problems faced by the lack of a tactical air doctrine in the RAF, see Vincent Orange, *Coningham* (Washington, D.C.: Center for Air Force History, 1992), 77–110.

51. Air Marshal Harris, chief of the RAF Bomber Command, believed in early 1944 that strategic bombing alone would win the war. See David Mets, *Master of Airpower: General Carl A. Spaatz* (Novato, Calif.: Presidio Press, 1988), 200.

52. Haywood Hansell, *The Air Plan That Defeated Hitler* (Atlanta: Longino and Porter, 1972), 273–77.

Bibliography

PRIMARY SOURCES

U.S. National Archives, Washington, D.C.

German Army Records, File T-78 (microfilm)

Roll 128	Army General Staff Records
Roll 152	Weapons Office, Description of Foreign Equipment
Roll 153	Weapons Office, File on Weapons Tested and Under Development
Roll 177	Weapons Office, File on Weapons Testing, 1932/1933
Roll 178	Weapons Office, Weapons Development and Supply, 1920s
Roll 179	Weapons Office, Russian-German Cooperation, 1930
Roll 180	Weapons Office/Wehrwirtschaft, Planning Papers on Economic Aspects
Roll 201	Air Office, General Staff, Study on Training and Leadership of Luftwaffe, 1934
Roll 392	Truppenamt Mobilization Appendixes, 1928–1940
Roll 430	Truppenamt T-1/T-2, Mobilization Plans for a Twenty-One-Division Army, 1924–1925
Roll 441	Truppenamt T-1, Army Expansion, 1925

German Air Force, File T-177 (microfilm)

Roll 1	Reichsluftfahrtministerium, Sammung ausländische Aufsätze über Luftkriegsfragen (Übersetzungen), 1 March 1937
Roll 2	Reichs Air Ministry
Roll 9	Army Files
Roll 10	Luftkriegsakademie Curriculum, 1937
Roll 18	Reichs Air Ministry, Weapons Office
Roll 72	Reichs Air Ministry

German Air Force Records, File T-321 (microfilm)

Roll 1	Reichs Air Ministry
Roll 2	Reichs Air Ministry
Roll 4	Reichs Air Ministry

Roll 7	Reichs Air Ministry
Roll 8	Reichs Air Ministry
Roll 9	Reichs Air Ministry
Roll 10	Reichs Air Ministry
Roll 18	Reichs Air Ministry
Roll 68	"Vorläufige Richtlinen für die Ausbildung der Offizieranwärter gemeinsamer Luftkriegschullehrgang," Berlin, 1936
Roll 76	Reichs Air Ministry
Roll 90	Reichs Air Ministry
Roll 104	Reichs Air Ministry
Roll 107	Reichs Air Ministry
Roll 113	Reichs Air Ministry-Flak Inspectorate, 1937–1939
Roll 157	Reichs Air Ministry-Luftschutzgesetze 1934–1937
Roll 163	Reichs Air Ministry
Roll 172	Reichs Air Ministry-Operational Directives, 1939
Roll 176	"Die Entwicklung der deutschen Shlachtfliegerwaffe," 1 December 1944, ed. Major Brücke
Roll 177	Reichs Air Ministry, "Instructions for Fall, Weiss-Invasion of Poland," 1939
Roll 185	Reichs Air Ministry
Roll 242	Reichs Air Ministry—Officer Training
Roll 243	Reichs Air Ministry—Civil Defense
Roll 245	Oberbefehlshaber der Luftwaffe, "Bemerkungen des Oberbefehlshabers der Luftwaffe zur Ausbildung und zu den Übungen in Jahre 1935"
Roll 260	Reichs Air Ministry

German Army Records, File T-405 (microfilm)

Roll 6	German Army Operational Records

Von Seeckt Papers, File M-132 (microfilm)

Roll 1	Military Correspondence, 1915–1926, and Personal Correspondence, 1919–1926
Roll 21	Correspondence Relating to Groener, Versailles, and Other Matters
Roll 25	World War I Battle Maps and Memos on Military Matters, 1919–1926

Bundesarchiv/Militärarchiv Potsdam (formerly Militärarchiv der DDR) BA/MA Potsdam

Documents: R 06 10/4	Inspektionen der Waffenschulen, Late 1920s and Early 1930s

W 10/50097 Kriegsgeschichtliche Forschungsanstalt on 1916–1917 Air Operations Correspondence from Early 1920s
W 10/50099 Kriegsgeschichtliche Forschungsanstalt on German Fourth Army Aviation, 1917, ca. 1928
W 10/50163 Kriegsgeschichtliche Forschungsanstalt, Study of Bombing Effort, 1917–1918, June 1934
W 10/50824 Von Rieben, ed., "Luftschiffen, Flugwaffe, Flak," August 1940
W 10/50845 "Die Luftstreitkräfte des Deutschen Reichs," Kriegsgeschichtliche Abteilung der Luftwaffe, ca. 1945, ed. Dr. Klemp
W 10/50865 Kriegsgeschichtliche Forschungsanstalt, On Aviation of the 6th Army, January 1917–April 1917, ca. 1930
W 10/50868 Kriegsgeschichtliche Forschungsanstalt: Home Air Defense in World War I, February 1939
W 10/52110 German Intelligence Files, 1920s
W 10/52127 German Intelligence
W 10/52139 Reichsarchiv Historical Study, 1930s
W 10/52143 Reichsarchiv Historical Study, ca. 1930

Bundesarchiv/Militärarchiv, Freiburg im Breisgau. BA/MA Freiburg
Archival Files:
N 52/2 General Werner von Blomberg, "Lebenserrinerungen"
N 176 Nachlass, General Karl Drum
N 179 Nachlass, Erhard Milch
N 671/1 Nachlass, Feldmarschal von Richthofen
N 671/2 Nachlass, Feldmarschal von Richthofen
PH 9/3 Aviation Inspectorate-Training, pre-1914
PH 9/14 Aviation Inspectorate-Training, pre-1914
PH 9/47 Files of the Aviation Inspectorate, 1907–1913
PH 9/82 Aviation Inspectorate, 1909-1912: Technical and Organizational Development
PH 9/160 Report on foreign military aviation, 1911
PH 9/161 Report on foreign military aviation, 1912
PH 9/162 Report on foreign aviation, 1912
PH 17/19 Air Service, Tactical Manual for Ground Support, 1918
PH 17/55 Reichsarchiv, Historical Study on American Air Service, 1925
PH 17/96 Air Service Files, 1918
PH 17/98 Air Service, Training Plan for Aircraft in Ground Support, 1918
RH 2/69 Army Commander's Report, 1921
RH 2/70 Army Commander's Report, 1925
RH 2/101 Army Commander's Report, 1923
RH 2/1603 Truppenamt T-3, Report on British Army, 1925

RH 2/1820	Truppenamt T-3, Officers' Report on Foreign Visits, 1923–1927
RH 2/1822	Truppenamt T-3, Officers' Report on Foreign Visits, 1928
RH 2/1823	Truppenamt T-3, Officers' Report on Foreign Visits, 1928
RH 2/2187	Air Organization Office Correspondence File
RH 2/2195	Reichsarchiv Historical Study on Air Tactics, 1918; Assorted Studies and Correspondence, 1926
RH 2/2197	Air Organization Office
RH 2/2198	Air Organization Office, Mobilization Information, Early 1920s
RH 2/2200	Weapons Office, Rearmament Programs
RH 2/2206	Weapons Office, Reports on Foreign Equipment, 1925
RH 2/2207	Air Organization Office, Correspondence, 1919–1921
RH 2/2244	Truppenamt Air Office Luftschutz Übungsreise, 1924
RH 2/2273	Air Organization Office
RH 2/2275	Air Organization Office, Tactical Studies
RH 2/2277	Commander's Report, 1926
RH 2/2279	Truppenamt T-2/L Truppenamt Air Staff Training Plans, 1926
RH 2/2656	Truppenamt T-4 Training, Kurt Hesse manuscript
RH 2/2901	Air Office, Mobilization Information, 1920s; Tactical Studies
RH 2/2963	Army Commander's Report, 1920
RH 2/2987	Army Commander's Report, 1922
RH 8/v906	Waffenamt. Tactical Requirements for the Air Force, 1929–1932
RH 8/v923	Waffenamt Correspondence, 1925–1932
RH 8/v957	Waffenamt, Aircraft Development, 1928
RH 8/v997	Waffenamt, Armaments Program for Army, Air Force, and Navy, June 1930
RH 8/v1366	Waffenamt, Armaments Plans, 1926–1928
RH 8/v3591	Heereswaffenamt, Correspondence Files, late 1920s
RH 8/v3592	Waffenamt, Medical Studies on Aviators, 1928
RH 8/v3593	Luftstreitkräfte (Weapons Office), 1931–1933
RH 8/v3603	Denkschrift on Education of Luftwaffe Officers, 1930–1933
RH 8/v3608	Tactical Requirements, 1930–1932
RH 8/v3610	Technical Requirements for 4-Engine Night Bomber, 1927
RH 8/v3613	Plans for Air Mobilization, 1927–1928
RH 8/v3616	Sturtzflug Versuche
RH 8/v3617	"Grundsätze für Einsatz der Luftsteitkräfte"
RH 8/v3618	Airplane Gas Delivery, 1925–1928
RH 8/v3622	Lipetsk Records, Summer Report of 1929
RH 8/v3624	Bombing Tests, Russia, 1928–1929
RH 8/v3659	Versuchbericht HD 33, 1927
RH 8/v3665	Cooperation with German Air Industry
RH 8/v9916	Waffenamt Correspondence, 1932
RH 12-1/15	Truppenamt T-4, Officer Training, 1920s

RH 12-1/53 Air Organization Office, Includes Tactical Studies, 1920s
RH 12-2/21 Army Commander, Correspondence, 1924-1925
RH 12-2/22 Army Commander, Correspondence with Weapons Office, 1919-1926
RH 12-2/51 Truppenamt T-3, Reports and Correspondence on Foreign Armies
RH 12-2/54 Heeresinspektionen and T-4 Files, Officer Training, 1920s
RH 12-2/94 Army Commander Correspondence, Reports from Inspectorates, 1920-1927
RH 12-2/95 Truppenamt T-4, Wehrkreisprüfung, 1928; Winter Exercises 1928/1929
RH 12-2/101 Reports from Branch Schools, Beginning in 1925
RH 12-2/150 Weapons Office, Reports on Weapons Tests, 1918-1924
RL 2/230 Bericht Wehrmachtmanöver (Luftwaffe) 1937, B and 1
RL 2 II/1 Abteilung 1, General Staff of the Luftwaffe, "Planstudie 1939, Heft 1: Aufmarsch und Kampfanweisungen der Luftwaffe," 7 February 1939
RL 2 II/24 Abteilung 1, Luftwaffe General Staff, "Luftkriegführung gegen England," 22 November 1939
RL 2 II/73 Luftwaffe Chief of Staff, Requirements for Fighter Aircraft, December 1936
RL 2 II/76 Luftwaffe Exercises, Wargames, 1930s
RL 2 II/77 Luftwaffe Exercises, Wargames, 1930s
RL 2 II/78 Luftwaffe Exercises, Wargames, 1930s
RL 2 II/83 Luftwaffe Gereralstab Records
RL 2 II/101 Lecture by General Kesselring, 1939
RL 2 II/141 Ausbildung Taktik: Jagdflieger, 1934
RL 2 II/154 Luftwaffe General Staff, "Verlauf der Wehrmachtmanövers, 1937," Band 1, 2, 3, and 4
RL 2 II/159 Luftwaffe General Staff 3rd Section, Bericht Wehrmachtmanöver (Luftwaffe) Sonderdruck zivile Luftschutz, 1 June 1937
RL 2 II/160 Luftwaffe Exercises, Wargames, 1930s. Luftwaffe General Staff, "Planspiel: Krieg gegen Frankreich, Polen, Belgien," October 1935
RL 2 II/163 Luftwaffe General Staff, Ausbildung von Fallschirmtruppen, 1937
RL 2 II/164 General Staff of the Luftwaffe, Training Section, 1935-1937 Training Plans
Luftwaffe General Staff, Ausbildung, 1935-1937
RL 2 II/165 Reichsluftministerium, Abteilung 1, Luftwaffe General Staff, "Generalstabsreise der Luftwaffe 1939," 24 April 1939
RL 2 II/280 "Taktik Luftwaffe: Taktischen Erfahrung NR 2," ca. late 1939

RL 2 II/283	Fighter Operations Manual, ca. 1939
RL 2 II/364	"Taktik Luftwaffe, Einsatz der Luftstreitkräfte," study, ca. 1931
RL 2 II/835	Luftwaffe General Staff, 3rd Section, Bericht Wehrmachtmanöver (Luftwaffe) 1937 Anlagen, Teil II, Teil III
RL 4/15	Luftkreiskommando 5, Training Program, winter 1937–1938
RL 4/16	Luftwaffe General Staff, Abt. 3, Training Plans, 1938
RL 4/18	Reichsluftministerium, "Übungsbestimmungen der Luftwaffe für die Teilnahme an der Mobilisation-Übungen der motorisierte Verbände," 1939
RL 4/79	General der Heeresflieger, Development of Training and Recon Planes, 1929–1932
RL 4/80	General Lieth-Thomsen, Denkschrift on World War I Experience, November 1931
RL 4/81	Reichsluftministerium, Correspondence Files, 1933–1934
RL 4/231	Inspektion der Jagd und Sturzkampfflieger Organisation, May 1936
RL 4/237	Fliegerinspektion 3, Merkblatt, "Über die Verlegung von Jagdverbände auf Feldflugplätze," 10 September 1936
RL 4/313	Civil Defense Studies, 1931–1933
RL 4/316	Reichsluftministerium, Civil Defense Organization, 1934
RL 4/317	Reichsluftministerium, Civil Defense Organization, 1936
RL 7/4	Luftflotte 2, Discussion of War Plans, May 1939
RL 7/41	Luftflotte 2, "Beiheft für die Blaue Partei: Manöver der Luftflotte 2," 1939
RL 7/42	Luftflottenkommando 2, "Schlussbesprechung der Planspiels 1939," 13 May 1939
RL 7/43	Luftwaffekommando 2, "Schlussbesprechung der Planspiels 1939," 13 May 1939
RL 7/57	Condor Legion Records
RL 7/155	Luftwaffe Gruppenkommando 3, "Bericht über die Reise für Führer obere Dienststellen," 23 May 1938
RL 7/156	Fliegerdivision 5, "Bemerkungen, Planspielen, Übungen, Manöver," 25 April 1939
RL 7/158	Luftflotte 3, Report on Army General Staff Tour 1939, May 1939
RL 7/160	General Staff of the Luftwaffe, "Generalstabsreise der Luftwaffe," 29 June 1939
RL 7/162	Luftflottenkommando 3, "Kriegsspiel Luftflotte 3," 17 August 1939
RL 7/169	Luftflottenkommando 3, "Besprechung beim Lehrstab für Heerestaktik: Manöver der Schnellen Truppen," 23 June 1939

RL 7/171	Luftflottenkommando 3, "Allgemeine Übungsbestimmungen für der Manöver Luftflotte 3 in 1939," 17 July 1939
RL 7/174	Luftflottenkommando 3, "Manöver der Luftflotte 3 in 1939; Lage Rot," 1939
RL 33	Inspectorate of Paratroops, on Unit Formation
RL 33/97	Inspectorate of Paratroops
RL 33/113	Fourth Paratroop Regiment, Movement to Austria, 1938
RL 35/4	Legion Kondor, Lagebericht, 1938
RL 35/5	Legion Kondor, Lagebericht, 1938
RL 35/6	Legion Kondor, Lagebericht, 1938
RM 7/1	Reichsmarine, Tagesbuch, Operations in Spain 1936–1937
RM 7/168	Reichsmarine, Staff Correspondence, 1939

Personnel Files

Altrock, Konstantin von
Cochenhausen, Friedrich von
Deichmann, Paul
Drum, Karl
Felmy, Helmuth
Haehnelt, Wilhelm
Jeschonnek, Hans
Knauss, Robert
Lieth-Thomsen, Hermann von der
Plocher, Hermann
Richthofen, Wolfram von
Schwabedissen, Walter
Sperrle, Hugo
Student, Kurt
Stumpf, Hans-Jürgen
Udet, Ernst
Wever, Walter
Wilberg, Helmuth
Wimmer, Wilhelm

Manuscripts

Crocker, Major Harrison. *The Use of Aviation in the Spanish War.* USAF HRA, Doc. 168.7045-34.

Dickey, D. A., USAAF. *Report on the State of the Luftwaffe's Research Effort, June–July 1945.* USAF HRA.

Drum, Karl (General der Flieger). *Die deutsche Luftwaffe im Spanischen Bürgerkrieg: 1936–1939.* USAF HRA, Karlsruhe Collection, Doc. K113.106-150.

Rohden, Hans-Detlef von. *Die deutsche Luftrüstung.* Maxwell AFB, Ala.: Air University Library, ca. 1950.

———. *Die Luftwaffe im Polenfeldzug 1939.* USAF HRA, Karlsruhe Collection.

———. *Entwicklung und Planung in der deutschen Luftwaffe.* Maxwell AFB, Ala.: Air University Library, ca. 1950.

———. *Luftkrieg Heft 5: Die Planungen und Vorbereitungen des Luftkrieges gegen Polen 1939.* Maxwell AFB, Ala.: Air University Library.

Smith, Truman. *The Papers of Truman Smith.* Carlisle Barracks, Pa.: U.S. Army War College Library.

Speidel, Wilhelm. *The Campaign for Western Europe, Parts I, II.* USAF HRA, Karlsruhe Collection.

Deutsches Museum, Munich

Special Collections—Records of Aircraft Manufacturers

Heft Henschel

Heft Heinkel

Heft Dornier

Heft Focke Wulf

German Official Documents

Deutschland und der spanischen Bürgerkrieg 1936–1939. Akten zur Deutschen Auswärtigen Politik 1918–1945. Series D (1933–1945), Vol. 3.

Französische Truppenführung. *Vorschrift für die taktische Verwendung der grossen Verbände.* Berlin: Verlag Offene Worte, 1937.

Generalstab der Luftwaffe. *Die Luftwaffe: Militärwissenschaftliche Aufsatzsammlung.* Vol. 2, no. 3. 31 Dec. 1937.

Generalstab des Heeres. "Die französischen Besfestigungen." *Grosses Orientierungsheft Frankreich.* 1935/36, 1 August 1936, chapter 14.

Generalstab des Heeres. *Landschaftsbilder aus den Niederlanden.* Berlin, 1939.

Generalstab des Heeres. *Militärgeographisches Überblick über die Niederlanden.* 1939.

Heeresdienstvorschrift 52. Kriegsakademie Vorschrift. 14 May 1938.

Heeresdienstvorschrift 81/2. Besichtigungsbemerkungen 1936. N.p Berlin: Oberbefehlshaber des Heeres, January 1937.

Heeresdienstvorschrift 124/1. Bildheft: Landesbefestigung der Tschechoslowakei. N.p. Generalstab, 10. Abt., 1938.

Heeresdienstvorschrift 300. *Truppenführung.* Part 1 (1933); Part 2 (1934).

Heeresdienstvorschrift 467. *Ausbildungvorschrift für Fahrtruppen.* Berlin: High Command, 1923.

Heeresdienstvorschrift 487. Führung und Gefecht der verbundenen Waffen. Berlin: Verlag Offene Worte, 1921, 1923, 1925.

Kommandierende General der Luftstreitkräfte. *The Infantry Aircraft and the Infantry*

Balloon [Translation of a captured German document dated September 1917]. U.S. Army War College translation, February 1918.

Kommandierende General der Luftstreitkräfte. *Utilization and Role of Artillery Aviators in Trench Warfare.* Early 1917. Translation by U.S. Army War College, July 1917.

Kommandierender General der Luftstreitkräfte. *Weisungen für den Einsatz und die Verwendung von Fliegerverbänden innerhalb einer Armee.* Generalstab des Feldheeres, May 1917.

Kommandierende General der Luftstreitkräfte. *Weisungen für die Einsatz und die Verwendung von Fliegerverbänden innerhalb einer Armee.* May 1917.

Kriegsministerium. *Anhaltspunkte für den Unterricht bei der Truppe über Luftfahrzeuge und deren Bekämpfung.* Berlin: Reichsdruckerei, March 1913.

Luftwaffedienstvorschrift 2/3, Der Aufklärungsflieger (Land), Luftaufklärung für die Kriegführung des Heeres. Berlin, 1938.

Luftwaffedienstvorschrift 2/2. Der Aufklärungsflieger (Land) Teil II, Luftaufklärung für den Luftkrieg. Berlin, 1938.

Luftwaffedienstvorschrift 7, Richtlinien für die Ausbildung in der Luftwaffe. Part 6 (Offizierausbildung), 1937.

Luftwaffedienstvorschrift 10, Der Kampfflugzeug, 1934.

Luftwaffedienstvorschrift 21, Die Flugzeugführerausbildung (land). Berlin, 1937.

Luftwaffedienstvorschrift 90, Die Versorgung der Luftwaffe im Kriege. 1938.

Luftwaffedienstvorschrift 410, Luftschutz in Unterkünften, Anstalten und Anlagen der Wehrmacht. 1937.

Oberkommando der Wehrmacht. *Anlagen zum Bericht über die Wehrmachtmanöver 1937.* Berlin, 1938.

Reichsarchiv. *Die Organisation des deutschen Heeres im Weltkrieg,* ed. Hermann Cron. Berlin: E. Mittler und Sohn, 1923.

Reichsluftministerium. *Merkblatt über die Führung von Kampfverbänden,* 1936.

Reichsluftministerium. *Vorläufige Offiziergänzungsbestimmungen der Luftwaffe,* 1936.

Reichsluftministerium. *Vorlaufige Ortsanweisung für den Luftschutz der Zivilbevölkerung.* Abschnitt VII, Luftschutzsanitätsdienst, 1936.

Reichsminister der Luftfahrt. *Merkblätter über Flakartillerie,* 1935.

Truppenamt (Luft). *Richtlinien für die Führung des operativen Luftkrieges,* 1926.

Truppenamt (Luft). *Studie eines Offizers über die Fliegerwaffe und ihre Verwendung,* ca. 1925.

Urkunden der Obersten Heeresleitung, ed. Erich von Ludendorff. Berlin: E. Mittler und Sohn, 1920.

French Official Documents

Ministère de la Defense. *Instruction sur l'Emploi Tactique des grandes unités.* 1936.

Ministère de l'Air. *Instruction sur l'Emploi Tactique des grandes unités aériennes.* 31 March 1937.

SECONDARY SOURCES

Books and Articles Published before World War II

Adler, Hermann. *Ein Buch von der neuen Luftwaffe.* Stuttgart: Franckh'sche Verlagshandlung, 1938.
Alexander, Axel. *Die Schlacht über Berlin.* Berlin: Verlag Offene Worte, 1933.
Armengaud, General. "La Guerre d'Espagne: La Combinaison des forces de l'air avec les forces navales et avec l'armeé de terre." *Revue Militaire Générale* (March 1938): 259–82.
——. "La Guerre d'Espagne: Technique et Tactique des forces de l'air." *Revue Militaire Générale* (April 1938): 413–19.
Arnold, General Hap. "Air Lessons from Current Wars." *U.S. Air Services* (May 1938).
Balck, Lt. Gen. a.D. W. von. *Entwicklung der Taktik im Weltkrieg.* Berlin: Verlag R. Eisenschmidt, 1922.
Bartz, Major. "Kriegsflugzeuge, ihre Aufgaben und Leistungen." *Militärwissenschaftliche Rundschau* 1 (1936): 204–29.
Bley, Wulf and Richard Schulz. *Luftwarmeen Ringsum.* Berlin: Verlag Deutsche Kultur-Wacht, 1935.
Bodenschatz, Karl. *Jagd in Flanderns Himmel.* Munich: Verlag Knorr und Hirth, 1935.
Bongartz, Heinz. *Luftmacht Deutschland.* Essen: Essener Verlagsanstalt, 1939.
Bülow, Freiherr von. "Die Luftverteidigung des britischen Weltreiches." *Militärwissenschaftliche Rundschau* 3 (1936): 392–422.
——. *Geschichte der Luftwaffe.* Frankfurt a.M.: Verlag Moritz Diesterweg, 1934.
——. "Luftpolitik und Luftkriegführung im Stillen Ozean." Parts I and II. *Militärwissenschaftliche Rundschau* 5 (1937): 690–706 and 6 (1937): 814–33.
Challener, Richard D., ed. *United States Military Intelligence.* Vols. 23–26. New York: Garland, 1978.
Cochenhausen, Friedrich von. "Was muss der Generalstabsoffizier der Luftwaffe von der Kriegsführung auf der Erde wissen?" *Die Luftwaffe: Militärwissenschaftliche Aufsatzsammlung* 4 (1936): 5–10.
Cot, Pierre. *L'Armeé de L'air.* Paris: Éditions Bernard Grasset, 1938.
Deutsche Kämpfen in Spanien. Berlin: Wilhelm Limpert Verlag, 1939.
Deutsches Reichsarchiv. *Der Weltkrieg, 1914 bis 1918.* 14 vols. Berlin: E. Mittler und Sohn, 1925–1940.
Douhet, Giulio. *The Command of the Air.* New York: Arno Press, 1972 (reprint of 1927 revised edition).
Eichelbaum, Dr., ed. *Jahrbuch der deutschen Luftwaffe 1939.* Leipzig: Verlag von Breitkopf und Hörtel, 1939.
Feuchter, Georg. *Flieger als Hilswaffe.* Potsdam: Ludwig Boggenreiter Verlag, 1939.
——. *Probleme des Luftkrieges.* Potsdam: Ludwig Boggenreiter Verlag, 1939.

Franke, Maj. Gen. Hermann. *Handbuch der neuzeitlichen Wehrwissenschaften.* Vol. 2: *Die Luftwaffe.* Berlin: Verlag von Walter de Gruyter, 1939.

Fuller, J. F. C. *On Future Warfare.* London: Sifton Press, 1928.

——. *The Reformation of War.* New York: Dutton, 1923.

Gehrts, Erwin. "Gedanken zum operativen Luftkrieg. Eine Studie." *Die Luftwaffe* 2 (1937): 16–39.

Grey, C. G. *Jane's All the World's Aircraft: 1919.* London: David and Charles, 1969 (reprint of 1919 edition).

Guderian, Heinz. *Achtung-Panzer!* Stuttgart: Union Deutsche Verlagsgesellschaft, 1937.

Hansen, Admiral. "Über Seetaktik: Ein Blick auf ihre Entwicklung und Zukunft." Part 2. *Militärwissenschaftliche Rundschau* 6 (1936): 794–813.

Harten, Leutnant von. "Die Luftaufklärung." *Militärwissenschaftliche Rundschau* 6 (1936): 734–45 and 1 (1937): 115–26.

Hearne, R. P. *Aerial Warfare.* London: John Lane, 1909.

Hirschauer, L. and C. H. Dolphus, eds. *L'Anneé Aéronautique 1928–1929.* Paris: Dunoud, 1929.

Hitler, Adolf. *Mein Kampf.* New York: Reynal and Hitchcock, 1940.

Hoeppner, Gen. der Kavallerie Ernst. *Deutschlands Krieg in der Luft. Ein Rückblick auf der Entwicklung und die Leistungen unserer Heeres-Luftstreitkräfte im Weltkriege.* Koehler und Amelang Verlag, 1921.

Jaenecke, Oberst. "Lehren des spanischen Bürgerkrieges." In *Jahrbuch des deutschen Heeren.* Leipzig: Verlag von Breitkopf und Hörtel, 1940.

Jones, H. A. *The War in the Air.* Oxford: Clarendon Press. Vol. IV (1934), Vol. V (1935), Vol. VI (1937).

Junger, Ernst, ed. *Luftfahrt ist Not!* Leipzig: Deutschen Luftfahrtverbandes, 1931.

Justrow, Oberstleutnant Karl. *Der technische Krieg.* Berlin: Verlag Wehrfront Rudolf Klaasen, 1938.

Kenney, George. "The Airplane in Modern Warfare." *U.S. Air Services* (July 1938): 17–21.

Knauss, Robert (under pseudonym Major Holders). *Luftkrieg 1936: Die Zertrümmerung von Paris.* Berlin: Verlag Tradition Wilhelm Kolk, 1932.

Knipfer, E. H., ed. *Die Zivile Luftschutz.* Berlin: Verlagsanstalt Otto Stollberg, 1937.

Krauser, Hauptmann Friedrich Ritter von, "Schlacht und Nachtflüge in Flandern 1917." In *In der Luft Unbesiegt,* ed. Georg Neumann, 79–91. Munich: J. F. Lehmanns Verlag, 1923.

Kriegswissenschaftliche Abteilung der Luftwaffe. *Die technische Entwicklung der Flakwaffe bis zum Ende des Weltkrieges,* Vol. V. Berlin: E. Mittler und Sohn, 1942.

Kürbs, Dr., ed. *Jahrbuch der deutschen Luftwaffe 1936.* Leipzig: Verlag von Breitkopf und Hörtel, 1937.

——. *Jahrbuch der deutschen Luftwaffe 1937.* Leipzig: Verlag von Breitkopf und Hörtel, 1937.

Lanza, Colonel Conrad. "Open Warfare." *Field Artillery Journal* (Nov./Dec. 1939): 538–40.

Liddell Hart, Basil. *Paris, The Future of War.* London: K. Paul, Trench, Trubner and Co., 1925.

——. *The Real War, 1914–1918.* Boston: Little, Brown, 1930.

——. *The Remaking of Modern Armies.* Boston: Little, Brown, 1928.

Loewenstern, Baron Elard von. *Der Frontflieger.* Berlin: Bernard und Graefe Verlag, 1937.

Ludendorff, Gen. Erich von. *Der Totale Krieg.* Munich: Ludendorffs Verlag, 1935.

——. *The Coming War.* London: Faber and Faber, 1931.

——. *The Nation at War [Der Totale Krieg].* London: Hutchinson, 1936.

Mackin, Major Robert. "Airplanes Can Be Stopped." *The Coast Artillery Journal* (Sept./Oct. 1937).

Maginel, General. "L'Intervention de l'aviation dans la lutte terrestre." *Revue Militaire Générale* (October 1938): 505–29.

McCudden, James. *Flying Fury.* London: Aviation Book Club, 1930.

Mecozzi, Major Amadeo. "Il volo Rasente e le sue Possibilita Tattiche." *Rivista Aeronautica* (June 1926): 53–69.

——. "La grandi unità Aviatori." *Rivista Aeronautica* (March 1929): 533–76.

Mehler, Colonel. *Der Soldat der Zukunft.* Berlin: Verlag Offene Worte, 1931.

Metzner, Kapitänleutnant. "Die Luftwaffe im Seekrieg." *Militärwissenschaftliche Rundschau* 4 (1936): 473–92.

Miksche, Ferdinand Otto. *Attack: A Study of Blitzkrieg Tactics.* New York: Random House, 1942.

Mitchell, William. *Memoirs of World War I.* New York: Random House, 1960; originally published in *Liberty Magazine* in 1926.

Neumann, Georg. *Die Deutschen Luftstreitkräfte im Weltkriege.* Berlin: E. Mittler Verlag, 1921

Neumann, Georg, ed. *In der Luft Unbesiegt.* Munich: J. F. Lehmanns Verlag, 1923.

Nordhoff, Charles, and James Norman Hall. *Falcons of France.* N.Y.: Little, Brown and Co., 1929.

Orlovius, Heinz, ed. *Die Deutsche Luftfahrt: Jahrbuch 1937.* Frankfurt a.M: Verlag Fritz Knapp, 1937.

——, ed. *Die Deutsche Luftfahrt: Jahrbuch 1938.* Munich: Verlag Fritz Knapp, 1938.

Rabenau, Friedrich von. *Seeckt: Aus seinem Leben, 1918–1936.* Leipzig: Hase-Koehler Verlag, 1941.

Ritter, Capt. Hans. *Der Luftkrieg.* Berlin: F. Koehler Verlag, 1926.

——. *Der Zukunftskrieg und seine Waffen.* Leipzig: F. Koehler Verlag, 1924.

Roeingh, Rolf. *Wegbereiter der Luftfahrt.* Berlin: Deutscher Archiv-Verlag, 1938.

Rohden, Herhudt von. "Gedanken zum Luftkrieg." *Deutsche Luftwacht* 6 (1939): 2–13.

——. *Vom Luftkrieg. Gedanken über Führung und Einsatz moderner Luftwaffe.* Berlin: E. Mittler und Sohn, 1938.

——. "Vom Wesen des Luftkrieges." In *Jahrbuch der deutschen Luftwaffe 1938,* 151–64. Leipzig: Verlag von Breitkopf und Hörtel, 1938.

Röhrig, Georg. *Die Ziele selbständiger Luftangriffe.* Königsberg: Ost-Europa Verlag, 1938.

Rougeron, Camille. *Das Bombenflugwesen.* Berlin: Rowohlt Verlag, 1938.

Schoszberger, Hans. *Bautechnischer Luftschutz.* Berlin: Bauwelt Verlag, 1934.

Schrott, Col. Ludwig. *Die Vorbereitung auf der Wehrkreisprüfung.* Berlin: E. Mittler und Sohn, 1929.

Schwabedissen, Oberstleutnant Walter. *Der Kampffliegerverband.* Berlin: Bernard und Graefe Verlag, 1937.

Schwarte, Max. *Der grosse Krieg, 1914–1918,* Vols. 1–10. Berlin: E. Mittler und Sohn, 1922–1923.

——. *Die militärischen Lehren des grossen Krieges.* Berlin: Verlag Offene Worte, 1920.

——. *Die Technik in Zukunftskriege.* Berlin: Verlag Offene Worte, 1923.

——. *Kriegslehren im Beispiel aus dem Weltkrieg.* Berlin: Verlag Offene Worte, 1925.

Seeckt, Hans von. *Aus Meinem Leben, 1866–1917,* ed. Lt. Gen. Friedrich von Rabenau. Leipzig: Hase-Kohler-Verlag, 1938.

——. *Die Reichswehr.* Leipzig: R. Kittler Verlag, 1933.

——. *Gedanken eines Soldaten.* Berlin: Verlag für Kulturpolitik, 1928

——. *Thoughts of a Soldier.* Trans. Gilbert Waterhouse. London: Ernest Benn, 1930.

Siebert, Major. *Atlas zu F.u.G.I.: Ein Anschauungs-Lehrbuch.* Berlin: Verlag Offene Worte, 1929.

Slessor, John. *Air Power and Armies.* London: Oxford University Press, 1936.

Soldan, Georg. *Der Mensch und der Schlacht der Zukunft.* Oldenburg: Gerhard Stalling, 1925.

Speier, Hans. "Ludendorff: The German Concept of Total War." In *Makers of Modern Strategy,* ed. Edward Meade Earle, 306–21. Princeton, N.J.: Princeton University Press, 1943.

Supf, Peter. *Das Buch der deutschen Fluggeschichte.* Vols. I and II. Berlin: Verlagsanstalt Hermann Klemm, 1935.

Thomsen, Lt. Gen. Hermann. "Die Luftwaffe vor und im Weltkriege." In *Die Deutsche Wehrmacht,* ed. General Georg Wetzell, 487–522. Berlin: E. Mittler und Sohn, 1939.

Triandafrillov, V. K. *The Nature of the Operations of Modern Armies.* Trans. Willams Buhrans. London: Frank Cass, 1994; originally published in Russian in 1929.

Vauthier, Lieutenant Colonel P. *La Danger Aerienne de Pais.* Paris: Bérgère-Levrault, 1930.

——. *La Doctrine de Guerre de Général Douhet.* Paris: Bérgère-Levrault, 1934.

Wachenfeld, Gen. der Flieger Edmund. "Die Luftwaffe nach dem Weltkriege." In *Die Deutsche Wehrmacht,* ed. Gen. Georg Wetzell, 528–57. Berlin: E. Mittler und Sohn, 1938.

Warner, Edward. "Douhet, Mitchell, Seversky: Theories of Air Warfare." In *Makers of*

Modern Strategy, ed. Edward Earle, 485–503. Princeton, N.J.: Princeton University Press, 1943.

Wells, H. G. *The War in the Air.* London: George Bell and Sons, 1908.

Wiesinger, General der Infanterie. "Der Bürgerkrieg in Spanien." In *Militärwissenschaftliche Mitteilungen.* All issues (1937–1938).

Wittlesey, Derwent. "Haushofer: The Geopoliticians." In *Makers of Modern Strategy,* ed. Edward Meade Earle, 388–414. Princeton, N.J.: Princeton University Press, 1943.

Personal Interviews

Freiherr Götz von Richthofen, son of Field Marshal Wolfram von Richthofen, 21 June 1992 and 4 September 1993, Aumühle, Germany.

Dr. Professor Heinrich von Sietencron, stepson of General der Flieger Robert Knauss, 11 September 1993, Tübingen, Germany.

Dr. Professor Manfred Siess and Frau Wietrand Siess, daughter and son-in-law of General der Flieger Robert Knauss, 11 September 1993, Tübingen, Germany.

Diplom Ingineur Hans-Joachim Wilberg, son of General der Flieger Helmuth Wilberg, 19 June 1992 and 9 September 1993, Bonn, Germany.

Books and Articles Published after World War II

Abendroth, Hans Henning. "Guernica: Ein fragwürdiges Symbol." *Militärgeschichtliche Mitteilungen* 1 (1987): 111–26.

Absolom, Rudolf, ed. *Die Wehrmacht im Dritten Reich,* Vol. 1. Boppard: Harald Boldt Verlag, 1969.

Adamthwaithe, Adam. *France and the Coming of the Second World War.* London: Frank Cass, 1977.

Allward, Morris. *An Illustrated History of Seaplanes and Flying Boats.* New York: Dorset Press, 1981.

Angelucci, Enzo. *The Rand McNally Encyclopedia of Military Aircraft 1914–1980.* New York: Military Press, 1981.

Aznar, Manuel. *Historia Militar de la Guerra de España,* Vol. 1. Madrid: Editoria Nacional, 1958.

Barclay, Glen. *The Rise and Fall of the New Roman Empire.* London: Sidgwick and Jackson, 1973.

Barnett, Coreeli, ed. *Hitler's Generals.* New York: Grove Weidenfeld, 1989.

Baumbach, Werner. *The Life and Death of the Luftwaffe.* New York: Ballentine, 1967.

Bennett, Edward. *German Rearmament and the West, 1932–1933.* Princeton, N.J.: Princeton University Press, 1979.

Birkenfeld, W. *Geschichte der deutschen Wehr-und Rüstungswirtschaft, 1918–1945.* Boppard am Rhein: Harald Boldt Verlag, 1966.

Boelcke, Willi. "Stimulation and Attitude of the German Aircraft Industry During Rearmament and War." In *The Conduct of the Air War in the Second World War,* ed. Horst Boog, 55–84. New York: Berg, 1992.

———. "Stimulation und Verhalten von Unternehmen der deutschen Luftrüstungsindustrie während der Aufrüstungs und Kriegsphase." In *Luftkriegführung im Zweiten Weltkrieg,* ed. Horst Boog. Herford: E. S. Mittler, 1993.

Boog, Horst. *Die deutsche Luftwaffenführung 1935–1945.* Stuttgart: Deutsche Verlags-Anstalt, 1982.

———. "Die Luftverteidigung in der deutschen Luftkriegsdoktrin und der Aufbau der deutschen Luftverteidigung im Frieden." In *Das Deutsche Reich und der Zweite Weltkrieg,* Band 6, ed. Militärgeschichtliches Forschungsamt. Stuttgart: Deutsche Verlags-Anstalt, 1990.

———. "Higher Command and Leadership in the German Luftwaffe, 1935–1945." In *Airpower and Warfare,* ed. Alfred Hurley, 128–58. Washington, D.C.: USAF Office of History, 1979.

———. "The Luftwaffe and Indiscriminate Bombing up to 1942." In *The Conduct of the Air War in the Second World War,* ed. Horst Boog, 373–404. New York: Berg, 1992.

———. "Luftwaffe und unterschiedloser Bombenkrieg bis 1942." In *Luftkriegführung im Zweiten Weltkrieg,* ed. Horst Boog, 435–68. Herford: E. S. Mittler Verlag, 1993.

Boog, Horst, and Jürgen Förster. *Der Angriff auf der Sowjetunion. Das deutsche Reich und der Zweite Weltkrieg,* Band 4. Stuttgart: Deutsche Verlags-Anstalt, 1983.

Boyne, Walter. *Messerschmitt Me 262: Arrow to the Future.* Washington, D.C.: Smithsonian Institution Press, 1980.

Bremer, Wulf, and Hans Dollinger. *Die deutsche Reichswehr.* Frankfurt a.M.: Bernard und Graefe Verlag, 1972.

Brooks, Peter. *The Modern Airliner: Its Origins and Development.* London: Putnam Press, 1961.

Brown, Eric. *Wings of the Luftwaffe.* Novato, Calif.: Presidio Press, 1987.

Buffotot, P. "La perception du Réarmament Allemand par les organismes renseignements françaises de 1936 à 1939." *Revue Historique des Armeés* 3 (1979): 173–84.

Bulloten, Burnett. *The Spanish Civil War: Revolution and Counterrevolution.* Chapel Hill: University of North Carolina Press, 1991.

Burdick, Charles. "Die deutschen militärischen Planungen gegenüber Frankreich, 1933–1938." *Wehrwissenschaftliche Rundschau* 6, 12 (1956): 678–81.

Cannistraro, Philip, ed. *Historical Dictionary of Fascist Italy.* Westport, Conn.: Greenwood Press, 1982.

Citino, Robert. *The Evolution of Blitzkrieg Tactics: Germany Defends Itself Against Poland, 1918–1933.* Westport, Conn.: Greenwood Press, 1987.

Cooper, Mathew. *The German Air Force, 1922–1945: An Anatomy of Failure.* London: Jane's, 1981.

Corum, James. "From Biplanes to Blitzkrieg: The Development of German Air Doctrine Between the Wars." *War in History* 3, 1 (1996): 85–101.

———. "The Luftwaffe and the Coalition Air War in Spain, 1936–1939." *Journal of Strategic Studies* March (1995): 68–90.

———. "The Luftwaffe's Army Support Doctrine, 1918-1941." *Journal of Military History* January (1995): 53–76.

———. "The Old Eagle as Phoenix: The Luftstreitkräfte Creates an Operational Air Doctrine 1919–1920." *Air Power History* (spring 1992): 13–21.

———. *The Roots of Blitzkrieg: Hans von Seeckt and German Military Reform.* Lawrence: University Press of Kansas, 1992.

Coverdale, John. *Italian Intervention in the Spanish Civil War.* Princeton, N.J.: Princeton University Press, 1975.

Craig, Gordon. *The Politics of the Prussian Army, 1640–1945.* Oxford: Clarendon Press, 1955.

Crane, Conrad. *Bombs, Cities and Civilians: Airpower Strategy in World War II.* Lawrence: University Press of Kansas, 1993.

Craven, Wesley, and James Cate. *The Army Air Forces in World War II.* Vols. 1–7. University of Chicago Press, 1948.

Creveld, Martin van. *Fighting Power.* Westport, Conn: Greenwood Press, 1982.

Cross, Robin. *The Bombers.* New York: Macmillan, 1987.

Deichmann, P. *German Air Force Operations in Support of the Army.* (USAF Historical Study 163.) Maxwell Air Force Base, Ala.: Air University Press, 1962.

Deist, Wilhelm et al. *The Build-up of German Aggression. Germany and the Second World War,* Vol. 1. Oxford: Clarendon Press, 1990.

Devereaux, Tony. *Messenger Gods of Battle.* London: Brassey's, 1991.

Dierich, Wolfgang. *Kampfgeschwader 55 "Greif."* Stuttgart: Motorbuch Verlag, 1994.

Divine, David. *The Broken Wing: A Study in the British Exercise of Air Power.* London: Hutchinson, 1966.

Doughty, Robert. *The Breaking Point.* Hamden, Conn.: Archon, 1990.

Dressel, Joachim, and Manfred Greihl. *Bombers of the Luftwaffe.* London: Arms and Armour Press, 1994.

Dülffer, Jost. "Aufrüstung zur Weltmacht: Die deutsche Marinepolitik 1919–1941." *Revue Internationale d'Histoire Militair* 73 (1991): 101–18.

Dupuy, Trevor N. *A Genius for War: The German Army and the General Staff, 1807–1945.* Englewood Cliffs, N.J.: Prentice-Hall, 1977.

———. *The Evolution of Weapons and Warfare.* New York: Da Capo Press, 1984.

Erfurth, Waldemar. *Die Geschichte des deutschen Generalstabes von 1918 bis 1945,* 2nd ed. Göttingen: Masterschmidt Verlag, 1960

Erickson, John. *The Soviet High Command: A Military-Political History, 1918–1941.* Boulder, Colo.: Westview Press, 1984.

Estado Mayor del Ejercito. *Historia Militar de la Guerra de España,* Vol 3. Madrid: Altimira S. A., 1963.

Façon, Patrick. "Douhet et sa Doctrine à Travers la Literature Militaire et Aéronautique Française de l'Entre Deux Guerres: Étude de Perception." In *La Figura et l'Opera de Giulio Douhet,* eds. Caserte-Pozzuoli. Rome: Società di Historia Patria, 1988.

Finney, Robert. *History of the Air Corps Tactical School 1920–1940.* Washington, D.C.: Center for Air Force History, 1992.

Forget, Michel. "Die Zusammenarbeit zwischen Luftwaffe und Heer bei den französischen und deutschen Luftstreitkräfte im Zweiten Weltkrieg." In *Luftkriegführung im Zweiten Weltkrieg,* ed. Horst Boog, 479-526. Herford: E. S. Mittler Verlag, 1993.

Franks, Norman. *Aircraft Versus Aircraft.* New York: Crescent, 1986.

Fredette, Raymond. *The Sky on Fire: The First Battle of Britain, 1917-1918, and the Birth of the Royal Air Force.* New York: Holt, Rinehart and Winston, 1966.

Frieser, Karl-Heinz. *Blitzkrieg-Legende: Der Westfeldzug 1940.* Munich: Oldenbourg Verlag, 1995.

Fritzsche, Peter. "Machine Dreams: Airmindedness and the Reinvention of Germany." *American Historical Review* June (1993): 685–709.

———. *A Nation of Fliers: German Aviation and the Popular Imagination.* Cambridge: Harvard University Press, 1992

Futrell, Robert. *Ideas, Concepts, Doctrine: Basic Thinking in the United States Air Force, 1907-1960,* Vol. 1. Maxwell Air Force Base, Ala.: Air University Press, 1989.

Geyer, Michael. "German Strategy in the Age of Machine Warfare, 1914–1945." In *Makers of Modern Strategy,* ed. P. Paret, 527–97. Princeton, N.J.: Princeton University Press, 1986.

Glanz, David. *A History of Soviet Airborne Forces.* London: Frank Cass, 1994.

Green, William. *Warplanes of the Third Reich.* New York: Galahad, 1990.

Greenhous, Brereton. "Evolution of a Close Ground-Support Role for Aircraft in World War I." *Military Affairs* 39 (1975): 22–28.

Greer, Thomas. "Air Arm Doctrinal Roots, 1917-1918." *Military Affairs* 20 (1956): 202–16.

———. *The Development of Air Doctrine in the Army Air Arm, 1917-1941.* (USAF Historical Study 89.) Maxwell Air Force Base, Ala.: Air University Press, 1955.

Griffin, David. "The Battle of France 1940" *Aerospace Historian* (fall 1974): 144–53.

Groehler, Olaf. *Geschichte des Luftkrieges 1910 bis 1980.* Berlin: Militärverlag der DDR, 1981.

Gröner, Erich. *Die deutschen Kriegsschiffe 1815-1945,* Vol. 1. Koblenz: Bernard und Graefe Verlag, 1989.

Gundelach, Karl. "Gedanken über die Führung eines Luftkrieges gegen England bei der Luftflotte 2 in dem Jahren 1938/39." *Wehrwissenschafliche Rundschau* (January 1960): 33–46.

Gunston, Bill. *The Development of Piston Engines.* Somerset, U.K.: Patrick Stephens Ltd., 1993.

———. *World Encyclopedia of Aero Engines.* Wellingborough, U.K.: Patrick Stephens Ltd., 1986.

Guttmann, Allen. *The Wound in the Heart: America and the Spanish Civil War.* New York: Free Press, 1962.

Hackenberger, Willi. *Die Alten Adler: Pioniere der deutschen Luftfahrt.* Munich: J. F. Lehmanns Verlag, 1960.

Hallade, Jean. "Big Bertha Bombards Paris." In *Tanks and Weapons of World War I,* ed. Bernard Fitzsimons, 141–47. London: Phoebus, 1973.

Hallion, Richard. *Rise of the Fighter Aircraft, 1914–1918.* Baltimore: Nautical and Aviation Press, 1984.

———. *Strike from the Sky: The History of Battlefield Air Attack, 1911–1945.* Washington, D.C.: Smithsonian Institution Press, 1989.

Hansell, Haywood. *The Air Plan That Defeated Hitler.* Atlanta: Longino and Porter, 1972.

———. *The Strategic Air War Against Germany and Japan.* Washington, D.C.: Office of Air Force History, 1986.

Hansen, Ernst W. *Reichswehr und Industrie, Rüstungswirtschaftliche Zusammenarbeit und wirtschaftliche Mobilmachungsvorbereitungen, 1923–1932* [*Militärgeschichtliche Studien* No. 24.]. Boppard am Rhein: Harald Boldt Verlag, 1978.

Hastings, Max. *Bomber Command.* New York: Simon & Schuster, 1989.

Hebrand, J. *Vingt-cinque Anneés de l'Aviation Militaire,* Vol. 1. Paris: Alvin Michel, 1946.

Heiman, Bernard, and Joachim Schunke. "Eine geheime Denkschrift zur Luftkriegskonzeption Hitler-Deutschlands vom Mai 1933." *Zeitschrift für Militärgeschichte* 3 (1964): 72–86.

Heinkel, Ernst. *He 1000.* London: Hutchinson, 1956.

———. *Stürmisches Leben.* Stuttgart: Mundus Verlag, 1953.

Hildebrand, Karl Friedrich. *Die Generäle der deutschen Luftwaffe 1935–1945.* Vols. I–III. Osnabrück: Biblio Verlag, 1990.

Holley, I. B., Jr. *Ideas and Weapons.* Washington, D.C.: Office of Air Force History, 1983.

Homze, Edward L. *Arming the Luftwaffe: The Reich Air Ministry and the German Aircraft Industry, 1919–1939.* Lincoln: University of Nebraska Press, 1976.

———. "The Continental Experience." In *Air Power and Warfare,* eds. Alfred Hurley and Robert Ehrhart, 36–39. Washington, D.C.: Office of Air Force History, 1979.

Hooton, E. R. *Phoenix Triumphant: The Rise and Rise of the Luftwaffe.* London: Arms and Armour Press, 1994.

Horne, Alistair. *To Lose a Battle: France, 1940.* New York: Penguin, 1969.

Howson, Gerald. *Aircraft of the Spanish Civil War 1936–1939.* Washington, D.C.: Smithsonian Institution Press, 1990.

Hoyt, Edwin. *Angels of Death: Göring's Luftwaffe.* New York: Forge, 1994.

Hyman, Neal. "NEP and Industrialization to 1928." In *Soviet Aviation and Airpower,* eds. Robin Higham and Jacob Kipp. Boulder, Colo.: Westview Press, 1977.

Irving, David. *Göring: A Biography.* New York: Avon, 1989.

———. *The Rise and Fall of the Luftwaffe: The Life of Luftwaffe Marshal Erhard Milch.* London: Weidenfeld and Nicolson, 1973.

Jones, Neville. *The Beginnings of Strategic Airpower: History of the British Bomber Force 1923–1939.* London: Frank Cass, 1987.

———. *The Origins of Strategic Bombing.* London: Kimber, 1973.

Keegan, John. *The Second World War.* New York: Penguin, 1989.

Kehrig, Manfred. *Die Wiedereinrichtung des deutschen militärischen Attachedienstes nach dem ersten Weltkrieg (1919–1933).* Boppard am Rhein: Harald Boldt Verlag, 1966.

Kennett, Lee. "Developments to 1939." In *Case Studies in the Development of Close Air Support,* ed. B. J. Cooling. Washington, D.C.: Office of Air Force History, 1990.

———. *The First Air War, 1914–1918.* New York: Free Press, 1991.

Kens, Karl-Heinz, and Heinz Nowarra. *Die deutsche Flugzeuge 1933–1945.* Munich: J. F. Lehmann Verlag, 1961.

Kesselring, Albert. *The Memoirs of Field Marshal Kesselring.* Novato, Calif.: Presidio Press, 1989.

Kilduff, Peter. *Germany's First Air Force 1914–1918.* Osceola, Wis.: Motorbooks International, 1991.

———. *Richthofen: Beyond the Legend of the Red Baron.* New York: John Wiley and Sons, 1993.

Killen, John. *The Luftwaffe: A History.* London: Muller, 1967.

Kleinfeld, Gerald, and Louis Tambs. *Hitler's Spanish Legion: The Blue Division in Russia.* Carbondale: Southern Illinois University Press, 1979.

Koch, Horst-Adalbert. *Flak: Die Geschichte der Deutschen Flakartillerie 1935–1945.* Bad Neuheim: Verlag Hans-Hennig, 1954.

Köhler, Karl. "Auf dem Weg zur Luftwaffe." *Wehrwissenschaftliche Rundschau* 10 (October 1966): 553–62.

Kosin, Rüdiger. *The German Fighter Since 1915.* London: Putnam, 1988.

Köstring, Gen. Ernst. *Der militärische Mittler zwischen dem deutschen Reich und der Sowjetunion 1921–1941,* ed., Hermann Teske. Frankfurt a.M.: E. S. Mittler Verlag, 1966.

Kühn, Volkmar. *Deutsche Fallschirmjäger im Zweiten Weltkrieg.* Stuttgart: Motorbuch Verlag, 1993.

Kuropka, Joachim. "Die britische Luftkriegskonzeption gegen Deutschland im Ersten Weltkrieg." *Militärgeschichtliche Mitteilungen* 27 (1980): 7–25.

Lamberton, W. M. *Reconnaissance and Bomber Aircraft of the 1914–1918 War.* Letchworth, U.K.: Harleyford Press, 1962.

Larrazabal, Jesús Salas. *Air War Over Spain.* London: Ian Allen, 1969.

———. *La Guerra de España desde el Aire.* Barcelona: Ediciones Ariel, 1969.

Lee, Asher. *The German Air Force.* New York: Harper and Brothers, 1946.

Lerma, José Larios. *Combat Over Spain.* London: Neville Spearman, 1965.

Liddle, Peter. *The Airman's War: 1914–1918.* New York: Blandford Press, 1987.

Lusar, Rudolf. *Die deutschen Waffen und Geheimwaffen des 2. Weltkrieges und ihre Entwicklung.* Munich: J. Lehmanns Verlag, 1962.

——. *German Secret Weapons of the Second World War.* New York: Philosophical Library, 1959.

Maass, Bruno. "Vorgeschichte der Spitzengliederung der frühen deutschen Luftwaffe 1920–1933." *Wehrwissenschaftliche Rundschau* 7, 9 (1957): 505–22.

Maier, Klaus, ed. *Die Errichtung der Hegemonie auf dem Europäischen Kontinent. Das Deutsche Reich und der Zweite Weltkrieg,* Vol. 2. Stuttgart: Deutsche Verlags-Anstalt, 1979.

——. *Guernica 26.4.1937: Der deutsche Intervention in Spanien und der Fall Guernica.* Freiburg im Breisgau: Verlag Rombach, 1975.

——. "Total War and German Air Doctrine before the Second World War." In *The German Military in the Age of Total War,* ed., Wilhelm Deist, 210–19. Leamington Spa, U.K.: Berg, 1985.

Mason, Herbert Molloy. *The Rise of the Luftwaffe.* New York: Ballantine, 1973.

Mathews, Herbert. *Half of Spain Died.* New York: Charles Scribner's Sons, 1973.

McFarland, Stephen, and Newton Wesley. *To Command the Sky: The Battle for Air Superiority Over Germany, 1942–1944.* Washington, D.C.: Smithsonian Institution Press, 1991.

Meier-Welcker, Hans. *Seeckt.* Frankfurt a.M.: Bernard und Graefe Verlag, 1967.

Mencarelli, J. *Amadeo Mecozzi.* Rome: Offizio Historico Aeronautica Militare, 1979.

Merkes, Manfred. *Die deutsche Politik gegenüber dem spanischen Bürgerkrieg: 1936–1939.* Bonn: Ludwig Rohrscheid Verlag, 1961.

Messerschmidt, Manfred. *Aussenpolitik und Kriegsvorbereitung. Das Deutsche Reich und der Zweite Weltkrieg,* Vol. 1. Stuttgart: Deutsche Verlags-Anstalt, 1979.

——. *Die Wehrmacht im N. S. Staat.* Hamburg: R. E. Dekkers Verlag, 1969.

——. "German Military Effectiveness between 1919 and 1939." In *Military Effectiveness,* Vol. 2, ed. Allan Millett and Williamson Murray, 218–54. Boston: Allen and Unwin, 1988.

Mets, David. *Master of Airpower: General Carl A. Spaatz.* Novato, Calif.: Presidio Press, 1988

Middlebrook, Martin, and Chris Everitt. *The Bomber Command War Diaries.* London: Penguin Books, 1985.

Militärgeschichtliches Forschungsamt. *Die Militärluftfahrt bis zum Beginn des Weltkrieges 1914.* 3 Vols. Frankfurt a.M.: E. Mittler und Sohn. *Textband,* 1965. *Technischer Band,* 1966. *Anlageband,* 1966.

——. *Handbuch zur deutschen Militärgeschichte, 1648–1939,* Vol. 7, ed., Michael Salewski. Munich: Bernard und Graefe Verlag, 1978.

Miller, Ronald, and David Sawers. *The Technical Development of Modern Aviation.* London: Routledge and Kegan Paul, 1968.

Mitcham, Samuel. *Men of the Luftwaffe.* Novato, Calif.: Presidio Press, 1989.

Model, Hans Georg. *Der deutsche Generalstabsoffizier: Seine Auswahl und Ausbildung in Reichswehr, Wehrmacht und Bundeswehr.* Frankfurt a.M.: Bernard und Graefe Verlag, 1968.

Morrow, John. *German Air Power in World War I.* Lincoln: University of Nebraska Press, 1982.

——, *Building German Airpower, 1909–1914.* Knoxville: University of Tennessee Press, 1976.

——. *The Great War in the Air.* Washington, D.C.: Smithsonian Institution Press, 1993.

Mueller, Rolf-Dieter. "World Power Status Through the Use of Poison Gas? German Preparations for Chemical Warfare, 1919–1945." In *The German Military in the Age of Total War,* ed. Wilhelm Deist. Leamington Spa: Berg, 1985.

Mueller-Hillebrand, Burkhart. *Das Heer, 1933–1945, Entwicklung des organisatorischen Aufbaues,* Vol. 1. Darmstadt: E. Mittler und Sohn, 1954.

Mueller, Klaus-Jürgen. *Das Heer und Hitler. Armee und nationalsozialistisches Regime 1933–1940.* Stuttgart: Deutsche Verlags-Anstalt, 1969.

Muller, Richard. *The German Air War in Russia.* Baltimore: Nautical and Aviation Press, 1992.

Munson, Kenneth. *Aircraft of World War I.* Garden City, N.Y.: Doubleday, 1977.

Murray, Williamson. *Strategy for Defeat: The Luftwaffe, 1933–1945.* Maxwell Air Force Base, Ala.: Air University Press, 1983.

Nielson, Andreas. *The German Air Force General Staff.* USAF Historical Study No. 173. Maxwell Air Force Base, Ala.: USAF Historical Division, 1968.

Neufeld, Michael. *The Rocket and the Reich.* New York: Free Press, 1995.

Niehaus, Werner. *Die Rädarschlacht 1939–1945.* Stuttgart: Motorbuch Verlag, 1977.

Nowarra, Heinz. *50 Jahre Deutsche Luftwaffe 1910–1960,* Band 1. Berlin: Heinz Nowarra, 1961.

——. *Die deutsche Luftrüstung 1933–1945.* 4 vols. Koblenz: Bernard und Graefe Verlag, 1985.

Nowarra, Heinz, and Kimbrough Brown. *Von Richthofen and the Flying Circus.* Letchworth, U.K.: Garden City Press, 1958.

Orange, Vincent. *Coningham.* Washington, D.C.: Center for Air Force History, 1992.

Overy, R. J. "Air Power, Armies and the War in the West, 1940." In *The Harmon Memorial Lectures in Military History.* U.S. Air Force Academy, 1989, 1–24.

Overy, R. J., and Andrew Wheatcroft. *The Road to War: The Origins of World War II.* London: Macmillan, 1989.

Payne, Stanley. *Politics and Military in Modern Spain.* Stanford, Calif.: Stanford University Press, 1967.

——. *The Franco Regime: 1936–1975.* Madison, Wis.: University of Wisconsin Press, 1987.

Peszke, Michael. "The Forgotten Campaign: Poland's Military Aviation in September 1939." *The Polish Review* 1 (1994): 51–72.

Philpott, Bryan. *The Encyclopedia of German Military Aircraft.* London: Bison, 1981.

———. *History of the German Air Force.* New York: Gallery, 1986.

Piekaliewicz, Janusz. *The Air War: 1939–1945.* Poole, Dorset: Blandford Press, 1985.

Pisano, Dominick, ed. *Legend, Memory and the Great War in the Air.* Washington, D.C.: Smithsonian Institution Press, 1992.

Pletschacher, Peter. *Die Königlich Bayerischen Fliegertruppen, 1912–1919.* Munich: Aviatic Verlag, 1992.

Price, Alfred. *Luftwaffe Handbook, 1939–1945.* New York: Charles Scribner's Sons, 1977.

Probert, H. A. *The Rise and Fall of the German Air Force, 1933–1945.* London: Arms and Armour Press, 1983.

Proctor, Raymond. *Hitler's Luftwaffe in the Spanish Civil War.* Westport, Conn.: Greenwood Press, 1983.

Questor, George. *Deterrence Before Hiroshima.* New Brunswick, N.J.: Transaction, 1986.

Raeder, Admiral Erich. *My Life.* Baltimore: U.S. Naval Institute, 1960.

Rahn, Werner. *Reichsmarine und Landesverteidigung, 1919–1928. Konzeption und Führung der Marine in der Weimarer Republik.* Munich: Bernard und Graefe Verlag, 1976.

Redemann, Hans. *Innovations in Aircraft Construction.* West Chester, Pa.: Schiffer Military History, 1991.

Richards, Dennis. *The Royal Air Force, 1939–1945.* London: Her Majesty's Stationery Office, 1953.

Richardson, R. "The Development of Air Power Concepts and Air Combat Techniques in the Spanish Civil War." *Air Power History* (spring 1993): 13–21.

Ries, Karl. *The Luftwaffe: A Photographic Record, 1919–1945.* London: B. T. Batsford, 1987.

Ries, Karl, and Hans Ring. *The Legion Condor: A History of the Luftwaffe in the Spanish Civil War, 1936–1939.* West Chester, Pa.: Schiffer Military History, 1992.

Rust, Eric. *Naval Officers Under Hitler: The Story of Crew 34.* New York, Praeger, 1991.

Salewski, Michael. *Die bewaffnete Macht im Dritten Reich 1933–1939.* Munich: Bernard und Graefe Verlag, 1978.

Schliephake, Hanfried. *The Birth of the Luftwaffe.* Chicago: Henry Regnery, 1971

Schmidt-Richberg, Wiegand. *Die Generalstäbe in Deutschland, 1871–1945.* Beiträge zur Militär- und Kriegsgeschichte 3. Stuttgart: Deutsche Verlags-Anstalt, 1962.

Schneider, Erich. "Waffenentwicklung, Erfahrungen in deutschen Waffenamt." *Wehrwissenschaftliche Rundschau* 3 (1953): 24–35.

Segre, Claudio. "Balbo and Douhet: Master and Disciple." In *La Figura e l'Opera di Giulio Douhet,* ed. Caserte-Pozzuoli. Rome: Società di Historia Patria, 1988.

Shirer, William. *The Rise and Fall of the Third Reich.* New York: Simon & Schuster, 1960.

Showalter, Dennis. *Tannenbeg: Clash of Empires.* Hamden: Archon, 1991.

Simpkin, Richard. *Deep Battle: The Brainchild of Marshal Tukhachevskii.* London: Brassey's, 1987.

Speiers, David. *Image and Reality: The Making of a German Officer, 1921–1933.* Westport, Conn.: Greenwood Press, 1984

Stegemann, Bernd. "Der Minenkrieg." In *Das Deutsche Reich und der Zweite Weltkrieg: Die Errichtung der Hegemonie auf dem Eurpäische Kontinent,* Vol. 2., ed. Klaus Maier, 180–81. Stuttgart: Deutsche Verlags-Anstalt, 1979.

———. "Der Zweite Anlauf zur Seemacht." In *Das Deutsche Reich und der Zweite Weltkrieg,* Vol. 2., ed. Klaus Maier. Stuttgart: Deutsche Verlags-Anstalt, 1979.

Stephens, Alan. "The True Believers: Air Power Between the Wars." In *The War in the Air 1914–1994,* ed. Alan Stephens, 47–80. Fairbairn, Australia: Air Power Studies Centre, 1994.

Stokesbury, James. *A Short History of Airpower.* New York: William Morrow, 1986.

Stone, Norman. *The Eastern Front, 1914–1917.* New York: Charles Scribner's Sons, 1975.

Suchenwirth, Richard. *Command and Leadership in the German Air Force.* USAF Historical Study 174. New York: Arno Press, 1969.

———. *The Development of the German Air Force, 1919–1939.* USAF Historical Study 160. New York: Arno Press, 1968.

Taylor, Michael. *Warplanes of the World: 1918–1939.* New York: Charles Scribner's Sons, 1981.

Taylor, Telford. *The March of Conquest.* Baltimore: Nautical and Aviation Press, 1958 (reprint, 1991).

———. *Sword and Swastika.* New York: Simon & Schuster, 1952.

Tessin, Georg. *Deutsche Verbände und Truppen, 1918–1939.* Osnabrück: Biblio Verlag, 1974.

Tessin, Georg. *Formationsgeschichte der Wehrmacht.* Koblenz, Harald Boldt Verlag, 1959.

Thomas, Georg. *Geschichte der deutschen Wehr und Rüstungswirtschaft, 1918–1945.* Boppard am Rhein: Harald Boldt Verlag, 1966.

Thomas, Gordon, and Max Witts. *Guernica: The Crucible of World War II.* New York: Stein and Day, 1975.

Thomas, Hugh. *The Spanish Civil War.* New York: Harper and Row, 1961.

Udet, Ernst. *Ein Fliegerleben.* Berlin: Ullstein Verlag, 1954.

Völker, Karl-Heinz. "Daten zur Gliederung und Organisation der Luftwaffe 1933–1939." *Wehrwissenschaftliche Rundschau* 4 (April 1967): 113–17.

———. *Die deutsche Luftwaffe, 1933–1939, Aufbau, Führung, Rüstung.* Stuttgart: Deutsche Verlags-Anstalt, 1967.

———. *Die Entwicklung der militärischen Luftfahrt in Deutschland, 1920–1933.* Stuttgart: Deutsche Verlags-Anstalt, 1962.

———. "Die geheime Luftrüstung der Reichswehr und ihre Auswirkung auf den Flugzeugbestand der Luftwaffe bis zum Beginn des Zweiten Weltkrieges." *Wehrwissenschaftliche Rundschau* 12, 9 (1962): 540–49.

———. "Die geheimen deutschen Luftstreitkräfte und Luftschutzprogramm von der

Befehlsübernahme des Reichsminister der Luftfahrt am 15. Mai bis zum Ende des Jahres 1933." *Wehrwissenschaftliche Rundschau* 4 (April 1967): 199–213.

——. *Dokumente und Dokumentarfotos zur Geschichte der Deutschen Luftwaffe.* Stuttgart: Deutsche Verlags-Anstalt, 1968.

Walle, Heinrich. "Das Zeppelinische Luftschiff als Schrittmacher technologischer Entwicklung im Krieg und Frieden." In *Militär und Technik: Wechselbeziehung zu Staat, Gesellschaft und Industrie im 19. Und 20. Jahrhundert,* ed. Roland Foerster, 161–218. Herford: E. S. Mittler, 1992.

Weinberg, Gerhard. *A World at Arms: A Global History of World War II.* New York: Cambridge University Press, 1994.

Werrell, Kenneth. *Archie, Flak, AAA and SAM.* Maxwell Air Force Base, Ala.: Air University Press, 1988.

Whealey, Robert. *Hitler and Spain: The Nazi Role in the Spanish Civil War, 1936–1939.* Lexington: University Press of Kentucky, 1989.

Wohlfeil, Rainer. *Heer und Republik. Handbuch zur deutschen Militärgeschichte, 1648–1939,* Vol. 6. Frankfurt a.M.: Bernard und Graefe Verlag, 1970.

Wohlfeil, Rainer, and Hans Dollinger. *Die Deutsche Reichswehr.* Frankfurt a.M.: Bernard und Graefe Verlag, 1972.

Wood, Derek, and Derek Dempster. *The Narrow Margin.* Washington, D.C.: Smithsonian Institution Press, 1990.

Wyden, Peter. *The Passionate War: The Narrative History of the Spanish Civil War.* New York: Simon & Schuster, 1983.

Zeidler, Manfred. "Luftkriegsdenken und Offizierausbildung an der Moskauer Zukovskij Akademie im Jahre 1926." *Militärgeschichtliche Mitteilungen* 27 (1980): 127–74.

——. *Reichswehr und Rote Armee 1920–1933.* Munich: Oldenbourg Verlag, 1993.

Doctoral Dissertations

Williams, George. *Statistics and Strategic Bombardment: Operations and Records of the British Long-Range Bombing Force During World War I and Their Implications for the Development of the Post-War Royal Air Force, 1917–1923.* Oxford: Oxford University, 1987.

Index